C000130173

A DICTIONARY OF THE SOCIAL SCIENCES

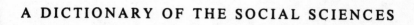

A Dictionary of the Social Sciences

Hugo F. Reading

Routledge & Kegan Paul
London, Henley and Boston

First published in Great Britain and the USA in 1977
by Routledge & Kegan Paul Ltd
39 Store Street,
London WC1E 7DD,
Broadway House,
Newtown Road,
Henley-on-Thames,
Oxon RG9 1EN and
9 Park Street,
Boston, Mass. 02108, USA
Printed in Great Britain by
Billing & Sons Ltd, Guildford, London and Worcester
Copyright © Hugo F. Reading, 1976
No part of this book may be reproduced in
any form without permission from the
publisher, except for the quotation of brief
passages in criticism

ISBN 0 7100 8650 4

Preface

This dictionary of over 7,500 terms covers all the social sciences with the exception of economics and linguistics.

Those economic and linguistic terms which are frequently used in the other social sciences have, however, been included. It has also been found necessary to include terms from subjects peripheral to the social sciences.

This dictionary is intended for students of the social sciences, public administration, social administration and social work, and should prove useful to the personnel of the specialized agencies and other international organizations.

This is not an encyclopaedic dictionary. The literary approach involving short articles in alphabetical order, too long for a dictionary and too short to be adequate as articles, is a tradition from which the author has departed. An encyclopaedic treatment has certain advantages and a dictionary treatment has certain limitations, but these are limitations which the author accepts and considers acceptable. A dictionary has its own function and forms part of the armamentarium of the student, along with text-books, monographs, and articles in journals and encyclopaedias.

The entries are thus purely analytic and no empirical information is given.

The definitions are as concise as possible without loss of meaning.

The definitions are hierarchical and interrelated, the definitions employing terms, printed in italics, which are defined elsewhere in the dictionary. Thus the dictionary possesses a logical unity.

A superscript shows the sense in which a term is being used by giving the number of the definition in the entry indicated.

Compounds are reversed. Thus, **aspirational reference group** is entered in the form **group, reference, aspirational.** An exception is made in the case of vital statistics where the first two words are given in normal order.

With a phrase such as *qualitative* or *quantitative data*, look up **data, qualitative** and **data, quantitative.** With a phrase such as *organized, negative sanction*, look up **sanction, organized** and **sanction, negative.**

The symbol ‖ in compounds, e.g. *primitive* ‖ *society*, means that each word is separately defined but not the compound.

The proper treatment of polysemous terms is controversial. However, experience with students has shown that polysemous terms such as 'culture', 'institution', 'role' can be treated in the same way as other terms and are comprehensible without further elucidation.

Terms of material culture and also vernacular terms have been omitted as no criteria exist for their inclusion or exclusion, and their inclusion in previous dictionaries has been purely arbitrary. Pressure of space has also resulted in the omission of proper names.

Only the most important statistical terms have been included as dictionaries of statistics are available for reference. However, terms relating to surveys, questionnaires, scales, and interviewing have been included.

Only observers' concepts are explicated and not folk concepts.

Alphabetization follows the rules of the American Library Association.

The author is extremely grateful for the encouragement he received from colleagues, and especially to Evangelos Vlachos, Earl Hopper, and Paul Baxter.

The author dedicates this book to all those who remain unconvinced by the arguments for restricting scientific method in its application to the social sciences.

HUGO F. READING

Athens, June 1976

Abbreviations

a.	adjective
archaeol.	archaeology
Dem. Y.	United Nations Demographic Yearbook
FAO	Food and Agricultural Organization
genet.	genetics
hum. ecol.	human ecology
ILO	International Labour Organization
jurid.	juridical
L of N	League of Nations
MDD	Multilingual Demographic Dictionary
n.	noun
NQ	Notes and Queries on Anthropology
OECD	Organization for Economic Co-operation and Development
pers n.	personal noun
sociom.	sociometry
SOUN	Statistical Office, United Nations
stats.	statistics
UN	United Nations
USBC	United States Bureau of the Census
usu.	usual
v.	verb
vi.	intransitive verb
vt.	transitive verb
WHO	World Health Organization

abduction 1. carrying off or detention of woman with intent to marry or mate.2. movement of limb away from axis of body. 3. process of producing a new *model*. (Pask,G.).

abient pertaining to behaviour tending to remove organism from exposure to a given *stimulus*. **abience** *n.*

ablineal a *consanguine* who is neither a *lineal* nor a *colineal*.

ablineality the state of being an *ablineal*.

abnormal 1. atypical. 2. deviating by more than two *standard deviations*. 3. see *dysfunctional*. **abnormality** *n.*

abortion the premature expulsion from the uterus of the nonviable products of conception.

abortion, artificial see *abortion, induced.*

abortion, eugenic an *induced abortion* having a *eugenic* purpose.

abortion, induced an intentional *abortion.*

abortion, natural see *abortion, spontaneous.*

abortion, provoked see *abortion, induced.*

abortion, spontaneous an unintentional *abortion.*

abortion, therapeutic an *induced abortion* intended to safeguard the mother's health.

abreaction the discharge of affect attaching to a previously repressed experience. **abreactive** *a.* see also *catharsis.*

absenteeism 1. failure to report to work. 2. the percentage of employees failing to report to work during a given period. 3. the failure of owners of the means of production or distribution to be regularly present to supervise the production or distribution.

absolute, cultural *value* or *norm* thought by a particular people to be applicable to all peoples of all times.

absolutism 1. *government* in which the governed play no part in governmental *decision-making*. 2. disposition to think in terms of absolutes.3. doctrine that all *values* are known.

absolutism, group tendency for *group* members to believe that their *usages* are the only correct ones.

absorption, economic absorption of *immigrants* into the *economy.*

abstinence 1. postponement of enjoyment or use. 2. voluntary avoidance of satisfaction of an appetite.

abstraction 1. separating a partial aspect or quality from a total object. 2. taking characteristics common to several individuals.

abstractionism the doctrine that all *concepts* are formed by *abstraction*[2]. (Geach, P.).

acathexis absence of *cathexis*. see also *cathection.*

acceleration, social rate of increase in a social *variable*. see also *deceleration, social; celeration, social.*

accessibility ease with which members of a given *social category* may be contacted. see also *inaccessibility.*

accessory, social functionally-independent social or cultural element. (LaPiere).

accident an event unpredictable from the point of view of a given *system.*

accommodation 1. a mixture of *co-operation* and *opposition*. 2. effecting changes to reduce *conflict*. 3.non-biological *adjustment* or *adaptation*. (MacIver). 4. see *co-operation, tertiary.*

accordance harmony or agreement between individuals or *groups*.

accretion increase in magnitude by addition.

acculturation 1. process of communicating the *culture* to a child. 2. conditioning a member of an *out-group* for incorporation into *group*. 3. see *assimilation, cultural*. 4. assumption by one *society* of part of culture of another society through contact. 5. cultural change in one or both *populations* resulting from contact. see also *assimilation; enculturation*.

acculturation, antagonistic the borrowing of certain *culture traits* for defence from the *society* from which they are borrowed.

acculturation, bilateral cultural change occurring to both *populations* in contact and as a result of the contact.

acculturation, controlled see *acculturation, selective*.

acculturation, directed see *acculturation, planned*.

acculturation, linguistic linguistic change in one or both *populations* resulting from contact.

acculturation, marginal culture interchange in the border region of two areas.

acculturation, planitational cultural interchange over a wide area.

acculturation, planned deliberate *acculturation* of one *group* by another.

acculturation, selective *acculturation* in which recipient *group* is selective.

acculturation, unilateral cultural change occurring to only one of two *populations* in contact and as a result of the contact.

acculturation, voluntary voluntary assumption by one *society* of part of *culture* of another society through contact.

accumulation, capital the growth by successive additions of a *society's real capital*.

accumulation, cultural the growth of a *culture* by successive additions of *culture traits*.

accumulation, primitive *capital accumulation* occurring in *primitive‖societies*.

accuracy 1. absence of mistake or *error*. 2. closeness of estimated to true *value*[6]. see also *precision*.

acephalous without a central *government*.

acquisition, data sensing or recording of *raw data*. see also *reduction, data; transcription, data*.

act 1. a unit of behaviour. 2. a sequence of behaviours dominated by a common motive. 3. an accomplished *action*. (Schutz, A.).

act, social *act* of an *actor* involving another person.(Parsons, T.).

act, unit *act* constituting the minimal unit of analysis.(Parsons, T.).

act-pollution *pollution* resulting from an *act* or contact.(Orenstein, H.). see also *pollution, internal; pollution, external; pollution, relational*.

action 1. purposive behaviour. 2. behaviour to which *actor* attaches subjective meaning. (Weber, M.). 3. a series of *acts*. 4. behaviour which takes other persons into account.

action, charismatic *action* backed by *charismatic authority*. (Weber, M.). see also *charisma*.

action, compliant an *action* in response to and in accordance with a *directive action*.

action, consensual involuntary *action* with awareness of performance.

action, corporate *action* taken by a *group* involving authorized decision-making procedures and employing authorized methods.

action, direct *political action*[1] which is non-constitutional, but not necessarily illegal.

action, directive a *communication* indicating what another is to perform.

action, expressive *action* which expresses internal state.

action, instrumental *action* which is a means to an end.

action, logical *action* in which the objective end and the subjective purpose are identical. (Pareto).

action, mass random *activity* of infant.

action, military-civic involvement of the military in *economic* and *social welfare* programmes.

action, non-logical *action* in which the objective end differs from the subjective purpose. (Pareto).

action, police a relatively localized military action undertaken by regular armed forces for the maintenance of internal peace.

action, policy *action* which seeks to influence *policy* by *competition* in *power*. (Southall, A.).

action, political 1.*action* concerned with *power*. 2. action concerned with power, ultimately sanctioned by physical force. (Weber, M.; Southall, A.).3. (Smith, M.G.). see *action, policy*.

action, rational-legal *action* legitimated and defined by *law* and performed by legally qualified office-holder. (Weber, M.).

action, serial see *reflex, chain*.

action, social 1. *action* of individual in a *social situation*. (Thomas, W.I.). 2. action having person or *group* as object. 3. organized action aimed at *reform*. 4. that aspect of human behaviour which can only be accounted for culturally.

action, traditional *action* based on piety for what is thought to have always existed. (Weber, M.).

action-sequence a sequence of *actions* through a *network*.

action-set those persons with whom *ego* has created direct or indirect links of various kinds for a particular purpose.

activity 1. any one of the types of things people do.(Homans). 2. associated *drive*, behaviour, and *goal*. (Slotkin). 3. the functioning of an organism. 4. organized *set¹* of *responses*.

actone observable behavioural bit consisting of body motion and environmental effect. (Harris, M.).

actoneme a class of *actones*. (Harris, M.).

actor 1. person actuating an *institution*. (Nadel).2. any acting unit. (Parsons, T.).

adaptation 1. changing to fit changed conditions. 2. *adjustment* of a *group* to its *environment*. 3. systemic change in response to change in environment of *system*. 4. process whereby individual or group is fitted to its environment. 5. state of being fitted to environment.6. biological or cultural *adjustment* resulting from natural selection. (Harris, M.). 7. overcoming environmental constraints and manipulation of the scarce resources of both environment and system. (Parsons, T.). see also *adjustment*.

adaptation, communal *adaptation* to *environment* achieved indirectly through the *organization* of the *population*.

adaptation, external *adaptation* of the *social structure* to its *natural* or *social environment*.

adaptation, genetic *adaptation* of individual to *environment* resulting from *genotype*.

adaptation, individual *adaptation* to *environment* achieved directly by individual and not indirectly through the *organization* of the *population*.

adaptation, internal 1. the controlled relations of individuals within the social unity. (Radcliffe-Brown). 2. mutual *adaptation* of social or cultural elements.

additivity treatable by the process of addition.

address, term of term used when speaking to a relative.

adhesion, cultural tendency for *culture traits* to be associated in *diffusion¹*.

adient pertaining to behaviour tending to expose organism to more of a given

11

stimulus. **adience** *n.*

adjudication 1. settling disputes peacefully by authoritative decision aimed at justice between the parties. 2. the use of *authority* in resolving *conflicts* between persons or *groups*. **adjudicate** *v.*

adjudication, administrative *adjudication* carried out by public administrative agencies.

adjustment 1. changing to fit established conditions. 2. change within *system* in response to other change within system. 3. response of individual producing tension-release. (Watson). 4. fitting of individual to *social environment.* 5. fitting of individual to *norms.* 6. process whereby individual or *group* deliberately fits itself to its *environment.* 7. correcting numerical data for *constant errors.* see also *adaptation.*

administration 1. establishing organizational aims. 2. the formal *hierarchy* for achieving the *goal* of an *organization.* (Bendix, R.). 3. the implementation of *policy decisions.* 4. the *co-ordination* of *activity* to achieve a goal. 5. installing and implementing *procedures.* **administrative** *a.*

administration, area *delegation of powers* to area officials without transfer of *final authority* from the ministry.

administration, comparative the comparative study of *administration.*

administration, correctional that branch of *administration* concerned with correctional institutions and services.

administration, development *administration* of the process of *economic development.*

administration, educational *administration* of educational services.

administration, field see *administration, area.*

administration, general the *principles* common to all branches of *administration.*

administration, industrial that branch of *administration* concerned with *economic organizations².*

administration, medical that branch of *administration* concerned with medical services.

administration, paternalistic *administration* characterized by *paternalism.*

administration, personnel the *administration* of the human resources of an *organization.*

administration, public 1. the implementation of government *policy.* 2. the study of the executive branch of *government.*

administration, social *administration* of the *social services.*

administration, systems *administration* based on *systems analysis.*

administration, urban *administration* of an *urban system².*

adoption acquisition by an individual, through a normatively-regulated process, of new *kinship* ties that are socially-defined as equivalent to the *congenital* ones and which supersede the old ones either wholly or in part.

aeromancy *divination* from the air, air currents, winds, or atmospheric condition. **aeromantic** *a.*

affective concerned with feeling.

affectivity—affective neutrality the incompatible alternatives facing an *actor* of immediate gratification or taking evaluative considerations into account. (Parsons, T.).

affines relatives by *marriage.*

affines, primary *affines* without linking relative.

affines, secondary *affines* related through one linking relative.

affines, tertiary *affines* related through two linking relatives.

affinity relationship by *marriage.* **affinal** *a.*

after-care services rendered person after discharge from *total institution.*

agamy absence of *rule* prescribing *marriage* outside or inside a given *group.*

see also *endogamy*; *exogamy*.

age, anatomical the age for which a certain degree of anatomical *development*[2] is typical.

age, chronological (C.A.) the time elapsed since birth.

age, chronological, corrected postnatal *chronological age* of a prematurely born child minus estimated difference between child's gestation period and full term.

age, conceptional the time elapsed since conception.

age, educational the age for which a certain degree of educational *development*[2] is typical.

age, life see *age, chronological*.

age, mental (M.A.) the age for which a certain level of intelligence is typical.

age, personality the age for which a certain degree of *personality*‖*development*[2] is typical.

age, physiological the age for which a certain degree of physiological *development*[2] is typical.

age, social the age for which a certain degree of social development is typical.

age, true see *age, conceptional*.

age-category see *age-grouping*.

age-ceremony *ceremony* marking passage of individual from one *age-group*[3] to the next. see also *passage, rites de*.

age-class 1. organized, compulsory *group* of coevals.2. number of *age-sets* combined for a specific purpose.

age-grade 1. organized, compulsory *group* of coevals. 2. *age status* and associated *role*. (Gulliver, P.H.). 3. *age-set*[1] possessing an *age role*. (Bohannan, P.).4. stage through which *age-set*[1] passes.

age-group 1. organized *group* of coevals. 2. local *age-set*[1]. (Gulliver, P.H.). 3. see *age-grouping*.

age-grouping those persons lying within specific age limits.

age-mates fellow-members of an *age-set*.

age-organization 1. an *organization* based on *age-grouping*.2. the *system* of *age-sets* in a *society*.

age-set 1. organized, compulsory *group* of coevals. 2. *set*[1] of concurrent *age-groups*[2]. (Gulliver, P.H.). 3. corporate *age-grade*[3] or corporate division of *age-grade*[3]. (Bohannan, R.).

age-system see *age-organization*[2].

age-village a *village* of coevals.

ageing, index of ratio of dependent aged to dependent children.

agglomerate 1. see *aggregate*[1]. 2. see *agglomeration*[1].

agglomeration 1. any concentration of *population*. 2. the process of separate urban nuclei coalescing.

agglomeration, rural *agglomeration* having a *rural* character.

agglomeration, urban 1. city of over a million inhabitants. (Dem. Y.). 2. *agglomeration* having an *urban* character.

aggregate 1. plurality of units without *integration*[1] or interdependence. 2. plurality of persons without *integration*[1] or interdependence. 3. plurality of persons. 4. figure summarizing numerical data.

aggregate, attention an *aggregate*[3] which is polarized.

aggregate, loose non-polarized, transitory, contiguous *collectivity*.

aggregate, panic *aggregate*[2] lacking *rapport* formed by a *panic* situation.

aggregate, population any concentration of *population*.

aggregate, power the persons having *power* in a given *power relationship*. (Lasswell, H.D.).

aggregate, social see *aggregate*[2,3].

aggregate, statistical see *aggregate*[1,4].

aggregate, status a plurality of persons of approximately equal *status* who interact infrequently. see also *group, status*.

aggregate, subject the persons over whom *power* is had in a given *power relationship*. (Lasswell, H.D.).

aggregation 1. any concentration of *population*. 2. the growth of *agglomerations* and *organizations*.

aggression 1. behaviour aimed at injury of a person or thing.(Dollard). 2. initiating an attack. (Scott, J.P.). 3. a *state'* s *use of force* which initiates an armed conflict. see also *hostility*.

aggression, anti-social *aggression* against others which is not intended for the benefit of *society*.

aggression, authoritarian disposition to seek out and condemn and punish persons who violate conventional *values*.

aggression, competitive *aggression* in the course of *competition*.

aggression, covert *aggression* existing at the level of phantasy.

aggression, deflected see *aggression, displaced*.

aggression, direct *aggression* towards the frustrating object.

aggression, displaced *aggression* displaced from the frustrating object to another subject.

aggression, extrapunitive *aggression* directed towards others.

aggression, free-floating *aggression* which is not directed towards a particular object.

aggression, generalized see *aggression, free-floating*.

aggression, in-group *aggression* towards another member or members of the *in-group*.

aggression, instrumental *aggression* which is employed as a means to an end.

aggression, intropunitive *aggression* directed towards self.

aggression, overt *aggression* existing at the behavioural level.

aggression, projected *aggression* attributed by *ego* through *projection*, to another person or persons.

aggression, pro-social *aggression* intended for the benefit of *society*.

aggression, protective *aggression* for the protection of other persons or the *group*.

aggression, reactive *aggression* which is a *reaction* to *frustration* or anger.

aggression, socialized *aggression* which has been channelled into socially-approved directions.

aggression, unsocialized *aggression* which has not been channelled into socially-approved directions.

aggressiveness tendency towards *aggression*.

aggressivity see *aggressiveness*.

agist to take in livestock for feeding at an agreed price.

agister a person who agists.

agistment 1. taking in livestock for feeding at an agreed price. 2. price paid for agisting. 3. agreement to agist.

agitation attempting to produce mass discontent with the social order. **agitate** *v*. **agitator** *pers n*.

agitation, group *agitation* undertaken by a *group*.

agitation, individual *agitation* undertaken by an individual.

agnates relatives related through males.

agnation see *descent, agnatic*.

agrarian pertaining to cultivation or *land tenure*.

agrarianism 1. the agricultural way of life. 2. the doctrine of the superiority of the agricultural way of life.3. the doctrine of *agrarian reform*.

agribusiness the *system* of production, processing and marketing of food and nonfood farm commodities.

agriculture 1. cultivation employing animal traction.2. cultivation employing animal traction or *animal husbandry*.3. cultivation of the soil to produce edible *food crops*.4. *activities* of persons settled on the land utilizing natural growth processes to produce vegetable and animal products. (Zimmerman, E.W.). see also *horticulture*.

agriculture, commercial *agriculture* for external consumption.

agriculture, extensive see *cultivation, extensive*.

agriculture, fire (Smith, T.L.) see *cultivation, shifting*.

agriculture, hydraulic cultivation which is aided   by centrally organized large-scale *irrigation*. (Wittfogel, K.A.).see also *hydro-agriculture*.

agriculture, intensive see *cultivation, intensive*.

agriculture, plantation large-scale cultivation of *cash crops*.

agriculture, sedentary *agriculture* practised by settled *farmers* or *peasants*.

agriculture, shifting see *cultivation, shifting*.

agriculture, shifting-field see *cultivation, shifting*.

agriculture, subsistence *agriculture* all the produce of which is internally consumed.

agriculture, swidden see *cultivation, shifting*.

agriculture, textile cultivation of crops to obtain fibres for the production of textiles.

agrofact a product of *agriculture*. (Bidney, D.). see also *artifact*; *mentifact*; *socifact*.

albinocracy rule by a *society'* s Caucasoid element.

aleatory pertaining to the unpredictable.

alectromancy see *alectryomancy*.

alectryomancy *divination* in which a cock selects grains placed on the letters of the alphabet. **alectryomantic** *a*.

aleuromancy *divination* by means of flour.

alienation 1. *isolation* from any aspect of *society*. 2. a feeling of powerlessness. 3. a feeling of meaninglessness. 4. see *alienation, political*. 5. see *alienation, normative*.6. see *alienation, work*. 7. see *alienation, role*.8. rejection of the beliefs and *values* of one's society. 9. inability of individual to find self-rewarding *activities*. 10. the right of owner or tenant to dispose of his interest.

alienation, normative rejection of or uncertainty concerning the *norms* or *values* of one's *society*.

alienation, political noninvolvement in or a feeling of meaninglessness concerning *politics*.

alienation, role *isolation* of the individual from his *roles* in *society*.

alienation, work the felt powerlessness to control one's own work conditions.

alliance 1. a co-operative relationship between two or more autonomous *groups* for the achievement of a specified *objective*. 2. a promise of mutual military assistance between two or more *states*.

alliance, asymmetric the unilateral transfer of women by *alliance*‖*groups*.

alliance, defensive *alliance* for defensive purposes.

alliance, formal *alliance¹* involving an express agreement. (LaPiere).

alliance, informal *alliance¹* involving a tacit agreement. (LaPiere).

alliance, marital *alliance¹* created between two *groups* by *marriages* or *marital exchanges* between them.

alliance, military see *alliance²*.

alliance, offensive *alliance* for offensive purposes.

alliance, political *alliance* having a political *objective*.

alliance, symmetric the bilateral transfer of women by *alliance*‖*groups*.

allodial 1. held in absolute ownership. 2. pertaining to the holding of land in absolute ownership.

allodialism land-tenure system in which the land is held in absolute ownership. see also *allodial*; *tenure, land*.

allo-empathy awareness of other persons' acceptance and rejection of one another.

allokurtic see *heterokurtic*.

allopatric (of a *group*) possessing a totally exclusive *territory*. see also *sympatric*.

allotheism the *worship* of foreign or forbidden gods.

alomancy *divination* by means of salt. **alomantic** *a*.

alphitomancy *divination* by means of barley-meal. **alphitomantic** *a*.

alter another person from the point of view of *ego*.

alternatives, behaviour the possible behaviours in a given situation from which an individual or *group* may make a choice.

alternatives, cultural alternative forms of behaviour permitted by a *society*.

amalgamation intermixture of *gene pools*, irrespective of the degree of similarity.

ambience the *set¹* of persons with whom *ego* interacts in a given *network*. (Caplow, T.).

ambiguity, role lack of clarity of *role expectations* for a given *position*.

ambilineage all the descendants through male or female links of a pair of *ancestors*.

ambilineality see *descent, ambilineal*.

ambilocality see *residence, ambilocal*.

ambivalence, cultural ambivalence of individual towards a *culture* resulting from *culture conflict*.

ambivalence, structural incompatibility of expectations faced by a statusholder. see also *status*.

ambiversion *personality type* balanced or oscillating between *introversion* and *extraversion*.

amentia intellectual deficiency. see also *oligophrenia*.

amentia, deprivative *amentia* due to lack of some environmental element necessary for complete cerebral development.

amentia, isolation *amentia* resulting from individual's early *isolation*.

amentia, secondary environmentally-determined *amentia*.

amentia, subcultural *amentia* resulting not from pathology but from heredity.

amimia inability to make or interpret *signs* or *gestures*.

amimia, motor inability to make or imitate appropriate *gestures*.

amimia, sensory inability to perceive or interpret *gestures*.

amita-clan a *clan³* based on *patrilineal descent* and *amitalocal residence*.

amitate 1. especially close ties between niece and aunt. 2. especially close ties between child and father's sister. 3. especially close ties between nephew and father's sister.

amnesty *pardon* given to a group of offenders.

amniomancy *divination* by means of a new-born baby's amnion. **amniomantic** *a*.

amusement passive, non-participating *play*.

analogue 1. a thing that resembles something else in a certain way in its properties, behaviour, or mode of functioning. 2. physical *model* in an analogue computer.

analysis, cohort study of a *cohort* through time.

analysis, componential discovering the dimensions of meaning underlying a *semantic domain* and mapping the *values⁶* of these dimensions on to a *lexical set*.

analysis, content a research *technique* for the objective, systematic, and quantitative description of the manifest content of *communication*. (Berelson,

B.).

analysis, data the use of distributions to test *hypotheses*. (Galtung, J.).

analysis, dependence (Boudon, R.) see *analysis, path*.

analysis, diachronic analysis of a *society* through time.

analysis, dynamic analysis of a *society* in which change is involved.

analysis, equilibrium the analysis of *systems* in *equilibrium*.

analysis, factor *procedures* for isolating the smallest number of *factors* which account for the observed variation in a *set[1]* of intercorrelated *variables*.

analysis, functional analysis of a *society* or an *organization* which reveals the functional interdependence of its elements.

analysis, interaction counting and categorizing *interactions* amongst members of a *group*.

analysis, job the analysis of a *job* into its tasks, processes and operations.

analysis, levels of functional relationships are found between *variables* each of which subsumes variables at a lower level of analysis and is itself subsumed with others under a variable at a higher level of analysis.

analysis, near-neighbour *techniques* for determining the departure from randomness of a distribution of points in an area, based on the distance between each point and its nearest neighbour.

analysis, occupational see *analysis, job*.

analysis, path analysis of a *set[1]* of *variables* into *determining variables* and *dependent variables[2]*.

analysis, population 1. see *demography, theoretical*. 2. *theoretical demography* employing mathematical methods. 3. analysis of particular *populations*.

analysis, role the analysis of *roles, role concepts*, and *systems* and *sets[1]* of roles.

analysis, roll-call analysis of voting record of group members on a series of issues.

analysis, sequential *sampling* in which cases are added to the *sample* until the minimum sample has been accumulated which will provide the required significance. see also *significance, level of*.

analysis, static analysis of a *society* in which change is not involved.

analysis, statistical that branch of *statistics[1]* concerned with the analysis of numerical data.

analysis, structural-functional analysis of a *society* which reveals the functional interdependence of its structural elements.

analysis, survey the analysis of *survey data* to identify *variables* of theoretical importance.

analysis, synchronic analysis of a *society* at a fixed point of time.

analysis, systems the application of *systems theory* to a *field* of phenomena.

ancestor a person from whom another person or persons are socially-defined as descended.

ancestor, apical the *ancestor* at the apex of a *lineage* from whom the members of a *descent group* trace *descent*.

ancestor, focal see *ancestor, apical*.

ancestor, reference an *ancestor* used as a point of reference.

androcentrism using masculine traits as criteria of evaluation. **androcentric** *a*.

androcracy rule by men. **androcratic** *a*.

androlepsy seizure of citizens of another *state* to force it to observe its obligations. **androlepsic** *a*.

animatism belief in impersonal spiritual force.

animism belief in indwelling spirits throughout nature.

anisogamy *marriage* in which one of the partners marries upwards. **anisogamous** *a*. see also *hypergamy*; *hypogamy*.

annexation 1. taking possession by a *state* of further *territory*. 2. incorporation by a city of territory previously outside its administrative boundaries. **annex** *v*

anomie 1. absence of common *values* in a *society*. 2. limitation of access to the institutionalized means to *cultural goals*. (Merton).

anomie, acute *societal* condition in which common *values* are absent. (DeGrazia, S.).

anomie, objective strain in the *social structure*.

anomie, simple *societal* condition of conflicting *value systems*. (DeGrazia, S.).

anomie, subjective the individual's normative uncertainty or *perception* of normative disagreement. see also *norm*.

antagonism active *opposition* to another person or *group*.

anthropic pertaining to pre-cultural man as an animal amongst other animals.

anthropism see *anthropocentrism*.

anthropocentrism regarding man as the central fact of the universe. **anthropocentric** *a*. "

anthropogeography the study of the relations between man and his *geographical environment*.

anthropolatry the *worship* of deified persons or of persons believed to be visible deities. **anthropolatric** *a*.

anthropology the study of human physical and social variation.

anthropology, action that branch of *anthropology* in which research directly facilitates *social change*.

anthropology, aerospace the application of *anthropology* to the solution of aerospace problems.

anthropology, applied the application of *anthropological theory* to the solution of concrete problems.

anthropology, biocultural the fusion of *physical anthropology* and *sociocultural anthropology*. (Thompson, L.).

anthropology, biological the study of human biological variation, including the effect of behaviour on human *organic evolution*.

anthropology, cognitive the study of *cognitive*, linguistic, and *semantic* phenomena in their social context.

anthropology, constitutional that branch of *anthropology* concerned with human *constitution*⁵ and its effects on behaviour.

anthropology, criminal that branch of *physical anthropology* concerned with the explanation of *criminality*.

anthropology, cultural field embracing *social anthropology* and *ethnography*, with emphasis on *culture* and history.

anthropology, development the application of *anthropological theory* to the *planning* of socioeconomic *development*.

anthropology, diffusionist body of *theory* in *social* and *cultural anthropology* based on the doctrine of *diffusionism*.

anthropology, economic the study of the *economic systems* of *primitive∥societies* in their social context.

anthropology, evolutionary body of *theory* in *social* and *cultural anthropology* based on social evolutionism.

anthropology, functionalist body of *theory* in *social* and *cultural anthropology* based on the doctrine of *functionalism*.

anthropology, historical *sociocultural anthropology* involving *diachronic analysis*.

anthropology, legal see *law, anthropology of*.

anthropology, linguistic branch of *anthropology* concerned with language as a part of *culture*.

anthropology, medical the study of the diseases and medical beliefs and practices of *primitive‖societies* in their social structural and cultural context.

anthropology, philosophical 1. see *metaanthropology*.2. that branch of *anthropology* which is concerned with man's place in nature.

anthropology, physical the study of human physical variation.

anthropology, political the study of the *political systems* of *primitive‖societies* in their social context.

anthropology, prehistoric the study of *prehistoric‖cultures*.

anthropology, psychiatric see *anthropopsychiatry*.

anthropology, psychological the study of the distributions of *personality traits* and *personality types* in *populations* and the interrelations of *culture* and *personality*.

anthropology, social the *sociology* of *primitive‖societies*.

anthropology, sociocultural the theoretical study of both the social structural and cultural features of *primitive‖societies*.

anthropology, somatic see *anthropology, physical*.

anthropology, structural *anthropology* having a *structuralist* approach. see also *structuralism*.

anthropology, symbolic a theoretical orientation in *anthropology* which stresses the interrelations of and manipulations of *symbols* in *society*.

anthropology, systems the application of *systems theory* to *sociocultural anthropology*.

anthropology, theoretical the body of *theory* and *metatheory* concerning human physical and social variation.

anthropology, unified see *anthropology, biocultural*.

anthropology, urban social studies employing anthropological techniques in an *urban* setting.

anthropomancy *divination* by means of human entrails. **anthropomantic** *a.*

anthropometry science of *measurement* of the human body. **anthropometric** *a.*

anthropomorphism attributing human characteristics to nonhumans. **anthropomorphic** *a.*

anthropomorphism, physical attributing human physical characteristics to nonhumans.

anthroponymy study of the derivation of personal names.

anthropopathism attributing human feelings to nonhumans.

anthropopathy see *anthropopathism*.

anthropophuism attributing human nature to nonhumans.

anthropopsychiatry the comparative study of mental disorders in different *societies*.

anti-clericalism opposition to the intervention of *religious‖leaders* in *politics*. see also *clericalism*; *religion*.

anticonformity see *rebellion⁴*.

anti-natalist pertaining to *population policy* designed to decrease the *birth rate*.

anti-nativism opposition to *nativism*.

anti-statism opposition to *statism*.

anxiety, covert anxiety of which the individual is unaware.

anxiety, general anxiety experienced in a wide variety of situations.

anxiety, overt anxiety of which the individual is aware.

anxiety, socialization anxiety resulting from underindulgence of a *drive* in the *socialization process*.

anxiety, test anxiety which is specific to test situations.

aperiodicity absence of *periodicity*. **aperiodic** *a.*

apolemity the degree to which the *energy* available to a *society* is not employed in *war* or military preparations.(Andreski, S.). **apolemitic** *a.* see also *polemity*.

apopathetic pertaining to behaviour not directed towards others but influenced by their presence.

apotropaic pertaining to a *ritual* designed to avert evil. **apotropaism** *n.*

appanage land or other source of revenue assigned to a member of a ruler's *family*. see also *fief*; *benefice*; *seigniory*.

arbitration method of dispute settlement in which the parties to a dispute appeal to a third party whose decision is binding on them. **arbitral** *a.* **arbitrate** *vi.* see also *mediation*; *conciliation*.

arbitration, compulsory *arbitration* to which the parties to a dispute are compelled to go.

arbitration, voluntary *arbitration* to which the parties to a dispute are not compelled to go.

archaism 1. survival of something from the past. 2. survival of primeval characteristics in a *primitive‖society*. (Lévi-Strauss).

area, administrative 1. an area officially delimited for the *administration* of one or more *governmental‖functions*.2. a territorial unit defined by its political boundaries.

area, agricultural area consisting of arable land, land under tree crops, or pasture. (FAO).

area, attention those persons sharing a common focus of attention.

area, blighted socially diseased *urban area* of deteriorated buildings, overcrowding, *crime, delinquency,* vice, *broken homes.*

area, built-up the area in a town or city actually covered with buildings.

area, census an area for which *census* data are collected.

area, contact area of individual's contacts of a particular type, or area of common contacts.

area, core area of greatest commercial and *population density* in a city or *metropolitan area.*

area, culture an area the *cultures* of which are more like one another than any are like the cultures of adjacent areas.

area, delinquency *urban, subcultural, natural area* possessing very high *crime* and *delinquency rates* and in which *crime* and *delinquency* are socially approved.

area, demographic an area delimited for *demographic* purposes.

area, deviant area possessing high *prevalence* of *deviance.*

area, disorganized 1. *urban area* where *values* and *behaviour patterns* deviate from those of general *population.* 2. urban area characterized by *social disorganization.*

area, distributional area over which a *culture trait* is distributed.

area, economic an area delimited by economic criteria.

area, focal 1. see *area, prestige.* 2. see *region, nodal.*

area, homogeneous area characterized by the uniform distribution of a specified phenomenon.

area, interstitial *blighted area* occurring in *urban* pocket.

area, isogloss area bounded by an *isogloss.*

area, marginal 1. a part of a *culture area* where the complex of *culture traits* peculiar to the area is found in its least extreme fofm. 2. an area at the boundaries of two culture areas displaying cultural features of both areas.

area, metropolitan a *metropolis* plus its *hinterland.*

area, natural unplanned, *urban area* of interdependent persons and activities.

area, negative an *uninhabitable* area.

area, refuge area into which *immigration* has resulted from pressure of other *tribes.*

area, registration an area for which *registration data* are collected.

area, rural an area possessing a *rural* character.

area, rurban an area having both *rural* and *urban* characteristics.

area, segregated area into which a *group* has been segregated. see also *segregation*.

area, service the area served by a library, hospital, etc.

area, social *set[1]* of contiguous *neighbourhoods* which possesses *demographic* and ecological homogeneity. (Tryon).

area, statistical an area delimited for the collection of *statistics*.

area, substandard an area which is below the national average in housing and in the services available to its inhabitants.

area, tribal an area regarded by a *tribe* as its *territory*.

area, underdeveloped an area characterized by *underdevelopment*.

area, urban 1. an *urbanized area* as a whole. 2. see *area, urbanized*.

area, urban, developed the *built-up area* plus streets of an *urban area*.

area, urban, total the *built-up area* plus streets plus open spaces of an *urban area*.

area, urbanized an area possessing an *urban* character.

area, urbanizing 1. an area in which *urbanization* is increasing. 2. an area which is in the process of acquiring an *urban* character.

armomancy *divination* from the shoulders of animals. **armomantic** *a.*

arena a stabilized conflict pattern with outcomes within certain bounds.

array items arranged according to magnitude.

artifact 1. man-made object. 2. device constructed to simulate some aspect of behaviour. 3. a finding which reflects an arbitrary *treatment* of the data.

artifact, statistical a *statistical inference* resulting from *bias*.

ascendancy 1. superiority in *power* or *status*. 2. the ability to induce another person or persons to violate *norms*.

ascendancy, impersonal *ascendancy[2]* in which those controlled are not known personally to the *ascendant[1]*.

ascendancy, individual *ascendancy[1]* of one individual over another.

ascendancy, personal 1. *ascendancy[1]* based on individual's personal attributes. 2. *ascendancy[2]* in which those controlled are known personally to the *ascendant[1]*.

ascendant 1. person in a position of *ascendancy*. 2. being in a position of ascendancy. *a.* 3. *ancestor,* living or dead.

ascription—achievement the incompatible alternatives facing an *actor* of orienting to a social object on the basis of some attribute it possesses or on its performance. (Parsons, T.).

asemasia inability to communicate by *signals* or words.

asemia inability to understand or communicate by *signs* or *gestures*.

asocial 1. indifferent to *norms*. 2. not instrumental to a socially-desired end.

aspiration, level of standard with reference to which individual has feeling of success or failure.

aspiration, mobility *level of aspiration* with regard to *social mobility*.

aspiration, occupational *level of aspiration* with regard to *occupational mobility*.

assemblage 1. loosely organized or fortuitous, contiguous *collectivity[1]*. 2. everything made and used by a particular extinct *culture*. 3. complex of *industries[9]* found at a *site[1]*. (archaeol.). 4. (LaPiere). see *audience[1]*.

assembly 1. see *audience[1]*. 2. a legislative or deliberative body. 3. *set[1]* of functionally interdependent *culture complexes*. 4. a part of the real world selected for observation.

assembly, constituent *assembly[2]* formed to frame or modify a *constitution[2]*.

assembly, consultative *assembly[2]* which may be consulted by the *government* but whose *function* is purely advisory.

assembly, national *assembly[2]* representing the whole *nation*.

21

assembly, popular *assembly*[2] representing the people.

assimilation 1. *acculturation,* structural incorporation, *amalgamation* or psychological *identification* of an *immigrant‖group.* 2. see *assimilation, structural.* 3. complete *acculturation.* 4. disappearance of cultural differences and rivalries between *populations.* 5. incorporation of individual or group into another group or fusion of groups in a common cultural life. see also *acculturation; enculturation.*

assimilation, behavioural see *assimilation, cultural.*

assimilation, civic absence of *value* and *power‖conflict* between *immigrants* and *host society.*

assimilation, cultural acquisition by *immigrants* of *culture* of *host society.*

assimilation, external *immigrant's* decreased distinguishability from members of *host society.*

assimilation, group *assimilation* occurring to a *group.*

assimilation, identificational *identification* of *immigrants* with *host society.*

assimilation, individual *assimilation* occurring to an individual.

assimilation, marital intermarriage of *immigrants* with members of *host society* resulting in *amalgamation.*

assimilation, occupational the *economic absorption* of *immigrants.*

assimilation, planned *assimilation* resulting from *planning* on the part of an *organization.* see also *acculturation, planned.*

assimilation, political incorporation of *immigrants* in the *political group.*

assimilation, structural incorporation of *immigrants* in the *social structure.*

assimilation, subjective *immigrant's identification* with *host society.*

association 1. *group* deliberately formed for a purpose. 2. group which is not a *kinship group.* 3. social intercourse. 4. interdependence between *quantitative* or *qualitative data.* 5. interdependence between qualitative data.

association, credit, rotating *association* the members of which have as a consequence of equal or unequal contributions a rotating, regular or premature access to the whole or a proportionate part of a continually reconstituted capital fund.

association, differential, Sutherland's theory of criminal behaviour is learned, in *interaction,* in process of *communication,* within intimate personal *groups, learning* comprising criminal techniques, *drives, attitudes* and *rationalizations;* learning of criminal associations involves all the mechanisms involved in any other learning; non-criminal behaviour expression of same *needs* and *values;* person becomes a criminal as result of excess of definitions favourable to violation of *law* over definitions unfavourable to violation of law.

association, ethnic an *association*[1] serving the interests of an *ethnic group.*

association, face-to-face *association*[3] involving *face-to-face contacts.* (Cooley, C.H.).

association, illusory a statistically significant *association* between two *attributes* which are not causally connected.

association, instrumental an *association*[1] which is directed towards the behaviour of nonmembers.

association, majoral an *association* serving the interests of one of the major *institutions* of *society.*

association, medial an *association* which mediates between major segments or *institutions* in the *society.*

association, minoral an *association* serving the interests of a *minority* in the *society.*

association, primary *association*[1] involving *primary contacts.* (Davis, K.).

association, promotional see *group, promotional.*

association, protective see *group, protective.*

22

association, secondary *association[1]* involving *secondary contacts*. (Davis, K.).

association, specialized *association[1]* serving a particular interest of a *group*. (MacIver).

association, spurious see *association, illusory*.

association, unspecialized *association[1]* serving total interests of a *group*. (MacIver).

association, voluntary 1. nonstate, common-purpose *organization* with voluntary membership. 2. nonstate, common-purpose organization with voluntary membership, with majority of members unpaid.

assumption, role taking on a *role* by an individual. see also *role-playing*; *role-taking*.

astragalomancy *divination* by means of small bones or dice. **astragalomantic** *a.*

astrolatry *worship* of the stars. **astrolatric** *a.*

asymbolia inability to comprehend *symbols*.

asymboly see *asymbolia*.

atom, social an individual and his relations of reciprocal attraction and repulsion with the other members of the *group*. (*sociom.*).

atomism, social view that the individual takes precedence to the *group* or *society* in explaining *sociocultural* phenomena.

attitude 1. a cluster of *cognitive, affective* and *conative* dispositions, inferred from a *sample* of behavioural *responses*. 2. an acquired mental and neural state of readiness influencing the individual's response to all objects and situations with which it is related. (Allport, G.). 3. the evaluative meaning possessed by an object or *concept* for an individual or *group*. (Osgood, C.E.). 4. the evaluative dimension of a concept. (Fishbein, M.).

attitude, associative an *attitude* which encourages social contacts.

attitude, cognitive a cluster of *cognitive* dispositions.

attitude, collective an *attitude* shared by a *collectivity*.

attitude, dissociative an *attitude* which discourages social contacts.

attitude, ethnic an *attitude* towards an *ethnic group*.

attitude, group an *attitude* shared by members of a *group*.

attitude, ideational an *attitude* expressed through speaking or writing. (Znaniecki, F.). see also *attitude, realistic*.

attitude, intergroup an *attitude* of one *group* towards another.

attitude, interpersonal an *attitude* of one person towards another.

attitude, mass an *attitude* shared by a *mass*.

attitude, negative an unfavourable *attitude* towards a thing, person, or *group*.

attitude, occupational an *attitude* forming part of an *occupational culture*.

attitude, positive a favourable *attitude* towards a thing, person, or *group*.

attitude, professional an *attitude* forming part of a *professional culture*.

attitude, realistic an *attitude* expressed through *action*. (Znaniecki, F.). see also *attitude, ideational*.

attitude, restrictive an *attitude* which restricts social contacts.

attribute 1. see *variable, qualitative*. 2. see *variable, dichotomous*.

attrition 1. cumulative loss of elements by a *set[1]*. 2. cumulative loss of elements by a *population*. 3. cumulative loss of members by a *birth cohort*.

audience 1. institutionalized, transitory, polarized, contiguous *collectivity*. 2. transitory, polarized collectivity whether or not institutionalized or contiguous. 3. collectivity without inter-member *communication*, exposed to a certain type of communication. 4. those persons who are exposed to a communication or *set[1]* of communications.

audience, captive *audience* unable to control its exposure to *communication*.

audience, casual *audience* characterized by accidental *polarization*. (LaPiere).

audience, concrete *audience* which is contiguous.

audience, conversional transitory, polarized *collectivity* formed in order to be the object of persuasion. (Young, K.).

audience, intentional *audience* characterized by intentional *polarization*. (Lapiere).

audience, mass a large *collectivity* without inter-member *communication*, exposed to a certain type of communication.

audience, passive *audience* in which *reaction* is covert.

audience, reactive *audience* in which *reaction* is overt.

audience, significant the *set¹* of persons who interact with and are of significance to a given individual.

augury *divination* by the interpretation of *omens*. **augur** *pers n.* **augural** *a.*

autarky national, economic self-sufficiency.

authoritarianism 1. authoritarian disposition in an individual. 2. see *personality, authoritarian*. 3. authoritarian procedures. 4. see *ideology, authoritarian.*5. the concurrence of authoritarian dispositions, procedures and ideology in a *society*. 6. *government* in which the governed play no part in governmental *decision-making*. see *absolutism¹*.

authority 1. legitimate *power*; power possessed with approval of those concerned. 2. the legitimate exercise of power. (Weber, M.). 3. the capacity, innate or acquired, for exercising *ascendancy* over a *group*. (Michels). 4. see *power, formal*. 5. see *authority, technical*.

authority, adjudicative *authority* to adjudicate. see also *adjudication*.

authority, administrative *authority* to plan, direct, or control the *activities* of a *group*. see also *planning*; *directing*; *control*.

authority, advisory the right to advise in an *organization*. see also *authority, staff*.

authority, charismatic *authority* based on the extraordinary quality of a particular person. (Weber, M.).

authority, coercive *authority* involving *coercive power*.

authority, colleage see *authority, collective*.

authority, collective *authority* which is vested in a *group*.

authority, control the right to command in an *organization*.

authority, de facto *power* possessed with approval of those concerned.

authority, de jure *power* where there is *rule* authorizing agent to issue *commands*.

authority, delegated *authority* conferred on a subordinate to exercise discretion on specified matters.

authority, discretionary see *power, discretionary*.

authority, domestic *authority* exercised in the *household*.

authority, echelon see *authority, line¹*.

authority, executive *authority* based on incumbency of *office*.

authority, final see *authority, ultimate*.

authority, formal 1. *authority* exercised in a *formal organization*. 2. see also *authority, de jure*.

authority, functional a right to command which is limited to a specialized area of *activity*.

authority, impersonal *authority* which is not based on an individual's personal attributes.

authority, informal *authority* exercised in an *informal organization*.

authority, jural *power* where there is a *rule* authorizing agent to issue *commands*. (Homans).

authority, line 1. the right to command in an *organization*. 2. the right to exercise the main *function* in an organization. 3. the right to command which is not limited to a specialized area of *activity*. see also *authority, staff*.

authority, normative *authority* involving *normative power*.

authority, personal *authority* based on an individual's personal attributes.

authority, positional *authority* based on incumbency of a *position* or *office*.

authority, rational-legal *power* legitimated and defined by *law* and held by legally qualified office-holder. (Weber, M.).

authority, reinforcing *authority* to enforce *conformity* to *norms*.

authority, remunerative *authority* involving *remunerative power*.

authority, sapiential the right to advise others in an *organization*.

authority, seignorial see *jurisdiction, seignorial*.

authority, shared *authority* possessed by two or more officials to make joint *decision*.

authority, splintered the pooling of *authority* by two or more officials in order to make *decisions*.

authority, staff 1. the right to advise in an *organization*. 2. the right to exercise a supportive *function* in an organization. see also *authority, line*.

authority, structural the right to command in an *organization*.

authority, sub-delegated *authority* which is the result of further *delegation* of *delegated authority*.

authority, technical the acceptance by others of a person's opinion because he is a recognized expert in the field concerned.

authority, territorial *authority* exercised over all the inhabitants of a certain *territory*.

authority, traditional *power* legitimated and defined by *tradition* and held by persons qualified by tradition; traditional authority thus rests on piety for what is thought to have always existed. (Weber, M.).

authority, ultimate the *authority* which is the ultimate source of a particular individual's authority.

autobiography, focused autobiography produced by *focused interview*||*technique*. see also *semi-autobiography*.

autocompetition attempt to improve on one's own performance.

autocracy rule by one person exercising unlimited *authority* without accountability. **autocratic** *a.* **autocrat** *pers n.*

autocracy, legitimate *autocracy* established in accordance with pre-existing *norms*.

automation *mechanization* involving mechanical self-correction and self-programming. see also *automatization*; *mechanization*.

automation, office the *computerization* of organizational *data processing*.

automatization the introduction of *automation*.

autonomy, external autonomy possessed by a *group* in external affairs.

autonomy, functional 1. the degree to which any one part of an *organization* can continue to survive after separation from the others. 2. functional interdependence of a psychological mechanism.

autonomy, group freedom of a *group* from external control.

autonomy, internal autonomy possessed by a *group* in internal affairs.

autonym a name applied to a person independent of his relation to other relatives, living or dead.

autostereotype a *group's stereotype* of itself.

autostereotype, reflected a *group's perception* of the *stereotype* held of it by another group.

autotelic 1. having itself as its *goal*. 2. pertaining to the central purposes of an individual.

autotomy the temporary or permanent expulsion, formal or informal, of a *group* member. (Slater, P.E.).

aversion, social a culturally-conditioned aversion. see also *conditioning, cultural*.

avoidance see *relationship, avoidance*.

avoidance, avuncular *avoidance relationship* between nephew and mother's brother.

avoidance, deferential avoiding reference to a matter out of *deference[1]* to another. (Goffman, E.).

avoidance, food the prescribed avoidance of a particular food.

avoidance, name the prescribed avoidance of the mention of the name of a person or *supernatural*.

avoidance, referential avoiding reference to a matter embarrassing to self or others. (Goffman, E.).

avoidance, sibling *avoidance relationship* between siblings.

avulsion the removal of teeth for ritual purposes.

avuncuclan *clan* based on *matrilineal descent* and *avunculocal residence*. (Murdock).

avuncu-family see *family, extended, avunculocal.*

avunculate especially close ties between nephew and mother's brother.

avunculocality see *residence, avunculocal.*

avuncupotestal with *authority* concentrated in mother's brother.

award decision of an arbitrator or arbitrators. see also *arbitration*.

axiology the investigation of the nature, types, criteria, and metaphysical status of *values*. **axiological** *a.*

axiom 1. an assertion without proof in an *axiomatic theory*. 2. a basic *proposition* common to all disciplines. see also *postulate*; *theorem*; *corollary*.

axiom-set a *set[1]* of *axioms* whether or not constituting an *axiomatic theory*.

axiometry the science of measuring *value*.

axis, development a corridor of development along a transport route linking two or more *metropolitan regions*.

ballot 1. process by which votes are gathered from those qualified to vote. 2. a paper, ball, or other object used to register a vote.

ballot, chain method of vote-buying according to which the vote-buyer obtains an unmarked *ballot[2]*, marks it, gives it to a voter who casts it and is paid after handing to the vote-buyer the unmarked *ballot[2]* he has received at the polling-station, which is then given to another voter, and so on.

ballot, exhaustive taking successive *ballots[1]*, the candidate with the fewest votes being eliminated on each *ballot[1]*, until one candidate secures an *absolute majority*.

ballot, office-block see *ballot, office-group.*

ballot, office-group *ballot[1]* in which all the candidates for a single *office* are arrayed together.

ballot, party-circle *ballot[1]* in which voter places a mark in a circle representing all the candidates of a particular *party*.

ballot, party-column *ballot[1]* in which candidates are listed by *party* vertically and by *office* horizontally.

ballot, party-emblem *ballot[1]* in which emblems are used for the identification of *parties* in addition to the names of parties or candidates.

ballot, second a second *election* which occurs if an *absolute majority* is not obtained by one of the candidates, all the candidates below the top two dropping out.

ballot, secret any method of casting votes which conceals the identity of the voter.

band a migratory *community*. see also *horde*.

band, collateral 1. a *band* consisting of many unrelated *families* and lacking *patrilineality, patrilocality,* and *band exogamy.* 2. see *band, unilateral.*

band, composite a *band* consisting of bilaterally-related *families.* (Martin, M.K.).

band, familistic a *band* consisting of an *independent nuclear family.* (Martin, M.K.).

band, matrilineal a *band* based on *matrilineal descent.*

band, patrilineal 1. a *band* characterized by *patrilineality, patrilocality,* and *band exogamy.* 2. a band based on *patrilineal descent.*

band, patrilocal see *band, patrilineal.*

band, unilateral a *band* having *residence rules,* membership of which is based not on an *ancestral ego* but on a *contemporary ego.* (Martin, M.K.).

band, unilineal 1. a *band* consisting of a single *lineage.* (Martin, M.K.). 2. a band based on *unilineal descent.*

barter *exchange* of goods for goods.

barter, dumb see *trade, silent.*

barter, intercommunity *barter* between *communities* at fixed rates on a permanent basis.

barter, money *barter* in which the exchange goods or other goods are used as standards of *value[5].*

barter, pure the complete dependence on *barter* for economic *exchanges.*

barter, silent see *trade, silent.*

base, culture those *culture traits* constituting a base for a particular *innovation.*

base, export the exportable commodities and services of a *region.*

baseline *value[6]* or values from which changes in a *variable* are measured. see also *criterion; standard.*

baseline, complex *baseline* whose *value[6]* varies predictably according to circumstances.

baseline, constant *baseline* with same *value[6]* under all circumstances.

baseline, stable *baseline,* constant or complex, whose *value[6]* can be ascertained.

baseline, zero *baseline* whose *value[6]* is zero.

behaviour, abient behaviour tending to remove organism from exposure to a given *stimulus.*

behaviour, adient behaviour tending to expose organism to more of a given *stimulus.*

behaviour, avoidance prescribed mutual avoidance between certain relatives. see also *relationship, avoidance.*

behaviour, circular 1. *behaviour cycle* stimulating its own repetition. 2. see *interaction, serial.*

behaviour, collective a noninstitutionalized mobilization of a generalized belief. (Smelser, N. J.).

behaviour, cross-sex behaviour between persons of opposite sex.

behaviour, cultural behaviour which is culturally-determined.

behaviour, deference behaviour intended to convey respect and appreciation on the part of one person for another. (Goffman, E.). see also *ritual, avoidance; ritual, presentational.*

behaviour, detour goal-directed behaviour following an indirect course resulting from an obstacle.

behaviour, emitted see *behaviour, operant.*

behaviour, expressive behaviour which expresses internal state.

behaviour, institutionalized behaviour which has become standardized and norm-controlled in a *collectivity.*

behaviour, instrumental behaviour which is a means to an end.

behaviour, irrelative making judgments on one *stimulus* at a time, e.g., rating individuals on a *rating scale* or expressing like or dislike for each of a number of items. see also *behaviour, relative.*

behaviour, joking disrespectful behaviour implying a privileged familiarity between relatives of specified categories. see also *relationship, joking; partners, joking*.

behaviour, kinesic communicative body motion behaviour.

behaviour kinship behaviour of relatives towards one another qua relatives.

behaviour, mass *collective behaviour* resulting from *mass communication*.

behaviour, normative behaviour prescribed by *norms*.

behaviour, operant behaviour which does not occur in response to *eliciting stimuli* but acts upon the *environment*.

behaviour, organizational behaviour of individuals in *interaction* occurring in *organization*.

behaviour, pluralistic the behaviour of a *plurel*.

behaviour, proxemic space-handling behaviour. see also *proxemics*.

behaviour, reflex see *behaviour, respondent*.

behaviour, relative judging between two or more *stimuli*, e.g., expressing preference or judging which of two individuals has more of a given characteristic. see also *behaviour, irrelative*.

behaviour, respondent behaviour occurring in response to *eliciting stimuli*.

behaviour, role see *performance, role[1]*.

behaviour, segmental behaviour involving *segmental contacts*.

behaviour, serial behaviour consisting of *reflex chains*.

behaviour, social 1. behaviour of an individual in response to his *interpersonal environment*. 2. behaviour having person or *group* as object.

behaviour, spontaneous see *behaviour, operant*.

behaviourism the view that psychology should be restricted to the study of behaviour. **behaviourist** *a.* & *pers n.*

behaviourism, dogmatic *behaviourism* involving a denial of consciousness.

behaviourism, methodological *behaviourism* in which restriction to the study of behaviour is advocated on methodological grounds.

beneceptor *receptor* which is aroused by beneficial *stimuli*. see also *nociceptor*.

benefice a grant of land that can be withdrawn at will. see also *fief; appanage; seigniory*.

berdache person who takes over dress and manner of living of opposite sex.

betrothal, infant betrothal of a person in infancy.

bias systematic distortion influencing the outcome of research.

bias, contagious influence of interviewer's behaviour in the interview on *respondent's responses*.

bias, downward a *bias* tending to produce a *value[6]* below the true *value[6]*.

bias, experimenter *bias* in *experiment* due to unintentional behaviour of experimenter.

bias, frame *bias* resulting from defects in *sampling frame*.

bias, interviewer *bias* in the *responses* or recorded information directly resulting from interviewer's behaviour.

bias, negative see *bias, downward*.

bias, net difference between total *positive bias* and total *negative bias*.

bias, nonresponse *bias* due to *nonresponse*.

bias, nonsampling *bias* which is not due to sampling variability.

bias, positive see *bias, upward*.

bias, re-interviewing influence on *respondent's responses* of being re-interviewed.

bias, sampling *bias* due to sampling variability.

bias, theoretic exaggeration used as a heuristic device in *theory* construction. (Bierstedt, R.).

bias, upward a *bias* tending to produce a *value[6]* above the true *value[6]*.

bias, volunteer *bias* resulting from self-selection of members for the group studied.

bicultural 1. pertaining to *biculturism.* 2. in which two *cultures* are represented. 3. pertaining to two cultures.

biculturalism the presence of two *cultures* in a *community* or *political unit.*

biculturism the employment, by an individual under different circumstances where appropriate, of two modes of behaviour learned in *culture contact.*

bifurcation applying one term to a relative if the relative linking him to *ego* is male and another if the linking relative is female.

bilaterality see *descent, bilateral.*

bilocality see *residence, bilocal.*

bimodal (of a *frequency distribution*) having two *modes.*

biocultural involving both biological and cultural *factors.*

bio-cybernetics the *cybernetics* of organisms.

biogenic of biological origin.

biograms partial autobiographies of group members written under specific instructions of investigator for obtaining data on *group.*

biologism attributing to biology supreme importance for the *explanation* of human behaviour. **biologistic** *a.*

biometrics see *biometry.*

biometry statistical analysis of biological data. **biometric** *a.*

biopsychology the interrelations of biology and *psychology.*

biosocial 1. involving both biological and social *factors.* 2. pertaining to social phenomena in which biological factors are predominant.

biosociology the interrelations of biology and *sociology.*

biosphere that part of earth's crust and atmosphere favourable to life.

biostatistics see *statistics, vital.*

biotic pertaining to life.

biotype 1. group of individuals of approximately the same *genotype.* 2. see *somatotype.*

birth, live any product of conception showing any signs of life after birth.

birth rate *general, specific* or *standardized rate* concerning *natality.*

birth rate, central *birth rate* based on *population* at mid-point of period.

birth rate, completed total number of *live births* of a *cohort* when all members have reached end of reproductive period.

birth rate, crude number of *live births* per specified number of persons over a specified period of time.

birth rate, cumulative total number of *live births* of a *cohort* from beginning of exposure to *risk*[2] until a specified date.

birth rate, live a *birth rate* concerning *live births* and excluding late foetal deaths.

birth rate, nuptial number of *live births* per specified number of married women over a specified period of time.

birth rate, parity-specific number of *live births* per specified number of women of a specified *parity* over a specified period of time.

birth rate, specific *birth rate* calculated for a homogeneous *sub-population.*

birth rate, stable *crude birth rate* of a *stable population.*

birth rate, standardized *birth rate* permitting comparability of *populations.*

birth rate, total number of *live births* and late foetal deaths per specified number of persons over a specified period of time.

bloc 1. combination of persons, *groups,* or *states* with a common interest or purpose. 2. group of states united for mutual support or joint action. 3. group of legislators who vote together for a particular interest.

block 1. group of items receiving a particular *treatment*[3]. 2. obstacle to action. 3. group of buildings which it is possible to go round without crossing a street or which is bounded by an obstacle.

borrowing, cultural adoption by one *culture* of *culture traits* of another culture.
botanomancy *divination* by means of leaves. **botanomantic** *a.*
boundary, cultural the coinciding of the distributional boundaries of a *set¹* of *culture traits.*
boundary, sentient the boundary of a *sentient group* or *sentient system.* (Miller, E. J.).
boundary, systems boundary between *system* and *environment.*
boundary-maintenance resistance of *system* to external attack.
boxhead section of *statistical table* which contains *column captions* and which specifies units.
bride-price *wealth* which passes at *marriage* from husband's *kin* to wife's kin.
bride-price, token *bride-price* consisting of a small or symbolic payment.
bride-service work done by husband for his parents-in-law.
bride-service, postmarital *bride-service* performed after the *marriage.*
bride-service, premarital *bride-service* performed before the *marriage.*
bridewealth see *bride-price.*
bridewealth, token see *bride-price, token.*
broker a middleman who recruits followers who believe him able to influence a person who can dispense favour. see also *patron.*
brokerage the *activities* of a *broker* qua broker.
brotherhood, ritual a fictive brotherhood established by a *ritual.*
budget estimate of future income and expenditure.
budget, family financial statement of recorded and projected revenue and expenditure of a *family.*
budget, household financial statement of recorded and projected revenue and expenditure of a *household.*
budget, time a record of an individual's *activities* giving the exact time at which the various activities begin and end.
bureau a subdivision of a government department or agency.
bureaucracy the organizational characteristics of *specialization, hierarchy, system* of *rules,* impersonality. **bureaucratic** *a.*
bureaucracy, agrarian *bureaucracy* found in an *irrigation state.*
bureaucracy, caste *public bureaucracy* which favours certain *social strata* in recruitment and security in office. (Marx, F.M.).
bureaucracy, governmental see *bureaucracy, public.*
bureaucracy, guardian *public bureaucracy* with an *ideology* of devotion to the common good, with its officials as exemplars. (Marx, F.M.).
bureaucracy, merit *public bureaucracy* with recruitment and promotion based on merit. (Marx, F.M.).
bureaucracy, patrimonial *bureaucracy* involving unfree officials. (Weber, M.).
bureaucracy, patronage *public bureaucracy* in which *positions* are filled according to political affiliation or personal favouritism. (Marx, F.M.).
bureaucracy, private *bureaucracy* in the private sector.
bureaucracy, public *bureaucracy* in the public sector.
bureaucracy, punishment-centred *bureaucracy* based on the imposition of *norms* and on obedience for its own sake. (Gouldner, A.W.).
bureaucracy, representative *bureaucracy* based on agreed-upon *norms.* (Gouldner, A.W.).
bureaucracy, state see *bureaucracy, public.*
bureaucratization the acquisition of *bureaucratic* character.
bypassing misinterpretation of a *message* by a recipient.
bystander an individual present who is not a ratified member of the *encounter.* (Goffman, E.).

cabal a plurality of persons secretly united and using devious and undercover means for the seizure of *power*.

cadastral pertaining to land ownership.

calculus an uninterpreted *axiomatic system*.

calendar, ceremonial the annual *cycle* of *rites* whose performance can be anticipated.

calendar, religious the annual cycle of *religiousǁceremonies* and observances.

call-back a later call to reach a *respondent[1]* not initially at home.

camarilla an unoffical *group* of personal advisers to a ruler.

canalization restriction of affect or a type of behaviour to a certain direction.

canon a *principle* guiding scientific *procedure*.

capacity, carrying *maximum population* of a *territory*.

capacity, metatask ability of a *system* to reorganize itself or the *environment* so as to prevent environmental disturbances. (Kaplan).

capacity, task ability of a *system* to reduce environmental disturbances. (Kaplan).

capital 1. anything permitting *society* to undertake *activites* having a deferred reward. 2. produced means of production. 3. *wealth* which produces more wealth. 4. a society's stock of material assets. 5. that which produces interest. (Thurnwald). 6. resources directed to productive ends. (Firth, R.). 7. all sources of income streams. (Fisher, I.).

capital, auxiliary all the equipment used in production.

capital, circulating *capital* which is consumed in one use.

capital, conventional see *capital, material*.

capital, fixed *capital* which can be used repeatedly.

capital, human produced human abilities which constitute a source of income.

capital, instrumental see *capital, auxiliary*.

capital, material *capital* which is not *human capital*.

capital, real raw materials and equipment used in production.

capital, social assets publicly owned.

capital-intensive pertaining to production employing a high ratio of *capital* to *labour[1]*. see also *labour-intensive*.

capnomancy *divination* by means of smoke. **capnomantic** *a.*

caption, column heading of column in a *statistical table*.

caption, row heading of row in a *statistical table*.

caption, scale verbal description or number assigned to a *scale point*.

career 1. an individual's sequence of *occupations*. 2. a standardized sequence of occupations of increasing *prestige* for an individual to pass through. 3. a predictable course through a *bureaucracy*. (Mannheim, K.). 4. an individual's movement through a series, not predetermined, of *statuses* or *roles*.

career, criminal an individual's sequence of sustained criminal activities.

career, delinquent an individual's sequence of sustained delinquent activities.

career, deviant an individual's sequence of sustained deviant activities.

career, graded see *career[2]*.

career, life the movement of an individual through a series, not predetermined, of all the *statuses* or *roles* of his life.

career, occupational see *career[1,2]*.

cartogram map showing an *areal distribution*.

cartomancy *divination* by means of cards or playing cards. **cartomantic** *a.*

case, custodial a psychiatric or criminal case in which *treatment[1]* is restricted to custody.

case-load. 1. the number of cases being simultaneously dealt with by a caseworker. 2. the number of persons requiring a particular *social service* from a particular social agency.

caste a *social stratum* in a *caste system.*

category 1. a *set[1]* whose membership is determined by defining characteristics or by limits of *measurement.*2. a rule for *classification* of *stimulus objects* as equivalents. (Triandis, H. C.).

category, analytic a *category* applied by social scientists to social phenomena.

category, folk a *category* applied by a *society* to its own social phenomena.

category, observational any one of a *set[1]* of *categories* employed in the *systematic observation* of behaviour.

category, occupational see *family, occupational.*

category, kinship a *category* of relatives.

category, social a *category* of persons in a *society.*

catharsis 1. the method by which *abreaction* is achieved. 2. the therapeutic effect of abreaction. **cathartic** *a.*

cathection the process by which affect is attached to an object. **cathect** *vt.*

cathexis affect attached to an object. see also *acathexis.*

catoptromancy *divination* by means of a mirror. **catoptromantic** *a.*

caucus a meeting of a small group within a larger *party* or *faction* for the consideration of *organization* or *policy.*

celeration, social rate of change in a social *variable.* see also *acceleration, social*; *deceleration, social.*

cell 1. rectangle in a contingency table. 2. rectangle in a grid. 3. rectangle representing a group or plot in a *research design* diagram. 4. any one of the many *subgroups* constituting a *cellular organization.*

cell, gossip plurality of persons regularly exchanging *gossip.*

cenogamy see *marriage, group.*

censorship the restriction by *authority* of any public expression regarded as dangerous to that authority or to the political or moral order it sustains.

censorship, advance see *censorship, preventative.*

censorship, preliminary see *censorship, preventative.*

censorship, preventative *censorship* exercised before the issuance of the material in question.

censorship, punitive *censorship* exercised after the issuance of the material in question.

census 1. study of entire *population* instead of a *sample.* 2. universal, simultaneous, individual *enumeration* of population of defined *territory*, with data compiled by geographic areas and basic *demographic‖variables.* (SOUN). 3. statistical count of *population distribution* or production.

census, complete *census* involving complete coverage of the *population* intended to be completely covered.

census, de facto *census* based on *de facto populations.*

census, de jure *census* based on *de jure populations.*

census, family 1. collection and *tabulation* of data concerning all members of a *family.* 2. collection and tabulation of data concerning all the families in a particular area.

census, general complete *enumeration* of *population* of *state territory.*

census, incomplete *census* involving incomplete coverage of the *population* intended to be completely covered.

census, linguistic an *enumeration* of languages and their speakers in a given area, or of individuals with the languages they speak.

census, partial complete *enumeration* of a specified section of a *population.*

census, population see *census[2].*

centiles see *percentiles.*

centrality, individual degree of access of a given position to all others in *network.*

centrality, total sum of individual *centralities* in *network.*

centralization 1. *(hum. ecol.)* concentration of activities. 2. concentration of *decision-making* concerning *policy* of the more general type.

centre, culture that part of a *culture area* where the complex of *culture traits* peculiar to the area is found in its most extreme form.

centre, power the most powerful position in a *group.*

centre, prestige locality from which *culture traits* diffuse as a result of the *prestige* of its inhabitants. see also *diffusion[1].*

centre, radiating see *area, prestige.*

ceremonial a *system* of *ceremonies.* see also *rite; ritual.*

ceremonialization the making ceremonial of an *activity.* **ceremonialize** *v.*

ceremony 1. standardized combination of *rites.* 2. rites signalizing important event. see also *ceremonial; ritual.*

ceremony, degradation communicative work aimed at *actor's degradation[1].*

ceremancy *divination* from figures formed by melted wax dropped into water or on the floor. **ceromantic** *a.*

cession giving up *territory* to another *state.* **cede** *v.*

chain, migration the flow of migrants involved in a *chain migration.*

chain, reflex see *reflex, chain.*

chain, scalar the entire chain of officials having a superior-subordinate relationship in an *organization.*

change, autonomous change resulting from *factors* within the *system.*

change, endogenous see *change, autonomous.*

change, exogenous change resulting from *factors* external to the *system.*

change, group changes in *group structure* over time.

change, incremental change which is quantitative and not qualitative.

change, prostructural change in a structural element determined by its structural context.

change, repetitive change in personnel without change in the *social structure.* (Bailey, F. G.).

change, social changes in *social structure* or *culture* over time.

change, sociocultural changes in a *sociocultural system* over time.

change, structured change occurring in well-organized steps.

channel, asymmetrical a one-way *communication channel.*

channel, code a *communiation channel* for coded *messages.*

channel, communication a part of a *communication system* along which *messages* are conveyed.

channel, information a *communication channel* for the transmission of information.

channel, symmetrical a two-way *communication channel.*

chaomancy *divination* by the observation of atmospheric changes. **chaomantic** *a.*

character 1. refers to stability, strength, or goodness of *personality.* 2. personal variant of the *basic personality structure.* (Kardiner). see also *personality.*

character, affectionless a *personality* possessing inability for affection towards another person.

character, national 1. see *personality, modal.* 2. see *structure, personality, basic.*

character, social the nuclear component of a *social personality.* (Honigmann, J.J.).

character, status the nuclear component of a *status personality.*

characteristics, diacritical characteristics which are the conscious badge of a *group,* distinguishing it from others of the same kind, e.g., dress, manners, etiquette. (Nadel, S.F.).

Characteristics, Index of Status (I.S.C.) total of weighted *ratings,* on seven-point *scales[2],* of four *status* characteristics, namely, *occupation,* source of income, house type, dwelling area, which is an *index of an individual's socioeconomic* status and *social class*. (Warner).

characteristics, syncretic characteristics of a *group* which are not *diacritical characteristics*. (Nadel, S.F.).

charisma an extraordinary quality of a person, the belief in which gives rise to his acceptance as a *leader*. **charismatic** *a.*

charisma, attenuated *charisma* which has become reduced in intensity. (Shils, E.).

charisma, concentrated *charisma* which is concentrated in one person or a few persons, or a few of the *roles, statuses,* or *institutions* of a *society*. (Shils, E.).

charisma, dispersed *charisma* which is dispersed through the personnel, *roles, statuses,* or *institutions* of a *society*. (Shils, E.).

charisma, personal *charisma* which is attached to a particular person and not to a *role, status, office,* or *institution*.

charisma, prophet *charisma* resulting from an individual's acceptance as a *prophet*.

charisma, routinized *charisma* which has become dispersed or hereditary.

chart, activity a diagram showing the breakdown of a process plotted against a time scale.

chart, alignment see *nomograph*.

chart, authority a chart showing the *authority structure* of an *organization*.

chart, band combination of *line graphs* showing not only total *values[6]* but also component *values[6]*.

chart, bar diagram consisting of a series of horizontal bars proportional in length to the quantities they represent. see also *chart, column*.

chart, bar, component see *chart, bar, subdivided*.

chart, bar, grouped *bar chart* in which the bars showing total *values[6]* are grouped with bars representing the components of these *values[6]*.

chart, bar, simple *bar chart* in which the bars show total *values[6]* and are not grouped with bars representing the components of the *values[6]*.

chart, bar, subdivided *bar chart* in which each bar is subdivided to show constituents as well as the total *value[6]*.

chart, circular chart in which the components of a total are represented by sectors of a circle, the angles showing the proportions.

chart, column diagram consisting of a series of vertical bars proportional in length to the quantities they represent. see also *chart, bar*.

chart, column, component see *chart, column, subdivided*.

chart, column, grouped *column chart* in which the columns showing total *values[6]* are grouped with columns representing the components of these *values[6]*.

chart, column, simple *column chart* in which the columns show total *values[6]* and are not grouped with columns representing the components of these *values[6]*.

chart, column, subdivided *column chart* in which each column is subdivided to show constituents as well as the total *value[6]*.

chart, communication a chart showing the *communication network* in an *organization*.

chart, coordinate see *graph, line*.

chart, curve see *graph, line*.

chart, flow 1. a graphic representation of a sequence of operations. 2. a graphic representation of a sequence of computer operations.

chart, line see *graph, line*.

chart, man-machine chart showing relationship between work of operator and that of a single machine.

chart, organization a chart showing the *formal organization*.

chart, organization, circular an *organization chart* representing the *organization* by means of concentric circles, the nearer a circle is to the centre the higher the *organizational level* represented.

chart, organization, vertical an *organization chart* representing the *organization* in pyramidal form.

chart, pie see *chart, circular*.

chart, process chart showing sequence of operations involved in a *group task*.

chart, silhouette *line graph* showing the positive deviations and negative deviations from a *baseline* with the area between the baseline and the curve filled in.

chart, stratum see *chart, band*.

chart, surface see *chart, band*.

chart, work-flow chart showing sequence of *activities* through an *organization*.

charter the explicitly-formulated *norms* of an *institution* or *constitution* as distinct from its practice or personnel.

chief a *leader* in a *society* which is on a low technological level. (Lewis, J.).

chiefdom a large, *primitive, polysegmentary, society* which possesses a central *government*.

child-price see *progeny-price*.

child-wealth see *progeny-price*.

chiliastic see *millenarian*.

chiromancy *divination* by inspection of the hands. **chiromantic** *a*.

chreod the buffered path along which a *homeorhetic system* develops. see also *homeorhesis*.

chthonic pertaining to subterranean spirits.

cicatrice decorative or symbolic scar. see also *cicatrization*; *scarification*; *moko*; *moxa*; *keloid*.

cicatrization see *scarification*.

cicisbeism permitted sexual access of a man to another man's wife who is not also his own wife. see also *polyandry*; *levirate, anticipatory*.

cicisbeism, fraternal permitted sexual access of a man's brothers to his own wife who is not also their wife.

cicisbeo a man who has permitted sexual access to another man's wife who is not also his own wife.

circle, divided see *chart, circular*.

circle, exchange plurality of persons who restrict *gift exchange* to one another.

circle, interest non-localized *interest group*.

circle, magic a circle around a person constituting a magical defence.

circle, social non-institutionalized, informal *interest group* having moderate degree of directness of member *interaction*. (Simmel, G.). see also *salon, social*; *set, social*.

circulation, ecological the intranational and international movements of goods, passengers, information, ideas, and *capital*.

circulation, internal degree of movement of group members to new positions in same *group*.

circulation, social 1. the movement of individuals into and out of *groups* and from group to group. 2. degree of change in group membership, group size held constant.

circumambulation ritual walking round of a *sacred* object. **circumambulate** *v*.

circumcision partial or total removal of prepuce.

circumcision, female removal of the labia minora in the female.

circumcision, pharaonic causing scar tissue to join the labia minora in order to prevent copulation. see also *infibulation*.

circumcision, symbolic a ritual action, such as making a scratch or scratches on the prepuce, which is regarded by a *community* as symbolic of *circumci-*

35

sion.

city, central the city which dominates a *metropolitan area.*

city, commercial a city commercially-oriented in its activities.

city, dispersed cluster of spatially-separated urban places with a degree of *functional specialization.*

city, dominant the city which dominates a specified area.

city, industrial a city industrially-oriented in its   activities.

city, inner 1. the central high density area of a city. 2. the area of deterioration near the *central business district.*

city, linear a linear-shaped planned city planned to retain a linear shape during its expansion. (Doxiades).

city, metropolitan see *metropolis.*

city, millionaire see *million-city.*

city, mononucleated a city which has developed from a single nucleus.

city, orthogenetic see *city, mononucleated.*

city, overbounded city whose political limits extend beyond the *urban area.*

city, polynucleated a city which has developed from several nuclei, either simultaneously or in succession.

city, primate the *dominant city* of a *state.*

city, regional the city dominating a *metropolitan region.*

city, satellite a city in a *metropolitan area* not totally dependent on the *metropolis* for employment.

city, strip an urbanized band connecting two cities.

city, underbounded city that includes within its political limits only part of the *urban area.*

civilization 1. the cumulative part of *culture.* 2. the utilitarian part of culture. 3. the property possessed by a *society* of sophistication, in the sense of reflecting on its own culture. (Bierstedt). 4. the presence of towns and writing. 5. the presence of writing in a society. (Sjoberg). 6. the presence of two of the following: towns, writing, complex ceremonial centres. (Kluckhohn, C.). see also *culture.*

civilization, hydraulic a *civilization* based on large-scale *irrigation.*

civilization, irrigation see *civilization, hydraulic.*

clan 1. a *consanguineal kin group* based on *unilineal descent* but with descent untraced.   2. see *matriclan.* 3. localized, *corporate kin group* with compatibility of *residence rule* and unilineal descent rule, with in-marrying spouses as members. (Murdock, G.P.).

clan, conceptional a group consisting of individuals living and dead thought to have been conceived in the same place.

clan, dispersed *clan* the members of which are interspersed with members of other clans.

clan, localized *clan* the members of which are not interspersed with members of other clans.

clan, multilocal see *clan, dispersed.*

clan, unilocal see *clan, localized.*

clan, uterine see *matriclan.*

clan-barrios the constituent *clans* of a *kin-community.* (Murdock). see also *clan-community.*

clan-community *clan* which is also a *community.* (Murdock). see also *clan-barrios.*

clan-mates fellow-members of a *clan.*

clan-section *set¹* of *sub-clans* forming part of *clan.*

claque *group* of subservient followers always ready to applaud their *leader.*

class, closed a *social class* in a *closed-class system.*

class, dependent a *social class* sharing considerably in the benefits of the rule, but not participating in it. (Lasswell, H.D.).

class, kin labelled *set[1]* of *kin-types*. (Loundsbury, F.G.).

class, marriage see *section, marriage*.

class, open a *social class* in an *open-class system*.

class, ruling the *social class* from which rulers are recruited and in whose interest they exercise *power*. (Lasswell, H.D.).

class, self-assigned see *class, social, subjective*.

class, self-rated see *class, social, subjective*.

class, social 1. major social *group*, members of which are of approximately same economic position. 2. major social group, members of which are of approximately same economic position, *prestige*, occupational rank, *power*, value orientations, and characterized by *interaction* and *class consciousness*.

class, social, subjective the *social class* of which an individual believes himself to be a member.

class, subject the *social class* sharing least in both *power* and other *values*. (Lasswell, H.D.).

classification 1. an arrangement of classes. 2. creating an arrangement of classes. 3. examining individuals for their place in an arrangement of classes. 4. assigning and re-assigning prisoners to classes and segregated *groups* in the course of their *treatment[2]*. see also *taxonomy*.

classification, duties *ranking* of *public offices* based on *position classification*, promotion depending on possession of relevant qualifications.

classification, manifold a *set[1]* of more than two co-ordinate classes.

classification, monothetic *classification* based on one or only a few characters, all the objects allocated to one class necessarily sharing the character or characters under consideration. see also *classification, polythetic*; *taxonomy, numerical*.

classification, natural *classification* yielding *taxa* whose members are in some sense more similar to one another than they are to members of other taxa.

classification, polythetic *classification* based on many characters and which does not require any one character to be universal for a class. see also *classification, monothetic*; *taxonomy, numerical*.

classification, position *classification* of a *set[1]* of administrative *positions* by skill, resulting from the analysis of the duties attached to the positions and their re-allocation and re-clustering.

classification, rank *ranking* of *public offices* not based on *position classification*, promotion depending on seniority and general competence.

classification, residence *classification* of residential location of married couples. see also *residence*.

clearance upward or lateral referral in *organization* for approval of *decision*.

clearance, lateral referral to *staff* for approval of *decision*.

clearance, multiple referral to a number of specialists of different type for approval of *decision*.

clericalism 1. the intervention of *religious‖leaders* in *politics*. 2. the doctrine that religious leaders should intervene in politics.

cleromancy *divination* by lots. **cleromantic** *a*.

climax, culture see *centre, culture*.

cliometrics the application of mathematical and statistical methods to history. (Conrad, A.H.). **cliometric** *a*. **cliometrician** *pers n*.

cliometrician *pers n*.

clique 1. small, spontaneous, informal *subgroup* of larger formal *group*. 2. regularly associating *primary group*.

clique, friendship *clique* formed by and aimed at the furtherence of common friendship.

37

clique, generalized *clique* which is socially heterogeneous.

clique, horizontal *organizational clique* whose members are drawn from the same *rank* of the same *department*.

clique, mixed *organizational clique* whose members are drawn from different *ranks* and from different *departments*.

clique, natural *clique* arising spontaneously from common friendship.

clique, organizational *clique* present in an *organization*.

clique, power *clique* aimed at the furtherence of *power*, either its own power or the power of another person or *group*.

clique, random see *clique, mixed*.

clique, social see *clique, friendship*.

clique, vertical an *organizational clique* whose members are drawn from different *ranks* of the same *department*.

clique, work 1. *clique[1]* forming part of a larger *work group*. 2. *clique[2]* whose members associate freely on the *job*.

clitoridectomy removal of the clitoris.

clitoridotomy see *circumcision, female*.

club 1. a *group* specifically organized for the pursuit of a special interest. (Lewis, J.). 2. a free *association*. (Hsu, F.L.K.).

club, contribution see *association, credit, rotating*.

cluster, behaviour a series of *behaviour items*.

cluster, correlation a *set[1]* of intercorrelated *variables*.

cluster, family (Goodwin, G.) see *family, extended*.

cluster, population any concentration of *population*.

cluster, role *set[1]* of *roles* associated with a *status-set*.

coaction working together without *communication* or task *interaction*. see also *group, coacting*.

co-actors the *group* responsible for the actuation of an *institution* from which the *actors* are drawn. (Nadel, S.F.).

co-adaptation *adaptation* of behaviour to the behaviour of others. (Nadel, S.F.).

coalition 1. defensive alignment of dissimilar *groups*. 2. defensive alignment of persons in group. 3. an agreement between two or more players to co-operate to defeat the others in a *game*.

coalition, civil-military a governmental *coalition* of the military and civilians, whether politicians or bureaucrats. (Putnam, R.D.).

coalition, dyadic defensive alignment of two persons or two dissimilar *groups*.

coalition, horizontal defensive alignment of same-status persons or *groups*.

coalition, polyadic defensive alignment of more than two persons or more than two dissimilar *groups*.

coalition, triadic defensive alignment of three persons or three dissimilar *groups*.

coalition, vertical defensive alignment of different-*status* persons or *groups*.

co-archy a *structure* of equal *power relationships*. (Lasswell, H.D.). **co-archic** *a*.

code 1. *set[1]* of *symbols* and *rules* for expressing information. 2. a *system* of legal *rules* created by a single enactment.

code, elaborated a linguistic *code[1]* in which the speaker selects from a wide range of syntactic alternatives. (Bernstein, B.). see also *code, restricted*.

code, kinesic see *system, kinesic*.

code, restricted a linguistic *code[1]* in which the speaker selects from a narrow range of syntactic alternatives. (Bernstein. B.). see also *code, elaborated*.

code, social a *system* of societal *norms*.

codification 1. creating *system* of legal *rules* or systematizing existing rules. 2. systematization of scientific findings. 3. theory-building.

coding 1. categorizing data, assigning a *symbol* to each answer which falls into a predetermined class. 2. reducing size of numbers for ease of computation. 3. categorizing the manifest content of *communication.*

coding, field *coding¹* of *schedules* before reception at field offices.

coding, multiple placing the same *response,* behaviour, or content unit into more than one *category.*

coding, office *coding¹* of *schedules* when received at office.

coding, qualitative *coding¹* of qualitative material

coding, quantitative *coding¹* of quantitative material.

coefficient, literacy percentage of speakers of a language who are able to read and write the language.

coercion controlling persons by the use of or threat of *force* or *deprivation.*

coercion, armed controlling persons by the use of or threat of armed *force.*

coercion, physical controlling persons by the use of or threat of *force.*

coercion, political *secular coercion* backed by the *force* of politically organized *society.*

coercion, psychological controlling persons by the use of or threat of *deprivation.*

coercion, ritual controlling persons by threatening to invoke supernatural forces.

coercion, secular controlling persons by other means than threatening to invoke supernatural forces.

co-ethnics members of the same *ethnic group.*

cognates relatives related through males, through females or through both.

cognation see *descent, cognatic.*

cognitive concerned with knowing.

cohesiveness resultant of all forces acting on members to remain in *group.*

cohort *group* of persons experiencing a certain event within a specified period of time.

cohort, birth *group* of persons born within a specified period of time.

cohort, fictitious see *cohort, hypothetical.*

cohort, hypothetical *cohort* which is not real but which is assumed for purposes of demographic analysis.

cohort, marriage *group* of persons marrying within a specified period of time.

cohort, synthetic see *cohort, hypothetical.*

co-husbands men who are husbands to the same woman.

colineal a *nonlineal* all of whose *ancestors* are included in *ego's* ancestors or whose ancestors include all ego's ancestors.

colineality the state of being a *colineal.*

collaterals relatives not related as *ascendant³* and descendant.

collation the processing of data after *editing* to *tabulation.*

collecting obtaining wild vegetable products. see also *food-gathering.*

collection see *aggregate¹⋅²⋅³.*

collection, data the steps and techniques involved in filling a *data matrix.* (Galtung, J.).

collectivity 1. plurality of persons. 2. *set¹* of persons with common *values* and solidarity. (Parsons, T.). 3. *group* with strong element of solidarity. (Etzioni, A.). 4. a *social system* capable of acting as a unit.

collision, role incompatibility of *roles* of different individuals.

command 1. an authoritative order. 2. an order backed by threats. (Austin).

command, chain of see *command, line of.*

command, line of the alternative sequences of *positions* down the *command hierarchy* through which a *command* is permitted to pass.

command, unity of the reception by an *organization* member of all *commands* from a single superior.

commensalism co-existence of unlike *groups* or persons without benefit or harm to either partner or which benefits one without harming the other.

commensalistic *a.* see also *symbiosis*; *mutualism*; *parasitism*; *helotism*.

communality see *circle, interest*.

communicand the receiver in a *communication process*.

communicant see *communicator*.

communication 1. intentional transfer of information from one person or *group* to another. 2. transfer of information from one person or group to another, whether intentional or not. 3. any event that triggers another organism.(Hockett, C.F.). 4. the transmission of information. (Price, J.L.). 5. the process of transmission and reception. (Williams, R.). 6. the eliciting of a *response*. (Dance, E.X.). 7. the *theory* of the origination, sending, receiving, and interpreting of *messages*. (Dance, E.X.).

communication, centralized *communication* in a *communication network* which is mediated by a *central person²* or central unit.

communication, consummatory *communication* resulting from the expression of *affective* or motivational states.

communication, decentralized *communication* in a *communication network* which is not mediated by a *central person²* or central unit.

communication, elite *communication* from, to, or amongst *elite* members.

communication, expressive 1. *communication* of affect. 2. communication of *normative* or *affective* information.

communication, face-to-face *communication* involving the co-presence of *communicator* and *communicand*. see also *media, basic*.

communication, formal the official transmission of information.

communication, horizontal *communication* between *positions* on the same *organizational level*.

communication, human form of *communication* which is peculiar to humans. (Dance, E.X.).

communication, impersonal *communication* by means other than *face-to-face interaction*.

communication, incidental *communication* which is unintended by *communicator*.

communication, informal the unofficial transmission of information.

communication, instrumental 1. *communication* which is intended by *communicator*. 2. communication of *cognitive* information.

communication, interpersonal *communication* between two persons.

communication, involuntary unintentional transfer of information from one person to another person or persons.

communication, kinesic *communication* through body motion behaviour.

communication, mass *communication* through *mass media*.

communication, multichannel *communication* employing several modalities, e.g., vision, hearing.

communication, nonlexical see *communication, nonverbal¹*.

communication, nonverbal 1. *communication* which is not by means of verbal *symbols*. 2. communication which is not by means of *conventional signs*.

communication, paralinguistic *communication* through *gestures* and tone-of-voice *signals*.

communication, personal *communication* by *face-to-face interaction*.

communication, preparatory any *communication* found in *preparatory propaganda*.

communication, proxemic *communication* resulting from the way in which the *communicator* handles space.

communication, subliminal *communication* involving *subliminal perception*.

communication, symbolic *communication* by means of *conventional signs*.

communication, therapeutic *communication* which has a therapeutic purpose or which occurs in a therapeutic setting.

communication, verbal 1. *communication* by means of verbal *symbols*. 2. see *communication, symbolic*.

communication, vertical *communication* between *organizational levels*.

communication, vocal *communication* by speech.

communication, voluntary intentional transfer of information from one person to another person or persons.

communicator the sender in a *communication process*.

community 1. a *subgroup* occupying a *territory,* less self-sufficient than a *society* and with closer *association³* and with deeper *sympathy*. 2. a territorially-bounded *social system*. (Bernard, J.). 3. non-overlapping area of a trade centre's trade zone. (Galpin, C.J.). 4. people who share some common interest or *function*.

community, campsite a *community* on the *band* level.

community, centrifugal a *community* with *norms* tending to drive out its members.

community, centripetal a *community* with *norms* tending to hold or draw back its members.

community, client *community* subject to *community development*.

community, closed a *community* relatively closed to outside influencies, *in-migrants,* and trade.

community, corporate *peasant‖community* selling less than half its produce to the outside world. (Wolf, E.R.).

community, cumulative *community* united by more than one social bond.

community, face-to-face *community* in which it is possible for every member to know every other member.

community, functional see *community⁴*.

community, fused area common to the various *service areas* of a trade centre.

community, geographic see *community¹·²·³*.

community, house see *family, composite*.

community, jural the widest *group* within which there is a moral duty and the machinery for the peaceful settlement of disputes. (Middleton, J.).

community, language a *community* whose members all claim to speak the same language or languages.

community, metropolitan the *community* formed by a *metropolis* plus its dependent integrated communities.

community, moral the widest *group* whose members are prepared to make moral judgments about one another. (Bailey, F.G.).

community, nomadic a *community* characterized by *nomadism*.

community, nucleated a *community* the dwellings of which are concentrated round a central point.

community, open 1. a *community* relatively open to outside influences, *in-migrants,* and trade. 2. *peasant‖community* selling at least half its produce to the outside world.(Wolf, E.R.).

community, open-country *community* consisting of dispersed farmsteads.

community, planned a *community* whose area has been physically planned.

community, political (Schapera, I.) see *unit, political*.

community, regional a *set¹* of economically independent cities and their *hinterlands* forming a *community*.

community, rurban a *community* of *rurban* character.

community, satellite *community* which is economically dependent on a larger community.

community, segmented *community* consisting of *clan-barrios*. (Murdock). see also *community, unsegmented*.

community, societal a *society's integrative subsystem*. (Parsons, T.).

community, speech see *community, language*.

community, subsistence *community* all the production of which is internally consumed.

community, trade-centre *community* consisting of trade centre plus surrounding farm *population*.

community, transhumant a *community* characterized by *transhumance*.

community, unsegmented *community* which is neither a *clan* nor a *deme* and is not segmented into *clan-barrios*. (Murdock). see also *community, segmented*.

community, village autonomous *village* with land collectively owned and cultivated.

commutation the substitution of a lesser sentence for the one which has been given. see also *pardon*; *amnesty*; *remission*; *reprieve*; *respite*.

competence scope of *authority* attached to an *office*.

competition 1. direct pursuit of mutually exclusive *goals*. 2. *norm*-regulated *conflict*. see also *co-operation*; *opposition*; *contravention*; *accommodation*.

competition, impersonal unrecognized, impersonal struggle between individuals or *groups*.

competition, intergroup *competition* between *groups* as units.

competition, interindividual see *competition, interpersonal*.

competition, interpersonal *competition* between individuals.

competition, intragroup *competition* between individuals or *subgroups* of a *group*.

competition, public (Dahl, R.A.) see *politics, competitive*.

complementarity the right of one person creating a correlative duty for another. see also *reciprocity³*.

complex a repressed *sentiment* which is in conflict with conscious sentiments.

complex, authority a *complex* concerning *authority*, which disposes an individual to react to authority as he originally did.

complex, creative *complex* resulting in *creativity* in individual.

complex, culture functionally integrated cluster of *culture traits*.

complex, discovery functionally integrated cluster of *discoveries* or *inventions*.

complex, ecological the *set¹* of functionally interrelated *variables* consisting of *environment, population, social organization*, and *technology*.

complex, exploration the *culture complex* focused on the exploration undertaken by a *society*. (Thompson, L.).

complex, institutional α *set¹* of functionally interrelated *institutions*.

complex, matrilineal the *set¹* of social and cultural elements associated with *matriliny*.

complex, organizational a *set¹* of functionally interrelated *organizations*.

complex, shamanistic the *culture complex* focused on *shamanism* in a given *society*.

complex, symbol *set¹* of associated *symbols*.

complex, technological functionally integrated cluster of technological elements.

complex, totemic *set¹* of *totemic* traits. see also *totemism*.

complex, trait see *complex, culture*.

complex, value *set¹* of associated *values*.

compliance 1. see *conformity, expedient*. 2. agreeing to act in a particular way. see also *consensus*; *conformity*.

composition, age see *distribution, age*.

composition, population 1. distribution within *population* of one or more individually carried characteristics. 2. alterable characteristics of population.

compromise *accommodation* in which each party yields something to the other.

computerize to introduce computer operations into a process. **computerization** *n.*

conative concerned with volition.

concentration, ethnic *residential segregation* of *ethnic groups.*

concept 1. being able to distinguish X's from everything that is not an X. 2. some criterion-in-mind, that is, some kind of mental content enabling us to distinguish X's from everything that is not an X.

concept, classificatory a *concept* having a classificatory purpose.

concept, conjunctive the common characteristics of the individuals of a class.

concept, definitive *concept* which precisely delimits area of meaning.

concept, disjunctive possession of either one characteristic or possession of a different characteristic makes the individual a member of the class.

concept, external see *concept, observers'.*

concept, folk a *concept* used by a *society* or *community* under investigation.

concept, internal see *concept, folk.*

concept, natural a *concept* which reflects the *structure* of reality.

concept, observers' a *concept* used in the study of a *society* by observers from outside.

concept, polar a *concept* representing one pole of a *continuum.*

concept, role any *concept* concerned with *role,* e.g., *role, role-set, role-sequence, role-relationship.*

concept, qualitative a *concept* having a qualitative character.

concept, quantitative a *concept* having a quantitative character.

concept, sensitizing *concept* with vague boundaries of meaning, but for that very reason scientifically useful.

conception, role *role* performer's *perception* of the expectations of others.

conceptualization creating or explicating *concepts* for use in research.

conciliation effecting a settlement between the parties to a dispute through a commission or agency which studies the facts and makes proposals which the parties are free to reject. see also *arbitration; mediation.*

conciliation, compulsory *conciliation* to which the parties to a dispute are compelled to go.

conciliation, voluntary *conciliation* to which the parties to a dispute are not compelled to go.

concubinage legalized, permanent cohabitation in which *status* of female partner is lower than that of a wife.

concubinage, group *concubinage* involving two or more men sharing two or more concubines.

concubinage, hypergamous *concubinage* in which a woman becomes a concubine to a man of higher *social status.*

concubinage, hypogamous *concubinage* in which a woman becomes a concubine to a man of lower *social status.*

concubinary 1. pertaining to *concubinage.* 2. a person living in concubinage.

concubinacy mutual marriageability.

conditionability susceptibility of an individual to conditioning.

conditioning, approximation differentially reinforcing successive approximations to a final form of behaviour.

conditioning, classical conditioning a *response* by pairing *unconditioned stimulus* with *conditioned stimulus.*

conditioning, cultural the acquisition of *cultural behaviour* by conditioning.

conditioning, inhibitory see *inhibition, conditioned.*

conditioning, instrumental see *conditioning, operant.*

conditioning, negative see *inhibition, conditioned.*

conditioning, operant increasing the probability of an *operant* by *reinforcement* which follows *operant behaviour.*

conditioning, respondent see *conditioning, classical.*

conditioning, subliminal conditioning involving *subliminal perception.*

condominium 1. joint rule of a *territory* by two or more *states.* 2. a territory ruled jointly by two or more states.

conduciveness, structural degree to which a *social structure* encourages a given type of *collective behaviour.*

conduct 1. deliberate behaviour. 2. see *behaviour, cultural.* 3. behaviour morally evaluated. 4. behaviour evaluated against *norms.* 5. behaviour to which *character* is relevant.

confederation a *political unit* or *organization* the units of which have greater autonomy than those of a *federation.* see also *federation.*

configuration, cultural *pattern* or *value* which polarizes and integrates a *culture.*

configuration, personality see *personality, configurational.*

configuration, symbolic *set¹* of *symbols* interrelated through the interrelation of their referents.

conflict 1. indirect pursuit of mutually exclusive *goals* by eliminating or weakening the opposition. 2. opposition process lacking a co-operative element. 3. situation of goal incompatibility between individuals or *groups.* 4. competitive situation in which each party seeks position he knows is incompatible with wishes of the other. (Boulding, K.). 5. fundamental opposition in *society* or group. 6. situation in which individual is faced with incompatible goals, two unpleasant alternatives, a goal with both *positive* and *negative valencies,* or two such goals.

conflict, approach-approach situation in which individual is faced with incompatible *goals.*

conflict, approach-avoidance situation in which individual is faced with a *goal* having both *positive* and *negative valencies.*

conflict, approach-avoidance, double situation in which individual is faced with two *goals* each having both *positive* and *negative valencies.*

conflict, avoidance-avoidance situation in which individual is faced with two unpleasant alternatives.

conflict, communal *conflict* within a structure of agreement.

conflict, continuous *conflict* the outcome of which is not conceived as permanent and which lacks scheduled episodes of regulated conflict. (Caplow, T.).

conflict. conventional *conflict* which is regulated by *norms.*

conflict, corporate *conflict* between *corporate groups.*

conflict, culture *conflict* between the *culture* acquired by an individual and that of a *group* in which he finds himself.

conflict, direct *social conflict* which is not mediated through one or more third parties. see also *conflict, indirect.*

conflict, dysfunctional *conflict* which is *dysfunctional* for the *social structure.*

conflict, episodic discontinuous *conflict* involving scheduled episodes of regulated conflict. (Caplow, T.).

conflict, expressive *social conflict* which is an end in itself. see also *conflict, instrumental.*

conflict, external *conflict* occurring between a specified *group* and one or more *out-groups.*

conflict, generational *conflict* between proximate *generations².*

conflict, heterogeneous *conflict* between parties of different type. (Boulding, K.E.).

conflict, homogeneous *conflict* between parties of the same type. (Boulding, K.E.).

conflict, ideological *social conflict* over basic *values.* see also *conflict, operational.*

44

conflict, indirect *social conflict* which is mediated through one or more third parties. see also *conflict, direct*.

conflict, individual *conflict* between one individual and another.

conflict, induced *social conflict* not inherent in a given situation but induced by an *actor*. see also *conflict, inherent*.

conflict, inherent *social conflict* inherent in a given situation. see also *conflict, induced*.

conflict, institutionalized *social conflict* regulated by *norms*. see also *conflict, noninstitutionalized*.

conflict, instrumental *social conflict* which is a means to an end. see also *conflict, expressive*.

conflict, intergroup *conflict* occurring between *groups*.

conflict, internal *conflict* occurring within a specified *group*.

conflict, inter-role a *role conflict* involving the incompatibility of *role requirements* belonging to different *roles*.

conflict, inter-societal *conflict* between *societies*.

conflict, intragroup *conflict* occurring within a *group*.

conflict, intrapersonal *conflict* occurring within an individual.

conflict, intrarole a *role conflict* involving the incompatibility of *role requirements* belonging to the same *role*.

conflict, intra-societal *conflict* within a *society*.

conflict, minus-minus see *conflict, avoidance-avoidance*.

conflict, noncommunal *conflict* which is not within a structure of agreement.

conflict, noninstitutionalized *social conflict* which is not *norm*-regulated. see also *conflict, institutionalized*.

conflict, non-interactive *conflict* in which *interaction* does not occur between those in conflict. (Rapoport, A.).

conflict, norm inconsistency in a *set[1]* of *norms*.

conflict, operational *social conflict* over the most efficient means to an end. see also *conflict, ideological*.

conflict, organized *conflict* in which the persons involved do not act independently.

conflict, plus-minus see *conflict, approach-avoidance*.

conflict, plus-plus see *conflict, approach-approach*.

conflict, pure *conflict* without any mutual dependence.

conflict, realistic *conflict* in which parties attempt to further their interests.

conflict, role inconsistency in a *role* or roles played by one person.

conflict, role, objective an actual *role conflict*.

conflict, role, subjective a *role conflict* which a role performer believes himself to be in, as a result of his *perception* of his *roles* or his *received roles*.

conflict, role-role see *conflict, inter-role*.

conflict, self-role *conflict* between *role* and a role performer's *values* or *needs*.

conflict, social *conflict* between individuals, between *groups*, or between individual and group.

conflict, societal *conflict* between *sub-populations* in a *society*.

conflict, terminal *conflict* the outcome of which is conceived as permanent. (Caplow, T.).

conflict, unorganized *conflict* in which the persons involved act independently.

conflict, unrealistic *conflict* aimed at *tension* release in one or both parties.

conformance change of *attitude* or belief as a result of *social pressure*. (Jahoda, M.). see also *consentience*.

conformism 1. see *conformity*. 2. extreme conformity. 3. the doctrine of the need for extreme conformity. 4. acceptance of both the *cultural goals* and the institutionalized means of a *society*. (Merton, R.K.). see also *retreatism*; *ritualism[2]*; *rebellion[5]*; *withdrawal*.

conformity 1. acting in accordance with *norms*. 2. acting in accordance with norms known to individual. 3. yielding to *group pressures* to adopt beliefs or behaviour of *group*. 4. acceptance by an individual of both the *cultural goals* and the institutionalized means of a *society*. (Merton, R.K.). see also *consensus*; *compliance*.

conformity, attitudinal internalization by an individual of a *value* or *norm*.

conformity, behavioural acting in accordance with a *value* or *norm*.

conformity, doctrinal stating to others acceptance of a *value* or *norm*.

conformity, expedient outwardly agreeing, under *group pressure*, or adopting behaviour of *group*, whilst inwardly disagreeing. see also *conformity*.

confusion, role disagreement in *group* as to expectations of *role*.

congenital present in individual at birth.

congeries, cultural *set[1]* of cultural elements which are not functionally interrelated.

congeries, social *set[1]* of social elements which are not functionally interrelated.

conglomeration any concentration of *population*.

congruence, status extent to which an individual's *positions* in different *hierarchies* are at a comparable level.

connate see *congenital*.

connotation 1. those characteristics by virtue of which a term is applied to a thing. 2. emotive meaning. 3. meaning implied by situation. **connotative** *a*. see also *denotation*.

connubium right to marry.

conquest 1. subjugation of a *territory*. 2. acquisition of supreme political *authority* in contravention of pre-existing *laws*. 3. the gaining of *ascendancy[1]* by an *organization* over nonmembers or over other organizations.(LaPiere).

consanguines 1. relatives by blood. 2. relatives socially-defined as genetically connected.

consanguines, primary *consanguines* without linking relative.

consanguines, secondary *consanguines* related through one linking relative.

consanguines, tertiary *consanguines* related through two linking relatives.

consanguinity 1. relationship by blood. 2. relationship between persons descended from a common *ancestor*. (Morgan, L.H.). 3. socially-defined relationship by blood. (Malinowski). **consanguineal** *a*.

consanguinity, biological real relationship by blood.

consanguinity, collateral relationship between persons descended from a common *ancestor* but not from each other.

consanguinity, fictive socially-defined relationship by blood which is not a real relationship by blood.

consanguinity, lineal relationship between persons one of whom is descended from the other.

consanguinity, putative commonly supposed relationship by blood.

consanguinity, real real relationship by blood.

consciousness, class the degree to which there is a common awareness of and *identification* with *social classes* on the part of members of a *community*. see also *identification, class*.

consciousness, group the degree to which there is a common awareness of and *identification* with a *group* on the part of its members.

consecration 1. dedication to a *sacred* purpose. 2. putting *mana* into a thing. see also *desecration*.

consensus 1. general *cognitive* and *affective* agreement between persons. 2. general agreement following *conflict*. 3. general agreement following any preceding difference. 4. mutual realization of others' awareness of agreement. 5. *opinion* in *group* on which all members agree to act. see also *conformity*; *compliance*.

consensus, cognitive see *consonance, cognitive.*

consensus, value general agreement in a *society* on basic *values.*

consentience change of *attitude* or belief as a result of relevant evidence. (Jahoda, M.). see also *conformance.*

consistency, status see *congruence, status.*

consolidation merging of administrative units.

consolidation, land reversing the process of *farm fragmentation.*

consonance, attitude a logical consistency amongst *attitudes.*

consonance, cognitive a logical consistency amongst cognitions.

constant a quantity whose *value*[6] remains fixed throughout a   particular investigation.

constant, absolute a quantity whose *value*[6] remains fixed in all situations.

constant, arbitrary a quantity to which any one of a *set*[1] of *values*[6] may be assigned, the assigned *value*[6] remaining fixed throughout the investigation.

constellation, attitude individual's total *set*[1] of *attitudes.*

constellation, ecological *set*[1] of interdependent ecological units having a common centre.

constitution 1. a *society*'s plan of *government.* 2. a society's plan of government plus *norms* limiting governmental *power.* 3. *rules* determining how the *decisions* of a *group* are made. 4. previously agreed method of resolving *conflicts* in a group. 5. the *set*[1] of rules of an *organization.* (Marschak, J.). 6. an individual's general physiological basis as modified by life expérience.

constitution, criminal a *constitution* [6] predisposing the   individual to *crime.*

constitution, federal the *constitution*[2] of a *federal state.*

constitution, flexible a *constitution*[2] which can be changed by   the ordinary processes of *legislation*[1].

constitution, rigid a *constitution*[2] which requires special processes for its change.

constitution, unitary the *constitution*[2] of a *unitary state.*

constitution, unwritten a *constitution*[2] which is uncodified.

constitution, written a *constitution*[2] enacted as a single *code*[2].

construct 1. higher-level abstraction constructed from *concepts* at a lower level of abstraction. 2. an explicated concept. see also *explication.* 3. a concept deliberately invented for a scientific purpose.

construct, hypothetical a *mediating construct* whose reality is thought probable.

construct, ideal see *type, ideal.*

construct, mediating a *variable* assumed to intervene between observables for the purpose of explaining their interrelationship. see also *variable, intervening*; *construct, hypothetical.*

consumption, conspicuous consumption for *prestige* of self or other of goods which are or were evidence of *wealth.* (Veblen, T.).

contact, categorical a social contact the content of which is determined by the *categories* of the persons and excludes their individual characteristics.

contact, collective contact between two *groups* or *societies.* (Maunier, R.).

contact, contrived a social contact that does not occur spontaneously.

contact, culture contact of a people with a more advanced *culture.*

contact, face-to-face a social contact involving the physical proximity of the persons.

contact, institutionalized contact between members of different *societies,* the persons in contact occupying *positions* both in their own society and the new *system* of interrelations between the societies. see also *contact, peripheral.*

contact, intercultural 1. contact between persons of different *cultures.* 2. reciprocal knowledge of each other's cultures by the bearers thereof.

contact, inter-ethnic contact between persons of different *ethnic groups*.

contact, interpersonal a social contact between two individuals.

contact, neighbouring a social contact between neighbours qua neighbours. (Keller, S.).

contact, peripheral contact between members of different *societies* which results in no change in the societies or in the persons in contact. see also *contact, institutionalized*.

contact, personal a social contact between two individuals of different *societies*. (Maunier, R.).

contact, primary a social contact intimate, personal, face-to-face.

contact, secondary a social contact non-intimate, impersonal.

contact, segmental a social contact involving only a segment of the other person's *activities*. (Davis, K.).

contact, sympathetic a social contact which includes the individual characteristics of the persons.

contact, tertiary transmission of influence without personal contact.

contagion diffusion of *response* through *population* by means of *interaction*.

contagion, affective spread of affect through a *population*.

contagion, behavioural spread of behaviour through a *population*.

contagion, crowd diffusion of *response* in a *crowd*.

contagion, hysterical diffusion of *response* through a *population*, resulting from hysteria.

contagion, mass diffusion of *response* through a *mass*.

contagion, psychic spread of affect, beliefs or information through a *population*.

contagion, semantic transference by conditioning of a *semantic* element from one word to another.

contestation, public (Dahl, R.A.) see *politics, competitive*.

continuum continuous series of quantitative variation in one dimension.

continuum. attitude continuous series of quantitative variation of an *attitude*.

continuum, folk-urban *concept* of *societies* lying on a *continuum* between the two polar *ideal types* of *folk society* and *urban society*.

continuum, hedonic *continuum* ranging from maximum pleasure to maximum unpleasure.

continuum, nomadic *continuum* from continuous *migration* to infrequent migration on the part of a whole *community*.

continuum, opinion continuous series of quantitative variation of an *opinion*.

continuum, polar *continuum* involving polar opposites.

continuum, reciprocity *continuum* of *reciprocity* from *generalized reciprocity* through *balanced reciprocity* to *negative reciprocity*.

continuum, rural-urban *concept* of *societies* lying on a *continuum* between the two polar *ideal types* of rural society and *urban society*.

continuum, telic curve showing *frequency distribution* of observance of *norm*.

continuum, totemic *continuum* on which *totemic complexes* may be located according to number of totemic traits.

contra-acculturative opposing *acculturation* by reviving *traditions* of *group*.

contract a legally-enforceable agreement.

contract, commercial a *contract* the terms of which are agreed upon by the contracting parties. see also *contract, status*.

contract, group the covert or implicit agreement or the *norms* binding together the members of a *group*.

contract, parole the agreement entered into by the *parolee* to observe the *parole* conditions.

contract, probation the agreement entered into by the *probationer* to observe the *probation* conditions.

contract, status a *contract* which results in *society* conferring a specified *status* on one or more of the contracting parties. see also *contract, commercial.*

contraculture the *culture* of a *group* hostile to the dominant culture.

contradiction, structural inconsistency in *social structure* tending to produce structural change.

contrasuggestibility disposition of some individuals to respond to attempt at *suggestion* by doing the opposite.

contravention *opposition* process between *competition* and *conflict.*

control 1. sending *messages* which change recipient's behaviour. (Wiener, N.). 2. evaluating performance and applying corrections. 3. keeping variations from *system objectives* within permissible limits. 4. the connectiveness of the elements of a *system.*

control, adaptive the control of a process in a changing *environment.*

control, boundary control of the transactions across a *systems boundary.*

control, built-in an element in a *system* which keeps variations occurring in the system within certain limits.

control, co-twin applying *experimental stimulus* to one of a pair of identical twins, thus controlling the hereditary factor.

control, culture 1. see *control, social, formal.* 2. planned cultural change.

control, ecological controlling the behaviour of a person by manipulating the person's *environment.*

control, face-to-face *organizational control* or *social control* obtained by *face-to-face contacts.*

control, formal *social control* maintained by *formal sanctions.*

control, informal *social control* maintained by *informal sanctions.*

control, institutional *social control* through *institutions.*

control, interpersonal mutual exercise of *social control* by role-partners.

control, line *organizational control* maintained by the *line.*

control, organizational control of performance in an *organization.*

control, primary *social control* exercised by a *primary group.*

control, religious *social control* maintained by *religious sanctions.*

control, secondary *social control* exercised by a *secondary group.*

control, social 1. maintenance of *equilibrium* in *social system.* 2. maintenance of *conformity* through *training* and *sanctions.*

control, social, external maintenance of *conformity* through *sanctions* or *manipulation[1].*

control, social, formal *social control* by means of institutionalized processes or *associations.*

control, social, informal *social control* by means of noninstitutionalized processes.

control, social, internal maintenance of *conformity* through *norm* internalization or *identification.*

control, span of the number of persons under the command of a particular official.

control, staff *organizational control* maintained by the *staff.*

control, subsocial control of individual obtained by *physical coercion.*

control, super-social use by ruler or ruling *group* threatened in *power* of all the technically possible *techniques* of *social control.*

conurbation 1. a continuous *urban area.* 2. a string of urban *settlements* connected by built-up strips.

convention 1. *custom* involving *conformity* to contemporaries rather than to *tradition,* and considered to be of minor importance. 2. *norm* which is not sanctioned. (Stammler). 3. norm involving an unorganized *moral sanction.* (Weber, M.). 4. sanctioned custom. (Parsons, T.). 5. formal, multilateral, international instrument. 6. a meeting of delegates of a *party* for making nominations and adopting *platforms*.

conventionalism rigid adherence to conventional middle-class *values*.

convergence independent development of similar features of *culture*.

conversion 1. a radical and relatively sudden change in an individual's world-view. 2. exchange of items belonging to different spheres of *exchange*. (Bohannan, P.).

conveyance exchange of items belonging to the same sphere of *exchange*. (Bohannan, P.). see also *conversion²*.

co-operation *chain of interaction* or *network of interaction* for achievement of common *goal,* the achievement possible to either all or none of the partici-pants.

co-operation, antagonistic see *co-operation, tertiary*; *accommodation⁴*.

co-operation, auxiliary-action *co-operation* in which some of the participants make up for the weakness of others.

co-operation, competitive see *co-operation, tertiary*.

co-operation, converging-action *co-operation* in which the participants do dis-similar things.

co-operation, direct *co-operation* involving performance of like *activities* side by side, which could be performed individually.

co-operation, indirect see *co-operation, converging-action*.

co-operation, joint-action *co-operation* in which the participants do similar or nearly similar things.

co-operation, primary *co-operation* in which the rewards are shared by the co-operating individuals.

co-operation, secondary *co-operation* in which each individual can separately enjoy the rewards of his co-operation.

co-operation, tertiary the use by two parties of common means to achieve an-tagonistic goals. see *accommodation⁴*.

cooptation 1. *election* into a *group* by the votes of its own members. 2. the process of absorbing new elements into the *leadership* or policy-determining structure of an *organization* to avert threats to its stability or existence. (Selznick, P.). **coopt** *v.* **cooptate** *v.* **cooptative** *a*.

cooptation, informal *cooptation* which is a response to the pressure of specific power centres. (Selznick, P.).

cooption see *cooptation*.

co-ordination the synchronization and the establishment of the functional in-terdependence of the *sub-goals, policies, procedures* and *methods* for achieving an *objective*.

co-ordination, horizontal *co-ordination* of *activities* of the same *organizational level* by a superior.

co-ordination, lateral see *co-ordination, horizontal*.

co-ordination, vertical *co-ordination* of *activities* of different *organizational levels*.

co-orientation simultaneous orientation of two persons towards something, the simultaneous orientation being controlled by reciprocal *communication*.

copresence sufficient mutual proximity for each to be fully perceived by the others and to perceive this *perception* by the others who perceive this perception of their perception. (Goffman, E.).

core, cultural a cultural regularity in a major feature of *culture*.

corollary an immediate consequence of a *theorem*.

correction 1. quantity added to an approximation to obtain a better approx-imation. 2. *action* in accordance with *norm,* or *punishment,* restitution or compensation, following violation of norm and *counteraction*. (Bohannan).

correlate a *variable* which is correlated with a specified variable.

correlation 1. interdependence between *quantitative* or *qualitative data*. 2. interdependence between quantitative data.

correlation, biserial method of measuring *correlation* between *continuous variables* which treats one of the variables as a continuous variable and the other as a *dichotomous variable*.

correlation, chance-half see *correlation, split-half.*

correlation, curvilinear a *correlation* in which there is not a constant ratio between the rates of change of two (or more) *variables* for the entire *range* of the observed *values*[6] of the variables. see also *correlation, linear*.

correlation, direct see *correlation, positive*.

correlation, ecological a *correlation* based on *grouped data* and involving *ecological distributions*.

correlation, illusory a statistically significant *correlation* between two *variables* which are not causally connected.

correlation, indirect see *correlation, negative*.

correlation, individual a *correlation* based on individual cases and not on *grouped data*.

correlation, inverse see *correlation, negative*.

correlation, linear a *correlation* in which there is a constant ratio between the rates of change of two (or more) *variables* for the entire *range* of the observed *values*[6] of the variables. see also *correlation, curvilinear*.

correlation, multiple a *correlation* between one *dependent variable* and a combination of two or more *independent variables*.

correlation, negative if one *variable* increases, the other decreases.

correlation, net see *correlation, partial*.

correlation, nonlinear see *correlation, curvilinear*.

correlation, partial the *correlation* between two *variables* when the effects of the other related variables are removed.

correlation, positive if one *variable* increases, the other increases.

correlation, rank *correlation* between *variables* with ranked *values*[6].

corelation, rectilinear see *correlation, linear*.

correlation, simple 1. a *correlation* between two *variables*. 2. see *correlation, linear*. 3. a *linear correlation* between two variables.

correlation, split-half *correlation* measuring *split-half reliability*.

correlation, spurious see *correlation, illusory*.

correlation, tetrachoric method of measuring *correlation* between *continuous variables*, which are assumed to be normally distributed, and which treats both as *dichotomous variables*.

cosatiation the extent to which *satiation* of desire to work on one *task* reduces *motivation* to work on another similar task.

coscinomancy sieve-turning, i.e., divining culprit by holding a sieve which is thought to turn over when name of culprit is mentioned. **coscinomantic** *a*.

cost that which must be given up to attain an end.

cost, opportunity the *cost* of anything in terms of the most desired alternative foregone.

cost, psychic the pain or loss of satisfaction incurred in attaining an end.

cost, real the efforts and abstinences incurred in attaining an end.

cost, social the total *cost* of anything to the *community*.

co-tradition, area *culture area* with time depth. (Bennett).

counteraction 1. an *action*, similar, equal and in opposite direction which cancels out another action. (Lévy-Bruhl).2. *reaction* decreasing *efficiency* of the original action. 3. the reaction of *society* to the violation of a *norm*, which reaction precedes the *correction*[2]. (Bohannan).

countercontrol *actions* aimed at counteracting *social control*.

counter-current, migration see *counterstream, migration*.

counter-curse a curse intended to counteract another curse.

counter-elites the *leaderships* of the *masses* in conflict with the *elite*.

counter-flow, migration see *counterstream, migration*.

counterformity see *rebellion*.

counter-gift a gift given in return for another gift.

counter-ideology 1. *ideology* which justifies patterns of *deviant‖group* without seeking to change the *society* as a whole. 2. minor variant of the conservative ideology.

counter-insurgency military operations designed to crush *insurrections*.

counter-magic *magic* intended to counteract other magic.

counter-mass those persons rejecting the *social structure*.

counter-mobilization *mobilization* by opponents in response to a particular mobilization.

counter-mores *norms* in conflict with the *mores*.

counter-obligation obligation of *reciprocation*.

counter-observation the observation of the observer by the subject. (Devereux, G.).

counter-payment *wealth* passing from bride's relatives to husband's relatives in recognition of *bride-price*.

counter-prestation a *prestation* given in return for another prestation.

counterpropaganda *propaganda* aimed at neutralizing the effect of other propaganda.

counter-spell a *spell* intended to counteract another spell.

counterstream, migration a body of migrants moving from the area of destination to the area of origin of a *migration stream*.

counter-suggestion *suggestion* intended to counteract earlier suggestion.

coup the forcible overthrow of the *government* by the infiltration of a small but critical segment of the state apparatus, which is then used to displace the government from its control of the remainder. see also *revolution*; *rebellion*; *putsch*; *insurrection*; *uprising*.

court a tribunal which adjudicates rationally and is capable of enforcing its decisions. see also *moot*.

couvade simulation of childbirth by father, or his confinement at parturition and observance by him of *taboos* designed to promote welfare of child.

couvade, psychosomatic *couvade* involving unconsciously motivated, unsanctioned, stress-induced behaviour on part of father.

couvade, social *couvade* involving deliberate, socially-sanctioned behaviour on part of father.

covering the minimizing by a stigmatized individual of the obtrusiveness of his *stigma*. (Goffman, E.). see also *passing*; *passer*; *visibility*.

co-wives women who are wives to the same man.

craze *fad* characterized by more than normal excitement. see also *fad*.

creativity 1. extent to which a contribution restructures our universe of understanding. (Ghiselin). 2. size of area of science affected by a contribution. (Lacklen). 3. the ability to be imaginative and original in the handling of words, ideas, materials.

credit total amount a person is permitted to borrow or to owe.

creed formal statement of a dogma.

creole a first language which is a *full language* derived from two or more natural languages. see also *pidgin*; *language, pidginized*.

crescive involving unplanned *growth*.

crime 1. a type of behaviour, the elements precisely specified, involving a *penal sanction*. 2. a violation of a *norm* involving a penal sanction. 3. a norm violation thought to threaten *society*.

crime, companionate a *crime* involving accomplices.

crime, conventional *crime* which is not an *occupational crime*.

52

crime, episodic a type of *crime* with low probability of repetition by the same individual.

crime, folk a common offence having its source in social complexity and which is regarded as minor by most members of a *society*.

crime, infamous a *crime* conviction for which confers on the offender the legal status of infamy.

crime, medical *crime* in which there is a diminution of *responsibility[1]* involving *factors* recognizable and, at some stage, treatable by medical means, the diminution excluding delusion or psychosis. (Stafford-Clark, D.).

crime, occupational *crime* committed by a person in the course of his *occupation* which utilizes his occupational skills.

crime, organized *crime* having an administrative structure.

crime, predatory a *crime* which does harm to another and benefits only the offender.

crime, self-reported *crime* reported confidentially to social investigators by those who have committed it.

crime, service purveying illicit goods or services.

crime, victimless a *crime* which does no harm to another or to *society*.

crime, white-collar *crime* committed by professional man in the course of his *profession* and which utilizes his professional skills.

criminalistics the science of crime detection. **criminalistic** *a.*

criminality 1. expected *relative frequency* over given period of time of criminal violation by persons under standard environmental conditions. 2. amount of *crime* of an area, *group* or person.

criminogenic crime-producing.

crimino-geographical pertaining to the *areal distribution* of *crime*.

criminology 1. the science of *crime*. 2. the *sociology* of criminal law. (Hall, J.). 3. the sociology of deviant behaviour. (Clinard, M.).

criminology, comparative the *cross-cultural* study of *crime*.

criminology, sociological the sociological study of *crime*.

criminology, theoretical the body of *theory* concerning *crime*.

crisis, axiological a crisis occurring in a *society's value system*.

crisis, cultural 1. a crisis occurring in a *culture*. 2. a *social crisis* resulting from cultural factors.

crisis, natural a *social crisis* resulting from physical or biological factors.

crisis, practical a non-ideational crisis occurring in a *society*.

crisis, social a turning-point faced by a *society*.

crisis, socialization a crisis existing in a *society* as to the *roles* for which the young should be prepared and as to how the task should be divided between the *family* and other *groups*.

crisis, succession a crisis concerning *succession* to an *office*.

crisis, survival a *social crisis* threatening the survival of the *society*.

crisis, theoretical an ideational crisis occurring in a *society*.

criterion *variable* used as a measure of *validity* for a *scale[2]*. see also *standard*; *baseline*.

crithomancy *divination* through the meal cast on the bodies of sacrificed animals. **crithomantic** *a.*

crop, cash crop grown primarily for sale.

crop, catch crop grown between two main crops or between the rows of a main crop or a substitute for a crop that has failed.

crop, commercial crop sold by producer or for which *credit* is extended.

crop, cover crop grown to protect cleared land from soil erosion.

crop, credit crop for which *credit* is extended to producer.

crop, feed crop grown to provide food for livestock.

crop, food crop grown to provide food for humans.

crop, industrial crop grown not to provide food but to provide a material for industrial use.

crop, irrigation a crop dependent on *irrigation*.

crop, pasture crop grown to be grazed by livestock.

crop, primary the main crop raised by a *productive unit*.

crop, row crop planted in rows spaced to permit intercropping.

crop, secondary crop which is not the *primary crop*.

crop, snatch see *crop, catch*.

crop, subsistence crop consumed by the *productive unit*.

crop, trade see *crop, commerical*.

cross-cousin child of father's sister or mother's brother.

cross-cousin, bilateral a *cross-cousin* who is both a *patrilateral* and a *matrilateral cross-cousin* to *ego*.

cross-cousin, matrilateral a *cross-cousin* on the mother's side.

cross-cousin, patrilateral a *cross-cousin* of the father's side.

cross-cultural pertaining to a comparison of features ot different *cultures*.

cross-dressing sęe *transvestitism*.

cross-national pertaining to a comparison of features of different *nations*.

cross-polity pertaining to a comparison of features of different *polities*.

cross-pressures contradictory pressures on an individual resulting from his membership of two *groups*.

cross-pressures, affiliative *cross-pressures* involving an affiliative *conflict*.

cross-pressures, attitudinal *cross-pressures* involving an attitudinal *conflict*.

cross-relatives relatives or offspring of *siblings* of the opposite sex.

cross-societal pertaining to a comparison of features of different *societies*.

crowd non-institutionalized, transitory, polarized, contiguous *collectivity*.

crowd, acting *crowd* possessing a *focus*.

crowd, casual a contiguous *collectivity* which has formed without the intention of its members.

crowd, dynamic a *crowd* which is excited. (Sombart).

crowd, expressive *crowd* lacking a *focus*.

crowd, focused *crowd* which has a *stimulus object* or event as a focus.

crowd, orgiastic *crowd* the members of which have reached an ecstatic state.

crowd, participant *crowd* the members of which have a sense of participation.

crowd, planned *crowd* deliberately formed.

crowd, simple transitory, unstable, amorphous, leaderless, contiguous *collectivity*. (Tarde, G.).

crowd, static a *crowd* which is calm. (Sombart).

crytallomancy *divination* which involves gazing at a piece of colourless quartz. **crytallomantic** *a*.

cult 1. *system* of beliefs, emotions and *rites* associated with an object. 2. individual-centred, minority religious *group* less organized than a *sect*. 3. specialized part of a *society*'s religious *institutions*. 4. totality of a society's religious institutions. 5. religious practice. **cultic** *a*.

cult, cargo a *revitalization movement* of a *magico-religious* character centred on a belief in the future arrival of ships' cargoes.

cult, millenarian a *cult* associated with *millenarism*.

cult, nativistic a *cult* which is part of a *nativistic movement*.

cult, negative the body of proscribing *rites*. (Durkheim).

cult, positive the body of prescribing *rites*. (Durkheim).

cult, possession *cult* centred on *spirit possession*.

cult-complex *set[1]* of associated *cults*.

cultigen a plant dependent on man for its survival.

cultism 1. tendency towards the formation of *cults*. 2. devotion to the doctrine and practice of a cult. **cultist** *a*.

cultivation, basin cultivation in a number of irrigated, artificial depressions.

cultivation, contour cultivation in which the rows follow the contours of the land.

cultivation, dry cultivation in which the necessary moisture is provided by rain.

cultivation, extensive cultivation producing a relatively low yield per specified area.

cultivation, hydraulic see *agriculture, hydraulic.*

cultivation, intensive cultivation producing a relatively high yield per specified area.

cultivation, mound cultivation on a number of artificial mounds.

cultivation, ridge cultivation along the top of parallel ridges.

cultivation, settled cultivation which permits at least a portion of the *population* to remain on the same residential sites for an indefinite period. (Gough, K.).

cultivation, shifting agricultural system in which fielda are cleared by firing and are cropped discontinuously, the periods of fallowing averaging longer than the periods of cropping. (FAO).

cultivation, shifting, obligatory *shifting cultivation* resulting from agricultural necessity. (Allan, W.).

cultivation, shifting, voluntary *shifting cultivation* not resulting from agricultural necessity. (Allan, W.).

cultivation, strip 1. cultivation in long strips each worked by an individual tenant or owner. 2. alternation of narrow strips of arable and pasture to check soil erosion.

cultivation, subsistence cultivation all the produce of which is internally consumed.

cultivation, terrace cultivation employing *terraces.*

cultivation, wet cultivation in which all or part of the necessary moisture is from a source other than rain.

culture 1. the totality of learned behaviour transmitted from one *generation²* to the next. 2. behaviours having the highest probability of occurrence in a *society.* (Wallace). 3. type of *tradition* in which *symbols* are transmitted from one *generation²* to the next by *social learning.* (Lorenz, K.). 4. all that is socially transmitted in a society. (Lewis, J.). 5. a way of life. (Harris, M.). 6. the non-cumulative part of culture. see also *civilization¹.* 7. the non-utilitarian part of culture. see also *civilization².* 8. an *assemblage³* which recurs repeatedly. *(archaeol.).* see also *industry⁹.*

culture, adaptive that part of the *nonmaterial culture* which adapts to changes in the *material culture.*

culture, adequate a *culture* achieving *societal‖adjustment.*

culture, adolescent the *subculture* of adolescents.

culture, agrarian a *culture* shared by people who are dependent primarily on *agriculture.*

culture, archaeological the totality of *assemblages³* characteristic of an extinct *group.*

culture, caste 1. the *subculture* of a *caste.* 2. the *culture* of a *caste society.*

culture, class the *subculture* of a *social class.*

culture, collection 1. a *culture* based on *collecting.* 2. a *prehistoric,* pre-*artifact* culture.

culture, control that part of a *culture* having the function of *social control².*

culture, core 1. *culture* common to all members of the *society.* 2. culture of the *core subsociety.*

culture, covert see *culture, implicit.*

culture, delinquent see *subculture, delinquent.*

culture, dominant the *culture* of the dominant *group* in a *society.*

culture, ethnic the *culture* of an *ethnic group.*

culture, explicit the surface structures of a *culture*.

culture, expressive that part of *culture* concerned with expressive and symbolic behaviour.

culture, extractive a *culture* based on hunting, fishing, *food-gathering* or *collecting*. (Aberle, D.F.).

culture, familistic a *culture* characterized by *familism*.

culture, folk the *culture* of a *folk society*.

culture, foraging a *culture* based on *foraging*.

culture, goal the *culture* which is the *goal* of a *revitalization movement*. (Wallace, A.F.C.).

culture, group 1. the standardized modes of behaviour of a *group* which lacks the scope of a *subsociety*. (Gordon, M.). 2. the established *values* and *norms* of a group. see also *ideology, group*.

culture, guilt a *culture* characterized by a high ratio of guilt to *shame²* reactions. see also *culture, shame*.

culture, high see *tradition, great*.

culture, holistic the whole *culture* of mankind.

culture, ideal that part of a *culture* consisting of ideals.

culture, immaterial see *culture, nonmaterial*.

culture, implicit the deep structures implicit in a *culture*.

culture, inadequate a *culture* failing to achieve *societal‖adjustment*.

culture, marginal the *culture* of a *marginal group*.

culture, mass that part of *culture* resulting from *mass communication*.

culture, material totality of *artifacts*.

culture, minority the *culture* of a *minority group*.

culture, neighbourhood *subculture* of a *neighbourhood*.

culture, nomadic a *culture* based on *nomadism*.

culture, nonmaterial that part of *culture* which does not consist of *artifacts*.

culture, occupational see *subculture, occupational*.

culture, oral *culture* which is orally-transmitted.

culture, overt see *culture, explicit*.

culture, parasitic a *culture* which benefits from another culture at the expense of the other culture. see also *parasitism*.

culture, partitive the specific *culture* of a particular *society*.

culture, peer a *subculture* shared by peers. see also *group, peer*.

culture, political the *attitudes, sentiments,* beliefs, ideals, and *norms* of a *polity*.

culture, professional the *subculture* of a particular *profession*.

culture, regional see *subculture, regional*.

culture, shame a *culture* characterized by a high ratio of *shame²* to guilt reactions. see also *culture, guilt*.

culture, structure of 1. combination of *culture traits* in complexes and *patterns*. (Herskovits). 2. underlying assumptions of a *society*. (Bateson).

culture, total a particular bounded *culture*. (Murdock, G. P.).

culture, value that part of a *culture* consisting of *values*.

culture, work the *subculture* of a *work group*.

culture-bound 1. limited to a particular *culture*. 2. (of a test or *scale²*) valid only with *respondents* of a particular culture or *subculture*. see also *culture-free*.

culture-free 1. not limited to a particular *culture* or cultures. 2. (of a test or *scale²*) validity not restricted to *respondents* of a particular culture or cultures. see also *culture-bound*.

culture-scheme the categories of universals in *culture*.

culturology the autonomous science of *culture*, with avoidance of lower-level analysis. **culturological** *a.* **culturologist** *pers n.*

cultus the *ritual system* of a *religion*.

currency *money* in the form of physical objects in current circulation.

currency, external *currency* restricted for use in external trade.

current, migration see *stream, migration.*

curve, frequency a curve representing a *frequency distribution.*

curve, percentile *ogive* showing *cumulative frequencies* as percentages.

curve, summation curve representing *ogive.*

curve, work curve showing change in work rate over the working day.

custom 1. (broad sense). see *usage.* 2. *usage* resting on long familiarity without *external sanction.* (Weber, M.). 3. usage legitimated by *tradition.* 4. a *norm* involving *unorganized sanctions.* **customary** *a.*

cybernation the combination of *computerization* and *automation.*

cybernetics the science of *communication* and control. (Wiener, N.). **cybernetic** *a.* **cyberneticist** *pers n.* see also *cybernation; bio-cybernetics.*

cybernetics, engineering the *cybernetics* of machines.

cycle series of events recurring as a whole. **cyclical** *a.*

cycle, agricultural the series of agricultural events in a *community* recurring as a whole.

cycle, aperiodic *cycle* lacking *periodicity.*

cycle, behaviour series of acts recurring as a whole.

cycle, calendric the *cycle* of *calendrical rites.*

cycle, ceremonial the year-long series of *ceremonies* recurring as a whole.

cycle, crisis characteristic series of events involved in the appearance and resolution of a specified type of crisis.

cycle, dynastic *cycle* consisting of deteriorating *government* resulting in *rebellion* and the establishment of a new dynasty.

cycle, festival the recurring series of festivals found in a particular *society.*

cycle, invasion characteristic series of changes involved in *invasion.*

cycle, life a characteristic series of changes occurring to a person in his lifetime.

cycle, life, biological the characteristic series of biological changes occurring to a person in his lifetime.

cycle, market the series of meetings held in rotation in a *set¹* of market places. (Bohannan, P. & L.).

cycle, migratory a *society's* annually recurring series of *migrations.*

cycle, periodic *cycle* possessing *periodicity.*

cycle, population the population growth and subsequent population decline characterizing preindustrial *civilizations.*

cycle, poverty characteristic series of changes in standard of living during lifetime of person near *poverty line,* resulting from number of dependent children, income from employed children, loss of income through *marriage* of children, and retirement.

cycle, race-relations characteristic sequence of *policies* towards immigrant *ethnic groups.*

cycle, seasonal the series of *activities,* in a given *society,* characteristic of the various seasons.

cycle, sectarian characteristic series of changes in the natural history of *sects.*

cycle, secular a very long-term *cycle.*

cycle, work-rest characteristic series of work and rest periods.

dactyliomancy *divination* by means of finger rings. **dactyliomantic** *a.*

dactylography the study of the use of fingerprints in crime detection.

dance, astronomical *magico-mimetic* dance concerning the heavenly bodies.

dance, celestial see *dance, astronomical.*

dance, chain *line dance* in which the performers form one long waving line.

dance, character dance in which the performer represents an animal or another person.

dance, couple a mimetic courtship dance.

dance, ecstatic dance in which trance is induced in performers by drumming or whirling.

dance, lift a *magico-mimetic* dance in which a woman is lifted by her male partner.

dance, line dance in which the performers form one or more straight lines or one or more lines which progress in serpentines or circles.

dance, longways dance in which the performers form two facing parallel lines.

dance, play dance which is not *magico-mimetic* or ritual but possesses only a *play‖function*.

dance, puberty dance which is performed in a *community* to mark the attainment of puberty.

dance, trance dance performed by *shaman* in a trance.

dance, votive dance performed or sponsored in fulfilment of *vow*.

dance, work a *magico-mimetic* dance concerning *work* or a dance performed by a *work group* which is conducive to its *effectiveness* or *efficiency*.

daphneomancy *divination* from the sound made by a dried laurel branch thrown into a fire. **daphneomantic** *a.*

data, attribute see *data, qualitative*.

data, basic 1. see *data, raw*. 2. non-derived data.

data, bivariate numerical data on two characteristics of a *population*.

data, continuous data on *continuous variables*.

data, crude see *data, raw*.

data, discontinuous see *data, discrete*.

data, discrete data on *discrete variables*.

data, enumeration data concerning *class frequencies*.

data, grouped numerical data summarized in classes.

data, hard 1. data concerning concrete observations. (Wootton, B.). 2. see *data, quantitative*.

data, integrated numerical data for periods which can be added together to produce data for longer periods.

data, localized data concerning cases located by map co-ordinates.

data, measurement data concerning a characteristic having intrinsic order, zero-point and equal intervals.

data, multivariate numerical data on more than two characteristics of a *population*.

data, period data referring to periods of time.

data, point data referring to points of time.

data, primary 1. see *data, raw*. 2. data drawn from *primary sources*.

data, punched data represented by holes punched in punched cards.

data, qualitative data on *qualitative variables*.

data, quantitative data on *quantitative variables*.

data, raw data in unprocessed state.

data, registration data concerning events recorded at time of occurrence in accordance with legal or administrative regulations.

data, secondary data drawn from *secondary sources*.

data, second-hand data consisting of statements made to observer by others.

data, soft 1. data concerning abstractions from concrete observations. (Wootton, B.). 2. see *data, qualitative*.

data, survey data from a *survey*.

data, type I see *data, enumeration*.

data, type II data concerning a *quasi-variable*.

data, type III see *data, measurement.*

data, ungouped numerical data not summarized in classes.

data, univariate numerical data on a single characteristic of a *population.*

death rate *general, specific* or *standardized rate* concerning *mortality.*

death rate, age-specific *death rate* calculated for a particular *age-grouping.*

death rate, central *death rate* based on *population* at mid-point of period.

death rate, crude number of deaths per specified number of persons over a specified period of time.

death rate, foetal ratio of foetal deaths registered in a given year to all births registered in the same year.

death rate, peri-natal 1. number of peri-natal deaths per specified number of *live births.* 2. number of peri-natal deaths per specified number of viable foetuses, whether or not they survive till after birth.

death rate, sex-age-specific *death rate* calculated for a particular sex in a particular *age-grouping.*

death rate, sex-specific *death rate* calculated for a particular sex.

death rate, specific *death rate* calculated for a homogeneous *sub-population.*

death rate, stable *crude death rate* of a *stable population.*

death rate, standardized *death rate* permitting comparability of *populations.*

debureaucratization the loss of *bureaucratic* character.

deceleration, social rate of decrease in a social *variable.* see also *acceleration, social; celeration, social.*

decentralization 1. *(hum. ecol.)* deconcentration of activities. 2. deconcentration of *decision-making* concerning *policy* of the more general type. 3. transfer of *authority* away from national capital by deconcentration (i.e. *delegation*) to field offices or by *devolution* to local authorities. (UN).

deciles *quantiles* dividing *array* into ten equal parts.

decision 1. a choice amongst alternatives. 2. the selection of a behaviour alternative.

decision, collective a *decision* in which a plurality of persons is involved in the *decision-making* process.

decision, communal see *decision, group.*

decision, composite a *decision* which is not the task of a single person, although a particular person is held accountable for it. (Simon, A. H.).

decision, consensual a *decision* of a *group* arrived at through consensus.

decision, corporate a *decision* made by a *group* involving authorized *decision-making* procedures.

decision, critical see *decision, strategic.*

decision, effective *decision* capable of implementation.

decision, group a *decision* of a *group,* whether a *corporate decision* or a *consensual decision.*

decision, maximax a *decision* which maximizes the maximum gain.

decision, maximin a *decision* which maximizes the minimum gain.

decision, minimax a *decision* which minimizes the maximum loss.

decision, nonprogrammed nonrepetitive *decision* not governed by a *procedure.*

decision, nonseriable a *decision* which is not a *seriable decision.* (Shakle, G. L. S.).

decision, optimal *decision* having an outcome at least as good as other possible decisions.

decision, planning any *decision* in the process of *planning.*

decision, policy a *decision* determining *policy.*

decision, programmed repetitive *decision* governed by a *procedure.*

decision, routine see *decision, tactical.*

decision, seriable a *decision* almost certain of repetition in similar circumstances. (Shakle, G.L.S.).

decision, strategic *decision* as to the *goals* of *organization*.

decision, tactical *decision* concerning operations in *organization*.

decision-making identifying problems for *decision*, devising alternative courses of action, and choosing one alternative. see also *problem-solving*; *policy-making*.

decision-making, consensual *decision-making* based on *consensus* in a decision-making *group*.

decision-making, impersonal *decision-making* carried out impersonally. (Blau, P.M.).

decision-making, participative (PDM) *decision-making* by those whose function is to execute the decisions.

decrease, natural excess of deaths over births. see also *increase, natural*.

decrement a unit decrease in a quantity. see also *increment*.

decrement, social decrease in quantity or quality of work, resulting from presence of *audience* or *group pressures*.

decrement, work decrease in output in a specified task per unit of time.

deculturation loss of cultural items by a *culture*. (Wolf, E.).

dedifferentiation loss of *differentiation*.

deduction inference from the general to the particular. **deductive** *a*. see also *induction*.

deference 1. behaviour intended to convey respect and appreciation on the part of one person for another. (Goffman, E.). 2. behaviour or *posture* symbolic of submissiveness. 3. the ritualistic acknowledgement of *power*. (Stephens, W. N.). **deferential** *a*.

defilement see *pollution*.

definition, conceptual definition in terms of *concepts*.

definition, extensional definition by enumeration of the members of the class. see also *definition, intensional*.

definition, intensional definition by giving the characteristics by virtue of which a thing has the term applied to it. see also *definition, extensional*.

definition, lexical a report of a meaning the term already has.

definition, nominal substitute expression for the definiendum.

definition, operational definition in terms of operations.

definition, ostensive see *definition, extensional*.

definition, pointing see *definition, extensional*.

definition, stipulative a definition stipulated by a particular writer for communication in his own writing.

degradation 1. loss of *status*. 2. human retrogression.

delegation downward transfer in *hierarchy* of *decision-making‖authority*.

delegation, formal *delegation* which is explicitly-formulated.

delegation, general *delegation* without delimitation of *delegated authority*.

delegation, informal *delegation* which is not explicitly-formulated.

delegation, specific *delegation* with delimitation of *delegated authority*.

delegation, total see *delegation, general*.

delinquency 1. socially disapproved behaviour. 2. socially disapproved behaviour of juveniles. 3. juvenile *crime*. **delinquent** *a*.

delinquency, adaptive *delinquency* resulting from an individual's *adaptation* to a hostile *environment*.

delinquency, defective *delinquency* in which the main *factor* is *amentia*.

delinquency, latent see *delinquency, potential*.

delinquency, maladaptive see *delinquency, psychiatric*.

delinquency, potential *delinquency* which an individual who is at present non-delinquent has a high probability of engaging in.

delinquency, primary an individual's *delinquency* which may result in his further delinquency.

delinquency, psychiatric *delinquency* resulting from *personality* maladjustment.

delinquency, secondary an individual's *delinquency* resulting from the effects on him of his original delinquency.

delinquency, self-reported *delinquency* reported confidentially to social investigators by those who have committed it.

delinquency, social *delinquency* resulting from *social learning* by a normal individual.

delinquency, subcultural *delinquency* resulting from *socialization* in a *delinquent subculture*.

deme *local group* lacking *unilineal descent*. (Murdock).

deme, endogamous *deme* characterized by *endogamy*. (Murdock).

deme, exogamous *deme* characterized by *exogamy*. (Murdock).

demobilization relatively rapid decrease in a social unit's control of resources. (Etzioni, A.). **demobilize** *v*. see also *mobilization*.

demography the quantitative study of human *populations*. **demographic** *a*.

demography, descriptive accounts of the quantitative properties of particular *populations*.

demography, economic the study of the relationships between demographic phenomena and economic phenomena.

demography, formal the study of the quantitative relationships amongst demographic phenomena, excluding non-demographic phenomena.

demography, historical 1. the study of the history of *population development*. 2. the study of the history of population development in the period prior to proper *statistics*[2].

demography, mathematical *demography* involving the application of mathematical techniques.

demography, pure see *demography, formal*.

demography, social the study of the relationships between demographic phenomena and social phenomena.

demography, theoretical see *demography, formal*.

demoralization the lowering of *morale*.

denomadization loss of *nomadic* character.

denominations large, doctrinal *groups* of a *religion*.

denotation the *set*[1] of things to which a term is properly applied. **denotative** *a*. see also *connotation*.

density, agricultural 1. number of males occupied with *agriculture*, hunting or forestry per specified area of cultivated land. 2. number of agricultural people per specified area of cultivated land.

density, arithmetic see *ratio, man-land*.

density, average see *ratio, man-land*.

density, building ratio of roof area to total ground area.

density, dynamic frequency and intensity of contact among members of *population*.

density, group number of *group* members per given area, or area per member.

density, moral (Durkheim) see *density, dynamic*.

density, optimum *population density* giving maximum per capita real income with given resources.

density, physiological ratio of *population* to land under cultivation.

density, population ratio of *population* to area.

density, real see *pressure, population*.

density, social degree to which *social relationships* are multi-stranded. (Banton).

department one of a *set*[1] of units in an *organization* in which *activities* are grouped in accordance with a specified characteristic.

department, service a *department* concerned with a group of auxiliary *ac-

tivities.

departmentalization see *departmentation*.

departmentation grouping *activities* in an *organization* to form *departments*.

departmentation, functional *departmentation* in which *activities* are grouped according to *function*.

departmentation, intermediate *departmentation* at *organizational levels* between the primary, i.e. highest, and the ultimate, i.e. lowest.

departmentation, primary *departmentation* at the primary, i.e. highest, *organizational level*.

departmentation, territorial *departmentation* in which *activities* are grouped by area.

departmentation, ultimate *departmentation* at the ultimate, i.e. lowest, *organizational level*.

dependency a *territory* and its *population* ruled by another *state*.

depoliticization 1. the loss of political character by a *group, institution* or *activity*. 2. the loss by an individual of political interests and activities. **depoliticize** *vt*.

depolitization see *depoliticization¹*.

deportee a person who has been deported. (MDD).

deprivation lack of satisfaction of *need*.

deprivation, cultural *deprivation* undergone by an individual or *group* of the cultural satisfactions obtainable in a *society*.

deprivation, maternal *deprivation* by child of presence or love of mother.

deprivation, parental *deprivation* by child of presence or love of one or both parents.

deprivation, relative 1. awareness by an individual of *deprivation* relative to others in the same *category*. 2. awareness by the members of a *group* of deprivation relative to other similar groups.

derivations *rationalizations¹* for *non-logical actions*. (Pareto, V.). see also *residues*.

descent 1. allocation at birth to *group* of relatives. 2. genealogical criteria for membership of unilineally bounded groups. 3. actual or socially-defined genealogical connection with *ancestor* or ancestors. 4. actual *genetic¹* relationship to an ancestor.

descent, agnatic see *descent, patrilineal*.

descent, alternating *descent* involving a regular alternation of *patriline* and *matriline*.

descent, ambilateral *descent* in which individual has choice of joining either a *group* of *patrikin* or a group of *matrikin*.

descent, ambilineal see *descent, non-unilineal*.

descent, asymmetric see *descent, mixed*.

descent, bilateral see *descent, non-unilineal*.

descent, bilineal see *descent, unilineal, double*.

descent, biological actual *genetic¹* relationship to an *ancestor*.

descent, cognatic see *descent, non-unilineal*.

descent, collateral *consanguinity* with a *collateral relative* in an *ascending generation*.

descent, cross-sex *descent* in which females are related to father's mother and males to mother's father.

descent, direct *consanguinity* with an *ascendant* who is a *lineal relative*.

descent, double see *descent, unilineal, double*.

descent, dual see *descent, unilineal, double*.

descent, duolineal see *descent, unilineal, double*.

descent, lineal see *descent, unilineal*.

descent, matrilineal allocation at birth to *group* of *matrikin*.

descent, mixed *descent* varies according to sex.

descent, multilineal see *descent, non-unilineal*.

descent, non-unilineal allocation at birth to *group* of relatives related to individual through males, females and through both.

descent, omnilineal see *descent, non-unilineal*.

descent, parallel see *descent, mixed*.

descent, patrilineal allocation at birth to *group* of *patrikin*.

descent, sex-linked *descent* in which females are related to females in the mother's line and males are related to males in the father's line.

descent, social see *descent[1,2]*.

descent, totemic *descent* in which *totem* is regarded as an *ancestor*. see also *totemism*.

descent, unilateral see *descent, unilineal*.

descent, unilateral, double see *descent, unilineal, double*.

descent, unilineal allocation at birth to one or more *groups* of relatives, the relatives in each group being related in a single line.

descent, unilineal, double allocation at birth to two *groups*, a group of *patrikin* and a group of *matrikin*.

descent, uterine see *aescent, matrilineal*.

description, job the description of a *job* as the result of *job analysis*.

desecration 1. removal of *sacred* character. 2. removal of *mana* from a thing. see also *consecration*.

desegregation the ending of *ethnic segregation*.

design, after-only *experimental design* in which relevant observations of *experimental group* and *control group* are confined to the period after *experimental manipulation*.

design, before-after *experimental design* involving relevant observations on one or more groups both before and after *experimental manipulation*.

design, classical *experimental design* involving two matched groups, namely, *experimental group* and *control group*.

design, cross-over see *design, switchback*.

design, ex post facto *experimental design* in which effect which has occurred is traced back to its causes.

design, experimental 1. the field concerned with the logical strategies of *experiments*. 2. the logical strategy of an experiment.

design, factorial plan for *experiment* in which effect of several *independent variables* on a *dependent variable* is studied.

design, job the determination of *tasks*, the method for performing each task and the combination of tasks into *jobs*.

design, matching *experimental design* which includes *matching*.

design, nonexperimental a *research design* which is not an *experimental design*.

design, randomized *experimental design* in which *treatments[3]* are randomly allotted to *experimental units*.

design, research an arrangement of conditions for the collection and analysis of data.

design, sample *sampling plan* plus method of estimation.

design, survey *sample design*, *questionnaire* and method of *measurement* employed in *survey*.

design, switchback an *experimental design* which relates to a three period sequence for two *treatments[3]*, e.g., ABA.

design, systematic *experimental design* in which *treatments[3]* are not randomly allotted to *experimental units*.

design, vertical see *design, after-only*.

desocialization loss by an individual of the changes produced by *socialization*.

despotism the exercise of unlimited *authority* without accountability.**despotic** *a.* **despot** *pers n.* see also *autocracy*; *dictatorship*; *absolutism*; *tyranny*; *totalitarianism*.

despotism, hydraulic *despotism* exercised over a *hydraulic society*.

destratification the loss of *stratification*.

determinism, biological 1. doctrine that human behaviour is basically *innate*. 2. doctrine that biological *factors* have a role in the *explanation* of particular phenomena.

determinism, climatic doctrine that *modal personality* and *social structure* are determined mainly by climatic *factors*.

determinism, cultural 1. doctrine that human behaviour is mainly determined by *culture*. 2. doctrine that culture must be explained at its own *level of analysis*.

determinism, economic doctrine that a *society* is determined in the way it is mainly as a result of economic *factors*.

determinism, geographic doctrine that a *society* is determined in the way it is mainly as a result of geographical *factors*.

determinism, ideological doctrine that a *society* is determined in the way it is mainly as a result of a *system* of beliefs.

determinism, racial doctrine that *cultural* differences are determined by differences in *race*.

determinism, techno-economic doctrine that a *society* is determined in the way it is mainly as a result of technological and economic *factors*.

deterrence, general deterring potential offenders through the *punishment* of actual offenders.

deterrence, individual deterring an actual offender from committing a further offence by punishing him.

deterrence, marginal an increase in *general deterrence* resulting from an increase in the *punishment* prescribed for a specified crime. (Morris, N.).

detribalization 1. movement from *tribal areas* into *urban areas*. 2. passage of an individual from the political control of the *tribe*. (Gluckman). 3. severing ties with tribe. 4. change from tribal standards of behaviour.

deurbanization 1. decrease in proportion of *urban population*. 2. the process of *population* deconcentration.

deutero-learning learning to learn. see also *learning*.

development 1. sequence of systemic changes. 2. increase in differentiation, complexity or integration.

development, agricultural technical advance in *agriculture*.

development, community the promotion of better living for the whole *community* with the active participation, initiative, and *co-operation* of the community. see also *organization, community*.

development, community, rural *community development* in a *rural community*.

development, community, urban *community development* in an *urban community*.

development, economic increase in economic complexity. see also *growth, economic*.

development, industrial industrial growth or increase in industrial complexity.

development, management methods of developing the competence of individual managers.

development, political 1. the efficiency of a *political system*. (Blondel, J.). 2. the combination of *massness*, liberalism and radical change in a *society*. 3. development towards liberal democracy. (Cutright, P.). 4. the ability of a society to sustain political demands and *organizations*. (Eisenstadt, S.N.). 5. the ability of a society to sustain *social goals* and *institutions*. (Diamant, A.).

development, population increase in differentiation in or complexity of a *population*. see also *dynamics, population*.

development, ribbon building houses along both sides of roads which radiate from towns.

development, social increase in social complexity.

development, socioeconomic increase in social and economic complexity.

deviance 1. motivated tendency for *actor* to contravene a *norm*. 2. considerable departure from the *modal personality*. 3. motivated disturbance of *equilibrium* of an *interactive system*. (Parsons, T.). **deviant** *a.* & *pers n.* **deviate** *pers n.*

deviance, felt *deviance* of an individual of which he is aware.

deviation 1. departure from a point of reference. 2. difference between *value[6]* and a measure of central tendency. *(stats.)*. 3. see *deviance*.

deviation, average see *deviation, mean*.

deviation, mean *arithmetic mean* of *deviations[2]* from average (signs ignored).

deviation, standard square root of *mean* of squared *deviations[2]* from mean.

deviation, step the *deviation[2]* of a mid-point from the *assumed mean*, divided by the size of the class interval.

devolution transfer of specified *powers[6]* including *final authority* from the central authority to other governmental or organizational units.

devolution, geographical *devolution* to geographical governmental units or organizational units.

devolution, political transfer of specified governmental *powers[6]* including *final authority* from the central authority to other governmental units.

devolution, territorial see *devolution, geographical*.

diagram, area diagram consisting of areas proportional to quantities represented.

diagram, bar diagram consisting of bars of length proportional to quantities represented.

diagram, branch a diagram in which branches are successively emitted at branch points.

diagram, circular see *chart, circular*.

diagram, flow see *chart, flow[1]*.

diagram, logic a diagram for representing logical relations.

diagram, path diagram in which one-way arrows link *determining variables* to *dependent variables[2]*.

diagram, pie see *chart, circular*.

diagram, scatter a graph with an arrangement of dots resulting from the plotting of two associated series, with one *variable* on the x-axis and the other on the y-axis.

diagram, tree see *diagram, branch*.

dialect variety of a language defined with reference to the *set[1]* of persons who use it. see also *register*.

diarchy rule by two persons. **diarchic** *a.*

dichotomy 1. a division into two parts. 2. a type of *division[3]*, or *classification*, in which at each stage the genus is divided into species according to a certain *set[1]* of differentiae.

dichotonymy the hyphenation of surnames.

dictatorship 1. *autocracy* not established in accordance with pre-existing *norms*. 2. unlimited *authority* possessed by one person or a *group* of persons acquired by *conquest[2]* and with no rule of *succession[1]*. see also *autocracy*; *despotism*; *absolutism*; *tyranny*; *totalitarianism*.

dictatorship, apparatic *dictatorship* serving the interests of a military and administrative apparatus which is alienated from the rest of the *society*.

dictatorship, classist *dictatorship* serving the interests of a *social class*.

65

dictatorship, collective *dictatorship* exercised by a *group* of persons.

dictatorship, constitutional a *dictatorship* of a temporary and emergency nature provided by the *constitution²*.

dictatorship, personal *dictatorship* exercised by one person.

dictatorship, provisional a *dictatorship* of a temporary and emergency nature, whether or not provided by the *constitution²*.

dictatorship, simple *dictatorship* through absolute control of the traditional instruments of *state‖power*. (Neumann, F. L.).

dictatorship, sovereign *dictatorship* aimed at a radical change in the form of *society*. (Schmitt, C.).

dictatorship, structural a *dictatorship* accounted for in terms of *socioeconomic development*. (Blondel, J.).

dictatorship, technical a *dictatorship* resulting from *factors* external to the *society*, e.g., colonization, foreign occupation. (Blondel, J.).

differential, semantic a technique for determining the emotive meaning of a word by rating the word on each of a number of seven-point *rating scales*, the extremes of which are defined by polar adjectives. (Osgood, C.E.).

differentiation, role 1. the number of distinct *roles* in a *society*. 2. the extent to which incumbency of one role is independent of the incumbency of other roles. (Banton, M.). 3. the process whereby the roles in a society become more numerous and specialized.

differentiation, social the differentiation in *society* of *occupations* and *roles*, *prestige*, *power*, and of *groups* according to *function*.

differentiation, structural *functional specialization* of structures.

diffuseness—specificity the incompatible alternatives facing an *actor* of a wide involvement or a narrow involvement with a social object. (Parsons, T.).

diffusion 1. spread of cultural feature beyond *community* in which it originated. 2. acceptance over time of some specific item by individuals, *groups* or other adopting units, linked to specific channels of *communication*, to a *social structure*, and to a given *system* of *values*, or *culture*. (Katz, E.). 3. spread of information from a source.

diffusion, antagonistic *diffusion¹* between hostile *groups*.

diffusion, contact *diffusion¹* resulting from direct contact.

diffusion, controlled *diffusion¹* in which recipient *group* is selective.

diffusion, cultural see *diffusion¹*.

diffusion, discontinuous *diffusion¹* between noncontiguous areas.

diffusion, industrial industrial *decentralization* to suburban or fringe areas.

diffusion, interpersonal *diffusion* in which the information spreads from person to person. see also *diffusion, source-personal*.

diffusion, message spread of a *message* or messages through a *population* from a source.

diffusion, natural see *diffusion, spontaneous*.

diffusion, planned deliberate spread of cultural feature by a *group*. (Kroeber).

diffusion, primary spread of new *culture trait* within *society* of origin.

diffusion, relay spread of *culture trait* by its relay from *community* to community.

diffusion, secondary spread of *culture trait* from *society* of origin to other societies.

diffusion, source-personal *diffusion* in which the information is transmitted directly to each person in the *group* from the source, i.e. the person or persons introducing the information to the group. see also *diffusion, interpersonal*.

diffusion, spontaneous *diffusion¹* which is not *planned diffusion*.

diffusion, stimulus *diffusion¹* involving only the general idea, not the specific form, of a *culture trait*.

diffusion, technological spread of technological *innovations*.

diffusionism the doctrine that most cultural similarities are the result of *diffusion[1]*. **diffusionist** *a. & pers n.* see also *parallelism[2]*.

diglossia the existence of two varieties of a language in same *speech community* used in different situations. see also *dialect*; *register*.

dilemma, role any situation of *role conflict* or *role ambiguity*.

diplomacy 1. peaceful *conflict* resolution between autonomous *groups*. 2. the use of accredited officials for intergovernmental *communication*.3. modes or techniques of foreign policy affecting the *international system*.

directing 1. guiding and supervising subordinates. 2. giving advice in an *organization*.

directive order or instruction issued by superior to subordinate.

disability 1. legal incapacity, general or special. 2. condition incapacitating person from his usual activity. 3. incapacity to work resulting from disease or other condition.

discovery the recognition of phenomena or relationships not previously perceived. see also *invention*; *innovation*.

discrimination treating a person differently for irrelevant reasons. see also *prejudice*.

discrimination, affirmative preferential treatment accorded to a *minority group,* a deprived socio-economic *group,* or a *social category* the members of which were previously discriminated against, sometimes involving the substitution of representation for equality of opportunity, and the maintenance of statistical parities amongst the various groups in *society,* whether or not intended to help eradicate the effects of previous discrimination.

discrimination, economic *discrimination* against a person which takes the form of preventing his entry to an *occupation* to which he is qualified or denying him material welfare.

discrimination, ethnic *discrimination* against a person because of his *ethnic group*.

discrimination, favourable see *discrimination, affirmative*.

discrimination, legal *discrimination* which takes the form of discriminatory laws or a lack of impartiality at any stage in the legal process.

discrimination, political I. *discrimination* against persons which takes the form of restricting their *political participation*. 2. discrimination by certain members of the *polity* against others.

discrimination, positive see *discrimination, affirmative*.

discrimination, racial 1. *discrimination* against persons because of their *race*. 2. distinction, exclusion, restriction, or preference based on race, colour, descent, or national or ethnic origin. (UN).

discrimination, reverse see *discrimination, affirmative*.

discrimination, social *discrimination* which takes the form of *involuntary segregation,* restrictions on or prohibition of intermarriage, or *degradation*.

disequilibrium, status a condition in which an individual's positions in different *hierarchies* are not at a comparable level.

disorganization, community I. *social disorganization* occurring in a *community.* 2. failure of one or more of the *subsystems* of a community to function at a specified level of effectiveness.

disorganization, social 1. decrease in influence of existing *norms* upon individual members of *group*. 2. disruption of an *activity* resulting from the violation of its constitutive *rules*. (Cohen).

dispersion how the observations are scattered around their average.

dispersion, industrial industrial *decentralization* beyond fringe areas. see also *diffusion, industrial*.

displacement 1. transference of *aggression* from the frustrating object to another object. 2. transference of affect from one object to another. 3. substitution of one *activity* for another which is frustrated.

displacement, ecological partial or complete displacement, in an area, of one *population* type or land-use type by another.

displacement, goal 1. an *instrumental value* becoming a *terminal value*. 2. see *succession, goal*.

displacement, military *military intervention* taking the form of the imposition by the military of civilians of their own choice.

displacement, population 1. partial or complete displacement, in an area, of one *population* type by another. 2. forced removal of a population or *sub-population*.

dissensus lack of *consensus*.

dissonance, attitude a logical inconsistency amongst *attitudes*.

dissonance, cognitive a logical inconsistency amongst *cognitions*.

distance, affinal distance between two pe ,ons in terms of number of *affinal* links.

distance, consanguineal distance between two persons in terms of number of *consanguineal* links.

distance, cultural see *distance, valuational*.

distance, genealogical distance between two persons in terms of number of *kinship* links.

distance, individual the minimum physical distance commonly maintained between individuals in a given *culture*. (Hediger, H.).

distance, interactive actual degree of *interaction* between two persons or *statuses*.

distance, kinship see *distance, genealogical*.

distance, normative prescribed degree of *interaction* between two persons or *statuses*.

distance, occupational difference in *status* between two *occupations*.

distance, personal degree of *empathy* between two persons or *statuses*.

distance, pheric distance in terms of time necessary to cover it.

distance, population any type of geographic distance or biological or linguistic difference between two *populations*. (Howells, W.W.).

distance, role the degree to which a *role* contradicts a player's *self-concept*.

distance, social distance on four dimensions (*normative*, interactive, valuational (cultural), and personal) between two persons or *statuses*.

distance, sociometric distance between two *group* members in terms of *sociometric status*. (*sociom.*).

distance, spatial distance in terms of spatial units.

distance, valuational degree to which two persons or *statuses* share *values*.

distoceptor *receptor* arousable by a *stimulus object* lying at a distance.

distribution, age the *frequency distribution* of a *population* or *sub-population* according to age.

distribution, areal distribution of items over a series of areas.

distribution, ecological *spatial distribution* of interrelated persons and activities.

distribution, frequency shows number of items which fall into various classes according to size.

distribution, frequency, cumulative see *ogive*.

distribution, historical see *distribution, temporal*.

distribution, income *frequency distribution* of income in the *population*.

distribution, occupational *frequency distribution* of a *population* by *occupation*.

distribution, parity *frequency distribution* of women according to number of births they have had.

distribution, percentage distribution in terms of *percentage frequences.*

distribution, population distribution of *population* over a series of areas.

distribution, profligacy see *distribution, parity.*

distribution, sampling the *frequency distribution* of an infinite number of *samples* of the same size selected independently and by the same prescribed procedure from the same *population.*

distribution, sex see *ratio, sex.*

distribution, spatial see *distribution, areal.*

distribution, temporal distribution of items over a series of time intervals.

distribution, truncated a distribution cut off so that there are no cases beyond a certain point.

district, central business (CBD) see *district, central commercial.*

district, central commercial area of greatest commercial and *population density* in a city.

district, central traffic see *district, central commercial.*

district, enumeration (ED) area assigned to one *enumerator.*

divination obtaining a knowledge of secret or future events from supernatural sources by means of *signs.* **divine** *v.* **diviner** *pers n.* see also *acromancy; alectoromancy; alectryomancy; aleuromancy; alomancy; alphitomancy; amniomancy; anthropomancy; armomancy; astragalomancy; augury; capnomancy; catoptromancy; chaomancy; chiromancy; cleromancy; coscinomancy; crithomancy; crytallomancy; dactyliomancy; daphneomancy; geomancy; gyromancy; haruspication; haruspicy; hepatoscopy; hydromancy; ichthyomancy; lampadomancy; lecanomancy; lithomancy; margaritomancy; necromancy; neomancy; nephelomancy; nomancy; oneiromancy; onychomancy; oomancy; ophiomancy; ornithomancy; ornithoscopy; pedomancy; pyromancy; rhabdomancy; scapulimancy; scatoscopy; sciomancy; scrying; somatomancy; spodomancy; theomancy.*

divination, automatic *divination* which does not depend on the state of the *diviner.*

divination, discovery *divination* of secret events. see also *divination, prediction.*

divination, hypnotic *divination* using a person in a hypnotic state.

divination, involuntary *divination* from *signs* which are not sought.

divination, magnetic *divination* through the immobilization of an object which normally moves freely on a flat surface.

divination, mechanical *divination* only involving the manipulation of material objects.

divination, mental *divination* through communication with the spirit world.

divination, pointing *divination* resulting from an instrument pointing at one of two *symbols* or at a suspect.

divination, reflecting *divination* from *signs* or images seen in water, mirrors, crystals, or polished stones.

divination, revolving *divination* through the direction or speed of movement of an instrument which revolves on its axis.

divination, possessive *divination* depending on the *diviner* being under *spirit possession.*

divination, prediction *divination* of future events. see also *divination, discovery.*

divination, voluntary *divination* from *signs* which are sought.

division 1. hereditary segment of a *society.* 2. see *department.* 3. breaking down a class into its subclasses, these into their subclasses, and so on.

division, self-contained highly independent *division²* in *organization.*

divisionalization see *departmentation.*

divorce rate 1. ratio of divorces to average *population* during a given period.2. ratio of divorces occurring to *marriages* extant in a population during a given period.

domain 1. *sub-population* on which numerical data is sought. 2. the *set[1]* of *values[6]* which a *variable* can take. 3. area of phenomena to which a generalization or *theory* applies. 4. the semantic range of a *lexical set*. 5. the range of phenomena that is represented in a *factor analysis*. (Thurstone, L.L.). 6. the right of control over a given area.

domain, administrative *state* ownership and management of land.

domain, familial the land on which a particular *family* resides and which it owns or controls.

domain, mercantile rights over land which is treated as a commodity to be bought and sold.

domain, patrimonial the heritable right of control over the occupants of a given area.

domain, prebendal the non-heritable right granted to an official to receive tribute from or attach a certain portion of the tribute from the occupants of a given area.

domain, semantic see *domain[4]*.

domain, territorial see *territory, state*.

domination 1. controlling the *actions* of others by making explicit the desired actions. see also *manipulation[1]*. 2. the process by which a person controls the actions of a *group* in the direction of *goals* chosen by himself.

dominance, ecological dominance of a city over the surrounding area.

dominance, metropolitan the *ecological dominance* possessed by a *metropolis*.

dominance, urban the *ecological dominance* possessed by a city.

double-bind the situation of being made the object of incompatible emotional demands by another.

double-blind pertaining to an *experimental design* in which neither the *subjects[1]* nor the experimental assistants know which subjects are in the *control group* and which are in the *experimental group*.

drama, ritual a symbolic enactment and resolution of a struggle between opposing forces.

dramatization demonstration of desired behaviour in a ritual or aesthetic context. (Nadel, S.F.).

dramatization, status demonstration of and reinforcement of a *society's* *statuses* in a ritual or aesthetic context.

drift, cultural deviation from normal by an increasing number of individuals.

drift, gene fluctuation of *gene frequencies* in a *population* from *generation[2]* to *generation[2]*. see also *flow, gene*.

drift, migratory gradual displacement of *transhumance* orbits.

drive central neural excitation, which activates organism, produced by *need*.

drive, acquired *drive* which is not *innate*.

drive, basic *drive* from which other drives are derived.

drive, biological *drive* which is *innate*.

drive, primary see *drive, biological*.

drive, secondary see *drive, acquired*.

drive, social 1. a *drive* to enter into certain social relations. 2. a socially-acquired drive.

drop-outs *observational units* which become unavailable for observation.

dualism the structural or territorial division of a *community* into two parts. (Lévi-Strauss). see also *triadism*.

dualism, concentric the territorial division of a *community* into two parts, one enclosing the other. (Lévi-Strauss).

dualism, diametric the territorial division of a *community* into two parts, the one not enclosing the other. (Lévi-Strauss).

duolineality see *descent, unilineal, double*.

duolocality see *residence, duolocal*.

duel a socially-recognised, *norm*-controlled combat between individuals.

duel, song a contest constituting a means of *adjudication* in which the parties to a dispute sing derisory songs. see also *duel, wrestling*.

duel, wrestling a contest constituting a means of *adjudication* in which the parties to a dispute engage in wrestling. see also *duel, song*.

duration, response time occupied by a *response*.

dwelling room or suite of rooms intended for habitation, having separate access to street or to a common landing or staircase having public access.

dwelling, conventional a room or suite of rooms and its accessories intended for habitation by one *household*, in a permanent building or structurally separated part thereof. (SOUN).

dwelling, core a sanitary unit plus at least one room around which a completed *dwelling* will eventually be constructed. (SOUN).

dwelling, semi-permanent *conventional dwelling* constructed of locally available crude materials. (SOUN).

dyad a *group* of two persons. **dyadic** *a*.

dynamics, administrative study of change in the *administration* of an *organization*. (Caiden, G.E.).

dynamics, attitude study of *attitude* change.

dynamics, cultural the study of the processes by which *cultures* change.

dynamics, group study of change in *groups*.

dynamics, organizational study of change in *organizations*.

dynamics, political study of political change.

dynamics, population study of *population* change. see also *development, population*.

dynamics, social analysis of changes or successive states of interrelated *social facts*. (Comte).

dysergy processes undermining social *equilibrium*. (Haesaert, J.).

dysfunction 1. those consequences which lessen the *adaptation* of the *system*. 2. disintegrative social consequences of social or cultural item. (Merton).**dysfunctional** *a*.

dysfunction, latent unintended *dysfunction*.

dysfunction, manifest intended *dysfunction*.

dysgenic conducive to undesirable *genetic[1]* qualities.

dysgenics the study of the determinants of the undesirable *genetic[1]* qualities of human *populations*. see also *eugenics*.

dysnomia 1. existence of *dysfunctional* element in a *society*. 2. social disintegration. (Radcliffe-Brown).

echelon a level of *command, authority*, or *rank*.

ecology, behavioural study of human behaviour in natural settings.

ecology, biological plant and animal ecology.

ecology, community the study of the relations between human *communities* and their *environment*.

ecology, cultural the study of the processes by which a *society* adapts to its *environment*. (Steward, J.H.).

ecology, economic the study of the social *factors* affecting the *economic system*.

ecology, factorial *human ecology* employing *factor analysis*.

ecology, general the *principles* common to all branches of ecology.

ecology, human 1. science concerned with spatial aspect of human communities and relationship between *community* and *habitat*. 2. study of the impersonal, *subsocial* aspects of communal structure. (Quinn, J.A.).

ecology, organizational the study of the relations between *organizations* and their *environment*.

ecology, political the study of the relations between *political systems* and their *environment*. (Russett, B.M.).

ecology, population the study of the relations between *population* and *habitat*.

ecology, psychological the psychologically relevent aspects of the *environment*. (Lewin, K.).

ecology, social see *ecology, human*.

ecology, urban that branch of *human ecology* concerned with *urban* phenomena.

ecology, work effect of spatial pattern of workers on *effectiveness* and *efficiency* of *work group*.

economics, comparative the comparative study of *economic systems*.

economics, primitive study of the *technology* and *economic systems* of *primitive‖societies*. (Firth, R.).

economizing applying scarce means to alternative ends. (Sahlins, M.D.).

economy 1. the *system* of relationships in a *society* determining the allocation of scarce economic resources and concerned with production, distribution and *exchange*. 2. any system of relationships determining the allocation of scarce resources.

economy, controlled *economy* under extensive governmental control.

economy, dual the existence within a single *political unit* of a traditional *peasant* sector and a capitalist sector in the hands of aliens.

economy, fire see *cultivation, shifting*.

economy, handicraft an *economy* dominated by handicrafts.

economy, household an *economy* dominated by domestically-produced goods.

economy, managed an *economy* the general direction of which is determined by *state* intervention.

economy, manorial the *economy* characteristic of the *manorial system*.

economy, market an *economy* regulated by market forces.

economy, metropolitan 1. a world *economy* the finance and *communications* of which are organized and integrated by *metropolises*. 2. an economy based on a *system* of *exchange* concentrated in the metropolis.

economy, mixed *economy* combining public and private ownership of the means of production.

economy, motion economizing of the motions necessary for a *job*.

economy, multicentric *economy* possessing two or more spheres of *exchange*.

economy, peasant an *economy* based on *peasant* production.

economy, planned an *economy* under *state planning*.

economy, power those operations of an *economy* which enhance the *government*'s internal and external *power*.

economy, prestige *economy* in which *economic surplus* can only be used by individuals for *prestige expenditure*.

economy, redistributive *economy* based on *redistribution*.

economy, robber the destruction of non-replaceable resources for short-term gains.

economy, subsistence *economy* all the production of which is internally consumed.

economy, unicentric *economy* possessing a single sphere of *exchange*.

ecosystem the interacting *environmental* and *biotic‖system*. (Allee, W.C.).

ectomorphy 1. one of the three primary components in physique concerned with the extent of surface area relative to mass and the degree of exposure of the nervous system. 2. the predominance of this component. (Sheldon, W.H.).**ectomorphic** *a.* **ectomorph** *pers n.* see also *endomorphy;*

mesomorphy; *somatotype*.

ecotype a *system* of energy transfers by which a *group* adapts to and exploits its *environment*. (Harris, D.R.).

ecumene 1. part of *state* with greatest *population density* and closest mesh of transportation lines. (Whittlesey, D.). 2. the permanently inhabited part of the earth. (Trewartha, G.T.). 3. the habitable part of the earth. (Houston, J.M.).

editing editing completed *schedules* for *accuracy* and *reliability,* consistency, uniformity, and completeness.

editing, check checking a *sample* of edited *schedules* to ascertain quality of *editing*.

editing, field *editing* of *schedules* before reception at field offices.

editing, intake *editing* of *schedules* on reception at field offices.

editing, regional *editing* of *schedules* at regional offices on reception from local field offices.

editing, specialized *editing* involving a number of editors each of whom specializes in a particular section of the *schedule*.

education 1. the transmission of knowledge or *values* by formal or informal means. 2. *systematic socialization* of the young *generation[2]* by adults. (Durkheim, E.).

education, comparative the *cross-cultural* study of *education*.

education, compensatory *training* intended to compensate for the lack of *educogenic* factors in the individual's *environment*.

education, correctional *education* or *training* given in prisons aimed at the rehabilitation of offenders.

education, extension *education* to help people improve themselves within their own *environment*.

education, fundamental basic *education,* by informal means, found in *community development*.

education, mass the extensive application of educational resources to a *population* as opposed to their intensive application to *sub-populations*.

education, social 1. teaching an individual to participate in group life. 2. formal *education* for *social participation*. 3. rehabilitative *training* given in the prison classroom. 4. rehabilitative training given in prisons.

educogenic conducive to a person's *education*.

effect, additive effect of a *set[1]* of *variables* on a *dependent variable* consisting of sum of effects of each of the variables acting alone.

effect, biased-viewpoint individual's misperception of his *group* resulting from his position in the group.

effect, halo tendency in a *rater* to rate traits on the basis of a previously formed general impression of the *ratee*. (Thorndike).

effect, interaction effect of a *set[1]* of *variables* on a *dependent variable* which does not consist of sum of effects of each of the variables acting alone.

effect, interviewer see *bias, interviewer*.

effect, leniency (Guilford) see *error, generosity*.

effect, sleeper an effect which is delayed.

effectiveness degree to which *group* achieves its *group goals*. see also *efficiency[7]*.

efficacy, political 1. the *perception* by a citizen that he is capable of influencing political *decisions*. 2. a legislator's feeling of effectiveness in his political *roles*.

efficiency 1. the attainment of maximum *values* with limited means. 2. ratio of actual output to actual input. 3. ratio of actual output to standard output. 4. ratio of actual output to possible output. 5. given fixed resources, the ratio of the results of an *activity* to the results of the alternative activities. (Simon,

H.). 6. degree to which a single organizational *objective* is obtained. 7. degree to which *group* produces member satisfaction. see also *effectiveness*.

efficiency, predictive the percentage of correct predictions made possible by a test.

efficiency, urban *efficiency* of an *urban system*[2].

ego 1. *personality* as subjectively perceived. (Kardiner). 2. individual acting as reference point in a *kinship system* 3. individual considered as a reference point in relation to others.

ego, ancestral dead *ancestor* acting as reference point in a *kinship system*.

ego, contemporary living person acting as reference point in a *kinship system*.

ego, female female acting as reference point in a *kinship system*.

ego, male male acting as reference point in a *kinship system*.

eidos non-*value* aspect of a *culture*. see also *ethos*.

election selection of office-holders by the votes of the electorate.

election, critical *election* in which the centres of gravity for voting oscillations for a large number of districts simultaneously undergo a step change. (Key, V.O.).

election, direct *election* in which votes of electorate are cast for candidates for *office*.

election, indirect *election* in which electorate selects delegates who in turn select the office-holders.

election, multiple *election* in which two or more *offices* are filled simultaneously from each constituency.

election, single *election* in which only one *office* is filled from each constituency.

element, culture see *trait, culture*.

element, population member of a *population*.

element, role a component of a *role*.

elite 1. a class of persons having the highest index in their branch of *activity*. (Pareto). 2. the *group* in *society* holding *positions* of eminence. 3. group in society holding positions in a particular field of eminence. 4. group of *actors* who have *power*. (Etzioni, A.). 5. those persons with most power in a group. 6. effective and responsible *minority* designated to serve a *collectivity* in a socially-valued way. (Keller, S.). 7. those persons in society who get most income, *deference* and safety. (Lasswell). 8. those persons who perform the most important *functions* in society.

elite, adaptive any *elite* concerned with the *group's* *adaptive subsystem*.

elite, divided an *elite* the members of which differ in social origin and source of *power*.

elite, external any *elite* concerned with the *group's* external problems. (Keller, S.).

elite, goal-attainment any *elite* concerned with the *group's* *goal-attainment subsystem*.

elite, governing see *elite, political*.

elite, hereditary *elite* characterized by *hereditary recruitment*.

elite, industrializing *political elite* which aims at industrializing its *society*.

elite, integrative any *elite* concerned with the *group's* *integrative subsystem*. (Keller, S.).

elite, internal any *elite* concerned with the *group's* internal problems. (Keller, S.).

elite, local the *elite* of a particular locality.

elite, migratory top *spiralists* with their characteristic of *areal mobility*.

elite, modernizing *political elite* which aims at modernizing its *society*.

elite, pattern-maintenance any *elite* concerned with the *group's* *pattern-maintenance subsystem*.

elite, political those persons with most political *power* in a *society* or com-

munity.

elite, power the *set[1]* of overlapping political, economic and military *cliques* sharing *decisions* having at least national consequences. (Mills, C.W.).

elite, ruling see *elite, political.*

elite, segmental an *elite* without a general and sustained social impact. (Keller, S.).

elite, strategic any *elite* which has a general and sustained social impact. (Keller, S.).

elite, traditional *political elite* which acts in accordance with the *traditions* of its *society.*

elite, unified an *elite* the members of which do not differ in social origin and source of *power.*

embourgeoisement the acquisition of bourgeois beliefs and *values.*

emergence, descriptive the occurrence of a property of a *system,* which property is not definable in terms of the components of the system.

emergence, explanatory the occurrence of *laws[10]* of a *system,* which laws are not derivable from the laws about components, including composition laws, by which is meant laws about how components of the system combine.

emic pertaining to the insider's view of a *society,* using *folk concepts* and *folk explanations.* see also *etic.*

emicist 1. a specialist in the *emic* approach. 2. a supporter of the emic study of individual *societies.* **emicism** *n.*

emigration *migration* out of a particular country. **emigrate** *vi.* **emigrant** *pers n.*

emigration, gross total amount of *emigration.*

emigration, mass *emigration* involving very large numbers.

emigration, net excess of *emigrants* over *immigrants.*

emigration, planned *emigration* resulting from *planning* on the part of an *organization.* see also *migration, planned; immigration, planned.*

emigré person who has left his country through fear but who hopes one day to return. (Petersen). see also *refugee; exile; expatriate; person, displaced; expellee.*

empathy reproduction in oneself of the affect of another person. **empathize** *v.* see also *sympathy; identification.*

empathy, interactive ability to sense the affect of another person and to communicate this understanding to him.

empathy, predictive ability to *empathize* and through this to predict the affect and behaviour of another person or class of persons.

empiricism doctrine that all knowledge is derived from experience.

empiricism, logical a philosophical movement combining *empiricism* and *positivism,* the scientific attitude, the logical analysis of language, symbolic logic, and *methodology.*

empiricism, scientific a philosophical movement combining *logical empiricism* with the doctrine of the unity of science.

emulation *rivalry* involving *imitation.*

enactment, role see *performance, role[2].*

enclave a portion of a foreign *territory* which a given territory encloses. see also *exclave.*

enclave, economic a portion of another *economy* which a given economy encloses.

encounter the *face-to-face interaction* of a *set[1]* of individuals on a given occasion. (Goffman, E.).

enculturation cultural *learning* by an individual. see also *acculturation; assimilation.*

enculturator a person contributing to a child's *enculturation.*

endo-conviviality entering into convivial relations only with other members of the *in-group*.

endo-deme see *deme, endogamous*.

endogamy 1. existence of *rule* prescribing *marriage* within a given *group*. 2. marriage within a given group. 3. mating within a given *population*. **endogamous** *a.* see also *exogamy*; *agamy*.

endogamy, band *endogamy* applying to the *band*.

endogamy, class *endogamy* applying to *social classes*.

endogamy, consanguine *endogamy* applying to a *set¹* of *consanguineal relatives*.

endogamy, kinship *endogamy* applying to a *set¹* of relatives. see also *endogamy, territorial*.

endogamy, local *endogamy* applying to the *local group*.

endogamy, occupational *endogamy* applying to an *occupation*.

endogamy, religious *endogamy* applying to a religious *group*.

endogamy, territorial *endogamy* applying to a *territory*. see also *endogamy, kinship*.

endogenous coming from within the *system*.

endomorphy 1. one of the three primary components in physique concerned with the degree of development of the digestive viscera. 2. the predominance of this component. (Sheldon, W.H.). **endomorphic** *a.* **endomorph** *pers n.* see also *mesomorphy*; *ectomorphy*; *somatotype*.

endtest see *post-test*.

energy 1. capacity to do work. 2. maximum amount of work that a *system* can do.

energy, psychic the tension of psychic activity. (Janet, P.).

energy, social total physical *energy* in a *society*.

engagement the number of aspects of its members' lives which a *group* regulates. (Merton, R.K.). see also *group, totalitarian*; *group, segmental*.

engineering, human (U.S.) see *ergonomics*.

enlargement, job adding dissimilar elements to a *job* and thus altering job content. see also *extension, job*.

entity, logical an entity to which reality is not attributed but which is assumed for scientific purposes. see also *variable, intervening*.

entropy 1. number of possible outcomes of an event. 2. the degree of randomness in a *system*. 3. the degree to which *psychic energy* cannot be transferred after being *cathected*.

entropy, social the degree of uncertainty in *social behaviour*.

enumeration the counting of a *population*.

enumerator any one of the individuals engaged in the actual counting of a *population*.

environment 1. surroundings to which *response* is made. 2. total surroundings of an individual. **environmental** *a.*

environment, abiotic the non-living *environment*.

environment, artificial an *environment* created for an organism for *experimental* purposes.

environment, behavioural that part of the *environment* to which an individual responds.

environment, biological see *environment, biotic*.

environment, biotic the living *environment*.

environment, cultural the *environment* consisting of cultural phenomena.

environment, external 1. the surroundings of an organism. 2. the surroundings of a *system* or *group*.

environment, geographical the *environment* consisting of geographical phenomena.

environment, internal 1. the intra-somatic surroundings of a particular organ. 2.

the intrasystemic surroundings of an element of a *system*.

environment, international an *environment* in which persons of different nations meet and which is similar to other environments having the same facilities (e.g. an international airport).

environment, interpersonal an individual's *environment* consisting of those persons with whom he has *interpersonal interaction*.

environment, linguistic the *cultural* or *subcultural[1]* linguistic patterns of an individual's *environment*.

environment, natural 1. see *environment, non-human*. 2. the ordinary *environment* of an organism. 3. environment of individual in a pre-industrial *society*.

environment, non-human that part of the *environment* which is not *sociocultural*.

environment, objective the *environment* as it is and not as perceived by the individual.

environment, physical see *environment, abiotic*.

environment, psychological *environment* as perceived by person, interactive product of person and *objective environment*.

environment, social the *environment* consisting of social phenomena.

environment, sociocultural the *environment* consisting of *sociocultural* phenomena.

environment, subjective see *environment, psychological*.

environment, symbolic the linguistic and non-linguistic *symbols* surrounding an individual.

environment, total see *environment[2]*.

envoûtement *magic* operating through an image of the person to be influenced.

eopolis the earliest and smallest type of *settlement[1]*.

epidemic, social rapid spread through a *population* of a social phenomenon.

epidemiology the study of the distribution of diseases or disabilities in *populations*. **epidemiological** *a*. **epidemiologist** *pers n*.

epidemiology, psychiatric the *epidemiology* of mental disorders.

epigenesis the acquisition of new *functions* by a *group*.

epistemology study of questions concerning the nature, possibility, limits, and sources of knowledge or of certain kinds of knowledge.

eponym the historical or mythical person who gives his name to a people, *tribe*, city or *group*. **eponymous** *a*.

equation, calendrical the correspondence of activities in a *society* with the calendar or calendars used.

equation, human see *equation, personal*.

equation, personal *factors* in the investigator tending to distort his judgement.

equifinality the condition of dissimilar initial conditions leading to similar end-states. see also *multifinality*.

equilibration, status tendency towards appearance of high degree of *correlation* between different forms of *rank*.

equilibrium a balancing of forces in a *system*.

equilibrium, cyclical *equilibrium* involving the indefinite repetition of a *cycle* of system-states.

equilibrium, dynamic *equilibrium* maintained by rates of change of *variables* of *system* being constant.

equilibrium, functional *equilibrium* involving the functional interdependence of social or cultural elements.

equilibrium, general a balancing of forces in the whole *system*.

equilibrium, generational the condition of no *generation[2]* believing that its energies and intelligence are being frustrated by the others. (Feuer).

equilibrium, moving continuous shift in *equilibrium* following a determinate pattern.

equilibrium, partial a balancing of forces in a *subsystem*.

equilibrium, quasi-stationary relative stability over a period of time of a *social process* in a field of forces.

equilibrium, self-corrective see *equilibrium, stable*.

equilibrium, stable loss of *equilibrium* automatically causes return to it.

equilibrium, static loss of *equilibrium* automatically causes return to the initial *values*[6] of the *variables*.

equilibrium, status a state in which an individual's positions in different *hierarchies* are at a comparable level.

equilibrium, unstable loss of *equilibrium* does not cause return to it.

ergonomics the scientific study of the relationship between man and his working *environment*. (Murrell, K.F.H.). **ergonomic** *a*. **ergonomist** *pers n*.

error 1. a mistake. 2. difference between estimated and true *value*[6]. 3. difference between actual state of *system* and criterion of desired state.

error, absolute difference between estimate and true *value*[6].

error, accidental see *error, random*.

error, biased see *error, constant*.

error, chance 1. see *error, random*. 2. see *error, sampling*.

error, compensating see *error, random*.

error, constant the *errors*, being in the same direction, do not cancel each other out in the long run. see also *error, random*.

error, contrast tendency in a *rater* to perceive *ratee* as opposite to himself in a trait.

error, cumulative see *error, constant*.

error, experimental 1. *error* in *experiment* due to probabilistic variation. 2. error in experiment, whether due to probabilistic variation or *bias*.

error, fortuitous see *error, random*.

error, generosity tendency in a *rater* to overestimate *ratee*'s desirable qualities.

error, grouping *error* resulting from assumption that data are concentrated at midpoints of class intervals.

error, instrumental *constant error* resulting from defect in instrument.

error, interviewer *error* due to interviewer.

error, logical tendency to give *ratee* similar *ratings*[2] on traits thought by *rater* to go together.

error, motivated *error* which appears accidental but is unconsciously motivated.

error, noncompensating see *error, constant*.

error, nonconstant see *error, random*.

error, observational deviation of observation from true *value*[6].

error, observer *error* due to observer.

error, persistent see *error, constant*.

error, process *error* introduced into data in the process of producing, measuring, recording, or computing.

error, random the *errors*, being in opposite directions, cancel each other out in the long run. see also *error, constant*.

error, relative *absolute error* divided by true *value*[6].

error, response lack of *reliability* or *validity* in *responses* to *structured questions*.

error, sampling difference between *mean* of *sample* and mean of *population*.

error, subjective *error* due to *personal equation*.

error, systematic see *error, constant*.

error, type I the rejection of a true *hypothesis*.

error, type II the acceptance of a false *hypothesis*.

error, unbiased see *error, random*.

error, variable see *error, random*.

esteem 1. social approval received for quality of performance. (Davis, K.). 2. social approval directed to person as a whole. (Parsons, T.). 3. total social approval received by individual. (Homans). 4. highly-emotionalized *prestige*. (Lasswell). 5. group approval commanded by a certain *role²*. (Mandelbaum,D.G.).see also *prestige*; *status*.

ethclass a *subsociety* resulting from the intersection of *ethnicity* with *social class*. (Gordon, M.M.).

ethnicity 1. membership of *ethnic group*. (U.S.). 2. sense of peoplehood.

ethnoanatomy the study of *primitive* anatomical beliefs.

ethnobiology the study of *primitive* biological beliefs.

ethnocentricism see *ethnocentrism*.

ethnocentrism centring of *positive attitudes* on own *ethnic group* or *race*. **ethnocentric** *a*.

ethnocracy rule by a particular *race* or *ethnic group*. **ethnocratic** *a*.

ethnoexpansionism imposition by a *society* of its *culture* on other societies for their own benefit. (Lapiere). **ethnoexpansionist** *a*.

ethnogeography the study of *primitive* geographical beliefs.

ethnography 1. the descriptive study of *primitive∥societies*. 2. the *ideographic* study of primitive societies. 3. description of the tribal and institutional distributions of an area. **ethnographic** *a*.

ethnography, survey *ethnography* employing the *survey method*.

ethnohistory 1. historical study of acculturative processes. 2. the study of *primitive* or *folk* historical beliefs.

ethnohoptology the study of the preparation and consumption of food in *primitive* and *peasant∥communities*. (Anderson, E.N.).

ethno-law the study of *primitive∥law* in its social context.

ethnolinguistics the science of the interrelations of *anthropology* and linguistics. **ethnolinguistic** *a*.

ethno-logic the study of *primitive* beliefs concerning logic. (Lévi-Strauss).

ethologism exaggerating the importance of *ethology* for the *explanation* of human behaviour. (Callan, H.). **ethologistic** *a*.

ethnology 1. descriptive, historical study of *primitive∥societies*.2. theoretical study of primitive societies, in contrast to *ethnography*. (US usage).

ethnology, applied the application of *ethnology* to the solution of concrete problems. (Nellemann, G.).

ethnology, comparative see *ethnology²*.

ethnology, regional the study of *folk culture* on a regional basis. (Erixon, S.).

ethnomedicine the study of *primitive* medical beliefs.

ethnomusicology the *cross-cultural* study of music.

ethnophaulism a derogatory term applied to members of an *ethnic group*.

ethnophilosophy the study of *primitive* philosophical ideas.

ethnophysiology the study of *primitive* physiological beliefs.

ethnopsychiatry 1. the study of mental disorders in *primitive∥societies*.2. the study of psychiatric beliefs and treatment found in primitive societies. see also *ethnopsychology*; *psychiatry, folk*; *anthropopsychiatry*.

ethnopsychology 1. the psychological study of *primitive∥societies*. 2. the study of primitive psychological beliefs.

ethnoscience the study of *primitive* scientific beliefs.

ethnosemantics see *semantics, anthropological*.

ethnospecific peculiar to a particular *ethnic group*.

ethology the science of the behaviour of animals in their *natural environments²*. **ethological** *a*. **ethologist** *pers n*.

ethos 1. the *ultimate values* and ideals of a *culture*. (Kroeber, A.L.).2. the *acquired drives* and *goals* of a culture. (Gillin, J.). 3. the *set¹* of *sentiments* towards reality found in a culture. (Bateson, G.). 4. the basic *set¹* of motivations found in a culture. (Honigmann, J.J.). 5. the general character of a culture. (Sumner, W.G.). see also *eidos*.

etic pertaining to the outsider's view of a *society*, using *observers' concepts* and scientific *explanations*. see also *emic*.

eticist 1. a specialist in the *etic* approach. 2. a supporter of the etic study of individual *societies*. **eticism** *n*.

etiquette ceremonial behaviour prescribed for person in one *category* towards person in another category.

etiquette, caste *etiquette* regulating behaviour between members of different *castes*.

etiquette, sibling *etiquette* regulating behaviour between *siblings*.

etiquette, spatial the way space is handled for purposes of *etiquette*.

eufunction integrative social consequences of social or cultural item. (Merton). **eufunctional** *a*. see also *dysfunction*.

eufunction, latent unintended *eufunction*.

eufunction, manifest intended *eufunction*.

eugenic conducive to desirable *genetic¹* qualities.

eugenics 1. science concerning methods of improving the *genetic¹* qualities of human *populations*. 2. *social movement* to secure the adoption of *eugenic policies*. see also *euthenics*; *dysgenics*.

eugenics, negative branch of *eugenics* concerned with the minimization of the undesirable *genetic¹* qualities of human *populations*.

eugenics, positive branch of *eugenics* concerned with the maximization of the desirable *genetic¹* qualities of human *populations*.

euhemerism the view that *myths* are allegories centred on real persons. **euhemeristic** *a*.

eunomia a high degree of *social integration*. (Radcliffe-Brown).

euthenics improving the non-*genetic¹* qualities of human *populations*. see also *eugenics*; *dysgenics*.

evacuation *migration* of endangered *population* supervised by authorities. (MDD).

events, vital events in the lives of persons which alter the size and composition of *populations*.

evolution increasing differentiation and specialization.

evolution, biological see *evolution, organic*.

evolution, convergent *evolution* involving convergence from different forms.

evolution, cultural *evolution* undergone by cultural phenomena.

evolution, divergent *evolution* involving divergence from an original common form.

evolution, emergent *evolution* involving the emergence of qualitatively new combinations of characteristics.

evolution, general increasing complexity of organization of cultural forms.

evolution, multilinear *social evolution* involving limited parallels of form, *function*, and sequence.

evolution, organic *evolution* undergone by organisms.

evolution, orthogenic see *evolution, unilinear*.

evolution, parallel *social evolution* in which the same feature evolves independently in two or more *societies*.

evolution, saltatory *evolution* by sudden variation.

evolution, social *evolution* undergone by social phenomena.

evolution, sociocultural *evolution* undergone by *sociocultural* phenomena.

evolution, specific differentiation of cultural forms.

evolution, sympodial *evolution* shifting in line of direction.

evolution, unilinear *social evolution* in which all *societies* pass through the same developmental stages.

evolution, universal *evolution* undergone by world *culture*.

evolutionism the doctrine of *evolution* applied to some field of phenomena.

exchange giving one thing for the receipt of another.

exchange, affinal *marital exchange* between *affines*.

exchange, ascriptive compulsory *gift exchange*.

exchange, ceremonial *gift exchange* with accompanying *ceremonial*.

exchange, customary *gift exchange* lacking a commercial character.

exchange, generalized *marital exchange* involving circulation through a *set[1]* of groups. see also *exchange, restricted*.

exchange, gift normatively-regulated exchange of gifts.

exchange, instrumental *gift exchange* for establishing solidarity.

exchange, labour exchange of labour between persons or *groups*.

exchange, marital exchange of women for *marriage* between individuals or groups.

exchange, market the exchange of goods at prices determined by the laws of supply and demand.

exchange, redistributive exchange of goods through *redistribution*.

exchange, restricted *marital exchange* restricted to mutual exchange between the members of pairs of *groups*. see also *exchange, generalized*.

exchange, social reciprocal *actions* which are contingent on rewarding *reactions* from others.

exchange, symbiotic exchange between *symbiotes*. see also *symbiosis*.

excision *clitoridectomy* plus removal of parts of labia minora and/or labia majora.

exclave separated portion of a *territory* lying inside another territory. see also *enclave*.

exclave, economic separated portion of an *economy* lying inside another economy.

excommunication 1. the exclusion of an individual from *association[3]* with other members of the *community*. 2. the exclusion of an individual from participation in religious *ritual*.

executive 1. executive branch of *government*. 2. the controlling body of an *organization*. 3. person with administrative *responsibility* in an organization.

executive, career a government *executive[3]* who is chosen from the civil service.

executive, middle an *executive[3]* belonging to the middle stratum of an *organization*.

executive, political a government *executive[3]* appointed by the chief executive from outside the civil service.

executive, top the highest *executive[3]* in an *organization*.

exile person compelled to live away from his native land. (MDD). see also *expatriate*; *refugee*; *emigré*.

exodus, rural mass *rural-urban migration* depopulating *rural areas*.

exogamy 1. existence of *rule* prescribing *marriage* outside a given *group*. 2. marriage outside a given group. 3. mating outside a given *population*. **exogamous** *a.* see also *endogamy*; *agamy*.

exogamy, band *exogamy* applied to the *band*.

exogamy, horde *exogamy* applying to the *horde*.

exogamy, kinship *exogamy* applying to a *set[1]* of relatives. see also *exogamy, territorial*.

exogamy, local *exogamy* applying to the *local group*.

exogamy, regional *exogamy* applying to a *region*.

exogamy, surname *exogamy* in which the *exogamous group* consists of those possessing the same surname.

exogamy, territorial *exogamy* applying to a *territory*. see also *exogamy, kinship*.

81

exogenous coming from outside the *system*. see also *endogenous*.

exolinguistics the science of the interrelations of language and other aspects of *culture*. **exolinguistic** *a*.

exonym name in a language for a foreign place.

expatriate person who chooses to live away from his native land. (MDD).see also *exile*; *refugee*; *emi ¬é*.

expatriation 1. legal right of *emigrant* who has acquired or is in a position to acquire a new nationality to renounce his old nationality. 2. banishment of citizen or *subject³*.

expectancy, life average future lifetime of the members of a *cohort* from a given point of 'time.

expectations, role the informal expectations attached to a *position*. (Lundberg). see also *prescriptions, role*; *requirements, role*.

expellee person expelled from *territory* by a *government*. (MDD).

expenditure, prestige see *consumption, conspicuous*.

experiment manipulation of some *variables* and observation of others under controlled conditions for discovery of concomitant variations. **experimental** *a*.

experiment, after-only see *design, after-only*.

experiment, before-after see *design, before-after*.

experiment, bivariate an *experiment* in which only two *variables* are allowed to vary simultaneously.

experiment, boundary *experiment* to d₁ cover the extreme *values⁶* to which a phenomenon applies.

experiment, critical *experiment* which will verify or falsify a given *hypothesis*.

experiment, crucial see *experiment, critical*.

experiment, determinate *experiment* where the relevant conditions are specified to the point that the outcome is known when the *value⁶* of the *independent variable* is known. (Galtung).

experiment, ex post facto *experiment* in which effect which has occurred is traced back to its causes.

experiment, field studying social phenomena under natural conditions and manipulating *independent variable*.

experiment, functional an *experiment* involving the manipulation of an *experimental variable* but lacking a *control group*.

experiment, laboratory *experiment* in which experimenter creates desired conditions, controls some *variables* and manipulates others.

experiment, methodological an *experiment* for improving *techniques* of inquiry.

experiment, multivariate an *experiment* in which many *variables* are allowed to vary simultaneously.

experiment, natural scientists observe effects of change produced by policy-makers.

experiment, nomological an *experiment* to establish a *law¹⁰* or generalization.

experiment, pure see *experiment, laboratory*.

experiment, replicable *experiment* where the *independent variables* and the relevant conditions can be reproduced at different points in time. see also *replication*.

experiment, simulation an *experiment* employing *simulation*.

experiment, stochastic *experiment* that is not determinate. (Galtung).see also *experiment, determinate*.

experiment, theoretical an *experiment* to test a *theory*.

experiment, trial-and-error all sorts of trials by laymen of new forms of *social behaviour*.

explanation accounting for a given phenomenon, *system*, generalization, or law¹⁰.

explanation, constructive accounting for a given phenomenon by reference to *constructs, principles,* or generalizations.

explanation, deductive-nomological accounting for a given phenomenon by deductive subsumption under general *laws[10]*.

explanation, folk an *explanation* offered by a *society* or *community* under investigation.

explanation, functional accounting for a given phenomenon by reference to its *function.*

explanation, genetic accounting for a later *system* by setting out the sequence of major events through which some earlier system has been transformed into it. (Nagel, E.).

explanation, inductive accounting for a given phenomenon by inductive subsumption under *statistical laws.*

explanation, nomological accounting for a given phenomenon by subsuming it under *laws[10]*.

explanation, probabilistic accounting for a given event or class of events by subsumption under *statistical laws.*

explanation, statistical see *explanation, probabilistic.*

explanation, structural accounting for a given phenomenon in terms of structural relations among units. (Harré, R.).

explanation, teleological accounting for a given phenomenon by its being a necessary and sufficient condition for a certain state of affairs.

expropriation 1. confiscation of foreign property. 2. confiscation of foreign property not resulting from a domestic *policy.*

extension, agricultural 1. dissemination of advice to farmers on agricultural matters. 2. teaching anything leading to improvement of rural life. see also *development, community.*

extension, goal the repeated re-adoption by an *organization* of a *goal* which has been achieved. see also *succession, goal.*

extension, job adding similar elements to a *job* without altering job content. see also *enlargement, job.*

exteroceptor *receptor* which is aroused by *stimuli* from outside the body. see also *interoceptor; proprioceptor.*

exterosystem complex somatic system relating organism directly to external world.

extinction, experimental extinction of acquired stimulus-response connection resulting from repeated evocations of *response* without *reinforcement.*

extrapolation estimating *values[6]* of a *variable* outside the limits of known values of the variable. **extrapolate** *v.* see also *interpolation.*

extraversion *personality type* characterized by interests being directed to external world. see also *introversion; ambiversion.*

extraversion, manipulative *personality type* characterized by the *need* to control the external world.

extraversion, social *personality type* characterized by the *need* to turn towards other people.

extrusion sending children to sleep away from parental home.

fable animal tale possessing a moral. see also *folktale; legend; myth.*

fable, cante story which is told partly in song.

facilitation, social 1. increase in quantity or quality of work, resulting from presence of *audience* or *group pressures.* 2. spiralling *social interaction* in *crowd.*

fact, social fact at the social level of analysis, e.g., crime rate, suicide rate. (Durkheim. E.). see also *analysis, levels of*.

factionalism 1. existence of *factions*. 2. tendency towards factions.

factions 1. conflict *subgroups* dysfunctional to the larger *group*. see also *clique*.

factor 1. anything contributing to a result. 2. component of a situation. 3. any one of the elements accounting for the variation in a *set¹* of intercorrelated *variables*.

factor, matching *factor* on which groups in *experiment* are matched. see also *group, control*; *group, experimental*; *matching*.

fads discontinuous, non-rhythmical, behavioural *innovations*, self-assertive and symbolic of *groups*. see also *craze*.

fallacy, particularistic overemphasizing a single *factor* or *set¹* of factors.

fallacy, type the fallacy of assuming a discontinuity between extremes and intermediate cases.

fallowing, bush see *cultivation, shifting*.

familialism 1. the character possessed by a *group* of being family-like. 2. the doctrine that certain *organizations* should be family-like. **familialistic** *a*. (Nakane, C.).

familialization conferring a familial character on extra-familial *social relationships*. **familialize** *v*.

familiar animal or bird servant of *witch* or *wizard*. see also *fetch*.

familism extreme emphasis on *family*; the *ideal type* characterized by feeling of belonging to family, co-ordination of activities of members for family objectives, aid for poor members, maintenance of continuity. **familistic** *a*. see also *familialism*.

familism, amoral extreme emphasis on an individual's duties towards his *nuclear family* to the neglect of duties towards other members of *society*. (Banfield, E. C.).

familsomatic pertaining to the contribution of *family* members to a somatic disorder. see also *psychosomatic*.

family two or more persons living together related by blood, *marriage*, adoption. see also *household*.

family, atomistic *family* having lowest degree of *group* unity and highest degree of *individuation*. (Zimmerman, C.C.). see also *family, trusteeship*; *family, domestic*.

family, bilateral *family* characterized by *non-unilineal descent*.

family, biological couple with their offspring living together.

family, broken a *nuclear family* with at least one of the natural parents not present in the home.

family, census see *family, statistical*.

family, commensal those members of the *family* who eat together.

family, companionship (ideal type) *family* whose unity results entirely from the mutual affection and *consensus* of its members. (Burgess, E. W.). see also *family, institutional*.

family, composite a familial aggregate consisting of two or more *nuclear families*.

family, compound *family* in which *half-siblings* are found.

family, compound, polyandrous a *compound family* resulting from *polyandry*.

family, compound, polygynous a *compound family* resulting from *polygyny*.

family, conjugal 1. *nuclear family* plays primary role in relation to other relatives. 2. see *procreation, family of*.

family, consanguine *nuclear family* which plays a secondary role in relation to other relatives.

family, denuded a *family* which has lost one or both parents.

family, domestic *family* which has more *group* unity and less *individuation* than the *atomistic family* but less group unity and more individuation than the *trusteeship family*. (Zimmerman, C.C.). see also *family, trusteeship*; *family, atomistic*.

family, educogenic *family* with psychological atmosphere conducive to the children's *education*.

family, elementary see *family, nuclear*.

family, extended *family* consisting of two or more *nuclear families* formed by joining the nuclear family of a married adult to that of his or her parents.

family, extended, avunculocal *extended family* formed by *avunculocal residence*.

family, extended, bilocal *extended family* formed by *bilocal residence*.

family, extended, classical *extended family* which is co-residential.

family, extended, matrilocal *extended family* formed by *matrilocal residence*.

family, extended, modified *extended family* which is not co-residential but with close inter-member contacts.

family, extended, patrilocal *extended family* formed by *patrilocal residence*.

family, extended, unilocal *extended family* formed by *unilocal residence[1]*. (Murdock).

family, filiocentric a *family* which is centred on the children.

family, grand see *family, extended*.

family, immediate see *family, nuclear*.

family, institutional (ideal type) *family* whose unity results entirely from *social pressures* on its members. (Burgess, E.W.). see also *family, companionship*.

family, intact a *nuclear family* consisting of offspring living together with their natural father and mother.

family, joint 1. *extended family* occupying a single *homestead*. 2. *family* consisting of two *siblings* living together with their spouses and children.

family, joint, fraternal *family* consisting of two brothers living together with their wives and children.

family, joint, matrilocal *joint family* formed by *matrilocal residence*.

family, joint, patrilocal *joint family* formed by *patrilocal residence*.

family, language *set[1]* of languages derived from the same parent language.

family, legal a class of *legal systems*.

family, limited see *family, nuclear*.

family, marital see *procreation, family of*.

family, maternal *family* characterized by *matrilineal descent*.

family, matricentric a *family* which is centred on the mother.

family, matrifocal a *family* with no regularly present male in the *role* of husband-father.

family, metronymic *family* in which the children inherit the mother's name.

family, natal see *orientation, family of*.

family, natural see *family, biological*.

family, nuclear married couple with their offspring living together.

family, nuclear, augmented husband and wife (with children, if any) and a parent of one spouse or other adult relatives.

family, nuclear, dependent a *nuclear family* which is part of a larger familial aggregate. (Murdock).

family, nuclear, independent a *nuclear family* which is not part of a larger familial aggregate. (Murdock).

family, nuclear, isolated *independent nuclear family* in the absence of *clans[3]*. (Murdock).

family, nuclear, multiple *extended family* or *joint family*.

family, nuclear, simple see *family, nuclear, independent*.

family, occupational *category* of *occupations*.

family, parental see *orientation, family of*.

family, paternal *family* characterized by *patrilineal descent.*

family, patriarchal *family* which is *patripotestal, patrilineal* and *patrilocal.*

family, patricentric a *family* which is centred on the father.

family, patrifocal a *family* with no regularly present female in the *role* of wife-mother.

family, patronymic *family* in which the children inherit the father's name.

family, politicized *family* characterized by substantial and sustained political interests and adult *political participation.*

family, polygamous two or more *nuclear families* linked through a common spouse. (Murdock).

family, polygamous, dependent a *polygamous family* which is part of a larger familial aggregate. (Murdock).

family, polygamous, independent a *polygamous family* which is not part of a larger familial aggregate. (Murdock).

family, primary 1. *household* head plus all other members of household related to head. 2. see *family, nuclear.*

family, problem a *family* thought of as the victim of a *social problem.*

family, restricted see *family, nuclear.*

family, secondary two or more related persons living in the *household* of a *primary family¹.*

family, simple see *family, nuclear.*

family, standard a hypothetical *family* employed as a *standard* in the study of various family characteristics.

family, statistical the unit taken as a *family* in a particular *demographic* investigation.

family, stem *family* which binds one married child to the parental *household* whilst permitting the other married children to reside elsewhere.

family, tertiary a *family* consisting of aged parents whose children have left them. (Golofast, V.).

family, trusteeship a *family* having the highest degree of *group* unity and the lowest degree of *individuation,* which is thought of as extending into the past and the future, and whose living members are regarded as trustees of the family's rights, property, name, and *status.* (Zimmerman, C. C.). see also *family, atomistic; family, domestic.*

family, unilateral *family* characterized by *unilineal descent.*

family, unstable *nuclear family* likely to become a *broken family.*

fanaticism sincere, passionate, narrow and persistent zeal in one cause which is believed to be so important that any means are justified. (Djamour, J.). **fanatical** *a.* **fanatic** *pers n.*

farmer an agriculturist who carries on *agriculture* for business and reinvestment, looking on the land as *capital* and commodity. (Wolf, E.R.). see also *peasant.*

farmer, part-owner *farmer* who owns part of the land he farms and rents the other part.

farmer, part-time an industrial worker having farming as a part-time *occupation.*

farming, cash see *farming, commercial.*

farming, commercial *farming* for external consumption.

farming, dry *farming* with insufficient rainfall and absence of *irrigation.*

farming, hydraulic see *cultivation, hydraulic.*

farming, mixed combination of *animal husbandry* and cultivation.

farming, subsistence *farming* all the produce of which is internally consumed.

farming, swidden see *cultivation, shifting.*

fashions relatively short-lived, socially-approved cultural *innovations,* with the appeal of newness, mere *conformity* conferring *prestige.* see also *fads;*

craze.

fasting voluntary, religiously-motivated total or partial abstention from food.

fasting, absolute *fasting* involving total abstention from food.

fasting, limited *fasting* involving partial abstention from food.

father-right rights over children are exercised by husband and his *kin.*

father-sib see *patrisib.*

fealty taking an *oath* of loyalty by a tenant to his lord.

fecundity 1. reproductive capacity of woman or *group* of women. 2. reproductive capacity of individual, couple, or group. (MDD). see also *fertility.*

fecundity, differential intergroup differences in *fecundity.*

federalism *geographical devolution* with guarantees for the autonomy of the governmental units or organizational units.

federalism, co-operative *federalism* involving bargaining between Regions or between Centre and Regions.

federalism, co-ordinate *federalism* characterized by the absence of formal subordination of the governmental units one to another.

federalism, dual see *federalism, co-ordinate.*

federalism, integrated see *federalism, organic.*

federalism, organic *geographical devolution* in which the area of autonomy of the governmental units is very small.

federation a *political unit* or *organization* characterized by *federalism.* see also *confederation.*

feedback change in *output[1]* of a mechanism causes change in *input[1].*

feedback, action *feedback* to an individual which arrives and can be used during a *response.* (Miller, R.B.).

feedback, controlled see *feedback, negative.*

feedback, goal-changing *feedback* to a *system* resulting in internal changes which produce a new *goal* or goals for the system.

feedback, learning *feedback* to an individual which arrives after the completion of the *response.* (Miller, R.B.).

feedback, negative increase in *output[1]* of a mechanism causes decrease in *input[1],* thus restoring *equilibrium.*

feedback, operational *feedback* which continuously controls the operations of an *organization.*

feedback, positive increase in *output[1]* of a mechanism causes increase in *input[1].*

feedback, runaway see *feedback, positive.*

feedback, stabilizing see *feedback, negative.*

fertility 1. actual reproductive performance of woman or *group* of women. 2. actual reproductive performance of individual or group. (MDD). see also *fecundity.*

fertility, age-specific *fertility* of women (or men) in a certain *age-grouping.*

fertility, cohort reproductive performance of a particular *birth* or *marriage cohort.*

fertility, completed *cumulative fertility* of a *cohort* when all members have reached end of reproductive period.

fertility, cumulative total reproductive performance of a particular *cohort* from beginning of exposure to *risk[2]* until a specified date.

fertility, differential intergroup differences in *fertility.*

fertility, duration-specific *fertility* of women (or men) married a specified length of time.

fertility, effective *fertility* in computing which late foetal deaths or late foetal deaths plus child deaths are excluded.

fertility, generation reproductive performance of a particular *birth cohort.*

fertility, incomplete *cumulative fertility* of a *cohort* which is expected to increase.

fertility, lifetime see *fertility, completed.*

fertility, marital reproductive performance of married women over specified period.

fertility, total *fertility* in computing which late foetal deaths are included.

fertility rate number of births per specified number of females (or males) of reproductive age over a specified period of time.

fertility rate, age-specific *fertility rate* calculated for women (or men) in a certain *age-grouping.*

fertility rate, duration-specific *fertility rate* calculated for women (or men) married a specified length of time.

fertility rate, female number of births per specified number of females of reproductive age ,over a specified period of time.

fertility rate, general number of births per specified number of females of reproductive age, irrespective of marital status, over a specified period of time.

fertility rate, male number of births per specified number of males of reproductive age over a specified period of time.

fertility rate, standardized *fertility rate* permitting comparability of *populations.*

fetch supernatural double of a living person. see also *familiar.*

feud lasting mutual homicidal relationship between two *groups* in a *society* which is socially regulated and terminable by peaceful settlement. see also *vendetta.*

feudalism 1. aristocratic or nobiliary rule. 2. see *manorialism.*3. see *latifundiarism.* 4. division of *society* into noblemen-warriors and *peasants* forbidden to bear arms. 5. a type of *social structure* characterized by *serfdom.* 6. the practice on a large scale of rewarding administrative and military services by grants of land. 7. a type of social structure characterized by the division of the *population* into noblemen-warriors and peasants forbidden to bear arms, the relative unimportance of other classes, *seignorial jurisdiction,* a simple *hierarchy,* and pronounced *devolution.* (Andreski, S.).

feudalism, contractual *feudalism* involving a *contract* between lord and *vassal.*

feudalization the process by which *feudalism* is established.

feudaloid possessing some, but not all, of the defining characteristics of *feudalism.*

feudatory see *vassal.*

fiction a social idea known to be false but assumed to be true for convenience.

fiction, legal a *fiction* held by the *law* for convenience.

fief an estate held under *feudal tenure.* see also *benefice*; *appanage*; *seigniory.*

field 1. *system* of coexisting interdependent events. 2. the entire, immediate situation which determines behaviour.3. see *field, phenomenal.* 4. see *field, stimulus.*

field, behavioral see *field².*

field, contact the *spatial distribution* of the acquaintances of an individual or *group.* (Morrill, R. L.).

field, occupational see *family, occupational.*

field, phenomenal total experiences of organism at given moment.

field, phenomenological see *field, phenomenal.*

field, political a *set¹* of two or more rival political structures which lacks a *set¹* of agreed *rules* regulating their *conflict.* (Bailey. F.G.).

field, psychological see *field².*

field, semantic the conceptual structure of a *semantic domain.*

field, social totality of *social stimuli* acting on an organism at a given moment.

field, stimulus totality of *stimuli* acting on an organism at a given moment.

field, urban see *hinterland, urban.*

figure, dark the amount of *crime,* or of a given type of crime, which is not reported to the police.

figure, string an intertwining of string on the fingers. see also *game, string.*

filiation the *rules* governing the attachment of children to their parents.

filiation, complementary the tie, in a *unilineal descent* system, between the child and the parent through whom *descent* is not traced and the relatives of that parent.

filiation, maternal see *matrifiliation.*

filiation, paternal see *patrifiliation.*

filiation, utrolateral a system of *filiation* in which an individual establishes a tie with the relatives of either parent but not both.

filiocentric centred on the children of a *family.*

fission, group 1. the process of internal subdivision of a *group.* (Fortes). 2. the process by which a group loses its unity by dividing into two or more groups. (Barnes).

flow, gene dispersal of genes through *population* by *migration* or admixture. see also *drift, gene.*

flow, migration see *stream, migration.*

focus *stimulus object* or event which is the object of roughly simultaneous attention by a *collectivity.*

focus, cultural the most emphasized aspect of the *culture.*

folk 1. pertaining to a cultural level between *primitive* and *peasant.*2. possessing the characteristics of the ideal-typical *folk society.* see also *continuum, folk-urban.* 3. the common people who share a basic store of *traditions.*

folklore 1. unwritten literature. 2. unwritten literature of a *preliterate‖culture.* 3. orally transmitted part of a culture. 4. culture lacking reliable ascription to inventor or author. 5. the science of folklore[1,2,3,4].

folktale a traditional tale of imaginary deeds or events. (Fontenrose, J.). see also *legend*; *myth.*

folk-wandering *primitive migration,* lacking destination, of a whole people.

folkways weakly-sanctioned *norms.* (Sumner). see also *mores.*

folkways, occupational *folkways* attached to a particular *occupation.*

folkways, professional *folkways* attached to a particular *profession.*

food-gathering obtaining food from landscape without *husbandry.*

foraging hunting, *food-gathering,* or *collecting.*

force 1. the physical manipulation of others by a power-holder.2. the actual or threatened use of *violence* to compel others to do what they might not otherwise do. see also *power*; *authority*; *influence*; *violence*; *coercion.*

force, labour those persons employed, self-employed or offering their services in the labour market during a specified week. (US).

force, labour, experienced those persons employed, self-employed or offering their services in the labour market during a specified week who have worked before. (US).

force, working 1. economically *active population.* (UN). 2. those persons employed, self-employed or offering their services in the labour market.

forecast 1. a foretelling, not a derivation from a given *set[1]* of assumptions. 2. foretelling on the basis of estimated *values[6]* and an incomplete knowledge of the *variables* involved. see also *projection[4]*; *prediction.*

forecast, population predicted development of a *population.* see also *projection, population.*

form, irrelevant non-functional part of the form of an *artifact.*

form, structural abstraction from those individual *social relationships* constituting *social structure* in the sense of a *set[1]* of individual social relationships.

formalogram a chart showing the network of mutually perceived *formal* *relationships* in an *organization*. see also *informalogram*.

formation, attitude process by which *attitudes* are established.

formation, elite process by which *elites* are established.

formation, group processes by which *groups* are established.

formation, habit process by which *habits* are established.

formation, policy process by which *policies* are established.

formation, reaction development in conscious behaviour of trend directly opposed to one in the unconscious.

formation, theory process by which *theories* are established.

formula, ending set form of words in which a particular *folktale* or class of folktale is ended.

formula, oath set form of words in which an *oath* is made.

fostering rearing another's child as one's own. **foster** *v.*

fostering, crisis *fostering* following the dissolution of the parents' *marriage*. (Goody, E.).

fostering, kinship the rearing of children by non-parental *kin*. (Goody, E.).

fostering, refuge see *fostering, crisis*.

fostering, voluntary *fostering* initiated whilst the parents' *marriage* is intact. (Goody, E.).

fraction, sampling proportion of *sampling units* selected for *sample* from *sampling frame*.

fragmentation, farm the interspersion of noncontiguous plots of one farm with noncontiguous plots of other farms.

frame, attention that part of *environment* reaching the focus of attention of person or *group*. (Lasswell, H.D.).

frame, incomplete *sampling frame* from which units of *target population* are missing.

frame, media *communication media‖signs* reaching the focus of attention. (Lasswell, H.D.).

frame, non-media part of *attention frame* not consisting of *communication media‖signs*. (Lasswell, H.D.).

frame, sampling list from which *sampling units* are selected.

fratrilateral pertaining to a relationship traced through a brother. (Goody, J.).

freedom the absence of an obstacle to action or to a personal state.

frequency, cell number of items in a cell.

frequency, class number of items in a class interval.

frequency, cumulative *class frequency* plus frequencies in all lower class intervals.

frequency, gene the percentage of individuals in a *population* having a certain gene.

frequency, genotype the percentage of individuals in a *population* having a certain *genotype*.

frequency, percentage *relative frequency* expressed as a percentage.

frequency, relative ratio of a particular *class frequency* or *cell frequency* to total number of items.

friendship, ceremonial *institutionalized friendship* created by a *ceremony*.

friendship, emotional friendship involving reciprocal satisfaction of emotional *needs*. (Wolf, E.R.). see also *friendship, instrumental*.

friendship, formalized see *friendship, institutionalized*.

friendship, guest temporary friendship, with specific duties, towards a guest.

friendship, hereditary an *institutionalized friendship* which is inherited.

friendship, informal friendship which is not *institutionalized friendship*.

friendship, institutionalized friendship, socially recognized, with specific duties.

friendship, instrumental friendship involving mutual assistance, with minimal element of affect. (Wolf, E.R.). see also *friendship, emotional*.

friendship, ritualized see *friendship, institutionalized.*

fringe, rural-urban see *fringe, rurban.*

fringe, rurban outermost city zone of mixed land-use, having both *rural* and *urban* characteristics.

fringe, urban that part of *urbanized area* which is outside *central city* or cities.

frustration 1. blocking of an active *drive* or of goal-striving behaviour. 2. blocking of goal-striving behaviour.

frustration, circular *frustration* resulting from a circular order of preferences.

frustration, primary blocking of an active *drive.*

frustration, secondary blocking of goal-striving behaviour.

full-siblings persons having both parents in common.

full-sibs see *full-siblings.*

function 1. the contribution of a part to the activity of the whole.2. consequences of social or cultural item. (Malinowski). 3. integrative social consequences of social or cultural item. (Merton). 4. the part played in the maintenance of *society* by a social or cultural item.(Radcliffe-Brown).5. *activities* assigned to occupant of *status*.6. activities logically implied by a status. (Peters, R.S.). 7. economic part played by a person. 8. class of organizational activities. 9. *variable* which responds to changes in other specified variables. **functional** *a.*

function, input impact of *environment* on *system.*

function, instrumental see *function, task.*

function, latent unintended consequences of social or cultural element.

function, line 1. a productive *function* in an *organization.* 2. a command function in an organization. see also *function, staff.*

function, maintenance any one of the classes of *activities* in a *group* which are means to the maintenance of the group. see also *synergy, maintenance.*

function, manifest intended consequences of social or cultural element.

function, negative see *dysfunction.*

function, output impact of *system* on *environment.*

function, personnel the class of *activities* in an *organization* concerned with the *administration* of its human resources.

function, positive see *eufunction.*

function, staff 1. a supportive *function* in an *organization.* 2. an advisory function in an organization. see also *function, line.*

function, step a relationship between *variables* such that a given variable has no effect on others until its *value^6* has been sufficiently changed.

function, task any one of the classes of *activities* in a *group* which are means to the achievement of the *group task.* see also *synergy, task.*

functionalism the doctrine that social or cultural elements are functionally interdependent.

functionalism, comparative the comparative analysis of social *functions.* (Goldschidt, W.).

functionalism, universal the doctrine that all social or cultural elements are functionally interdependent in all *social systems* and *cultural systems.*

functionalization *departmentation* according to *functions,* i.e. classes of organizational *activities.*

fund, ceremonial amount of *money* required by an individual or *community* to pay for culturally-prescribed *ceremonials.* (Wolf, E.R.).

fund, replacement amount of *money* required by an individual or *community* for replacement of minimum equipment for production and consumption. (Wolf, E.R.).

fundament see *landscape, natural.*

funnel *technique* in interviewing of beginning with an *open question* and then following with *closed questions.*

funnel, reverse *technique* in interviewing of beginning with *closed questions* and then following with an *open question.*

fusion, group merging of two or more *groups* into one group.

gait manner of walking or stepping. see also *posture*; *gesture.*

game 1. the *set¹* of *rules* under which a particular match is played.(von Neumann). 2. contest between two or more individuals or *groups* under the limitation of implicit or explicit rules. 3. any *activity* with the structure of a contest.

game, cultic *game²* forming part of a *cult.* (Jensen).

game, dual two-person zero-sum *game¹.*

game, dynamic *game¹* in which the *rules* change over time.

game, finite *game¹* with a finite number of *strategies.*

game, funeral *game²* forming part of a mortuary *ceremonial.*

game, heuristic an *all-man simulation* or *man-machine simulation* serving to stimulate investigation.

game, infinite *game¹* with an infinite number of *strategies.*

game, non-zero-sum *game¹* in which the *payoffs²* to the players do not add to zero.

game, plural *game¹* in which the active interests are not diametrically opposed.

game, singular *game* characterized by a single player.

game, slow slow-moving animals obtainable by collection.

game, static *game¹* in which the *rules* do not change over time.

game, string the playful intertwining of string on the fingers. see also *figure, string.*

game, zero-sum *game¹* in which the *payoffs²* to the players add to zero.

gaming *all-man simulation* or *man-machine simulation* of competitive situations.

gang, delinquent a gang of juveniles whose main aim is *delinquency* for material profit. (Yablonsky, L.).

gang, retreatist a gang the members of which are characterized by *retreatism.*

gang, social a gang of juveniles having the aim of nondelinqueut social *activities.* (Yablonsky, L.).

gang, violent a gang of juveniles whose main aim is *violence* for its own sake. (Yablonsky, L.).

gardening see *horticulture.*

gathering *set¹* of individuals characterized by *copresence.* (Goffman, E.).

gathering, fully-focused *gathering* in which an *encounter* includes all the persons. (Goffman, E.).

gathering, multifocused *gathering* in which more than one *encounter* is being carried on. (Goffman, E.).

gathering, partly-focused *gathering* in which an *encounter* excludes some of the persons. (Goffman, E.).

gathering, unfocused *gathering* in which no *focused interaction* occurs. (Goffman, E.).

Gemeinschaft (ideal type) *society* characterized by *primary relationships,* emphasis on *tradition.* (Tönnies). see also *Gesellschaft.*

genealogy 1. an account of the ancestry of a person or *group.* 2. an account of one's descent from an *ancestor* or ancestors by enumeration of the intermediate persons. 3. a genealogical statement made by an ethnographer as part of his field record or its analysis. (Barnes, J.A.). see also *pedigree².* 4. a genealogical statement which links a living person to others around him. (Yalman). 5. the study of genealogies[1,2,3,4]. **genealogical** *a.*

genealogy, concentric a *genealogy* in the form of a chart the highest *generation[2]* being located in the centre with successive *generations[2]* shown in concentric circles.

generation 1. group of persons born within a specified period of time. see *cohort, birth*. 2. descendants of a *group* of persons who themselves constitute a generation. 3. see *cohort*.

generation, ascending any *generation[2]* consisting of *ascendants[3]* of *ego*'s generation.

generation, descending any *generation[2]* consisting of descendants of *ego*'s generation.

generation, female the daughters of a *generation[2]* of females.

generation, male the sons of a *generation[2]* of males.

generation, marriage see *cohort, marriage*.

generation, political those persons who underwent the political experiences of a certain time.

genetic 1. pertaining to genetics. 2. genetically determined. 3. pertaining to origin.

genetrix physical mother. see also *mater*.

genitor physical father. see also *pater*.

genotype the bodily structure as determined exclusively by genes. see also *phenotype*.

gens see *patriclan[1]*.

geogroup see *group, territorial*.

geolatry *worship* of the earth. **geolatric** *a*.

geomancy *divination* from the features of the earth. **geomantic** *a*. **geomancer** *pers n*.

geomedicine study of the geographical distribution of diseases.

geophagism see *geophagy*.

geophagy eating earth or clay. **geophagous** *a*.

geopolitics application of human geography to the analysis of international *politics*. **geopolitical** *a*.

geotragia see *geophagy*.

geriatrics that branch of medicine concerned with old age. **geriatric** *a*.**geriatrician** *pers n*. see also *gerontology*.

geronticide the killing of the aged.

gerontocracy 1. rule by the aged. 2. situation in which the aged are influential and possess *arbitral||powers[6]*. (Davies, D.M.). 3. situation in which the older men are held in respect and are polygynists while the younger men are bachelors. (Spencer, P.). **gerontocratic** *a*. see also *index, gerontocratic*.

gerontology the scientific study of ageing or old age. **gerontological** *a*.**gerontologist** *pers n*. see also *geriatrics*.

gerontology, industrial the scientific study of ageing in relation to industry.

gerontology, psychosocial the scientific study of the psychological and social aspects of ageing or old age.

gerontology, social the scientific study of the social aspects of ageing or old age.

gerophobia pathological fear of late ageing.

Gesellschaft (ideal type) *society* characterized by *secondary relationships*, lack of emphasis on *tradition*. (Tönnies). see also *Gemeinschaft*.

gesture a bodily movement having a communicative *function*. **gestural** *a*.see also *posture*; *gait*.

gesture, contactual a *gesture* involving touching another person.

gesture, mimetic a *gesture* imitating that which is to be communicated.

gesture, plus behaviour intended to demonstrate superiority as compensation for feelings of inadequacy. (Adler, A.).

gesturing *communication* through bodily movements.

ghetto highly-congested *ethnic slum.*

ghost *soul* of the dead believed to be perceivable by human beings.see also *soul; spirit; supernaturals.*

gift, achievement gift presented in recognition of achievement.

gift, ceremonial a gift presented on a ceremonial occasion.

gift, fatal a gift given to an enemy, supposedly coming from a friend, intended to bring him death or misfortune.

gift, free see *gift, simple.*

gift, morning gift from husband to wife on morning after wedding.

gift, pure see *gift, simple.*

gift, simple a gift given without expectation of a return.

gift, status gift presented in recognition of *status.*

glosseme smallest meaningful unit of language.

glossolalia ecstatic vocalization in the form of incoherent sounds or foreign words. **glossolalic** *a.* see also *xenoglossia.*

glottopolitics *government*‖*policy* on language matters.

goal 1. aim involving cessation of effort upon achievement. 2.ultimate aim involving cessation of effort upon achievement. 3. the end towards which *actions* are moving. 4. the intended end of an acting organism. 5. the place or thing towards which actions are leading organisms.6. end towards which variable movements are directed. 7. *equilibrium* level maintained by a *cybernetic system.*

goal, accessory see *goal, secondary.*

goal, class-general a *goal* shared by the *social classes* of a *society.*

goal, class-specific a *goal* peculiar to a particular *social class.*

goal, collective *goal* achievable only by collective effort.

goal, cultural a *goal* prescribed by the *culture.*

goal, group 1. *goal* for the achievement of which the activities of a *group* are coordinated. 2. goal adopted by a group whether pursued individually or collectively.

goal, individual see *goal, private.*

goal, intermediate see *sub-goal.*

goal, national a *goal* pursued by a *nation.*

goal, official an authoritatively-stated *organizational goal.*

goal, organizational a *goal* pursued by an *organization.*

goal, primary the main *goal* pursued by an. *organization* or individual.

goal, private a *goal* that an individual desires for himself.

goal, secondary a *goal* other than the main goal pursued by an *organization* or individual.

goal, social see *goal, group².*

goal, societal a *goal* adopted by a *society.*

goal, subcultural a *goal* prescribed by a *subculture.*

goal, subordinate see *sub-goal.*

goal, subsystem the end served by a *subsystem.*

goal, system the end served by a *system.*

goal-attainment setting *goals,* establishing priorities amongst goals, and determining the best means of achieving these goals. (Parsons, T.).

gossip 1. talk about persons and their *conduct,* with an overt moral evaluation, following specific channels. (Bailey, F. G.). 2. talk intended to obtain information about absent persons and their *activities.* (Paine, R.). 3. idle talk which is largely about other persons' morals and *skills.* (Gluckman, M.). see also *scandal; rumour.*

gossip, informative talk intended to obtain information about absent persons. (Layton, R.).

gossip, scandalizing talk intended to discredit other persons. (Layton, R.).

government 1. the existence of persons with the *authority* to take *communal decisions*. 2. the machinery by which *values* are allocated in a *group*. 3. the *management*, *directing* and *control* of the public affairs of a *political unit*.
governmental *a*.

government, comparative the comparative study of *government*.

government, convention *government* in which legislature can dismiss *executive[1]* and can give it any orders.

government, crisis 1. a temporary concentration of *power* in the *executive[1]* within the framework of responsible *government*. 2. a temporary suspension, in accordance with the *constitution[2]*, of the democratic system and the rule of law enabling the *executive[1]* to enact *laws* on its own *authority*.

government, federal *government* characterized by *federalism*.

government, parliamentary *government* in which both legislature and executive[1] can dismiss the other and their *powers[6]* are largely mixed.

government, presidential *government* in which neither legislature nor *executive[1]* can dismiss the other and there is separation of powers.

government, unitary *government* not characterized by *federalism*.

grade, warrior *age-grade* consisting of those men who are of fighting age.

gradient magnitude sloping from high to low, or vice versa.

gradient, crime *gradient* of increasing *crime rate* towards city centre.

gradient, delinquency *gradient* of increasing *delinquency rate* towards city centre.

gradient, dominance decrease in *ecological dominance* with increase in distance from centre.

grading, job the *ranking* of *jobs* according to the kind of *decisions* involved.

graph, band see *chart, band*.

graph, bar see *chart, bar*.

graph, belt see *chart, band*.

graph, circle see *chart, circular*.

graph, coordinate see *graph, line*.

graph, curve see *graph, line*.

graph, line a graph consisting of a curve plotted against the *values[6]* of a horizontal axis (x-axis) and the *values[6]* of a vertical axis (y-axis).

graph, line, aggregate see *chart, band*.

graph, rectangular see *graph, line*.

gratification, deferred self-imposed postponement of gratification.

groom-service see *bride-service*.

group 1. see *aggregate[2,3]*. 2. homogeneous *aggregate[2,3]*. 3. plurality of interacting persons. (Lewin, K.). 4. plurality of co-operatively interacting persons. (French). 5. plurality of persons with shared *norms* and interlocking *roles*. (Newcomb). 6. plurality of persons interacting co-operatively in pursuit of common *goal* for satisfaction of individual *needs*. (Gibb, C.A.). 7. a plurality of persons characterized by relatively exclusive *interaction* in a given context for the achievement of a common aim.

group, accessible *social category* the members of which are relatively easy to contact. see also *group, inaccessible*.

group, acquaintance voluntary *face-to-face group*.

group, age-sex a single-sex *grouping[1]* consisting of persons lying within age limits.

group, artificial see *group, contrived*.

group, ascribed *group* the membership of which is ascribed.

group, bilateral see *group, descent, bilateral*.

group, closed group with *closed recruitment*.

group, coacting *group* the members of which work together without com-

munication or *task interaction*. see also *coaction*.

group, cognatic a *group* of *cognates* computed from an *ancestral ego* or based on a *contemporary ego*.

group, collateral *kinship group* based on *collaterality*.

group, command the *group* within an *organization* consisting of the *top executive* and his immediate subordinates.

group, compound a *group* consisting of two or more *subgroups*.

group, conflict *group* deriving its *integration* from *conflict* with another group.

group, consanguine *group* consisting of *consanguineal relatives*.

group, control the group not exposed to the *experimental stimulus*.see also *group, experimental*.

group, contrived a *group* established by an investigator for observation or experimentation.

group, core 1. the dominant *group* in a *community*. (Hollingshead).2. members of the dominant *subsociety* found in a particular *social class*.(Gordon, M.M.).

group, corporate *group* characterized either by collective action, representatives, or collective property.

group, crescive a *group* not resulting from *planning*.

group, cultural *group* possessing a common *culture*. see also *tribe*.

group, cumulative see *group, multibonded*.

group, demographic *social category* having *demographic* criteria.

group, descent 1. living members of *kinship group*. 2. *group* which is closed on *genealogical* grounds. 3. corporate *descent unit*. (Schneider, D.M.).

group, descent, ambilineal see *group, descent, bilateral*.

group, descent, bilateral a *descent group* based on *non-unilineal descent*.

group, descent, cognatic see *group, descent, bilateral*.

group, descent, cognatic, restricted *cognatic descent group* of which all descendants of founding *ancestor* have right of membership which can only be exercised under certain conditions. (Fox, R.).

group, descent, cognatic, unrestricted *cognatic descent group* of which all descendants of founding *ancestor* are members. (Fox, R.).

group, descent, corporate a *descent group* characterized either by collective action, representatives, or collective property.

group, descent lineal see *group, descent, unilineal*.

group, descent, local the members of a *lineage* who live in close, everyday contact. (Leach).

group, descent, omnilateral *cognatic group* based on *contemporary ego*.

group, descent, omnilineal 1. *cognatic group* computed from an *ancestral ego*. 2. see *group, descent, bilateral*.

group, descent, unilineal a *descent group* based on *unilineal descent*.

group, descent, unlimited see *group, descent, bilateral*.

group, direct-contact see *group, face-to-face*.

group, dispersed *group* the members of which are interspersed with members of other groups.

group, domestic a *group* of people who habitually share a common dwelling and a common food supply.

group, dyadic a *group* of two persons.

group, elementary see *group, unibonded*.

group, enacted a *group* resulting from *planning*.

group, endogamous the *group* outside which *marriage* is prohibited.

group, ephemeral a *group* which exists for only a short time.

group, ethnic *group* characterized by common *religion, racial* origin, *national* origin, or *culture*.

group, exogamous the *group* within which *marriage* is prohibited.

group, experimental the group exposed to the *experimental stimulus*.see also *group, control*.

group, extended a *group* consisting of spatially-separated *subgroups*.(Gree, S.A.).

group, face-to-face two or more persons in sufficient proximity to permit each to respond to *stimuli* or *signals* emitted by each of the others.

group, formal a *group* with explicit *role* definitions.

group, friendship non-*kin* congeniality *group*.

group, genetic *group* consisting of persons genetically-related to a common *ancestor*.

group, gossip see *cell, gossip*.

group, hearth the members of a *band* who share a common hearth.

group, horizontal 1. *group* composed of persons of the same *social status* 2. group possessing a low ratio of *ranks* to co-ordinate *positions*.

group, impermanent see *group, ephemeral*.

group, inaccessible *social category* the members of which are relatively difficult to contact. see also *group, accessible*.

group, informal a *group* without explicit *role* definitions.

group, interest a *collectivity* the members of which share overt interests.

group, interest, anomic *interest group* which is non-institutionalized, contiguous, transitory.

group, interest, associational *interest group*, permanent, bureaucratized, with *primary goal* of advancing interests.

group, interest, institutional *interest group*, permanent, bureaucratized, which has an existence and purpose apart from advancing interests.

group, intermittent a *group* which functions at intervals.

group, involuntary *group, recruitment* to which is involuntary.

group, kin see *group, kinship*.

group, kin, ambilineal see *group, kin, bilateral*.

group, kin, bilateral a *kin group* based on *non-unilineal descent*.

group, kin, consanguineal *kin group* consisting of *consanguineal relatives*.

group, kin, corporate a *kin group* characterized either by collective action, representatives, or collective property.

group, kin, occasional *kin group* which becomes operative only on specific occasions.

group, kin, residential *kin group* characterized by common residence.

group, kin, unilineal a *kin group* based on *unilineal descent*.

group, kinship *group* of relatives.

group, kinship, affectionate congeniality *group* consisting of *kin*.

group, kinship, dispersed *kinship group* the members of which are interspersed with members of other kinship groups.

group, kinship, localized *kinship group* the members of which are not interspersed with members of other kinship groups.

group, lineage living members of a *lineage*.

group, local *group* restricted to a locality.

group, locality see *group, territorial*.

group, localized *group* the members of which are not interspersed with members of other groups.

group, marginal 1. *group* which is in a *marginal situation*. 2. an incompletely assimilated group. 3. a low-status *minority group*. (Kerckhoff, A.C.).

group, membership a *group* to which a person belongs.

group, migratory a plurality of *migrants* compelled to migrate together. (Hägerstrand, T.).

group, minority 1. *group* having a *racial* or *cultural* distinctiveness leading to a self-definition or definition by others of alienage with resulting lower *esteem* and *discrimination* by dominant *group.* 2. group which is regarded by members or others as being the object of discrimination by dominant group.

group, multibonded a *group* the members of which are bound together by more than one social tie. see also *group, unibonded.*

group, natural a *group* which is not a *contrived group.*

group, nominal a *social aggregate, grouping,* or *social category.*

group, normalization see *group, standardization.*

group, occupational see *family, occupational.*

group, omnilateral see *group, descent, omnilateral.*

group, omnilineal see *group, descent, omnilineal.*

group, open *group* with *open recruitment.*

group, organized a *group* with *role differentiation.*

group, patronymic a *set[1]* of *families* sharing a *patronym.*

group, peer 1. *group* without *ranks.* 2. group whose members have the same index in their branch of activity.

group, political see *unit, political.*

group, power organized *power aggregate.* (Lasswell, H.D.).

group, pressure organized *subgroup* that tries to influence *group* in direction of subgroup's *goals.*

group, pressure, international a *group* able to influence an international *organization* or a *state* other than that to which the group juridically belongs.

group, primary 1. small, affectional, *face-to-face group.* 2. small *group* or that part of small group the members of which accept each other. see also *group, secondary.*

group, promotional 1. *group* defending a particular point of view. 2. group whose aim is to secure the adoption of an *innovation.*

group, protective *group* defending a class of persons.

group, reference any *group* which an individual uses as a point of reference for his aspirations or his appraisal of himself, his situation or a group to which he belongs.

group, reference, aspirational a *reference group* to membership of which an individual aspires.

group, reference, membership a *reference group* which is also a *membership group.*

group, reference, negative a negatively-valued *reference group.*

group, reference, nonmembership a *reference group* which is not also a *membership group.*

group, reference, normative a *reference group* constituting a point of reference for *norms.*

group, reference, positive a positively-valued *reference group.*

group, reference, status a *reference group* constituting a point of reference for *status.*

group, residential see *group, territorial.*

group, secondary formal, impersonal *group.* see also *group, primary.*

group, segmental a *group* which regulates only a segment of members' lives. (Merton, R.K.). see also *group, totalitarian*; *engagement.*

group, sentient *group* which demands and receives loyalty from its members. (Miller, E. J.). see also *system, sentient.*

group, sibling the *group* of *siblings.*

group, skill those exercising a common *skill* or *set[1]* of skills.

group, small any number of persons engaged in *interaction* in one or a series of face-to-face meetings in which each member receives an impression of every other sufficiently distinct to cause a *reaction* to him, if only to recall his presence, on being questioned at the time or later.

group, socializing *group* which acts as an agent of *socialization*.

group, socio-religious a *group* distinguished from others by both religious and social characteristics.

group, solidary *group* possessing high solidarity.

group, sorority *group* of true sisters dominated by a brother.

group, spatial see *group, territorial*.

group, spontaneous a *natural group* not deliberately created.

group, standardization *group* for establishing *norms[3]* for a test.

group, status 1. a *group* or *grouping* whose members are of approximately equal *status*. 2. a plurality of persons of approximately equal status who interact frequently. see also *aggregate, status*. 3. a group granting *specific status*. (LaPiere).

group, subject organized *subject aggregate*. (Lasswell, H.D.).

group, subsistence a *group* all the production of which is internally consumed.

group, synectics a *group* of diverse individuals for the creative solution of problems. see also *synectics*.

group, target 1. the *group* to which an investigator wants to generalize. 2. group which is the object of *social action[3]*.

group, task 1. a *group* organized for a *task*.2. formal organizational unit engaged on a particular task, which is part of a larger group.

group, task-oriented see *group, task*.

group, territorial *group* based on residence in a certain area.

group, tetradic see *tetrad* see *quartet*.

group, totalitarian a *group* which regulates all aspects of members' lives. (Merton, R.K.). see also *group, segmental*; *engagement*.

group, totem a *group* associated with a *totem*. see also *totemism*.

group, treatment group in *experiment* receiving a *treatment[3]*.

group, triadic a *group* of three persons.

group, unibonded a *group* the members of which are bound together by only one social tie. see also *group, multibonded*.

group, unorganized a *group* without *role differentiation*.

group, vertical 1. *group* composed of persons of different *social status*.2. group possessing a high ratio of *ranks* to co-ordinate *positions*.

group, volitional *group* the membership of which is not ascribed.

group, voluntary *group, recruitment* to which is voluntary.

group, work a *group* organized for production.

grouping 1. see *category, social*. 2. see *group*. 3. putting into *categories*. 4. summarizing numerical data in classes. 5. arrangement in categories. 6. see *aggregate[2]*.

grouping, occupational see *family, occupational*.

growth 1. increase in magnitude by addition. 2. change towards a more developed state.

growth, accretionary see *growth[1]*.

growth, axial urban expansion along roads radiating from city.

growth, economic increase in per capita real income. see also *development, economic*.

growth, horizontal 1. increase in *functions* or *positions* in an *organization* without increase in levels. 2. horizontal urban *growth*.

growth, natural see *increase, natural*.

growth, negative depletion occurring to an aggregate or decrease in structural complexity.

growth, peripheral urban *growth* involving progressive expansion of the periphery.

growth, radial see *growth, axial*.

growth, ring *population‖growth* in suburban and fringe areas.

growth, simple accretion or depletion occurring to an aggregate.
growth, structural increase in structural complexity. (Boulding).
growth, sympodial *growth* shifting in line of direction.
growth, vertical 1. increase in levels in an *organization*. 2. vertical urban *growth*.
guide, interview a list of topics for use in a *semi-structured interview*.
gynaecocracy rule by women. **gynaecocratic** *a.*
gynocracy see *gynaecocracy*.
gyromancy *divination* from the position of collapse of a person who has walked continuously round a circle. **gyromantic** *a.*

habit recurring manner of *response* to a given *stimulus* situation.
habit, position disposition to prefer accustomed place.
habitability suitability of an area for *settlement²*.
habitat 1. see *environment, abiotic*. 2. an inhabited area with distinctive physical and chemical conditions. 3. *abiotic environment* plus *social environment*. 4. area suited to the needs of a *community*.
habitat, biological see *environment, biotic*.
habitat, physical see *habitat¹·²*.
hagiotoponym a place name which is also the name of a saint.
half-culture the incomplete *culture* of a *society* or people depending on goods traded from other *groups*. (Kroeber).
half-marriage *marriage* characterized by half the ordinary *bride-price, matrilocal residence*, and *bride-service* to work off the balance.
half-siblings persons having only one parent in common.
half-siblings, agnatic see *half-siblings, paternal*.
half-siblings, maternal see *half-siblings, uterine*.
half-siblings, paternal *half-siblings* having a common father.
half-siblings, uterine *half-siblings* having a common mother.
half-sibs see *half-siblings*.
handling, data see *reduction, data*.
haruspication *divination* through the entrails of dead animals.
haruspicy see *haruspication*.
head *leader* imposed on a *group* from outside.
headman 1. the *leader* of a *primitive‖community*. 2. the leader of a *tribe* or smaller primitive *group* who employs persuasion but lacks *authority*.
headship *leadership* of a *group* resulting from outside imposition.
hegemony, closed low degree of *liberalization* combined with low degree of *political participation²*. (Dahl, R.A.).
hegemony, inclusive low degree of *liberalization* combined with high degree of *political participation²*. (Dahl, R.A.).
helotism co-existence of unlike *groups* or persons in which one partner functions as the slave of the other. **helotic** *a.* see also *symbiosis; mutualism; commensalism*.
henotheism belief that one *spirit* in pantheon plays most of the *roles* belonging to the other spirits.
heortology the study of festivals.
hepatoscopy *divination* by examining an animal's liver.
herding maintaining the relationship of herd to pasture necessary for the welfare of the animals. see also *husbandry, animal*.
hereditary pertaining to predictable parental contribution to body state. see also *genetic²*.

heresiarch a leader of heretics.

heresimach one who fights heresy.

hero a person, either mythical or real, alive or dead, who symbolizes by his supposed past or present *role* or deeds some important aspect of the *values* of a *culture* or *subculture*.

hero, culture a person, either mythical or real, who is supposed to have given a people the most important parts of their *culture*.

heterogamy *marriage* of unlike according to a specified characteristic. **heterogamous** *a.* see also *homogamy*.

heterokurtic having different degrees of *kurtosis*. **heterokurtosis** *n.*

heterophenogamy matings to a greater degree than would be expected by chance between individuals not resembling each other somatically. **heterophenogamous** *a.*

heterophily friendship between individuals who are unlike according to a specified characteristic. see also *homophily*.

heterosociality *sociation* between persons of opposite sex. **heterosocial** *a.* see also *homosociality*.

hierarchization 1. the process by which a *hierarchy* is formed. 2. the increase in the *hierarchical* character of a *society*.

hierarchy 1. a grading into successive levels. 2. a structure of unequal *power relationships*. (Lasswell, H.D.). **hierarchical** *a.*

hierarchy, all-embracing a *hierarchy* in which everyone in the *society* has his place. see also *hierarchy, restricted*.

hierarchy, authority the ascending, successive levels of *authority*.

hierarchy, caste the ascending, successive *prestige* levels of *castes* in a *society*.

hierarchy, class the ascending, successive *social classes*.

hierarchy, command the ascending, successive levels of *command*.

hierarchy, occupational the ascending, successive *occupational levels*.

hierarchy, power the ascending, successive *power* levels.

hierarchy, restricted a *hierarchy* which is restricted to a segment of the *society*. see also *hierarchy, all-embracing*.

hierarchy, segmentary a *hierarchy*, each of the similar, mutually exclusive *groups* on a given level being subdivided into similar, mutually exclusive groups on the level below.

hierarchy, status the ascending, successive levels of *status*.

hierocracy rule by priests. **hierocratic** *a.*

hierogram a *sacred‖symbol*.

hinterland 1. see *hinterland, urban*. 2. see *hinterland, metropolitan*. 3. the area behind a port to and from which passes the greater part of the goods which pass through the port.

hinterland, metropolitan sphere of influence of a *metropolis*.

hinterland, urban *urban* sphere of influence.

histogram a graph representing a *frequency distribution* made by constructing rectangles on the x-axis, the bases being equal to the class intervals and the areas being proportional to the frequencies in each class.

histogram, area *histogram* in which frequency is represented not by height but by area of each bar.

histogram, percentage a *histogram* representing a *percentage distribution*.

historicalism the study of specific *cultural* elements as they move through time and space. **historicalist** *a.*

historicism 1. the doctrine that history is essential to an understanding of the present. 2. the assertion of historical *laws[10]* enabling the prediction of the future. **historicist** *a. & pers n.*

historicity 1. historical authenticity. 2. the presence in research of an historical dimension.

historigram graph with *values*[6] of the *variable* measured along the y-axis and time measured along the x-axis.

history, culture the *diachronic analysis* of *culture*.

holdover, squatter a former tenant whom the landlord fears to evict.

holy the separation of anything from ordinary life on account of its supernatural significance.

homino-centricity (Kroeber) see *anthropocentrism*.

holocaust a completely burnt *sacrificial* offering.

homeorhesis the property possessed by a *system* of developing along a buffered path. **homeorhetic** *a.* see also *system, homeorhetic*; *chreod*.

homeostasis maintenance of *system* in *equilibrium* through automatic *adaptation*. **homeostatic** *a.*

homeostasis, dynamic *homeostasis* involving constant *adjustment*.

homeostasis, family *homeostasis* in the relationship system of a *family*. (Jackson, D.D.).

homestead 1. farm occupied by owner and his *family*. 2. habitation whose occupants constitute a *household*.

homogamy *marriage* of like to like according to a specified characteristic. **homogamous** *a.* see also *heterogamy*.

homokurtic having the same degree of *kurtosis*. **homokurtosis** *n.*

homophily friendship between individuals who are alike according to a specified characteristic. see also *heterophily*.

homosociality *sociation* between persons of same sex. **homosocial** *a.* see also *heterosociality*.

honour a person's legitimate claim to *esteem* based on his embodiment of the *values* of his *culture* or *subculture*. see also *shame*[1].

horde 1. *group* at *crowd* level of *organization* but more enduring. 2. *social aggregate* lacking *subgroups*. (Durkheim).3. *nomadic‖group* which wanders over a *territory* to which it lays claim. (NQ).

horticulture hand tillage, i.e., cultivation of the soil with hand tools. **horticultural** *a.* **horticulturalist** *pers n.*

hospitalism psychological harm resulting from hospitalization.

hostility 1. anger and *aggressiveness* towards another person or person. 2. a situation in which party 'A' seeks to worsen the position of party 'B'. (Boulding, K.). see also *aggression*.

hostility, displaced *hostility*[1] displaced from the frustrating object to another object.

hostility, malevolent a situation in which party 'A', irrespective of the effect on its own position, seeks to worsen the position of party 'B'. (Boulding, K.).

hostility, nonmalevolent a situation in which party 'A' to improve its own position seeks to worsen the position of party 'B'. (Boulding, K.).

household 1. entire *group* of persons sharing living quarters and principal meals. 2. all persons occupying a *housing unit*. 3. all persons occupying a *dwelling unit*.

household, composite *household* consisting of members of more than one *nuclear family*.

household, extended *household* consisting of two or more *nuclear families* formed by joining the nuclear family of a married adult to that of his or her parents.

household, family see *household, private*.

household, institutional inmates of a *total institution*.

household, non-family see *household, institutional*.

household, one-person an individual living by himself regarded as a *household* for *census* purposes.

household, private *household* which is not an *institutional household*.

102

husbandry production or use of domesticated animals or plants.

husbandry, animal *activities* aimed at maintaining a herd as a harvestable resource. see also *herding*.

hydro-agriculture cultivation aided by minor irrigation works which are a purely local responsibility. (Wittfogel, K.A.). see also *agriculture, hydraulic*.

hydromancy *divination* by means of water. **hydromantic** *a*.

hypercathexis a *cathexis* which is greater than optimum.

hypergamy *marriage* of a woman to a man of higher *status*. **hypergamous** *a*. see also *hypogamy*; *anisogamy*.

hypergamy, caste *marriage* of a woman to a man of a higher *caste*.

hypergamy, class *marriage* of a woman to a man of higher *social class*.

hypocathexis a *cathexis* which is less than optimum.

hypogamy *marriage* of a woman to a man of lower *status*. **hypogamous** *a*. see also *hypergamy*; *anisogamy*.

hypogamy, caste *marriage* of a woman to a man of a lower *caste*.

hypogamy, class *marriage* of a woman to a man of lower *social class*.

hypothesis *proposition* subject to future experimental testing.

hypothesis, age-area *hypothesis* that the age of a *culture trait* is proportional to the distance it has diffused. see also *diffusion*.

hypothesis, alternative the *hypothesis* which is accepted if the *null hypothesis* is rejected.

hypothesis, complex a *hypothesis* divisible into *propositions* which may be separately tested.

hypothesis, concentric zone see *theory, concentric zone*.

hypothesis, descriptive *hypothesis* concerning the presence or distribution of a *variable*.

hypothesis, extensionist the *hypothesis* that *classificatory terms* are the result of extension of the terms from single *kinship categories*.

hypothesis, generalization a *hypothesis* that a *proposition* or propositions established for a *sample* are generalizable to the *population*. (Galtung, J.).

hypothesis, heuristic see *hypothesis, working*.

hypothesis, J-curve *hypothesis* that *frequency curves* of *conformity* to *norms* are J-curves.

hypothesis, multi-nuclear see *theory, multi-nuclear*.

hypothesis, null the *hypothesis* that no *correlation* or *association* exists between two specified *variables*.

hypothesis, relational *hypothesis* concerning a relationship amongst *variables*.

hypothesis, sector see *theory, sector*.

hypothesis, substantive a *hypothesis* concerning *variables* relating to a *sample*. (Galtung, J.).

hypothesis, tenable a *hypothesis* which has received a satisfactory degree of confirmation. (Galtung, J.).

hypothesis, test a *hypothesis* intended to be tested. see also *hypothesis, working*.

hypothesis, valid a *hypothesis* which is deducible.

hypothesis, wedge see *theory, sector*.

hypothesis, working a *hypothesis* not for testing but intended to guide research. see also *hypothesis, test*.

hypothesis, zonal see *theory, concentric zone*.

ichthyolatry the worship of fishes. **ichthyolatric** *a*.

ichthyomancy *divination* by means of head or entrails of fishes. **ichthyomantic** *a*.

idealism, cultural 1. regarding *culture* as a *system* of *norms*. (DiRenzo, G.J.). 2.

the rejection of the prepotence of economic *factors* in the determination of culture. see also *materialism, cultural.*

identification accepting as one's own the beliefs and *values* of another person or a *group.* see also *sympathy*; *empathy.*

identification, class *identification* with a *social class.* see also *consciousness, class.*

identification, cross-parent *identification* with parent of opposite sex.

identification, defensive *identification* resulting from fear.

identification, developmental *identification* resulting from a positive relationship with a person on whom one is originally dependent.

identification, ethnic *identification* with an *ethnic group.*

ideographic pertaining to the investigation of the particular. see also *nomothetic.*

ideology 1. a *belief system* which protects the interests of an *elite.* 2. a socially-determined *set¹* of beliefs.3. a belief system which indicates the probable *social position* of the individual. 4. a *system* of beliefs.

ideology, authoritarian *ideology* supporting authoritarian behaviour, procedures and government.

ideology, existential that part of a *society's belief system* which consists of existential statements. (Service, E.R.).

ideology, family the beliefs and *values* shared by members of a particular *family.*

ideology, group the beliefs and *values* shared by members of a *group.*

ideology, latent an *ideology* which is not explicitly-formulated.

ideology, manifest an *ideology* which is explicitly-formulated.

ideology, militaristic *ideology* supporting military ideals.

ideology, normative that part of a *society's belief system* which consists of *normative* statements. (Service, E.R.).

ideology, occupational the beliefs and *values* shared by members of an *occupation.*

ideology, open-class the *ideology* of the *open-class system.*

ideology, religious an *ideology* consisting of *religious* beliefs and *values.*

ideology, sacred an *ideology* consisting of *sacred* beliefs and *values.*

ideology, secular an *ideology* consisting of *secular¹* beliefs and *values.*

idiocult person's distinctive *set¹* of non-genetic *behaviour patterns.* (Hull, R.A.).

idiolect person's distinctive *set¹* of language *habits.*

ignorance, pluralistic all members of *group* reject belief, each believing that all the others accept it.

imitation copying the behaviour of another.

imitation, suggestion *imitation* resulting from *suggestion.*

immigration 1. *migration* into a particular country. 2. joining a *population* or *sub-population.* *(genet.).* **immigrate** *vi.* **immigrant** *a.* & *pers n.*

immigration, chain *immigration* in which each *immigrant* pulls in another immigrant.

immigration, gross total amount of *immigration.*

immigration, mass *immigration* involving very large numbers.

immigration, net excess of *immigrants* over *emigrants.*

immigration, planned *immigration* resulting from *planning* on the part of an *organization.* see also *migration, planned; emigration, planned.*

immunity, seignorial exemption from taxes and services, and from intervention of *overlord* into relations between a lord and his *vassals* or *serfs.* (Andreski, S.).

imperatives, functional conditions necessary for the stability and effectiveness of a *social system.* see also *prerequisites, functional*; *requisites, functional*; *requirements, functional.*

imperatives, social the necessary characteristics of *social organization*.

impersonalization conferring an impersonal character on *social relationships*. **impersonalize** *v*.

impurity see *pollution*.

inaccessibility degree of difficulty in contacting members of a given *social category*. see also *accessibility*.

incentive a reward inducing a more than standard output or performance of individual.

incest 1. sexual intercourse between *consanguines* within the *nuclear family*. 2. sexual intercourse which is proscribed because of insufficient *genealogical distance*.

incest, dynastic see *incest, royal*.

incest, royal *incest[1]* which is permitted or prescribed within a royal family.

incidence see *rate, incidence*.

incision see *superincision*.

income, nominal income in terms of *money*.

income, psychic that part of income which consists of the satisfaction derived from a *job* or from the *status* conferred by it.

income, real income in terms of goods and services.

incompatibility, role incompatibility of *roles* of same individual.

incorporation, institutional incorporation of peripheral *groups* in *national institutions*.

increase, natural excess of births over deaths. see also *decrease, natural*.

increment a unit increase in a quantity. see also *decrement*.

increment, social see *facilitation, social[1]*.

incubation passing the night at a *sacred* place in order to receive divine aid.

indeterminism the doctrine that events are independent of antecedent events.

index 1. an indirect measure of a characteristic. 2. see *number, index*.

index, aggregative see *number, index, aggregative*.

index, arbitrary *composite index* resulting from the combination of two or more subjectively weighted indicators.

index, composite an indirect measure resulting from the combination of two or more indicators.

index, gerontocratic *polygyny* rate for older men, i.e. 40+, divided by polygyny rate for younger men. (Spencer, P.). see also *gerontocracy*.

index, simple an indirect measure consisting of a single indicator.

indexing that operation of *content processing* involving the assignment of *symbols* to units of content, considered as meaningful, for the purpose of information retrieval.

indigence the state of being near the *subsistence level*. see also *pauperism*; *poverty*.

individual, reference person with whom *ego* identifies and emulates.

individuation 1. the acquisition of a distinctive *role* by a *group* member. 2. the development of the individual from general to specific *responses*.

induction 1. inference from the particular to the general. 2. see *induction, social*.

induction, complete *enumerative induction* based on the study of the entire *population*.

induction, enumerative *induction[1]* in which probabilistic generalizations are derived from the analysis of cases in a defined *population*.

induction, incomplete *enumerative induction* based on the study of a *sample*.

induction, social process by which a person is prepared for and introduced into a *group*, *role*, *status* or *office*.

induction, statistical see *inference, statistical*.

induction, sympathetic the diffusion and intensification of affect in a *collec-*

tivity.

industrialization 1. extensive use of inanimate sources of power in production. 2. spread of *mechanized industry*. 3. any type of economic modernization.

industry 1. any field of full-time *work*. 2. extractive, productive or service activities. 3. productive activities. 4. factory production. 5. category of establishments manufacturing close-substitute products. 6. category of *productive organizations* using the same type of technology. 7. category of *productive organizations* based on criteria revelant to some analytic or policy-making purpose. 8. a particular type of *prehistoric||technology*. 9. all the *artifacts* of one kind found at a *site¹*. see also *occupation*; *job*.

industry, basic 1. *industry* producing goods and services for consumption outside *community* and bringing *money* into community. see also *industry, nonbasic*. 2. industry fundamental to an *economy*. 3. industry fundamental to a *set¹* of industries.

industry, extractive exploitation of non-replaceable natural resources.

industry, mechanized an *industry* with mass production resulting from *mechanization*.

industry, nonbasic *industry* producing goods and services for comsumption by residents of *community*. see also *industry, basic¹*.

industry, primary exploitation of natural resources.

industry, prison any field of extractive, productive or service activities performed by prisoners.

industry, rural 1. an *industry* located in a *rural area*. 2. a traditional industry located in a rural area. 3. an industry located in a rural area serving local needs.

industry, secondary *industry* which transforms materials.

industry, tertiary *industry* which does not transform materials but supplies services.

inertia 1. property of anything which tends to preserve its state of rest or direction of movement. 2. lag of physiological effect behind stimulation.

inertia, cultural tendency for cultural features to persist after ceasing to be *eufunctional*.

inertia, industrial tendency of an *industry* or industries to remain located in an area after the advantages of location in that area are no longer significant.

infecundity absence of reproductive capacity. see also *fecundity*.

inference, statistical estimating from a *sample* the distributions of characteristics in the *population*.

infertility absence of reproductive performance. see also *fertility*.

infertility, physiological *infertility* resulting from physiological factors.

infertility, voluntary voluntary absence of reproductive performance.

infeudation grant by a lord of whole or part of land to a tenant to hold of him in *feudal tenure*. see also *subinfeudation*.

infibulation attaching together the lips of the vulva or prepuce to prevent copulation.

influence 1. *power* involving persuasion. 2. non-coercive power. 3. see *power, spontaneous*. 4. indirect and unstructured power. 5. exercise of power. 6. changing the probability of a *decision*.

influence, mass *influence* achieved through *mass communication*.

influence, metropolitan the influence, varying in distance and degree, in various spheres, exercised by a *metropolis* over its *environment*.

influence, military *military intervention* taking the form of an attempt by the military to increase their resources or to shift *policies* relating to the military.

influential 1. person who influences *public opinion*. 2. person who influences *policy decision*.

influential, ascribed individual in a *position* which confers considerable *power* on the holder.

influential, attributed person receiving a large number of designations as an *influential* from the *set[1]* of *informants*.

influential, cosmopolitan *influential* oriented primarily towards national and international affairs.

influential, local *influential* oriented primarily towards local affairs.

informalogram a chart showing the network of mutually perceived *informal relationships* in an *organization*. see also *formalogram*.

informant 1. a member of the *group* under study chosen for *ethnographic* interviewing. 2. an individual sending information, whether or not intentionally. (Goffman, E.).

informant, key one of a few persons chosen for intensive *ethnographic* interviewing over an extensive period of time.

informant, key, focused *key informant* interviewed for information on a particular topic.

information, status information which does not change rapidly.

information, transient information which changes rapidly.

infracultural pertaining to phenomena below the cultural level of analysis or to *genetic[2]*‖*factors* in the behaviour of individuals and *populations*.

infrastructure the necessary pre-conditions for *industrialization*.

infrastructure, physical the necessary physical pre-conditions for *industrialization*.

infrastructure, social the necessary social as distinct from physical pre-conditions for *industrialization*.

in-group a *group* from the point of view of a member. see also *out-group*.

in-grouper a member of the *in-group*. see also *out-grouper*.

inheritance devolution of property on death.

inheritance, adelphic *inheritance* by a brother.

inheritance, bilateral *inheritance* in both the *patriline* and the *matriline*.

inheritance, circular *inheritance* by deceased's *collaterals* of goods allocated to him during his lifetime and not regarded as his property and which return on his death to the head of the *kinship group* who retains some of them and divides the rest amongst the collaterals. (Poirier).

inheritance, collateral *inheritance* by *collaterals*.

inheritance, double *inheritance* from both *patrilineal relatives* and *matrilineal relatives*.

inheritance, general *inheritance* which is not restricted to males.

inheritance, horizontal *inheritance* from brother to brother. (Poirier).

inheritance, lateral see *inheritance, collateral*.

inheritance, lineal *inheritance* by *lineals*.

inheritance, matrilineal *inheritance* in the mother's line.

inheritance, nepotic inheritance by a man of his uncle's widow as wife.

inheritance, oblique inheritance by a man from his mother's brother. (Poirier).

inheritance, patrilineal *inheritance* in the father's line.

inheritance, positional inheritance of a *position*.

inheritance, primogenitary see *primogeniture*.

inheritance, ultimogenitary see *ultimogeniture*.

inheritance, unigenitary see *unigeniture*.

inheritance, universal *inheritance* by an individual of the entire estate of another, including both assets and liabilities.

inheritance, widow inheritance of a man's widow as wife.

inheritance, widow, filial inheritance of father's widows as wives, except own mother.

inhibition a blocking or arrest of function.

inhibition, conditioned suppression of CR when CS is repeatedly paired with an indifferent *stimulus* and the US is not given.

inhibition, connective increased difficulty in recalling separate parts after the parts have been integrated.

inhibition, cortical *inhibition* of nerve impulses in the cortex.

inhibition, extinctive (Pavlov) see *extinction, experimental.*

inhibition, general (U.I.17) a *factor³* connected with a tendency to be generally cautious and timid.

inhibition, generalized *inhibition* occurring in a wide variety of situations.

inhibition, proactive increased difficulty in learning the later members of a series following learning of an earlier member.

inhibition, reactive tendency to lessened *response* consequent to effortful activity. (Hull).

inhibition, reciprocal *retroactive inhibition* used in the treatment of mental disorders.

inhibition, reflex *inhibition* of one *reflex* by another.

inhibition, retroactive destruction of old *learning* by new learning.

inhibition, social *inhibition* resulting from *social control.*

initiation *ceremonies* marking transition from one state or *status* to another.

initiative see *referendum, initiative.*

initiative, direct an *initiative* in which the proposed measure is referred directly to the voters.

initiative, indirect an *initiative* in which the proposed measure goes first to the legislature for possible adoption, and failing adoption is referred to the voters.

inmates persons managed in a *total institution.* (Goffman, E.).

in-migration *migration* into a particular area from another part of the same country. **in-migrant** *pers n.* see also *out-migration.*

in-migration, gross total *in-migration.*

in-migration, net excess of *in-migration* over *out-migration.*

innate see *genetic².*

inner-directed directed by *internalized norms.* (Riesman, D.). see also *tradition-directed; other-directed.*

innovation 1. a new cultural element. 2. acceptance by an individual of the *cultural goals* and rejection of the institutionalized means of a *society.* (Merton, R.K.).

innovation, material *innovation* in *material culture.*

innovation, nonmaterial *innovation* in *nonmaterial culture.*

innovation, secondary an *innovation* facilitating the functioning of a previous innovation.

innovation, social see *innovation, nonmaterial.*

input 1. that which enters a processing system. 2. the manipulations applied to a *model.*

input, maintenance an energetic *input¹* whose *function* is to help sustain a *system.*

instability, conjugal the de facto dissolution of *marriage.*

instability, jural the de jure dissolution of *marriage.*

instability, marital divorce or separation of married couple.

instinct complex, species-specific, invariant, *innate* disposition.

institution 1. standardized mode of behaviour. (Radcliffe-Brown). 2. *co-operation* in a regular and habitual fashion. (Allport). 3. behaviour standardized, recurrent, aim-controlled, in accordance with *norms,* implying specific *group.*(Nadel). 4. unit of organized human activity implying norms and personnel. (Malinowski). 5. *system* of *rules* generally acted upon which, by defining *offices* and *positions,* rights and duties, give form and structure to social activity. (Rawls). 6. complex of co-operative activities. 7. group organized for a purpose. (Coon, C. S.). 8. socially established *behaviour patterns* authoritatively enforced. 9. *set¹* of norms focused on a given functional requirement. 10. a normative pattern conformity with which is generally to be expected and failure to conform with which is generally met with the moral indignation of the personnel of the general *social system* concerned. (Parsons, T.). 11. a complex of institutional patterns.

institution, alternative see *institution, free.*

institution, associative *institution* actuated collectively by whole *group* for which it is valid. (Nadel, S.F.).

institution, compulsory *institution* which individuals are compelled to activate. (Nadel, S.F.).

institution, contingent *institution* actuated in given circumstances. (Nadel, S.F.).

institution, continuous *institution* actuated continuously.(Nadel, S.F.).

institution, crescive an *institution* not resulting from *planning.*

institution, crucial an *institution* which is a structural requisite of the *system* of which it forms a part. (Levy, M.J.).

institution, economic an *institution* which produces goods and services. (Parsons, T.).

institution, embracing *institution* whose actuation embraces the whole *group* for which it is valid. (Nadel, S.F.).

institution, enacted an *institution* resulting from *planning.*

institution, exclusive see *institution, compulsory.*

institution, free *institution* which individuals are free to activate or not. (Nadel, S.F.).

institution, governmental any *institution* exercising a governmental *function.*

institution, group a normatively standardized activity of a *group.* (Znaniecki, F.).

institution, national an *institution* which is nation-wide.

institution, operative 1. *institution* which is service-rendering rather than *normative.* (Becker-Wiese).2. institution which is mainly non-supportive of another institution. (Nadel, S.F.).

institution, parallel *institution* actuated in different instances by *subgroups* of *group* for which it is valid (Nadel, S.F.).

institution, pivotal the *institution* which dominates a given *society.*

institution, political any one of those *institutions* which possess a monopoly of legitimate *power.*

institution, primary one of the *institutions* of a *society* responsible for the *basic personality structure.* (Kardiner).

institution, redressive an *institution* which restores social equilibrium.(Bailey, F. G.).

institution, regulative 1. *institution* which is mainly *normative* rather than service-rendering. (Becker-Wiese).2. institution the main purpose of which is to support another institution. (Nadel, S.F.).

institution, repetitive *institution* actuated periodically. (Nadel, S.F.).

institution, secondary one of the *institutions* of a *society* resulting from the *basic personality structure.* (Kardiner).

institution, sectional *institution* whose actuation is allocated by the *group* for which it is valid to a special group. (Nadel, S.F.).

institution, self-regulating an *institution* which is not regulated by *public sanctions.* (Nadel, S.F.).

institution, total place where a large number of like-situated persons lead an enclosed, formally administered round of life.

institutionalization the standardization of *behaviour patterns* and behavioural expectations in a *collectivity.*

insurrection organized *revolt* against the *government*.

intake see *input¹*.

integration 1. making a whole out of elements. 2. see *assimilation, structural*. 3. acquisition of sufficient elements of *culture* of *host society* by *immigrant‖group* to permit unity in the *society*. 4. predictable co-*adaptation* of behaviour in a group. 5. conflict resolution through environmental changes which satisfy both parties or through a change or reconciliation of *values*. (Follett, M.P.). 6. the control of *conflict* and *deviance* in a *social system*. (Parsons, T.).

integration, communicative the extent to which a common *communication network* is operative throughout a *society*.

integration, community 1. co-ordination of activities in the *community*. 2. *structural assimilation* into the community.

integration, cultural the degree of interdependence amongst the elements of a *culture*.

integration, external the degree of *integration¹* of a *group* with other groups.

integration, functional the functional interdependence of social or cultural elements.

integration, group see *integration⁴*.

integration, horizontal single control of a *set¹* of *activities* or units which are at the same *organizational level*.

integration, internal the degree of *integration¹* within a *group*.

integration, interpersonal the degree of interdependence amongst persons.

integration, lateral see *integration, horizontal*.

integration, political the merging of previously separate *polities*.

integration, rite of a symbolic parade of the individual's new *status* before the members of his *community*. (Van Gennep).

integration, social the degree of interdependence amongst social elements.

integration, sociocultural the degree of interdependence amongst *sociocultural* elements.

integration, vertical single control of a *set¹* of *activities* or units which are at different *organizational levels*.

interactant see *interactor*.

interaction 1. stimulating and responding of persons to one another. 2. *act* of A to B. 3. the non-additivity of the separate effects of the *variables* comprising a *set¹* which is acting on a *dependent variable*.

interaction, binary interaction between two units.

interaction, chain of see *interaction, serial*.

interaction, cultural interaction between *cultures* or *cultural systems*.

interaction, direct see *interaction, face-to-face*.

interaction, ecological indirect and impersonal reciprocal modification of individuals or *groups* through their effect on limited sources of environmental supplies upon which the others depend.

interaction, face-to-face *interaction* involving the *copresence* of the interacting individuals.

interaction, focused *interaction* which occurs when persons co-operate to maintain a single focus of attention. (Goffman, E.).

interaction, group the *network of interaction* occuring in a *group*.

interaction, group, guided *group‖technique* for rehabilitation of offenders in which *leader* is active in the discussion and guides group members towards acceptance of legal restrictions.

interaction, immediate see *interaction, face-to-face*.

interaction, interpersonal see *interaction¹ʼ²*.

interaction, interpretative *interaction* in which *responses* are based on interpretation of the behaviour of others.

110

interaction, network of the *interactions* between more than two persons.

interaction, non-symbolic *interaction* between individuals which is not based on the interpretation by each of the other's behaviour. (Mead, G.H.).

interaction, range of number of persons with whom *ego* interacts.

interaction, scalar *interaction* in *organization* between subordinates and superiors.

interaction, serial *response* of B to *stimulus* of A is itself stimulus producing response of A, and so on.

interaction, situational *interaction* in response to cues implicit in situation.

interaction, social *social processes* involving *interaction* of individuals, *groups,* or individual with group.

interaction, spatial interaction and flows of all kinds involving spatially distributed objects or cultural items. (Ulmann, E.L.).

interaction, symbolic *interaction* between individuals which is based on the interpretation by each of the other's behaviour. (Mead, G.H.).

interaction, task *interaction* of persons in performance of *group task.*

interaction, transactional *interaction* which stresses mutual rights and obligations.

interaction, unfocused *interaction* which occurs when persons do not co-operate to maintain a single focus of attention. (Goffman, E.).

interaction-consciousness over-involvement by a participant in a conversation with the way in which the *interaction,* qua interaction, is proceeding. (Goffman, E.). see also *self-consciousness*; *other-consciousness*.

interactionism, symbolic the *theory* of *symbolic interaction.*

interactor a person engaged in *interaction.*

interoceptor *receptor* which is aroused by *stimuli* from the internal organs. see also *exteroceptor*; *proprioceptor*.

interpellation formal interrogation of a minister.

interpolation estimating *values*[6] of a *variable* between any two known values. **interpolate** *v.* see also *extrapolation.*

interstimulation 1. mutual stimulation of two or more persons. 2. *response* of person to his *perception* of another.

interval, median the class interval containing the *median.*

interval, migration time interval to which *migration statistics* relate.

interval, modal the class interval containing the *mode.*

intervention, military the constrained substitution of the military's personnel and/or *policies* for those of the civilian authorities. (Finer, S.E.).

interview, active interview in which *respondent*[1] does more than answer *closed questions.* (Festinger).

interview, check interview carried out in the process of checking a *sample* of another interviewer's work.

interview, demonstration interview for *training* purposes in which a supervisor plays the part of *respondent*[1].

interview, depth an interview involving considerable detail and flexibility.

interview, experimental interview forming part of an *experiment.*

interview, extensive see *interview, structured.*

interview, focused interview concentrating on selected aspects of a specific event or situation experienced by the *respondent*[1].

interview, formal see *interview, structured.*

interview, free-response see *interview, open-ended.*

interview, group interview involving two or more *respondents*[1] simultaneously.

interview, guided see *interview, structured.*

interview, informal see *interview, unstructured.*

interview, information interview for obtaining information from a *respondent*[1].

interview, intensive see *interview, unstructured.*

interview, nondirective *unstructured interview* both the subject and form of which is left to the *respondent[1]*.

interview, nonschedule interview not utilizing a *schedule*.

interview, open-ended interview without fixed response-alternatives.

interview, opinion interview for obtaining *opinions* of *respondent[1]*.

interview, passive interview in which *respondent[1]* merely answers *closed questions*. (Festinger).

interview, personal interview involving only one *respondent[1]* at a time.

interview, pilot interview forming part of a *pilot study*.

interview, pre-pilot an interview forming part of an *exploratory survey*.

interview, qualitative interview which does not permit quantification of the *responses*.

interview, quantitative interview which permits quantification of the *responses*.

interview, reconstructed interview recorded by interviewer after interview.

interview, research interview aimed at obtaining information aiding research.

interview, schedule interview utilizing a *schedule*.

interview, semi-structured interview involving predetermination of the general course but not the details.

interview, standardized *structured interview* with *closed questions* which is the same for all *respondents[1]*.

interview, stress interview in which the *respondent[1]* is deliberately exposed to *psychic stress*.

interview, structured interview with predetermined questions.

interview, structured, partially see *interview, semi-structured*.

interview, survey interview forming part of a *survey*.

interview, therapeutic interview having a therapeutic aim.

interview, trial interview for *training* purposes in which one trainee plays the part of interviewer and another the part of *respondent[1]*.

interview, unguided see *interview, nondirective*.

interview, unstructured interview the course of which is not predetermined.

interviewee person interviewed. see also *respondent[1]*.

introcision see *clitoridectomy*.

intracultural within a particular *culture*.

intrasocietal within a particular *society*.

intrasystemic within a *system*.

introspection, retrospective the *technique* of getting a *respondent[1]* to try to recall his feelings in a certain past situation.

introspection, sympathetic see *Verstehen*.

introversion *personality type* characterized by interests being directed to self. see also *extraversion*; *ambiversion*.

introversion, active *personality type* characterized by voluntary withdrawal from external world.

introversion, passive *personality type* characterized by involuntary withdrawal from external world.

invalidicide the killing of invalids.

invariant see *constant*.

invasion movement into a segregated area of a *population* type or land-use type displacing the existing type.

invasion, ecological see *invasion, residential*.

invasion, institutional movement of commercial or industrial *organizations* into an area used for another purpose.

invasion, residential movement of one *population* type into an area occupied by another type.

invention 1. *innovation* which is either synthesis of existing cultural elements or application of cultural element to a new situation. 2. any new application of a *discovery*. (Harrison, H.S.).

invention, basic an *invention* which is the key to a series of inventions.

invention, improving *invention* which is only an improvement of another invention.

invention, independent an *invention* originating in a given area and not borrowed from elsewhere.

invention, physical an *invention* involving traits of *material culture*.

invention, social an *invention* relating to *social organization*.

inventory, activity list of the *acts* performed by a given person in a given situation.

involvement 1. amount of attention given by individual to an *activity*. 2. activity receiving an individual's attention. 3. the cathectic-evaluative orientation of an *actor* to an object. (Etzioni, A.).

involvement, alienative negative *involvement³* of high intensity.

involvement, calculative negative or positive *involvement³* of low intensity.

involvement, dominant *activity* having first priority on individual's attention.

involvement, main *activity* receiving major part of individual's attention.

involvement, moral positive *involvement³* of high intensity.

involvement, side *activity* not receiving major part of individual's attention.

involvement, subordinate *activity* not having first priority on individual's attention.

ipsative taking the person's own typical behaviour as the *standard* of comparison.

irrigation supplying land with water required for cultivation. see also *subirrigation*.

irrigation, basin *irrigation* achieved by conducting flood waters into basins formed in the soil.

irrigation, perennial *irrigation* in which the land can be supplied with water at any time.

island, linguistic see *island, speech*.

island, speech small *settlement* totally surrounded by a language barrier. (Bloomfield).

isochrone cartographic line all points on which are of equal time-distance from a given point.

isodapane a cartographic line all points on which represent points of equal cost.

isogamy *marriage* in which partners are of equal *status*. **isogamous** *a*. see also *hypergamy*; *hypogamy*; *anisogamy*.

isogloss a cartographic line separating places which differ with respect to a given linguistic feature.

isogram see *isopleth¹*.

isoikete cartographic line all points on which represent points of equal *habitability*.

isokurtic see *homokurtic*.

isolate 1. *group* member without *primary contacts*. 2. see *isolate, sociometric*. 3. individual who feels isolated from others who are in physical proximity. 4. individual with no social contacts or only superficial ones. 5. individual who is only permitted by *communication network* to communicate with one other person. 6. see *isolate, breeding*.

isolate, breeding a subdivision of a *breeding population*.

isolate, genetic see *isolate, breeding*.

isolate, neglected individual who receives no sociometric choices. (*sociom.*).

isolate, sociometric individual who receives no sociometric choices, or who neither receives nor makes sociometric choices. (*sociom.*).

isolate, star individual who neither receives nor makes sociometric choices. (*sociom.*).

isolation 1. prolonged absence of social contact. 2. failure of individual to communicate with those about him. 3. absence of *social relationships*. 4. prescribed absence, minimizing, or restricting social contact. 5. extreme *segregation*. 6. lack of contact between one *group* and others.

isolation, circumstantial *isolation* due to external circumstances.

isolation, idiosyncratic *isolation* due to idiosyncratic attribute.

isolation, physical *isolation* due to distance from others.

isolation, sociopathic *isolation* forced by others on a *sociopath*.

isolation, vicinal absence of social contacts with persons or *groups* outside the immediate vicinity.

isolex a lexical *isogloss*.

isoline see *isopleth[1]*.

isometer see *isopleth[1]*.

isonymy recurrence of the same surnames in *affines*. **isonymous** *a*.

isophenogamy matings to a greater degree than would be expected by chance by individuals resembling each other somatically. **isophenogamous** *a*.

isophode cartographic line all points on which represent points of equal transport costs.

isopleth 1. cartographic line all points on which are of equal *value*. 2. cartographic line all points on which represent equal rates or ratios.

item 1. standardized statement plus *set[1]* of *response||categories*. 2. natural unit of *communication* content, e.g., book, article.

item, behaviour the smallest observable unit of human behaviour.

item, monotone *questionnaire* item to which the same *response* is only made by persons who are genotypically the same.

item, nonmonotone *questionnaire* item to which the same *response* may be made by persons who are genotypically different.

job 1. an employment in an *occupation*. 2. an assignment of duties accepted as a condition of employment. (Mundel, M.E.).

job, composite *job* consisting of a combination of different positions in different work flows.

job, decisive a *job* in which the *objectives* are specified but not the manner of performance.

job, direct a *job* involving *direct work*.

job, indirect a *job* involving *indirect work*.

job, repetitive a *job* in which both the *objectives* and the detailed sequences of *actions* are specified.

job, selective a *job* in which both the *objectives* and the manner of performance are specified but not the details of performance.

judicialization the conferring of judicial character on *adjudication*. **judicialize** *vt*.

juniority see *ultimogeniture*.

junta a *group* constituting or dominating a revolutionary *government*.

junta, caretaker see *junta, interim*.

junta, interim a *junta* which promises to act as a caretaker until new *elections*.

jurimetrics the scientific investigation of legal problems using computers, symbolic logic and quantitative methods. **jurimetric** *a*.

jurisdiction, seignorial full administrative and judicial *authority* held over the inhabitants of land by a tenant holding it on *feudal tenure* or *allodial tenure*.

jurisdiction, territorial *jurisdiction* exercised over a specified *territory*.

justice, coordinate justice administered not by a superordinate *chief* or *court* but by the *group* wronged.(Whiting, B.B.).

justice, superordinate justice administered not by the *group* wronged but by a superordinate *chief* or *court*.(Whiting, B.B.).

juxtaposition a state of internal subdivision of a *group* involving a linear series of segments. (Goody, J.). see also *segmentation⁴*.

kakina decoration produced by drawing a needle and soot-covered thread under the skin.

kathenotheism see *henotheism*.

keloid deliberately-produced raised scar. see also *moxa*; *moko*; *cicatrice*.

key see *diagram, branch*.

key, semantic a *branch diagram* representing a *semantic‖structure*.

key, strip scoring key having answers in a column on a strip permitting alignment with *responses* on *questionnaire*.

kin persons related by *real, putative* or *fictive consanguinity*.

kin, effective 1. see *relatives, intimate*. 2. relatives with whom *ego* interacts only occasionally but who can be relied upon for assistance. (Djamour, J.).

kin, intimate relatives with whom *ego* interacts frequently and who can be relied upon for assistance. (Djamour, J.).

kin, natal relatives amongst whom individual has been reared in common residence.

kin, nominal relatives with whom *ego* does not interact. (Djamour, J.).

kin, primary *consanguineal relatives* who are *primary relatives*.

kin-community a *community* that is a *kinship group*.

kin-type the *genealogical position* of a relative in relation to *ego*.

kindred 1. an individual's *cognates*. (Rivers).2. see also *group, descent, bilateral*.

kindred, asymmetrical *kindred* with *unisexual recruitment*.

kindred, consanguineal a *kindred* consisting of *consanguines*.

kindred, core those members of an *ego-centric kindred* with whom active membership is obligatory. (Hudson, A.B.).

kindred, descending see *group, descent, bilateral*.

kindred, ego-centric see *kindred, personal*.

kindred, nodal a *local group* consisting of the common overlap of the *personal kindreds* of all its members. (Goodenough, W.H.).

kindred, personal an individual's *cognates*.

kindred, skewed 1. *kindred* with *unisexual recruitment*. 2. kindred in which extension to *patrikin* and *matrikin* is not symmetrical.

kindred, stem the *group* of relatives with changing personnel having definite obligations towards a *genealogical line* of land-holders. (Davenport, W.).

kindred, symmetrical 1. *kindred* with *bisexual recruitment*. 2. kindred in which extension to *patrikin* and *matrikin* is symmetrical.

kineme a unit of *gestural* expression.

kinemics the study of units of *gestural* expression. **kinemic** *a.*

kinesics the science of communicative body motion behaviour. **kinesic** *a.*

kinship the social recognition and expression of *consanguineal* and *affinal relationships*.

kinship, actual actual *consanguineal* and *affinal relationships*.

kinship, artificial see *quasi-kinship*.

kinship, assumed socially-assumed *consanguineal* and *affinal relationships*.

kinship, fictive see *quasi-kinship*.

kinship, genetic *genetic¹* relationship between persons.

kinship, intersecting *kinship* obligations which cross-cut *groups*.

kinship, perpetual *quasi-kinship* in which successor to *office* succeeds to relationship of predecessor.

kinship, physical see *kinship, genetic*.

kinship, putative commonly supposed *consanguineal* and *affinal relationships*.

kinship, ritual *quasi-kinship* established between two persons by *ritual*.

kinship, social see *kinship[1]*.

kinship-centred pertaining to *kinship theory* which explains *kinship* elements by reference to other kinship elements. see also *matrix-centred[2]*.

kleptocracy rule by thieves. **kleptocratic** *a*.

knowledge, sociology of that branch of *sociology* concerned with the study of ideas in their social context.

kurtosis the peakedness of a *frequency curve*. see also *mesokurtosis; leptokurtosis; platykurtosis*.

labour 1. amount of *manpower* employed. 2. reserves of manpower. 3. the workers as a *social class*.

labour, contract *labour* involving migrant workers under *contract*.

labour, direct see *work, direct*.

labour, division of the degree to which the *tasks* of a *social system* are subdivided.

labour, division of, routinized *division of labour* resulting in specialists who use minimum skills.

labour, division of, sexual the allocation by sex of the *tasks* of a *social system*.

labour, division of, social the allocation of the *tasks* of a *social system*.

labour, division of, specialized *division of labour* resulting in the use of experts.

labour, forced *labour* given by workers under compulsion.

labour, free *labour* not given under compulsion.

labour, indirect see *work, indirect*.

labour, migrant *labour* undertaken by workers who migrate temporarily or seasonally for the purpose.

labour, prison *labour* undertaken by prisoners.

labour, target *labour* undertaken to acquire a specific amount of cash income for a specific expenditure.

labour-intensive pertaining to production employing a high ratio of *labour[1]* to *capital*. see also *capital-intensive*.

lag, cultural 1. lag of *immaterial culture* behind *material culture*. 2. lag of one part of a *culture* behind the rest of the culture.

lag, cultural, inverse lag of *material culture* behind *immaterial culture*.

lampadomancy *divination* by inspection of the flame of a lamp. **lampadomantic** *a*.

landlord, squatter a *squatter* who lets huts to others. see also *tenants, squatter*.

landscape, biological that part of the urban-industrial landscape consisting of vegetation conserved or employed.

landscape, cultural all the physical features of an area which have been modified by *culture*.

landscape, humanized see *landscape, cultural*.

landscape, natural all the physical features of an area which have not been modified by *culture*.

landscape, physical see *landscape, natural*.

language, artificial 1. language constructed as a substitute for a natural language. 2. a *formal* or *ideal language*.

language, constructed see *language, artificial*.

language, contact language used by persons with different first languages for intercommunication.

language, culture a language learned by members of other *speech communities* for obtaining access to the *culture* of which it is the vehicle.

language, creolized see *creole.*

language, formal language for the formalization of a particular *theory* or field.

language, formalized see *language, formal.*

language, full a language not restricted in content and use.

language, ideal language constructed to permit the expression of any cognitively meaningful *proposition.*

language, indigenous language which has not been imported into the area where it is found.

language, information a language of *concepts* employed in *indexing.*

language, liturgical a special language used in religious services.

language, minimal (Jespersen) see *pidgin.*

language, pidginized a second language which is a *restricted language* derived from two or more natural languages and which is markedly closer to one of these languages than the others. see also *pidgin; creole.*

language, prestige the language or *dialect* which confers most *prestige* on the user.

language, restricted a language restricted in content and use.

language, ritual a special language used for ritual purposes.

language, sociology of see *sociolinguistics.*

language, superimposed a non-indigenous language imposed on an area as the official language.

language, synthetic see *language, artificial.*

language, vehicular see *language, contact.*

latency, response time between onset of *stimulus* and onset of *response.*

latifundiarism an *agrarian system* of large estates.

law 1. sanctioned *norms.* (Malinowski). 2. norms involving *organized sanctions.* 3. norms involving the force of politically organized *society.* (Radcliffe-Brown). 4. norms applying to issues characterized by the entry of persons not personally involved. (Wilson, G.). 5. norms closely formulated, highly obligatory, with strong *negative sanctions* and involving organized *authority.* (Firth, R.). 6. any *rule* recognized as obligatory by the bulk of the *community.* (Goodhart, A.L.). 7. norms whose violation is followed by *counteraction.* (Bohannan, P. J.). 8. valued norms the violation of which is subject to *sanctions.* (Carlston, K.S.). 9. norms supported by the regularized application of *force.* (Hoebel). 10. a uniformity in nature.

law, adjective *law (jurid.)* concerning legal operations by which legal rights and duties are discovered and enforced.

law, administrative *law (jurid.)* regulating the executive branch of *government* and providing remedies for individuals and *groups* against administrative action.

law, anthropology of 1. the study of *primitive∥law (jurid.)* in its social context. 2. the unrestricted *cross-cultural* study of *law (jurid.)* in its social context. (Pospisil, L.).

law, comparative the comparative study of features of different *legal systems.*

law, constitutional *law (jurid.)* regulating the principal organs of *government* and their interrelationships.

law, customary 1. *law (jurid.)* resulting from judicial or legislative recognition of *custom.* 2. *law (jurid.)* of *stateless societies.*

law, declaratory *written law* which declares the existence of *law (jurid.)* which was previously unwritten.

law, enacted *law (jurid.)* made by the legislative and executive organs of *government.*

law, Engel's *hypothesis* that as *family* income increases, the percentage of income spent on necessities decreases.

law, esoteric secret *law(jurid.)* knowledge of which is restricted to certain persons. (Poirier, J.).

law, incipient practices so important to functioning *institutions* as to make eventual legal recognition highly probable.

law, personal *law (jurid.)* of a particular *social stratum* or *ethnic group* within a *society.* see also *law, territorial.*

law, private *law (jurid.)* defining the rights and duties of individuals inter se and the operations for their enforcement.

law, procedural see *law, adjective.*

law, public 1. field embracing *constitutional law, administrative law,* and criminal law. 2. study of all legal phenomena connected with *politics* and *government.*

law, sociology of the study of *law (jurid.)* in its social context.

law, statistical a uniformity in nature which is probabilistic.

law, statute *law (jurid.)* made by the legislature.

law, substantive *law (jurid.)* defining legal rights and duties.

law, sumptuary *law (jurid.)* governing the consumption patterns of the various *social strata* of a *society.*

law, territorial *law (jurid.)* which applies to all persons in a particular *territory.* see also *law, personal.*

law, unwritten *law (jurid.)* which is not constituted by a written declaration.

law, written *law (jurid.)* which is constituted by a written declaration.

law-ways rules of law created by *courts.* (Sumner). see also *state-ways.*

leader 1. person initiating *interaction* with other members of *group.* 2. person directing or controlling others in pursuit of *group goal.* 3. person who initiates interaction more frequently than anyone else in group. 4. person who moves group towards group goal. 5. person whose contribution to group *effectiveness* is mediated through direct efforts of others. 6. see *sociocentre.*

leader, nominal an individual who is *leader* in name only.

leader, positional one who leads as a result of his *offices.*

leader, specialist one who leads as a result of having specialized knowledge relevant to the *group goal.*

leader, status one who leads as a result of his *general status.*

leadership, distributed leadership the various *functions* of which are allocated to different persons.

leadership, formal leadership involving *de jure authority.*

leadership, informal leadership lacking *de jure authority.*

learning the acquisition of dispositions.

learning, accretion the acquisition of unrelated *responses* or facts by repeated association.

learning, avoidance *learning* what to do or what not to do in order to avoid an unpleasant event.

learning, avoidance, active *learning* what to do in order to avoid an unpleasant event.

learning, avoidance, passive *learning* what not to do in order to avoid an unpleasant event.

learning, blind see *learning, rote.*

learning, goal-path *learning* to reach the same *goal* by more effective means.

learning, group 1. *learning* by individual involving *social facilitation.* 2. *learning* by interacting *group* members resulting in a group product.

learning, incidental *learning* which is unintentional.

learning, meaningful *learning* involving the ability to recall the meaning of the

learning, mechanical see *learning, rote.*

learning, operant see *conditioning, operant.*

learning, passive see *learning, incidental.*

learning, rote memorizing a *set[1]* of *symbols* in the form presented without any concern for meaning or for understanding of relationships.

learning, social *learning* based on *social reinforcement.*

learning, subliminal *learning* involving *subliminal perception.*

learning, substance see *learning, meaningful.*

lecanomancy *divination* by inspection of water in a basin. **lecanomantic** *a.*

leech a *primitive* healer who treats illnesses which are not attributed by the *community* to *witches* or *sorcerers.*(Reynolds, B.).

legend 1. a *tradition,* unsupported by evidence, about a historical person or place. 2. a fictitious accretion to a historical event or the life of a historical person.

legend, local a *legend* explaining a local geographical or social feature.

legislation 1. see *law, statute.* 2. *law* made by legislative or executive organs of *government.* 3. law-making as distinct from declaring existing law. 4. making law whether domestic or international.

legislation, administrative *legislation* produced by public administrative agencies.

legislation, delegated *legislation* resulting from *delegation.*

legislation, direct *legislation* resulting from *initiative, referendum,* or *plebiscite.*

legislation, subordinate see *legislation, delegated.*

legislation, sumptuary *legislation* governing the consumption patterns of the various *social strata* of a *society.*

legislation, supreme *legislation* not resulting from *delegation.*

legitimacy 1. general acceptance of the *political system* as the most appropriate one for the *society.* 2. a political system's capacity to engender and maintain the belief that existing *political institutions* are the most appropriate ones for the society. (Lipset, S.M.). **legitimate** *a.* **legitimize** *v.* see also *legitimation; legitimization.*

legitimation establishment of *legitimacy.*

legitimization the process by which *legitimacy* is established.

leisure 1. see *time, residual.* 2. see *time, free.* 3. see *time, discretionary.*

leisure, commercialized *leisure‖activities* organized by others for profit.

leisure, conspicuous *leisure* indulged in for *prestige.* (Veblen, T.).

leisure, mass standardized *leisure‖activities* pursued on a large scale.

leptokurtic having peakedness greater than that of the normal curve. **leptokurtosis** *n.* see also *mesokurtic; platykurtic.*

level, genotypic a person's behavioural dispositions as distinguished from his actual behaviour type in a given situation. see also *level, phenotypic.*

level, latent see *level, genotypic.*

level, manifest see *level, phenotypic.*

level, occupational the relative degree of *skill* demanded by an *occupation.*

level, organizational a hierarchical level in an *organization.*

level, phenotypic a person's actual behaviour in a given situation as distinguished from his behavioural dispositions. see also *level, genotypic.*

level, scalar see *level, organizational.*

level, subsistence 1. level of nutrition below which life is impossible. 2. level of remuneration necessary to sustain family life at the degree of comfort expected in a particular *occupational stratum.*

levirate custom whereby a man must marry his brother's widow. **leviratic** *a.*

levirate, anticipatory the right of a man to sexual intercourse with his brother's wife in anticipation of a *leviratic marriage* with her.

levirate, junior custom whereby a man must marry his elder brother's widow.

levirate, prescribed the prescription in a *society* of *leviratic marriage*.

lexeme a lexical unit whose meaning cannot be inferred from anything else in the language. **lexematic** *a*.

libation ceremonial pouring out of a liquid.

liberalization the degree to which *competitive politics* is present. (Dahl, R.A.).

life, expecation of see *expectancy, life*.

life, social the functioning of the *social structure*. (Radcliffe-Brown).

life-chance probability of a person of specified *status* achieving a specified *goal* or suffering a specified disadvantage.

line 1. see *organization, line*. 2. those persons having a common *ancestor* placed one under the other in order of birth.

line, ascending all *ego's ascendants³* or ascendants through one sex.

line, career see *pattern, career²*.

line, collateral an independent *line²* branching off from a given *line²* at a common *ancestor*.

line, descending all *ego's* descendants or descendants through one sex.

line, direct those persons who are descended one from the other.

line, genealogical see *line²*.

line, isometric see *isoline*.

line, poverty point below which, income of *family* is insufficient for adequate diet, necessary clothing, fuel and light, and necessary *household* and personal sundries.

line, uterine see *matriline*.

lineage a *consanguineal kin group* based on *unilineal descent* and with traced descent from a common *ancestor*.

lineage, accessory see *lineage, attached*.

lineage, agnatic see *patrilineage*.

lineage, attached a *lineage* which is part of a larger lineage with which it has a fictive genealogical relationship.

lineage, client *attached lineage* possessing a client status.

lineage, dispersed *lineage* the members of which are interspersed with members of other lineages.

lineage, localized *lineage* the members of which are not interspersed with members of other lineages.

lineage, minimal *lineage* which is an operational unit.

lineage, multilocal see *lineage, dispersed*.

lineage, nuclear those *lineage* members who live close together under *authority* of senior male.

lineage, unilocal see *lineage, localized*.

lineage-mates fellow-members of a *lineage*.

lineals relatives related as *ascendant³* and descendant.

linguistics, anthropological the study of unwritten languages in their cultural contexts.

linguistics, area branch of linguistics concerned with the *areal distribution* of linguistic phenomena.

linguistics, geographical see *linguistics, area*.

linguistics, psychological see *psycholinguistics*.

list, source see *frame. sampling*.

listing an entry in a list used for selecting *sampling units*.

listings, duplicate *listings* that represent same *population element*.

listings, empty *listings* containing no elements of *target population*.

litholatry the *worship* of stones. **litholatric** *a*.

lithomancy *divination* by means of stones. **lithomantic** *a*.

lobbying attempting to directly influence governmental decision-makers.

lobbying, administrative see *lobbying, executive-branch*.

lobbying, executive-branch attempting to directly influence executive-branch decision-makers.

lobbying, legislative-branch attempting to directly influence legislative-branch decision-makers.

localism 1. a local linguistic peculiarity. 2. a local *cultural* peculiarity. 3. intense *sentiment* and loyalty towards one's local *community*.

localism, family-home a pattern of *social participation* which is limited to *interaction* with *neighbours, kin,* and friends. (Wilensky, H.L.).

locomotion, group movement of *group* towards its *goal.*

look, fatal a glance killing instantly.

loss, cultural loss by a *culture* of culture traits.

ludic pertaining to *play.*

machine, political a *party||organization* geared with the highest *efficiency* to securing votes. see also *politics, machine.*

machine, voting machine for the casting and automatic *tabulation* of votes.

macro-analysis analysis of social phenomena in terms of society-wide aggregates. see also *micro-analysis.*

macro-change change occurring to society-wide aggregates.

macrodemography *demography* involving *macro-analysis.* see also *microdemography.*

macrodiacritic (of an *ethnic group*) 80 per cent or more recognizable. see also *visibility; mesodiacritic; microdiacritic; pandiacritic.*

macrodynamics analysis of change occurring to the whole. see also *microdynamics.*

macroethnology large-scale *cross-cultural* research. see also *microethnology.*

macroexplanation accounting for the micro-properties of thing by reference to its macro-properties. (Harré, R.). see also *microexplanation.*

macro-functionalism the *functional analysis* of large-scale *social systems.* (Martindale, D.). see also *micro-functionalism.*

macrolinguistics the whole field concerned with language. **macrolinguistic** *a.* see also *microlinguistics; exolinguistics.*

macro-politics *political science* involving *macro-analysis.* see also *micropolitics.*

macrosociology *sociology* involving *macro-analysis.* see also *microsociology.*

macro-theory see *theory, wide-range.*

macro-time periods so long as to invalidate a given social structural schema. see also *micro-time.*

magic 1. techniques for influencing the supernatural automatically. 2. techniques for controlling nature by the commanding power of *spell.* (Frazer). 3. techniques for controlling nature by spell and *rite* for a definite practical end. (Malinowski). 4. application of *religion* to human affairs. (Piddington). **magical** *a.* see also *religion.*

magic, active *magic* to accomplish something.

magic, aversive *popular magic* for averting trouble.

magic, black *magic* socially-disapproved of in a particular *community.*

magic, contagious *magic* based on assumption that things that have been in contact continue to exert an influence on each other after separation.

magic, defensive *magic* for protection from, or destruction of, evil influences.

magic, destructive *magic* intended to have a destructive function.

magic effigy *magic* using an effigy as if it were the object of the magic.

magic, exuvial *magic* employing exuviae, i.e., bodily products, of intended *victim*[2].

121

magic, homeopathic see *magic, imitative*.

magic, imitative *magic* based on assumption that things that resemble each other can influence each other.

magic, menstrual *magic* to avert the dangers of menstruation.

magic, mimetic see *magic, imitative*.

magic, mortuary *magic* performed for the benefit of a dead person or persons.

magic, negative *magic* involving prohibitions.

magic, passive *magic* to avoid something.

magic, popular *magic* performed collectively by the *group* it is intended to benefit.

magic, positive *magic* involving prescriptions.

magic, private *magic* performed for the benefit of an individual.

magic, productive *magic* intended to have a productive function.

magic, protective *magic* intended to have a protective function.

magic, public *magic* performed for the benefit of the *community*.

magic, repetitive *magic* involving the attempt to initiate what is thought to be the sequence of events which lead to a certain event.

magic, sympathetic see *magic, imitative*.

magic, white *magic* socially-approved of in a particular *community*.

magico-mimetic pertaining to *miming* having a *magical* aim.

magico-religious possessing a *magical* or *religious* character or both.

majority, absolute a number of votes constituting more than half the number cast.

majority, overall see *majority, absolute*.

majority, simple less than half the number of votes cast but more than the minimum required to win in a situation where there are three or more candidates or choices.

malfunction socially-disapproved social consequences of social or cultural item. (Gillin, J.P.). **malfunctional** *a*.

malnutrition vitamin or mineral deficiency. see also *undernutrition*.

mana an impersonal spiritual force,'spiritual electricity'. see also *animatism*; *animism*.

management 1. *administration* of an *economic organization*[2]. 2. the creative element in administration. 3. controlling a *system* towards specified *goals*. 4. a body of knowledge concerning *management*[1,2,3]. 5. all those identified with the employers in an *organization*. 6. all those in an organization exercising managerial *functions*. 7. all those concerned with organizational *policy*.

management, administrative *management*||*functions* of *planning* and organizing.

management, comparative the comparative study of *management*.

management, conflict controlling *social conflict* so as to maximize its beneficial effects. (Boulding, K.E.).

management, executive *management*||*functions* of *directing* and controlling.

management, first-line the lowest level of *management*.

management, middle the stratum of *management* between *first-line management* and *top management*.

management, paternalistic *management* characterized by *paternalism*.

management, scientific the application of *scientific method* to *management*.

management, span of see *control, span of*.

management, systems *management* based on *systems analysis*.

management, top the highest stratum of *management*.

manaism see *animatism*.

mandate instruction from the electorate to their representatives to do certain things.

manifesto 1. published statement of the political beliefs and aims of a *social* *movement* or *party*. 2. see *platform*.

manipulation 1. controlling the *actions* of others without making explicit the desired actions. see also *domination¹*. 2. see *manipulation, experimental*.

manipulation, experimental changing the *value⁶* of an *independent variable* to discover whether there is a resulting change in the *dependent variable*.

manism 1. *worship* of the *spirits* of the dead. 2. *ghost* worship. 3. the view that *religion* emerged from *ancestor worship* and ghost worship. (Spencer, H.).

manners institutionalized behaviours for the expression of courtesy. (Mead, G. H.).

manor large estate, completely or nearly self-sufficient, a substantial part of which is cultivated for the benefit of its master by *peasants* rewarded with strips of land. **manorial** *a*.

manorialism see *system, manorial*.

manpower *working force* plus the *potential working force*.

mantic 1. pertaining to *divination*. 2. having the power of divination.

map, base map on which additional information is added for a particular purpose.

map, cadastral a map showing land ownership.

map, diagram a *base map* with superimposed graph or diagram.

map, dot see *map, spot*.

map, flow map using arrows, width representing size, to show *migration currents* or other flows.

map, graded see *cartogram*.

map, multiple-dot *spot map* on which the number of items is indicated by the number of dots.

map, nosographical see *map, nosological*.

map, nosological map showing distribution of diseases.

map, qualitative a map showing location and kind but not *value⁶* of phenomena.

map, quantitative a map showing not only location and kind but also *value⁶* of phenomena.

map, single-dot *spot map* on which the number of items is indicated by the size of the dot.

map, spot map showing *spatial distribution* of social phenomenon by means of dots, each dot representing a stated number of items.

map, spot, analytical *spot map* showing *spatial distribution* of two or more social phenomena and thus revealing any spatial coincidence of the phenomena.

map, statistical see *cartogram*.

map, thematic a map restricted to presenting the *spatial distribution* of a particular type of physical, social or economic phenomena.

margaritomancy *divination* from the position of pearls thrown on a flat surface. **margaritomantic** *a*.

marginality the state of sharing two *cultures* or *subcultures* and neither giving loyalty to either nor being fully accepted by the personnel of either. **marginal** *a*.

marginality, internal the characteristic possessed by a *culture* of being backward within a culturally advanced area.

marginality, psychological the subjective aspect of *marginality*.

market, peripheral a market in which factors of production are not transacted. (Bohannan, P.).

market, sectional a market in which the *communities* involved act as sections, each community contributing a particular type of commodity. (Wolf, E.R.).

marriage 1. union between a man and a woman such that children born to the woman are legitimate offspring of both. 2. union between a man and a woman establishing *inheritance* rights of the children. 3. union between a man and a woman leading a common life for establishment of a *family*.

marriage, adoptive *marriage* involving husband's *adoption* into wife's *family*, to which his children belong.

marriage, affinal see *marriage, continuation*.

marriage, broken 1. *marriage* not legally dissolved but with judicial or de facto separation. 2. marriage either legally dissolved, annulled, or with judicial or de facto separation.

marriage, child *marriage* in which one spouse is child, baby-husband being cared for by wife who becomes mother by authorized lover, baby-wife being cared for my husband until puberty.

marriage, companionship *marriage* based not on prescription, preference, parental choice or political, *status,* or economic considerations, but on the mutual attraction of the partners.

marriage, consanguineal *marriage* between close *consanguines*.

marriage, continuation a *marriage* between *affines* in which a dead spouse is replaced.

marriage, cross-cousin *marriage* of a man with a *cross-cousin*.

marriage, cross-cousin, bilateral 1. prescribed *marriage* of a man with a *bilateral cross-cousin*. 2. *ego* has choice of marriage to mother's brother's daughter or father's sister's daughter.

marriage, cross-cousin, double *cross-cousin marriage* in which mother's brother's daughter is also father's sister's daughter.

marriage, cross-cousin, duolateral *marriage* permitted with either *cross-cousin* but proscribed with a *parallel-cousin*.

marriage, cross-cousin, matrilateral *marriage* of a man with his mother's brother's daughter.

marriage, cross-cousin, patrilateral *marriage* of a man with his father's sister's daughter.

marriage, cross-cousin, unilateral prescribed *marriage* of a man with a *cross-cousin,* the side·being prescribed.

marriage, dissolved *marriage* legally dissolved.

marriage, dysgenic *marriage* likely to produce defective offspring.

marriage, fictive a sham *marriage* performed like a real marriage.

marriage, first 1. the first *marriage* contracted by a person. 2. marriage of bachelor to spinster.

marriage, full-sibling *marriage* between *full-siblings*.

marriage, ghost *fictive marriage* of a woman to a dead person.

marriage, group *marriage* of two or more men to two or more women.

marriage, group, fraternal *group marriage* in which the husbands are brothers.

marriage, half-sibling *marriage* between *half-siblings*.

marriage, kin *marriage* between *consanguineal relatives*.

marriage, left-hand see *marriage, morganatic*.

marriage, leviratic *marriage* of woman to dead husband's brother.

marriage, morganatic *marriage* with woman of lower *status* in which wife and offspring are debarred from husband's *rank* and *inheritance*.

marriage, pair *marriage* in which spouses have equal *status*.

marriage, parallel-cousin *marriage* of a man with a *parallel-cousin*.

marriage, parallel-cousin, matrilateral *marriage* of a man with his mother's sister's daughter.

marriage, parallel-cousin, patrilateral *marriage* of a man with his father's brother's daughter.

marriage, primary a person's first *marriage*.

124

marriage, ritual see *marriage, fictive*.

marriage, secondary a *marriage* which is not the first that a person contracts.

marriage, sequential see *polygamy, serial*.

marriage, service *marriage* involving *bride-service*.

marriage, sibling *marriage* between *siblings*.

marriage, sororatic *marriage* of man to dead wife's sister.

marriage, substitution see *marriage, continuation*.

marriage, term *marriage* entered into for a specified period.

marriage, tree a *fictive marriage* of a man or woman to a tree.

marriage, trial 1. a *marriage,* easily dissolved, intended to determine the compatibility of the couple. 2. cohabitation intended to determine the couple's *fecundity*.

marriage rate, crude 1. number of *marriages* per specified number of persons over a specified period of time. 2. number of persons marrying per specified number of persons over a specified period of time.

marriage rate, specific marriage rate calculated for a homogeneous *subpopulation*.

marriage rate, standardized marriage rate permitting comparability of *populations*.

mass 1. noncontiguous *collectivity*. 2. noncontiguous, leaderless, heterogeneous collectivity without inter-member *communication* or *interaction*. (Blumer, H.). 3. see *non-elite*. 4. a class of persons having the lowest index in their branch of activity.

mass, polarized a *mass* characterized by roughly simultaneous attention to some *stimulus object* or event.

massification the process by which a *mass society* is formed.

massness the societal characteristics of *mass behaviour* and *mass culture*.

matching in an *experiment,* equalizing initial groups to enable the accurate *measurement* of the effects of the *experimental stimulus*.

matching, frequency in an *experiment,* equalizing initial groups by ensuring the approximately equal distribution of the relevant *variables* in each of the groups.

matching, precision in an *experiment,* equalizing initial groups by pairing each element in one group with its exact match (in terms of relevant *variables*) in the other group or groups.

mater social mother. see also *genetrix*.

materialism, cultural the doctrine of the prepotence of economic *factors* in the determination of *culture*. see also *idealism, cultural²*.

maternity, age-specific frequency of births per woman in a specified *age-grouping*.

maternity rate frequency of births per woman.

mating, assortative mating in which the mate selection pattern in respect to a given characteristic differs from the frequency pattern that would have been obtained by random selection.

mating, random mating based on random selection.

mating, selective see *mating, assortative*.

matriarchate see *matriarchy*.

matriarchy 1. rule by women. 2. a combination of *matrilineal descent, matrilocal residence,* and *matripotestality*.

matricentric centred on the mother.

matriclan 1. *clan¹* based on *matrilineal descent*. 2. *clan³* based on matrilineal descent and *matrilocal residence*. (Murdock).

matri-cross-cousin see *cross-cousin, matrilateral*.

matri-deme *deme* with *matrilocal residence*. (Murdock).

matri-descent see *descent, matrilineal*.

matridominant characterized by the mother having dominance.

matri-family see *family, extended, matrilocal.*

matrifiliation the tie between mother and child. **matrifilial** *a.*

matrifocality lack, in the *family,* of a regularly present male in the role of husband-father. **matrifocal** *a.* see also *patrifocality.*

matrikin relatives related through females.

matrilateral on the mother's side. **matrilaterality** *n.*

matriline *line²* traced upwards by female links through mother.

matrilineage *lineage* based on *matrilineal descent.*

matrilineal 1. pertaining to *matriline.* 2. having an emphasis on *matrilineal descent, matrilineal inheritance* and *matrilineal succession.*

matrilineality see *descent, matrilineal.*

matrilinear see *matrilineal.*

matriliny see *descent, matrilineal.*

matrilocality 1. see *residence, matrilocal.* 2. area of residence of a person's *matrilateral‖kin.* (Velsen).

matri-moiety *moiety* based on *matrilineal descent.*

matrinominal see *matronymic¹.*

matri-parallel-cousin see *parallel-cousin, matrilateral.*

matripotestal with *domestic authority* concentrated in the mother.

matrisib *sib* based on *matrilineal descent.*

matrix a rectangular arrangement of numbers.

matrix, activity *matrix* showing the participation or nonparticipation of each *group* member in each of a number of *activities,* the rows and columns being arranged to reveal *subgroups.*

matrix, communication all the languages and varieties of a *language community.*

matrix, correlation *matrix* of the intercorrelations of a *set¹* of *variables.*

matrix, data *matrix* of *m* rows for the units to be explored and *n* columns for the *variables* used to explore them. (Galtung, J.).

matrix, decision *matrix* showing the outcomes of the alternative courses of action under various states of nature.

matrix, interaction *matrix* showing number of initiations of *interaction* of each *group* member to each of the other members and to the group as a whole.

matrix, payoff *matrix* showing the *payoffs* of the alternative courses of action under various states of nature.

matrix, response *matrix* showing *responses* of *subjects¹* to items and *item¹‖ categories.*

matrix, sociometric see *sociomatrix.*

matrix-centred 1. pertaining to *theory* which explains a systemic element by reference to elements of other *systems.* 2. pertaining to *kinship theory* which explains *kinship* elements by reference to economic, political, or *magico-religious* elements.

matronymic 1. pertaining to *inheritance* of the mother's name. 2. name inherited from one's mother or maternal *ancestor.*

matronymy *inheritance* of the mother's name.

maturation organismal growth and differentiation.

maximax choosing alternative which maximizes the maximum gain.

maximin choosing alternative which maximizes the minimum gain.

mean, arithmetic (mean) sum of items divided by number of items.

mean, assumed a point assumed to be the *mean* for the purpose of computing the mean.

mean, geometric *n*th root of product of *n* items.

mean, guessed see *mean, assumed.*

mean, harmonic reciprocal of *arithmetic mean* of reciprocals of items.

mean, quadratic square root of *mean* of the squares of the items.

mean, working see *mean, assumed.*

meaning, act the *explanation* given by an individual for his own *action.*

meaning, action the *explanation* given by a scientist for the *action* of another person.

meaning, connotative see *connotation.*

meaning, denotative see *denotation.*

measure a measuring instrument or observational *technique.*

measure, nonreactive an observational *technique* in which *subjects[1]* are not aware of being observed.

measure, unobtrusive research *technique* employable without awareness of *subjects[1].* (Webb, E.J.).

measurement 1. assignment of numbers to observations which permits analysis by manipulation. 2. a number assigned to an observation.

measurement, derived *measurement* which is not in terms of itself. see also *measurement, fundamental.*

measurement, fundamental *measurement* which is in terms of itself, e.g., length measured in terms of length.

measurement, qualitative *measurement* below the level of the *ratio scale* and *interval scale.*

measurement, quantitative *measurement* at the level of the *ratio scale* and *interval scale.*

measurement, social the *measurement* of social phenomena.

mechanism arrangement of parts which always produces same effect.

mechanization substitution of mechanical effort for human effort. see also *automation.*

media, basic *communication media* implying the *copresence* of *communicator* and *communicand.* (Doob, L.W.).

media, communication the various technological means of *communication.*

media, electronic *mass media* involving *communication* by electronic means.

media, extending *communication media* which imply that *communicator* and *communicand* are at a distance. (Doob, L.W.).

media, mass *communication media* used for *communication* with a *mass audience.*

median *value[6]* of middle item when items arranged according to size.

mediation method of dispute settlement in which the parties to a dispute appeal to a third party who participates in the discussions but whose proposals they are free to reject. **mediatory** *a.* **mediate** *vi.* see also *arbitration; conciliation.*

mediator a person or *group* engaged in mediating.

medicolegal involving both medical and legal *factors.*

mediopolis a medium-sized city. (Leiffer, M.H.).

mediumship, spirit the use by a *spirit* of a possessed human body for communication with other humans. see also *possession, spirit.*

megalopolis *urbanized region* consisting of several *metropolitan areas.* (Gottmann, J.).

membership, multiple-group individual is member of a number of *groups.*

menarche the first appearance of menstruation.

menstruation, male the practice of cutting the penile urethra to induce a flow of blood.

mentifact any ideational product of *society.* see also *artifact; agrofact; socifact.*

merging ignoring collaterality; grouping *lineals* and *collaterals* or relatives of different degrees under a single *classificatory term.*

mesh, urban the geometrical pattern of the interrelations of urban centres. (Smailes, A.E.).

mesodiacritic (of an *ethnic group*) 30-80 per cent recognizable. see also *visibility*; *macrodiacritic*; *microdiacritic*; *pandiacritic*.

mesokurtic having the peakedness of the normal curve. **mesokurtosis** *n*. see also *leptokurtic*; *platykurtic*.

mesomorphy 1. one of the three primary components in physique concerned with the degree of development of the somatic structures. 2. the predominance of this component. (Sheldon, W.H.). **mesomorphic** *a*. **mesomorph** *pers n*. see also *endomorphy*; *ectomorphy*; *somatotype*.

message transmitted series of *symbols* intended to convey information.

message, disembodied *message* which continues to exist after individual has stopped informing. (Goffman, E.).

message, embodied *message* which only exists while individual is informing. (Goffman, E.).

message, metacommunicative any *message* as to the *rules* governing the interpretation or flow of messages.

message, primary a *message* which moves through a *system* as a result of the system's interaction with the outside world.

message, secondary a *message* about a *primary message*.

message, socializing a *message,* intentional or unintentional, transmitted to an individual which has a high probability of producing a socializing effect. see also *socialization*.

metaanthropology philosophy of science in so far as it concerns *anthropology*.

metacommunication *communication* about communication.

meta-goal the *goal* towards which a particular goal is a means.

metahistory the philosophy of history.

metalanguage language which is used to refer to language.

metalepsis the spontaneous assignment of new meaning to a *culture trait*.

metalinguistics 1. see *exolinguistics*. 2. the science of *metalanguage*. **metalinguistic** *a*.

metapolicy the study of *policies* in order to improve *policy formation*.

metapolitics the philosophy of *political science*.

metapsychology the *philosophy of science* in so far as it concerns *psychology*.

metascience see *science, philosophy of*.

metasociology *philosophy of science* in so far as it concerns *sociology*.

meta-system see *supra-system*.

metataxis the spontaneous re-evaluation of a *culture trait*.

metataxonomy the *theory* of *taxonomies*.

meta-theory *philosophy of science* in so far as it concerns *substantive theory*.

methectics see *dynamics, group*.

method 1. type of reasoning used in investigation and verification. 2. see *technique, mid-range*. 3. prescribed way of carrying out step in *procedure*.

method, case 1. method which seeks *nomothetic* findings from the intensive study of particular cases. 2. diagnostic and remedial *procedure* based on the intensive study of the individual.

method, clinical the *case method²* employed in medical and psychiatric research.

method, comparative the comparison of matched *societies* and *institutions* for the discovery of *associations⁵* and *correlations*.

method, deductive *method* of inferring from general to particular.

method, genealogical ethnographic *method* according to which research is based on the construction of *genealogies³*.

method, householder completion of *census schedule* by household head.

method, inductive *method* of inferring from particular to general.

method, proband-sibship determining whether there is a hereditary *factor* in a clinical trait by observing whether the trait occurs more frequently amongst the *consanguineal relatives* of a *sample* of *probands* than in the general *pop-*

ulation.

method, prosopographic historical *method* of studying change by compiling the biographies of numerous individuals.

method, scientific the logic of scientific investigation.

method, survey *method* of social investigation involving the *survey.*

method, twin method of discovering hereditary element in various conditions by comparing *correlation* between pairs of fraternal (heterozygotic, binovular) twins (dissimilar inheritance) with pairs of identical (homozygotic, uniovular) twins (similar inheritance) brought up together, or by comparing correlation between identical twins brought up together with identical twins brought up apart.

methodology 1. the logic of scientific investigation. 2. the study of research *procedures* and *techniques.* 3. a *system* of research procedures and techniques. **methodological** *a.* **methodologist** *pers n.*

metropolis the largest city of an area having economic and social dominance over the area.

metropolis, international a *metropolis* with international influence.

metropolis, interregional a *metropolis* whose dominance spreads over more than one *region.*

metropolis, regional a *metropolis* having dominance over a *region.*

metropolitanism the character of being metropolitan.

metropolitanization 1. the process by which *metropolitan areas* are formed. 2. the high prevalence of metropolitan areas in a *territory.*

metropolitics the *politics* of a *metropolitan area.*

metropolity the *polity* of a *metropolitan area.*

micro-analysis analysis of social phenomena in terms of individual motivation. see also *macro-analysis.*

microculture the *culture* of a small, near-isolated *community.* (Thompson, L.). **microcultural** *a.*

microdemography *demography* involving *micro-analysis.* see also *macro-demography.*

microdiacritic (of an *ethnic group*) less than 30 per cent recognizable. see also *visibility*; *macrodiacritic*; *mesodiacritic*; *pandiacritic.*

microdynamics analysis of change occurring to a segment of the whole. see also *macrodynamics.*

microethnology small-scale *cross-cultural* research. see also *macroethnology.*

microexplanation accounting for the macro-properties of a thing by reference to its micro-properties, i.e., the properties and relationships of its constituent parts. (Harré, R.). see also *macroexplanation.*

micro-functionalism the *functional analysis* of small-scale *social systems.* (Martindale, D.). see also *macro-functionalism.*

microlinguistics the analysis of *language systems.* **microlinguistic** *a.* see also *macrolinguistics*; *exolinguistics.*

micro-politics *political science* involving *micro-analysis.* see also *macro-politics.*

micro-reduction see *microexplanation.*

microsociology *sociology* involving *micro-analysis.* see also *macrosociology.*

microstate a *state* of the lowest category in territorial size. see also *ministate.*

micro-time periods too short to invalidate a given social structural schema. see also *macro-time.*

mid-elite a class of people having an index in their branch of *activity* lower than that of the *elite* but higher than that of the *mass.* (Lasswell, H.D.).

migration 1. permanent movement of persons over a significant distance. 2. permanent movement of persons over at least one county line. (USBC). 3. assumption of new *transhumance* orbits by a sudden movement. 4. joining or leaving a *population* or *sub-population*. *(genet.)*. **migrant** *pers n.*

migration, alternating daily movement of persons out of and back to residential areas.

migration, balance of see *migration, net.*

migration, chain *migration* in which each *migrant* pulls in another migrant.

migration, collective *migration* in groups of *families* or individuals. (MDD).

migration, conservative *migration* in which the purpose of the activating agent is to prevent change. (Petersen). see also *migration, innovating.*

migration, controlled *migration* which is controlled by the authorities.

migration, crop movement of the cultivation of a crop through its transportation to other areas.

migration, differential see *migration, selective.*

migration, economic *migration* which is mainly the result of economic *factors*. (ILO).

migration, epiphenomenal *migration* resulting from dependency or from circumstances not economic or social.

migration, external *migration* across the boundaries of a particular area.

migration, family *migration* in which *families* move as units.

migration, forced 1. *migration* which is not free, i.e., involving *coercion*, social pattern or forcible removal. 2. migration involving forcible removal of persons.

migration, free *migration* not involving *coercion*, forcible removal, or social pattern. (Petersen).

migration, gross total amount of *emigration* and *immigration.*

migration, group (Petersen) see *migration, collective.*

migration, impelled *migration* involving *coercion*. (Petersen).

migration, incomplete *migration* in which the *migrants*, through unacceptability as *immigrants*, remain in displaced persons' camps.

migration, individual *migration* in which *migrants* do not travel in *groups*. (MDD).

migration, innovating *migration* in which the purpose of the activating agent is to produce change. (Petersen). see also *migration, conservative.*

migration, interlocal *migration* from one locality to another.

migration, intermetropolitan *migration* from one *metropolis* or *metropolitan area* to another.

migration, internal *migration* from one part of a country to another.

migration, international *migration* from one country to another.

migration, interregional *migration* from one *region* to another.

migration, interrural *migration* from one *rural* locality to another.

migration, interurban *migration* between *urbanized areas* separated by *rural areas.*

migration, intralocal *migration* within a locality.

migration, intraregional *migration* within a given *region.*

migration, intrarural *migration* within a *rural* locality.

migration, intraurban *migration* within an *urbanized area.*

migration, involuntary *migration* involving *coercion* or forcible removal.

migration, mass 1. *migration* involving very large numbers. (MDD). 2. migration involving very large numbers and established as a social pattern. (Petersen).

migration, net difference between *emigration* and *immigration.*

migration, oscillatory *migration* in which the *migrant* returns periodically to his place of abode.

migration, planned *migration* resulting from *planning* on the part of an *organization*. see also *immigration, planned*; *emigration, planned.*

migration, political *migration* which is mainly the result of political *factors.*

(ILO).

migration, primary *mass migration* to an uninhabited area.

migration, primitive *migration* resulting from an ecological push.

migration, resultant *migration* resulting from economic or social circumstances.

migration, return see *re-migration*.

migration, reverse *re-migration* of rural-urban migrants.

migration, rural-urban *migration* from the country to the town.

migration, rural-urban, net the excess of *in-migration* to the towns over *out-migration* to the country.

migration, seasonal seasonal movements on the part of an individual, a *collectivity*, or a whole people.

migration, secondary *mass migration* to an area with an indigenous *population*.

migration, selective *migration* which occurs to *population strata* disproportionately.

migration, simulated model-derived *migration*. see also *model*; *simulation*.

migration, social see *mobility, social, vertical*.

migration, transilient *migration* involving high propensity of *migrant* to move backwards and forwards between two or more countries. (Richmond, A.H.).

migration, urban-rural *migration* from the town to the country.

migration, voluntary *migration* not involving *coercion* or forcible removal. (MDD).

milieu 1. immediate *environment*. 2. immediate *social environment* of individual. 3. organism and its immediate *environment*. 4. see *frame, attention*.

militancy tendency to take military action. (Andreski, S.).

militarism 1. see *militancy*. 2. overemphasis on military *ceremonial*. 3. preponderance of the military in the *state*. 4. see *militarization*. 5. see *ideology, militaristic*. 6. the combination of *militancy*, preponderance of the military in the state, *militarization*, and *militaristic ideology*. (Andreski, S.).

militarization extensive political control by the military with the whole *society* subserving military needs. (Andreski, S.).

militocracy see *stratocracy*.

millenarian pertaining to *religious movements* that expect total, imminent, ultimate, this-worldly, collective salvation. (Talmon, Y.).

millenarism the quest for total, imminent, ultimate, this-worldly, collective, religious salvation. (Talmon, Y.).

milling aimless activity in *crowd*.

million-city city with a *population* of a million or over.

mimicry the imitation of one organism by another.

miming imitation of events by means of *actions* or *gestures*.

minimax choosing alternative which minimizes the maximum loss.

ministate a *state* of the second lowest category in territorial size. see also *microstate*.

minority 1. a socially significant *sub-population*. 2. see *group, minority*.

minority, assimilationist a *minority* desiring total assimilation into the dominant group. (Wirth, L.).

minority, ethnic a *minority* which is an *ethnic group*.

minority, linguistic a *minority* whose first language and language of everyday use is different from that of the majority.

minority, militant a *minority* seeking a dominant position. (Wirth, L.).

minority, pluralistic a *minority* desiring peaceful co-existence with the majority and with other minorities. (Wirth, L.).

minority, secessionist a *minority* seeking both cultural and political independence. (Wirth, L.).

miscegenation mating of persons of different *breeding populations*.

mob destructively active *crowd*.

mobiles persons who are socially mobile.

mobiles, downward persons who are downward mobile, i.e., undergoing *downward mobility*.

mobiles, upward persons who are upward mobile, i.e., undergoing *upward mobility*.

mobility, areal change of residence involving horizontal movement.

mobility, caste *vertical mobility* occurring to *caste* as a whole.

mobility, chronic frequent change of residence by an individual.

mobility, class movement up or down the *class hierarchy*.

mobility, collective large-scale *vertical mobility* occurring to persons as members of a *collectivity*.

mobility, contest *upward mobility* not controlled by the *elite*. see also *mobility, sponsored*.

mobility, downward see *mobility, social, downward*.

mobility, family *vertical mobility* of a *family*.

mobility, generational see *mobility, intergenerational*.

mobility, geographical see *mobility, areal*.

mobility, group *vertical mobility* occurring to a *group*.

mobility, habitual see *mobility, chronic*.

mobility, horizontal see *mobility, social, horizontal*.

mobility, individual *vertical mobility* occurring to an individual.

mobility, industrial change in the areal distribution of *industries*.

mobility, intergenerational difference between the *status* of an individual and that of his father.

mobility, intersitus movement of persons from one *situs* to another.

mobility, interstratic *vertical mobility* between *social strata*.

mobility, intragenerational *vertical mobility* of an individual during own lifetime.

mobility, intraoccupational *social mobility* within an *occupation*.

mobility, intrasitus *social mobility* within a *situs*.

mobility, job 1. movement from one *job* to another. 2. average number of jobs in the working life of a specified *category* of workers.

mobility, labour movement of persons between *jobs*, employers, *occupations, industries*, localities or *regions* in which employed, or between employment and unemployment.

mobility, manipulative *upward mobility* achieved by *manipulation*.

mobility, manpower *areal mobility* of *manpower*.

mobility, occupational 1. *vertical mobility* between *occupations*. 2. *horizontal mobility* between occupations. 3. vertical mobility occurring to an occupation as a whole.

mobility, personal see *mobility, individual*.

mobility, physical see *mobility, areal*.

mobility, power movement up or down the *power hierarchy*.

mobility, professional 1. *social mobility* between *professions*. 2. *vertical mobility* occurring to a profession as a whole.

mobility, residential change of residence involving limited horizontal movement. see also *mobility, areal*.

mobility, resource the degree to which resources are transferable to other ends.

mobility, social 1. movement from one *social position* to another. 2. movement of individuals in *social space*. 3. see *mobility, vertical*.

mobility, social, downward movement down the *class, status*, or *power hierarchies*.

mobility, social, horizontal movement from one *situs* to another without change of *stratum*.

mobility, social, upward movement up the *class, status,* or *power hierarchies.*

mobility, social, vertical movement up or down the *class, status,* or *power hierarchies.*

mobility, spatial see *mobility, areal.*

mobility, sponsored *upward mobility* controlled by the *elite.* see also *mobility, contest.*

mobility, status movement up or down the *status hierarchy.*

mobility, territorial see *mobility, areal.*

mobility, upward see *mobility, social, upward.*

mobility, vertical see *mobility, social, vertical.*

mobility, vicinal see *mobility, areal.*

mobilization 1. ratio of actual to possible number of *actions.* 2. relatively rapid increase in a social unit's control of resources. (Etzioni, A.). **mobilize** *v.*

mobilization, net *mobilization* minus the *counter-mobilization* of its opponents.

mode most frequent *value[6]* in series.

mode, computed see *mode, estimated.*

mode, crude midpoint of class interval containing highest frequency.

mode, estimated estimate of *mode* of *population* from which *sample* is drawn.

mode, inspection see *mode, crude.*

model 1. simplified *system* of *variables.* 2. exemplar in *child socialization.* 3. person imitated. see also *imitation.*

model, analogue *model* representing *set[1]* of *system* properties by another *set[1]* of properties.

model, analytical 1. see *model, unconscious.* 2. a *system* of functionally interdependent *variables.*

model, communication a representation of the steps in *communication.* (Shannon, C.E.).

model, conscious a *model* constructed by a people of their own *sociocultural system.*

model, decision *model* of the way an individual or player chooses a course of action.

model, deterministic *model* permitting prediction of entire future of a given *system.*

model, dynamic a *model* in which change is involved. see also *model, static.*

model, emulative a person intended to be emulated.

model, equilibrium a *model* which assumes that its constituent *variables* are in *stable equilibrium.*

model, folk see *model, conscious.*

model, historical a *model* in which the time element is particularly stressed.

model, home-made 1. see *model, conscious.* 2. see *model, immediate.*

model, hydraulic physical *model* consisting of water in tubes in which water flows simulate flows in real-world *system.*

model, iconic *model* which visually represents certain aspects of a *system.*

model, ideological a *subgroup's* believed-in traditional *model* of the wider *sociocultural system.* (Ward, B.).

model, immediate a *subgroup's model* of its own *sociocultural system.* (Ward, B.).

model, mathematical a *model* which is mathematical both in form and content. see also *model, protomathematical.*

model, metaphoric an *iconic model* which is speculative and static. (Hilgard, E.R.).

model, natural *model* consisting of an analogous real-world *system.*

model, normative *model* giving conditions for achieving a stated *objective.*

model, observers' see *model, unconscious.*

model, operating representation of a *system* that reproduces its processes.

model, predictive a *model* the purpose of which is prediction.

model, primary first important exemplar in *child socialization*. see also *model, secondary*.

model, probabilistic *model* which will only determine probabilities of certain future events.

model, protomathematical a *model* which is mathematical in form but not in content. see also *model, mathematical*.

model, role person whom *ego* emulates in one or a few *roles*.

model, scale *model* which, apart from its materials, differs only in scale from the real-world *structure*.

model, secondary exemplar in *child socialization* who is not the first important one. see also *model, primary*.

model, static a *model* in which change is not involved. see also *model, dynamic*.

model, stochastic *model* incorporating elements of randomness.

model, symbolic 1. *model* consisting of *symbols* representing *system* properties. 2. fictitious or dead person acting as exemplar.

model, unconscious a *model* of a *sociocultural system* constructed by observers from outside.

model, urban *model* of *urban* processes.

model, vernacular see *model, conscious*.

model, work practitioner of *occupation* emulated by another.

model, work, primary practitioner of *occupation* emulated by child.

model, work, secondary practitioner of *occupation* emulated by trainee.

moiety 1. one of two divisions of a *community*. 2. one of two exogamous *descent groups* of a community. (Lowie). 3. one of two *unilineal descent groups* of a community. (Linton).

moiety, ceremonial one of two divisions of a *community* divided for ceremonial purposes.

moiety, compound a *moiety* which is segmented into *sibs*.

moiety, descent one of two divisions of a *community* based on *descent*.

moiety, political one of two divisions of a *community* based on political allegiance.

moiety, residence one of two divisions of a *community* based on residence.

moiety, simple a *moiety* which is not segmented into *sibs*.

moko groove chiselled in skin with pigment rubbed in. see also *moxa*; *keloid*; *cicatrice*.

momentum, industrial tendency for an *industry* in a particular area to continue to grow after the conditions giving rise to it have ceased to exist.

monandry *marriage* in which there is one husband.

money anything which can at all times be used as a medium of exchange.

money, bride *money* forming part or whole of a *bride-price*.

money, commodity *money* consisting of things having intrinsic value.

money, milk a small amount of *wealth* which passes at *marriage* from husband's relatives to wife's mother.

money, token *money* consisting of things without intrinsic value.

monism, cultural absence of a plurality of *ethnic groups* in a *society*.

monism, ideological absence of a plurality of *ideologies* in a *society*.

monism, structural absence of a plurality of *social structures* in a *society*.

monitoring human or mechanical inspection of an operation, for detecting variations exceeding permissible limits.

monitoring, continuous *monitoring* involving the continuous inspection of an operation.

monitoring, system *monitoring* carried out by a *system* for detecting variations within the system exceeding permissible limits.

monocracy rule by one person. **monocratic** *a.*

monoculture the cultivation of a single crop in a particular area.

monoethnic pertaining to one *ethnic group.*

monogamy *marriage* of one man to one woman.

monogamy, serial having a succession of spouses on the part of one person, but only one at a time.

mono-hierarchic possessing only one *hierarchy.*

monorchy unilateral castration.

moot informal assembly of neighbours or relatives for settling a dispute. see also *court.*

morale 1. tendency for members of *group* to act together. 2. level of group functioning. 3. degree of participation of group members. 4. attractiveness of group for its members. 5. degree to which individual *needs* are gratified. 6. ability of individual or group to carry on a course of action to completion.

morale, general *morale* which is the property of a *society.*

morale, group *morale* which is a *group* property.

morale, individual ability of individual to carry on a course of action to completion.

morale, situational *group morale* which is situation-dependent.

morale, societal see *morale, general.*

morbidity *incidence* and *prevalence* of illness and *disability* in a *population.*

morbidity, general *morbidity* which is not restricted to a particular type of illness or *disability.*

morbidity, psychiatric *incidence* and *prevalence* of psychiatric illness in a *population.*

morcellation progressive subdivision of land resulting from equal division amongst children.

mores strongly-sanctioned *norms.* (Sumner).

morphogenesis change or elaboration of a *system*'s form, *structure,* or state. **morphogenic** *a.*

morphology, social the physical configuration of *society.* (Durkheim).

morphology, urban the study of the determinants of the physical pattern, both horizontal and vertical, of cities.

morphostasis the maintenance of a *system*'s form, *structure,* or state. **morphostatic** *a.*

mortality 1. frequency and effect of death on a *population.* 2. cumulative loss of elements by a *set[1].*

mortality, case cumulative loss of members of a *sample.*

mortality, cause *mortality* classified by cause of death.

mortality, differential intergroup differences in *mortality.*

mortality, disease *mortality* resulting from disease.

mortality, endogenous natural *mortality* which is not from infectious diseases.

mortality, exogenous *mortality* from infectious diseases.

mortality, experimental *attrition* of *observational units* during the course of an *experiment.*

mortality, foetal *mortality* prior to complete expulsion or extraction of product of conception, irrespective of duration of pregnancy. (WHO).

mortality, infant *mortality* between birth and under one year.

mortality, intra-uterine see *mortality, foetal.*

mortality, maternal *mortality* of women resulting from their pregnancy, labour or *puerperium.*

mortality, neo-natal *mortality* in the first four weeks.

mortality, occupational 1. inter-occupational differences in *mortality rate.* 2. *mortality* from occupational disease.

mortality, panel cumulative loss of members of a *panel.*

mortality, peri-natal *mortality* between time foetus becomes viable and one week after birth.

mortality, post neo-natal *mortality* between four weeks and under one year.

mortality, proportionate ratio of deaths from a certain cause to number of deaths from all causes.

mortality, puerperal see *mortality, maternal.*

mortality, semanatal *mortality* in the first week.

mortality rate *general, specific* or *standardized rate* concerning *mortality.*

mortality rate, infant number of deaths between birth and under one year registered in a given year per 1000 *live births* registered in the same year.

mother-right rights over children are exercised by wife and her *kin.*

mother-sib see *matrisib.*

motivation concerned with *a.* what makes an animal active rather than inactive *b.* what makes one form of activity dominant over others.

motivation, extrinsic *motivation* in which the *task* itself is not rewarding but is a means to a *goal.*

motivation, intrinsic *motivation* in which the *task* itself is rewarding.

move 1. an occasion on which a player can act. (von Neumann).2. selection of an alternative at a choice point in a *game[1].*

movement, agrarian a *social movement* aimed at *agrarian reform.*

movement, cargo see *cult, cargo.*

movement, charismatic a *social movement* led by a *charismatic person.*

movement, contra-acculturative a *social movement* which opposes *acculturation* by reviving *traditions* of group.

movement, mechanical a *population movement* taking the form of *migration.*

movement, millenarian a *social movement* characterized by *millenarism.*

movement, nativistic a *social movement* having a *nativistic* aim.

movement, natural a *population movement* taking the form of births or deaths.

movement, population any change in a *population.*

movement, religious a *social movement* having a *religious* aim.

movement, revitalization a deliberate, organized attempt by some members of a *society* to construct a more satisfying *culture* by rapid acceptance of a pattern of multiple *innovations.* (Wallace, A.F.C.).

movement, revolutionary a *social movement* aimed at bringing about a *revolution.*

movement, social an *informal organization,* which may include formally organized sub-units, of a large number of persons to gain a *social goal.*

movers those who have changed their residence within a single county. (USBC).

moxa scar produced for decorative purposes. see also *keloid; moko; cicatrice.*

multicultural 1. in which more than two *cultures* are represented. 2. pertaining to more than two cultures.

multiculturalism the presence of more than two *cultures* in a *community* or *political unit.*

multifinality the condition of similar initial conditions leading to dissimilar end-states. see also *equifinality.*

multigravida woman whose pregnancy is not her first. **multigravidous** *a.* (MDD).

multilineality see *descent, multilineal.*

multipara woman whose confinement is not her first. **multiparous** *a.***multiparity** *n.* (MDD).

mutualism see *symbiosis[2].*

myth 1. *sacred* story; *charter* for *ritual.* (Malinowski). 2. idea or group of ideas which secures obedience to *leadership.* (Pareto). 3. story which maintains the *status* of an individual or *group.* (Leach). 4. dogma in narrative form.

myth, aetiologic *myth* concerning origin of a particular thing.

myth, creation *myth* describing the creation of the universe or of mankind.

myth, culture a *society*'s *myth* accounting for the origin of its arts and sciences.

myth, emergence a *society*'s *myth* concerning its emergence from the ground or other place.

myth, eponymic *myth* of tribal parentage which identifies tribal name with name of imaginary *ancestor*. (Tylor).

myth, explanatory a *myth* which is purely explanatory.

myth, iterative a *myth* which is recited on ritual occasions.

myth, local *myth* accounting for a place name. (Tylor).

myth, operative a *myth* whose purpose is served by its recitation.

myth, origin a *society*'s *myth* concerning its origin.

myth, rite *myth* concerning origin and proper performance of a *rite*.

myth, speculative a *myth* embodying pre-scientific speculations.

myth, theogonic *myth* describing the origin of a god or gods.

myth, validatory a *myth* establishing the validity of the *social structure*.

mythicize to give a mythical character to.

mythography descriptive study of *myths*. see also *mythology*.

mythoheroic concerned with the deeds of heroes of *myths*.

mythologem a mythic theme.

mythology 1. the science of *myth*. 2. the *set¹* of myths found in a *society*. see also *mythography*.

mythopoeic 1. pertaining to myth-making. 2. giving rise to *myths*.3. preoccupied with mythological matters.

name, auspicious personal name bestowed to establish favourable auspices.

name, commemorative a place name given in honour of someone or something.

name, descriptive personal name descriptive of the person's appearance or character.

name, incident a place name resulting from an incident at the place.

name, possessive place name derived from name of individual or *group* at some time in possession of the place.

name, quasi-personal proper name of an animal, personified object or personified abstraction.

name, temporary personal name, intended to be temporary, bestowed at or shortly after birth.

natality frequency and effect of births on a *population*.

natality, differential intergroup differences in *natality*.

nation 1. a large *territorial group* with common citizenship rights and possessing characteristics differentiating it from other similar *groups*.(Smith, A.D.). 2. independent *political unit*. 3. a *state* which is coterminous with a *society*. (Olsen, M.E.). **national** *a.*

nationalism 1. an ideological movement for attainment and maintenance of self-government of a *group*, some of whose members conceive it to constitute an actual or potential *nation¹*. (Smith, A.D.). 2. doctrine that *nation¹* and *state* should coincide.

nationalism, ethnocentric *nationalism* involving *ethnocentrism*.

nationalism, polycentric *nationalism* not involving *ethnocentrism*.

nativism any conscious, organized effort of a people to revive or perpetuate selected aspects of their *culture*. **nativistic** *a.*

nativism, magical *nativism* employing irrational means. (Linton).

nativism, perpetuative *nativism* aiming at the perpetuation of selected aspects of the *culture*. (Linton).

nativism, rational *nativism* employing rational means. (Linton).

nativism, reformative aggressive or non-aggressive effort of a subordinated *society* to produce for its own use a synthesis of some of its own *cultural* features and those of the dominant society.

nativism, reformative, dynamic aggressive *reformative nativism.*

nativism, reformative, passive non-aggressive *reformative nativism.*

nativism, resistive aggressive or non-aggressive resistance by a subordinated *society* to the *culture* of the dominant society.

nativism, resistive, passive non-aggressive *resistive nativism.*

nativism, revivalistic 1. *nativism* aiming at the revival of selected aspects of the *culture.* (Linton). 2. aggressive *resistive nativism.*

necrolatry *worship* of the dead. **necrolatric** *a.*

necromancy 1. *divination* through communication with the dead. 2. *magic* performed with aid of the dead or *spirits* of the dead. **necromantic** *a.* **necromancer** *pers n.*

necronym a name applied to a person by virtue of his relation to a deceased relative.

necrophagy the eating of exhumed human corpses. **necrophagous** *a* **necrophager** *pers n.*

need 1. organismal deprivation which gives rise to *drive.* 2. inadequacy of provision when compared with a socially-accepted *norm.*

need, acquired *need* which is not *innate.*

need, basic *need* from which other needs are derived.

need, biological *need* which is *innate.*

need, cultural a *need* resulting from *cultural conditioning.*

need, manipulative individual's *need* to manipulate elements of the *environment.* (Hagen, E.E.).

need, primary see *need, biological.*

need, secondary see *need, acquired.*

need, tissue deprivation existing in a tissue.

negativism an *attitude* of not co-operating and conforming.

neglectee 1. individual who receives no sociometric choices. 2. an individual who is neglected.

negotiation discussion between the parties to a dispute, without the intervention of a third party, aimed at settlement of the dispute. see also *mediation*; *arbitration*; *conciliation.*

neighbourhood 1. area supplying necessary services for individual or *group.* 2. a *territorial group* with distinctive social characteristics living in an area with distinctive physical characteristics. 3. self-conscious, face-to-face, *residential group* exercising *social control* over its members.

neighbourhood, delinquent *neighbourhood* possessing very high *crime* and *delinquency rates* and in which *crime* and *delinquency* are socially approved.

neighbourhood, disorganized *neighbourhood* characterized by *social disorganization.*

neighbourhood, market the people who share a complete *market cycle.*(Bohannan, P. & L.).

neighbourhood, occupational immediate surroundings of individual's place of work supplying necessary services.

neighbourhood, open-country *neighbourhood* consisting of dispersed farmsteads.

neighbourhood, planned area designed as a physical unity containing all the public facilities needed by the *families* living there.

neighbourhood, residential immediate surroundings of individual's home supplying necessary services.

neighbourhood, roving area larger than *residential neighbourhood* for intensive cultivation of social reltions.

neighbourhood, stable *neighbourhood* without *social disorganization.*
neighbouring the *activities* of *neighbours* qua neighbours.
neighbourliness, latent the disposition towards neighbourliness in a crisis. (Mann, P.H.).
neighbourliness, manifest the amount of neighbourliness. (Mann, P.H.).
neighbours persons characterized by living in physical proximity and by the absence of ties of *kinship* or friendship who play a *role* based on this *set[1]* of characteristics. see also *neighbourhood*; *neighbouring*; *role, neighbour.*
nemoriculture see *food-gathering.*
neolocality see *residence, neolocal.*
neomancy *divination* from moles on the body. **neomantic** *a.*
neonate a newly-born infant. **neonatal** *a.*
neonatus see *neonate.*
neo-positivism sociological school defending *quantitativism, behaviourism* and *operationalism.*
nephelomancy *divination* by observation of the clouds. **nephelomantic** *a.* **nephelomancer** *pers n.*
nephew-right right of a nephew to inherit from or succeed to his mother's brother.
net, communication see *network, communication.*
network 1. *set[1]* of lines connected together in which shapes and lengths are irrelevant. 2. a *social field* consisting of relations between people. (Barnes, J.A.). 3. persons with whom *ego* interacts and others with whom they interact.
network, all-channel see *network, comcon.*
network, centralized *communication network* in which all or most *communication* is mediated through one person.
network, close-knit *personal network* with high interconnectedness of members.
network, comcon a *communication network* having all links open. see also *network, restricted.*
network, communication *set[1]* of *communication channels* linking individuals, *group* members, or units.
network, criminal a *network* of contacts between criminals.
network, decentralized *communication network* which is not centralized. see also *network, centralized.*
network, decision see *tree, decision.*
network, differentiated a *social network, role performance* in which is independent of role performance in any other. (Cohen, Y.A.).
network, effective that part of *personal network* which consists of persons who know one another. (Epstein, A. L.).
network, extended that part of a *personal network* which consists of persons who do not know one another. (Epstein, A.L.).
network, interpersonal a *network* existing between individuals as distinct from *positions.*
network, loose-knit *personal network* with low interconnectedness of members.
network, market *communication network* the nodes of which are market places.
network, megalopolitan a large group of cities with their connecting urbanized bands. (Matras, J.). see also *megalopolis.*
network, personal see *network[3].*
network, restricted a *communication network* which denies some members of a *group* direct contact with one or more other members. see also *network, comcon.*
network, settlement see *net, settlement.*
network, situational a temporary *personal network* meeting the needs of a particular situation.

network, social see *network, personal.*

network, undifferentiated a *social network, role performance²* in which is dependent on *role performance²* in another. (Cohen, Y.A.).

niche, ecological unique *set¹* of environmental *factors* capable of supporting a given form of life.

nociceptor *receptor* which is aroused by pain *stimuli.* see also *beneceptor.*

no-data tabulating category consisting of *nonresponse* and unclassifiable data.

noise 1. non-*signal* elements in *communication channel.* 2. distortion of *message* in transmission. 3. anything increasing difficulty in comprehension of problem communicated.

nomadism repetitive *migration* on the part of a whole *community.* **nomadic** *a.* **nomads** *pers n.*

nomadism, local *nomadism* involving a relatively small area. (Arbos, P.).

nomadism, pastoral *nomadism* practised by *pastoralists.*

nomadism, regional *nomadism* involving a relatively large area. (Arbos, P.).

nomadism, seasonal see *transhumance.*

nomancy *divination* from the letters in a name. **nomantic** *a.*

nominalism, cultural the doctrine that *culture* is logically but not ontologically distinct from the behaviour of individuals. see also *realism, cultural.*

nomogram see *nomograph.*

nomograph two or more scales arranged so as to permit calculation from relation of points on them.

nomothetic pertaining to the establishment of generalizations. see also *ideographic.*

noncoverage failure to include all units of *target population* in *sampling frame.*

noncoverage, net excess of *noncoverage* over *overcoverage.*

non-elite those persons who are not members of the *elite.*

nonliterate (of a *society* or *culture*) lacking writing. see also *preliterate.*

nonmobiles persons who are not socially mobile.

nonparametric refers to statistical methods which do not assume normality of distribution.

non-registration failure to register *vital statistics.*

non-registration, random *non-registration,* neither systematic nor selective, which occurs randomly as a result of the negligence or circumstances of officials.

non-registration, selective *non-registration* resulting from individual decisions concerning particular cases.

non-registration, systematic deliberate *non-registration* of a whole category of *vital events* in a *population.*

nonresponse tabulating category consisting of failures to respond to a particular item. see also *no-data.*

nonstate see *society, stateless.*

non-valuation see *value-freedom.*

norm 1. social *rule³.* 2. average behaviour of a specified *group.* 3. average performance of a specified *group.* **normative** *a.*

norm, absolute a *norm* possessing general application, general acceptance, and general enforcement. (Morris, R.T.).

norm, age a *norm* governing behaviour in a particular *age-grouping.*

norm, cohesive a *norm* conducive to *societal* or *group* cohesion.

norm, conditional a *norm* possessing limited application, limited acceptance, and limited enforcement. (Morris, R.T.).

norm, covert (Murdock, G.P.) see *norm, informal.*

norm, decision-making *norm* as to how a *group decision* is to be arrived at.

norm, deviant a *norm* in conflict with *societal norms* which governs the behaviour of a *deviant‖group.*

norm, emergent *norm* appearing in a special situation.

norm, explicit see *norm, formal.*

norm, flexible a *norm* which permits a latitude in observance.

norm, formal a *norm* which is explicitly-formulated.

norm, general a *norm* governing behaviour in a wide range of situations.

norm, implicit see *norm, informal.*

norm, imposed a *norm* created by a *decision-making unit.* (Blondel, J.). see also *norm, natural.*

norm, informal a *norm* which is not explicitly-formulated.

norm, institutional *norm* associated with an *institution.*

norm, kinship a *norm* regulating *kinship behaviour.*

norm, legal a *norm* involving an *organized sanction.*

norm, natural a *norm* which has emerged from a standardized *behaviour pattern.* (Blondel, J.). see also *norm, imposed.*

norm, neighbourhood a *norm* governing behaviour in a particular *neighbourhood.*

norm, permissive a *norm* which does not prescribe or proscribe but permits a particular form of behaviour.

norm, procedural a *norm* governing *procedure.*

norm, rigid a *norm* which permits no latitude in observance.

norm, sanctioning a *norm* prescribing *sanctions.*

norm, societal a *norm* the validity of which receives general acceptance in a *society.*

norm, specific a *norm* governing behaviour in a narrow range of situations.

norm, subcultural a *norm* governing the behaviour of a *subculture.*

norm, verbalized (**Murdock, G.P.**) see *norm, formal.*

normalization see *standardization²*.

nosometry the measurement of the *morbidity rate.* **nosometric** *a.*

nosology the *classification* of diseases. **nosological** *a.*

nucleation the concentration of *population.*

nucleation, defensive the concentration of *population* for defensive purposes.

nullifiability (**Merton, R.K.**) see *falsifiability.*

nullipara woman who has had no confinements. **nulliparous** *a.* **nulliparity** *n.*

number, index number showing *value⁶* of a quantity relative to a *base period.*

number, index, aggregative *index number* constructed by aggregating a number of items.

number, magic number believed to possess magical power.

number, pattern number which is preferred in a given *culture.*

number, scale number designating position on *attitude continuum.*

nuptiality frequency and effect of *marriage* on a *population.*

nuptiality, differential intergroup differences in *nuptiality.*

nuptiality, female frequency and effect of the *marriages* of females on a *population.*

nuptiality, male frequency and effect of the *marriages* of males on a *population.*

nurturance 1. ministering to an infant's vital processes. 2. ministering to an infant's vital processes and need for stimulation. 3. *drive* to provide nurture to the young or incapable.

oath conditional self-imprecation. (Westermarck).

oath, corporal see *oath, embodied.*

oath, embodied *oath* by or on some object.

oath, weapon *oath* made by a person on his weapon.

object, stimulus 1. *stimulus* consisting of smaller stimuli. 2. thing which is a source of stimuli.

objective 1. any aim, short-term, long-term, ultimate, or continuing. 2. outcome having a positive value for the decision-maker. see also *goal*; *target*. 3. to do with the external world. 4. impartial. 5. publicly verifiable.

objective, system *objective* served by a *system*.

oblation 1. offering something to a deity. 2. that which is offered to a deity. **oblatory** *a*.

obsecration *supplicatory prayer* mentioning *sacred* things.

observation, field observation of human behaviour in natural settings.

observation, mass intensive observation simultaneously carried out on a large number of persons in natural settings.

observation, objective observation which is publicly verifiable.

observation, participant observing a *group* by participating in its activities.

observation, participant, active *participant observation* in which participation is maximized.

observation, participant open *participant observation* in which the *group* is aware that it is under observation.

observation, participant, passive *participant observation* in which participation is minimized.

observation, random 1. observation which is unsystematic. 2. observation involving *techniques* to ensure *randomness*.

observation, systematic observation governed by a *procedure*.

observationalism the doctrine that knowledge is based on observation.

occupation 1. type of *work* regardless of *industry* in which it is performed. see also *job*. 2. a person's regular activity, paid or unpaid.

occupation, closed *occupation* with *closed recruitment*.

occupation, hereditary *occupation* which is inherited by a person.

occupation, open *occupation* with *open recruitment*.

occupation, primary *occupation* in a *primary industry*.

occupation, quaternary *occupation* requiring intellectual training. (Gottmann, J.).

occupation, secondary *occupation* in a *secondary industry*.

occupation, tertiary *occupation* in a *tertiary industry*.

ochlesis any disease due to overcrowding. **ochletic** *a*.

ochlocracy rule by the mob. **ochlocratic** *a*.

octiles *quantiles* dividing *array* into eight equal parts.

offering, votive an offering to a *spirit* in fulfilment of a *vow*.

office *status,* well-defined, rule-governed, created by *authority*.

office, appointive *office* to which the office-holder is appointed.

office, bureaucratic an *office* in a *bureaucratic‖organization*.

office, elective *office* to which the office-holder is elected.

office, public an *office* in the public sector.

office, responsible *public office* whose incumbent is directly responsible to the ultimate ruling *authority* or *group*.

ogive a distribution in which the frequencies are cumulated.

oligarchy rule by a few. **oligarchic** *a*.

oligarchy, competitive high degree of *liberalization* combined with low degree of *political participation*[2]. (Dahl, R.A.).

oligophrenia *amentia* resulting from mental retardation.

omen sign foretelling future event or revealing distant event.

omen, birth *omen* occurring during childbirth.

omen, chance *omen* occurring without being sought for.

omen-taker an interpreter of *omens*.

omnilineality see *descent, omnilineal*.

oneiromancy *divination* from dreams. **oneiromantic** *a.* **oneiromancer** *pers n.*

ontogenetic concerned with development of individual organism. see also *phylogenetic.*

onychomancy *divination* from the fingernails. **onychomantic** *a.***onychomancer** *pers n.*

oomancy *divination* by eggs. **oomantic** *a.* **oomancer** *pers n.*

operant any type of *operant behaviour.* (Skinner, B.F.).

operationalism the doctrine that scientific terms have meaning only in terms of the operations which enter into their definition.

operationalization substituting an *operational definition* of a term for a *conceptual definition.*

operationism see *operationalism.*

ophiolatry the *worship* of serpents. **ophiolatric** *a.*

ophiomancy *divination* by means of serpents. **ophiomantic** *a.* **ophiomancer** *pers n.*

opinion overt expression of an *attitude.*

opinion, public 1. the *opinions* prevalent in a *public.* 2. the opinions on public matters prevalent in a public.

opinionaire *questionnaire* for obtaining *opinions* of *respondent[1].*

opposition absence of *co-operation.*

opposition, public (Dahl, R.A.) see *politics, competitive.*

oracle 1. the agency by which a god speaks. 2. the place of an agency by which a god speaks. 3. a response given at the seat of a god.

ordeal test applied to suspect involving *magic* or an appeal to the supernatural.

ordeal, poison *ordeal* involving the administration of a particular poison to the suspect or to an animal representing the suspect.

order, birth see *rank, birth.*

order, world the aggregation of *norms, procedures,* and *institutions* that give shape and *structure* to international *society* at any given time. (Falk, R.A.).

ordinality condition of being measurable on *ordinal scale.*

orectic pertaining to the *affective* or *conative.* **orexis** *n.*

organicism using the analogy of an organism to explain *society.*

organization 1. a *group* with *role differentiation.* 2. *set[1]* of functionally interrelated *roles* designed to achieve *goal.* 3. a *system* of consciously coordinated *activities.* 4. a system of continuous purposive activity. (Weber, M.). 5. degree of role differentiation existing in *group.* 6. *social system* organized for attainment of particular type of goal. (Parsons, T.). 7. several persons agreeing to follow a *set[1]* of *rules.* (Marschak, J.). 8. structure-in-interaction. 9. the act of organizing. 10. arrangement of functionally interrelated parts.

organization, cellular a *political‖organization* which has a resistance or subversive aim consisting of many small *subgroups* most of the members of each subgroup having little or no knowledge of members of other subgroups. see also *cell[4].*

organization, commonweal *organization* the intended beneficiary of which is the general *public.*

organization, community promoting the *integration* of the *social services* in a *community.* see also *development, community.*

organization, dual *system* of *moieties* with complementary *functions.*

organization, ecological the spatial aspects of *population* and *institutions* at any given time.

organization, economic 1. see *economy.* 2. an *organization* whose primary aim is production, exchange, or organizing and manipulating monetary processes.

organization, educational 1. the *organization* of *education* in a *society.* 2. an organization having educational aims.

organization, formal the explicitly-formulated *organization*.

organization, functional *organization* based on *functional authority*.

organization, informal the *system* of relations, not explicitly-formulated, found in an *organization*.

organization, kinship network of *kinship‖statuses* and associated behaviour. (Gibbs, J.L.).

organization, lateral an *organization* possessing a low ratio of *organizational levels* to co-ordinate *positions*.

organization, line that part of the *organization* consisting of *line functions*. see also *organization, staff*.

organization, line-and-staff *organization* based on *line functions* and *staff functions*.

organization, maintenance an *organization* concerned with *socialization* or *training*. (Katz, D.).

organization, metropolitan the *organization* of a *metropolis* or *metropolitan area*.

organization, military arrangement of functionally interrelated military *statuses*, *roles*, and *groups*. see also *sociology, military*.

organization, mutual-benefit *organization* the intended beneficiary of which is the membership.

organization, official see *organization, formal*.

organization, power see *structure, power*.

organization, productive see *organization, economic*[2].

organization, regional an inter-governmental *organization* created by the *states* of a particular *region*[3].

organization, revolutionary see *structure, revolutionary*.

organization, scalar an *organization* based on the *scalar principle*.

organization, service *organization* the intended beneficiaries of which are clients.

organization, social 1. the maintenance machinery of *society* consisting of 'acts of choice and decision' and mutual-steering mechanisms. 2 the ways in which human behaviour becomes socially organized. (Blau, P.M.).

oreganization, social, urbanized a *social organization* of *urban* character which applies to both *rural* and urban inhabitants.

organization, staff that part of the *organization* consisting of *staff functions*. see also *organization, line*.

organization, status see *system, status*.

organization, tripartite structural division of *community* into three parts. (Lévi-Strauss).

organization, voluntary see *association, voluntary*.

orientation, family of *nuclear family* in which person was born and reared.

orientation, mobility discrepancy between achievement and *level of aspiration*.

orientation, respondent property possessed by *interview* or *questionnaire* of enlisting *co-operation* of *respondent*[1].

origin, family of see *orientation, family of*.

ornithomancy *divination* from the flight or cries of birds. **ornithomantic** *a*. **ornithomancer** *pers n*.

ornithoscopy see *ornithomancy*.

orphan dependent child who has lost one or both natural parents.

orphan, complete dependent child who has lost both natural parents.

orphan, incomplete dependent child who has lost only one of its natural parents.

orphan, maternal dependent child who has lost only its mother.

orphan, paternal dependent child who has lost only its father.

ortho-cousins *parallel-cousins* who are members of the same *unilineal descent* *group.*

ostracism temporary banishment by popular decision.

other, generalized the organized *community* or *society* to which an individual responds and the individual *attitudes* of which he generalizes. (Mead, G.H.).

other, role a person or *category* of persons towards which a *role* performer's *activities* are directed. (Goffman, E.).

other-consciousness over-involvement with another participant by a participant in a conversation at the expense of involvement in the topic of conversation. (Goffman, E.). see also *self-consciousness; interaction-consciousness.*

other-directed characterized by a close *behavioural conformity* to contemporaries through an exceptional sensitivity to the *actions* and wishes of others. (Riesman, D.). see also *tradition-directed; inner-directed.*

other-rating *rating* by person other than *ratee.*

others, affective others to whom *ego* attaches affect.

others, confirming others who confirm the correctness of *ego's* behaviour, *attitudes,* or beliefs.

others, intimate others with whom *ego* has *primary contacts.*

others, responding others who respond to *ego.*

others-group (Sumner) see *out-group.*

out-group another *group* from the point of view of a group member. see also *in-group.*

out-grouper a member of the *out-group.* see also *in-grouper.*

outliers extreme *values*[6] of a distribution.

out-marriage see *exogamy.*

out-migration *migration* out of a particular area to another part of the same country. **out-migrant** *pers n.* see also *in-migration.*

out-migration, gross total *out-migration.*

out-migration, net excess of *out-migration* over *in-migration.*

output 1. that which leaves a processing *system.* 2. the results of the manipulations applied to a *model.* see also *input.*

over-centralization *centralization* in excess of that required for maximum *efficiency* and which reduces efficiency.

overcoverage inclusion in *sampling frame* of units which do not belong to *target population.*

over-enumeration *enumeration* which, through error, is in excess of complete coverage.

overheards unobtrusively collected verbal behaviour.

overload, information an excess of information for processing or interpretation.

overload, role an excess of legitimate calls from more than one person upon the time of an office-holder.

overlooking casting the evil eye.

overlord in the lord-vassal relationship, the lord of a particular *vassal.*

overpopulation the condition in which a decrease in inhabitants will yield advantages to the remainder. see also *underpopulation; population, optimum.*

overpopulation, absolute *overpopulation* resulting in starvation or hunger.

over-registration registration of *vital statistics* which, through error, is in excess of complete coverage.

over-represented more frequent in a *sample* than in the *population.* see also *under-represented.*

oversampling selecting from a stratum a more than proportionate *sample.*

overspill displacement of *population* from an *urban area* through lack of accommodation.

overurbanization *urbanization* higher than that justified by *economic development.*

ownership, absentee ownership of the means of production or distribution by persons who are not regularly present to supervise the production or distribution.

pair *group* of two persons.

palaeodemography the quantitative study of *prehistoric* and *protohistoric* ‖ *populations*.

pandiacritic (of an *ethnic group*) every individual recognizable. see also *visibility*; *macrodiacritic*; *microdiacritic*.

panel 1. *sample* of persons repeatedly interviewed. 2. sample the elements of which are repeatedly measured.

panic a collective flight based on a hysterical belief. (Smelser, N.J.).

pantagamy see *marriage, group*.

parachronism referral of event to a later date than the true one.

paradigm 1. case employed as example. 2. framework of basic *concepts* and *postulates* within which research proceeds. (Kuhn). **paradigmatic** *a*.

paralinguistics 1. the study of tone-of-voice *signals* in speech. 2. the study of *gestures* and tone-of-voice signals in *communication*. **paralinguistic** *a*.

parallel-cousin child of father's brother or mother's sister.

parallel-cousin, matrilateral a *parallel-cousin* on the mother's side.

parallel-cousin, patrilateral a *parallel-cousin* on the father's side.

parallelism 1. see *convergence*. 2. the doctrine that most cultural similarities are the result of independent development. **parallelist** *a.& pers n*. see also *diffusionism*.

parameter 1. *population²* ‖ *value⁶* as distinguished from *statistic³*. 2. magnitude determined outside *system* and constant during period of study.

para-shamanistic pertaining to attempt at direct communication with supernaturals without spirit possession trance. see also *shamanism*.

parasitism co-existence of unlike *groups* or persons in which one partner benefits at the expense of the other. **parasitic** *a*. see also *symbiosis*; *mutualism*; *helotism*; *commensalism*.

parasitism, kin the economic *parasitism* of relatives upon *ego*.

parataxis attributing the *personality traits* of familiar persons to strangers who resemble them in appearance and manner.

pardon 1. full *remission* of a particular *punishment*. 2. removal of both sentence and conviction.

pardon, absolute see *pardon, full¹*.

pardon, conditional full *remission* of a particular *punishment* on condition that the person submits to some lesser punishment.

pardon, free full *remission* of a particular *punishment* without any condition that the person submits to some lesser punishment.

pardon, full 1. see *pardon, free*. 2. removal of both sentence and conviction.

pardon, unconditional see *pardon, free*.

pardonee a person who has received a *pardon*.

parity state of a woman with regard to the number of children she has borne.

parole conditional release granted to prisoner after serving part of sentence in penal institution, rest of sentence being served outside.

parole, mandatory *parole* to which an offender is legally entitled after a specified period of incarceration.

parolee a person on *parole*.

part-culture see *half-culture*.

participation, audience action on the part of members of an *audience* which aids the *communication* or *learning process*.

146

participation, cultural extent to which the entire *culture* is socially shared.

Participation, Evaluated(E.P.) six *techniques* for rating an individual's actual social-class participation. (Warner).

participation, objective amount of actual *influence* of *group* member on *group decisions*.

participation, political 1. the participation of an individual in political activity. 2. percentage of *population* entitled to participate in *government*. (Dahl, R.A.).

participation, psychological amount of self-perceived *influence* of *group* member on *group decisions*.

participation, respondent the degree to which a *respondent[1]* participates in an *interview*.

participation, social the participation of the individual in *social life*.

partiles see *quantiles*.

partners, joking the partners to a *joking relationship*. see also *behaviour, joking*.

part-society a *vertical segment, horizontal segment,* or formal *institution* of a complex *society*. (Steward, J.).

party *group* with open membership concerned with all matters facing the *polity*. (Blondel, J.).

party, cadre *party* structurally characterized by the absence of members,i.e., persons regularly paying a subscription to the party. (Duverger, M.).

party, confessional see *party, religious*.

party, direct *party* which does not consist of affiliated *groups* and which has individual membership. (Duverger, M.).

party, doctrinal see *party, ideological*.

party, ethnic *party* generated by an *ethnic group*.

party, extensive *party* which covers the whole *state territory*. (Blondel, J.).

party, ideological a *party* based on commitment to an *ideology*.

party, indirect *party* consisting of affiliated *groups*, with no individual membership but only membership of each group. (Duverger, M.).

party, intensive *party* which does not cover the whole *state territory*. (Blondel, J.).

party, mass *party* structurally characterized by the presence of members, i.e., persons regularly paying a subscription to the party. (Duverger, M.).

party, pragmatic a *party* with the dominant *goal* of gaining *power*.

party, religious *party* generated by a *religious‖group* or *set[1]* of religious groups.

party, secular party which is not a *religious party*.

pasimology the study of *communication* by *gestures*.

passability the capacity of an individual to *pass*. see also *passing*.

passage, rites de *ceremonies* marking passage of individual from one stage of *life cycle* to the next. (Van Gennep).

passer an individual engaged in *passing*.

passing 1. posing of *minority group* member as dominant *group* member. 2. concealment by individual of a discreditable characteristic. (Goffman, E.). **pass** v.

passing, reverse concealment by individual of a creditable characteristic. (Goffman, E.).

pastoralism the *herding* and *husbandry* of domesticated animals. **pastoral** *a.* **pastoralist** *pers n.*

pastoralism, nomadic *pastoralism* involving *nomadism*.

pastoralism, transhumant *pastoralism* involving *transhumance*.

pater social father. see also *genitor*.

paternalism managing individuals or *groups* in the manner of a father with respect to his children. **paternalistic** *a.*

147

paternity 1. the state of being a father. 2. descent from a father.
paternity, biological the state of being a physical father.
paternity, cultural see *paternity, social.*
paternity, physical see *paternity, biological.*
paternity, physiological see *paternity, biological.*
paternity, social the state of being a social father.
path, career see *pattern, career².*
pathogenic disease-producing.
patriarchate see *patriarchy.*
patriarchy 1. rule by men. 2. a combination of *patrilineal descent, patrilocal residence,* and *patripotestality.*
patricentric centred on the father.
patriclan 1. *clan¹* based on *patrilineal descent.* 2. *clan³* based on *patrilineal descent* and *patrilocal residence.* (Murdock).
patri-cross-cousin see *cross-cousin, patrilateral.*
patri-deme *deme* with *patrilocal residence.* (Murdock).
patri-descent see *descent, patrilineal.*
patridominant characterized by the father having dominance.
patri-family see *family, extended, patrilocal.*
patrifiliation the tie between father and child. **patrifilial** *a.*
patrifocality lack, in the *family,* of a regularly present female in the *role* of wife-mother. **patrifocal** *a.* see also *matrifocality.*
patrikin relatives related through males.
patrilateral on the father's side. **patrilaterality** *n.*
patriline *line²* traced upwards by male links through father.
patrilineage *lineage* based on *patrilineal descent.*
patrilineal 1. pertaining to *patriline.* 2. having an emphasis on *patrilineal descent, patrilineal inheritance* and *patrilineal succession.*
patrilineality see *descent, patrilineal.*
patrilinear see *patrilineal.*
patriliny see *descent, patrilineal.*
patrilocality 1. see *residence, patrilocal.* 2. area of residence of a person's *patrilateral‖kin.* (Velsen).
patri-moiety *moiety* based on *patrilineal descent.*
patrinominal see *patronymic¹.*
patri-parallel-cousin see *parallel-cousin, patrilateral.*
patripotestal with *domestic authority* concentrated in the father.
patrisib *sib* based on *patrilineal descent.*
patron a person who recruits followers through his *power* to dispense favours. see also *broker.*
patron, political a *patron* whose *power* to despense favours results from his political *office.*
patronage the *activities* of a *patron* qua patron.
patronage, political the *activities* of a *political patron* qua political patron.
patronym see *patronymic².*
patronymic 1. pertaining to *inheritance* of the father's name. 2. name inherited from one's father or paternal *ancestor.*
patronymy *inheritance* of the father's name.
pattern (applied to *culture*) the standardization, recurrence, organization, or direction of *cultural behaviour.*
pattern, behaviour 1. that which a group of *responses* which differ in detail have in common. 2. a type of behaviour serving as a *model.*
pattern, career 1. sequence of *occupations* found in the life of an individual. 2. sequence of occupations typical for persons in a particular *group.* 3. sequence of *jobs* expressing the development of a *career.*

pattern, communication see *network, communication*.

pattern, conceptual an *organization¹⁰* of *concepts*.

pattern, culture 1. consensus of the individual *behaviour patterns* of a *society*. (Herskovits). 2. a *group*'s pattern of value orientations. (Hill, R.). 3. distinctive *organization¹⁰* of *trait complexes*. (Wissler).

pattern, dominance the network of *dominance relationships* amongst a *set¹* of individuals. (Bartos, O.J.). see also *structure, dominance*.

pattern, need the *organization¹⁰* of an individual's *needs*.

pattern, universal the broad *categories* of *culture* which are found in all *societies*.

pattern, visiting network of visiting contacts and visiting frequences.

pattern-maintenance the maintenance of the *values* of a *social system*. (Parsons, T.).

pattern-part pattern which is part of a more general pattern. (Kluckhohn).

pauperism the state of being in relief. **pauper** *pers n*. see also *indigence*; *poverty*.

payoff 1. outcome stated in quantitative terms of a course of action. 2. resultant allocation from the *play⁸* of a *game¹*.

peace, market peace maintained in market places through policing.

peasant 1. an agriculturist producing only a *subsistence crop*. (Firth, R.). 2. an agriculturist having rights over the land and using a simple *technology* to raise *cash crops* in addition to subsistence crops. (Padilla, E.). 3. an agriculturist to whom *agriculture* is a livelihood and a way of life, not a business for profit. 4. a person who personally farms the land he controls. (Wolf, E.R.). 5. an agriculturist with little or no *education* and therefore resistant to *innovations*. (Martin, A.).

peasant, urban *rural-urban migrant* retaining *peasant‖values* and *attitudes*. (Suzuki, P.).

peasantism 1. the *peasant* way of life. 2. the doctrine of the superiority of the peasant way of life.

peasantization the acquisition by an *urban area* of *peasant* characteristics.

pedigree 1. the charter by which any particular person presents himself as the descendant of a specified *ancestor*. (Fortes). 2. a *genealogical* statement made orally, diagrammatically, or in writing by an *actor* or *informant*. (Barnes, J.A.). see also *genealogy³*. 3. a genealogical statement which links a living person with his dead ancestors. (Yalman).

pedomancy *divination* from the human feet. **pedomantic** *a*. **pedomancer** *pers n*.

peer, class a fellow-member of a *social class*.

peer, ethnic a fellow-member of an *ethnic group*.

penalty 1. an unpleasantness occurring to a person automatically as the result of his *action* or his violation of a *rule*. 2. see *punishment*.

penalty, primary the *punishment* imposed on an offender by the sentence of a *court*.

penalty, secondary an unpleasantness occurring to a person as the result of a *primary penalty*.

penology the science of the *treatment* of criminals. **penological** *a*.**penologist** *pers n*.

penology, administrative branch of *penology* concerned with *correctional administration*.

penology, comparative the *cross-cultural* study of the *treatment* of criminals.

penology, rehabilitative branch of *penology* concerned with criminal rehabilitation.

peonage condition of compulsory service based on indebtedness. **peon** *pers n*.

percentiles *quantiles* dividing *array* into a hundred equal parts.

perception *sensation* plus interpretation.

perception, asocial *perception* which is not socially-conditioned.

perception, depth *perception* of depth and the position of objects relative to one another.

perception, enriched *perception* greatly influenced by the *needs* and *values* of the *percipient*.

perception, genealogical the recognition and recall of relatives.

perception, impoverished *perception* under experimental conditions in a simplified *environment*.

perception, intersensory *perception* involving more than one sense modality.

perception, primary *perception* which is not *secondary perception*. (McKellar, P.).

perception, role the *perception* of *roles* by those who play them and by others.

perception, secondary receiving information concerning the *perceptions* of others. (McKellar, P.).

perception, social 1. social *factors* in *perception*. 2. conditions influencing our perception of other people. (Heider).

perception, sociometric a *group* member's perception of the *sociometric status* of self of others. *(sociom.).*

perception, subliminal *perception* below the threshold of consciousness.

perception, tendentious *perception* of what one expects to perceive.

percipient person who perceives.

performance 1. the manner in which an *action* or *task* is carried out. 2. an individual's total *activity* influencing a *set[1]* of observers continuously present on a particular occasion. (Goffman, E.).

performance, cultural the manner in which a particular individual meets *cultural* expectations.

performance, role 1. the manner in which a particular individual plays a *role*. 2. the enactment of a role.

period, base a period the rate for which is used as a *standard* for comparing future rates.

period, lochial period following childbirth during which woman remains inactive.

period, neo-natal the period between birth and four weeks.

period, planning period for which plan is designed.

period, post-parole the period following *parole*.

period, projection whole period for which derivations are made from a given *set[1]* of assumptions.

period, reference 1. see *period, base*. 2. period for which data are collected.

periodicity the characteristic of repeating the same *values[6]* at regular intervals.
  periodic *a*. see also *aperiodicity*.

periphery, power the least powerful positions in a *group*.

peri-urban around an *urban area*.

permeability 1. degree to which membership of *group* is open. 2. the ease of entrance to and exit from any *position* in *social system*. 3. the degree to which positions in social system are filled without respect to social origin or other characteristics determined at birth.

person, central 1. person controlling *actions* of *group*. (Redl). see also *leader*. 2. person in *communication network* mediating all or most *communications*.

person, charismatic person who has imputed to him and feels he possesses an intense *charismatic* quality. see also *charisma*; *authority, charismatic*.

person, displaced person forcibly removed from an area by a public authority. (MDD). see also *refugee*; *emigré*; *exile*; *expatriate*.

person, focal any individual whose *role* or *office* is under consideration. (Katz, D.).

personality 1. social-stimulus value of an individual. 2. *aggregate[1]* of an individual's dispositions. 3. *organization[10]* of an individual's dispositions. 4.

organization[10] of an individual's socially-relevant dispositions. 5. pattern or form of an individual's dispositions. 6. pattern of *adjustments* of an individual. 7. an individual's unique pattern of dispositions. 8. sum of individual's *roles*. 9. an individual's invariant reactive system. 10. subjective awareness of self as distinguished from other objects. see also *character*.

personality, antisocial see *personality, psychopathic*.

personality, authoritarian *personality* characterized by submission to *authority*, *aggressiveness, conventionalism, ethnocentrism, stereotypy*.

personality, basic see *structure, personality, basic*.

personality, bureaucratic the *modal personality* found amongst bureaucrats. see also *bureaucracy*.

personality, configurational *basic personality* structure underlying a *culture*'s polarizing and integrating *pattern* or *value*.

personality, inadequate condition characterized by lack of drive, aimlessness and inadequacy of achievement.

personality, marginal the *personality* typical of an individual characterized by *marginality*.

personality, modal the central or dominant *personality traits* more or less shared by all members of an *ethnic group*.

personality, nuclear the more general traits of the *personality*.

personality, occupational the *modal personality* found in a particular *occupation*.

personality, passive-aggressive a *personality* characterized by extreme *aggressiveness* manifested in passive ways.

personality, passive-dependent a *personality* characterized by extreme indecisiveness, emotional dependency, and lack of self-confidence.

personality, peripheral the more specific *responses* based upon the *nuclear personality*. (Honigmann, J.J.).

personality, private those aspects of the total *personality* which are not influenced by *norms* and which do not directly affect the individual's *social behaviour*. (Lewis, O.).

personality, psychopathic condition characterized by underdeveloped superego, impulsiveness and emotional blunting.

personality, public those aspects of the total *personality* which are influenced by *norms* and which directly affect the individual's *social behaviour*. (Lewis, O.).

personality, role that part of the *personality* consisting of the individual's *roles*.

personality, social the *ideal type*||*personality* of a particular *society*.

personality, sociopathic a *personality* characterized by *sociopathic* dispositions. see also *sociopathy*.

personality, status 1. *personality* type linked to a particular *status*. 2. status-linked *response* configuration. (Linton).

personalization conferring a personal character on *social relationships*. **personalize** *v.*

persuasibility susceptibility to *persuasive communication*.

pheno-motive a motive of which the individual is conscious.

phenotype the bodily structure resulting from *genetic*[1] plus other *factors*. see also *genotype*.

phratry *set*[1] of associated *clans*.

phratry-mates fellow-members of a *phratry*.

phylogenetic concerned with development of species. see also *ontogenetic*.

physicalism the misapplication to other disciplines of the terms, *concepts* and *methods* of the physical sciences. **physicalist** *a.* see also *scientism*.

physico-social pertaining to the interrelations of social phenomena and the *physical environment*.

physiodrama synthesis of sports and *psychodrama*. (Moreno).

physiolatry worship of nature. **physiolatric** *a.*

pidgin a second language which is a *restricted language* derived from two or more natural languages and which is not markedly closer to one of these languages than the others. see also *language, pidginized*; *creole*.

pie-graph see *chart, circular*.

plan, contingency a plan intended to be put into operation if certain contingencies arise.

plan, flexible plan adjustable to changed conditions without delay or serious loss of economy or effectiveness.

plan, master comprehensive plan within which subordinate plans are co-ordinated.

plan, parole proposed supervision and *treatment* of *parolee*.

plan, repeat-use see *plan, standing*.

plan, single-use plan used up on achievement of *objective*.

plan, standing plan followed whenever a given situation occurs.

plank a single proposal in a *platform*.

planning 1. determining *objectives* and determining and co-ordinating the *subgoals, policies, procedures* and *methods* for achieving them. 2. designing courses of action for achieving objectives, which may or may not be adopted.

planning, allocative determining the optimal allocation of resources for the achievement of an *objective*.

planning, central making general planning decisions.

planning, centralized restricting the making of general planning decisions to the highest administrative levels.

planning, community *planning* applied to a *community*. see also *organization, community*; *development, community*; *integration, community*.

planning, comprehensive *planning* having the greatest functional scope.

planning, decentralized permitting the making of general planning decisions at lower administrative levels.

planning, development the *planning* of *socioeconomic development*.

planning, indicative economic *planning* consisting of the setting of *targets* and *objectives* by the *state*, the state restricting itself to persuasion.

planning, innovative devising *strategies* for the acceptance of *objectives*.

planning, local *planning* restricted to a particular locality.

planning, manpower *planning* the development and utilization of the human resources of a *society* or *organization*.

planning, national *planning* for *national goals*.

planning, operational making more specific planning decisions based on central planning decisions.

planning, organization *planning* applied to an *organization*.

planning, overall *planning* applied to the *system* as a whole.

planning, partial *planning* applied to a *subsystem*.

planning, physical *planning* of the *physical environment*, e.g. of land use.

planning, regional *planning* of regional development at the national or regional levels.

planning, resource *planning* the development of natural resources.

planning, social 1. *planning* for *societal goals*. 2. planning for non-economic societal goals. 3. planning by a *group* as opposed to planning by an individual.

planning, societal see *planning, social[1]*.

planning, state *societal planning* by the *state*.

planning, strategic long-range *planning*.

planning, systems *planning* by means of *systems analysis*.

planning, technological *planning* of technological development.

plans, hierarchy of plans of increasing comprehensiveness, plans at each level depending on plans at a lower level which are aimed at the achievement of *sub-goals*.

platform the whole or a section of the *policy* proposals of a particular *party* produced during an *election* campaign. see also *plank*.

platykurtic having peakedness less than that of the normal curve. **platykurtosis** *n.* see also *mesokurtic*; *leptokurtic*.

play 1. non-instrumental and non-productive *activity* pleasurable to the *actor*. 2. non-instrumental and non-productive activity pleasurable to the child actor. 3. self-rewarding activity. 4. pleasurable *leisure* activities. 5. activity which is free, separated from ordinary life, non-productive, uncertain in its outcome, and involving either *rules* or make-believe. (Caillois, R.). 6. a particular possible realization of the rules of a *game¹*. 7. a path followed down a *game tree*. 8. a particular match of a game. (von Neumann).

play, automatic an infant's *play* centred on its own body.

play, ceremonial intrinsically satisfying *activity* with ceremonial element.

play, constructive *play* resulting in increased structuring of materials.

play, free *play* which is unsupervised.

play, group co-operative *play* of the members of a *group*.

play, individual the unco-operative *play* of an individual.

play, informal *play* without ceremonial element.

play, linguistic see *play, speech*.

play, manipulative child's manipulation of materials without any intention to construct.

play, organized 1. *play* characterized by *rules*. 2. play characterized by rules, *planning* and supervision.

play, parallel the side-by-side, unco-operative *play* of two or more persons.

play, projective children's *play* encouraged for diagnostic purposes involving *projection* on to the play materials.

play, speech speech modification to entertain, or conceal meaning or speaker's identity.

play, work strain-reducing *play* element in *work*.

plebiscite a direct *decision* by the people on an exceptionally important matter. see also *referendum*.

pluralism, cultural presence of a plurality of *ethnic groups* in a *society*.

pluralism, ideological presence of a plurality of *ideologies* in a *society*.

pluralism, local *political pluralism* in a *community*.

pluralism, political absence of a *power elite*.

pluralism, structural presence of a plurality of *social structures* in a *society*.

plurality the excess of votes received by the leading candidate over those received by the next candidate in an *election* in which there are three or more candidates.

plurel plurality of persons.

point, choice see *point, decision*.

point, decision a branch point in a *decision tree*.

point, sample a point representing a particular *sample* in an n-dimensional space.

point, scale point on a *scale²* showing magnitude.

poise ability to maintain composure. (Goffman, E.).

polarization 1. roughly simultaneous attention by a *collectivity* to some *stimulus object* or event. 2. degree to which *group* pursues a *goal* common to its members. 3. concentration of speaker on certain section of *audience*. 4. inducing individual to adjust to one pole of a bipolar relation. 5. clustering of observations at the poles of a *continuum*. 6. the tendency in a multiparty system for votes to be given to the two major *parties*.

polarization, mass *polarization* possessed by a *mass audience*.

polemity the degree to which the energy available to a *society* is employed in war or military preparations. (Andreski, S.). **polemitic** *a.* see also *apolemity*.

polemology the study of human *aggression* and *intergroup conflict*. **polemologist** *pers n.*

policy 1. aims and course of action followed by a *government, organization* or individual. 2. general *rule* guiding *decision-making*. 3. general rule in organization limiting discretion of subordinates. 4. general rule promulgated by *top management* limiting discretion of subordinates. 5. establishing ultimate *goals*.

policy, administrative *policy* followed in *planning* and organizing.

policy, anti-natalist *population policy* designed to decrease the *birth rate*.

policy, appealed *policy* resulting from request by subordinate for guidance in *decision-making*.

policy, basic organizational *policy* of the most general type.

policy, departmental organizational *policy* concerning activities at the departmental level.

policy, eugenic *population policy* designed to improve the genetic qualities of the *population*.

policy, executive *policy* followed in *directing* and controlling.

policy, general organizational *policy* more specific than a *basic policy* but less specific than a *departmental policy*.

policy, implied *policy* without formal written or verbal expression.

policy, imposed *policy* pursued by *organization* imposed on it from without.

policy, migration the *policy* of a *government* on *migration*.

policy, originated *policy* pursued by *organization* which it has itself initiated.

policy, population measures taken by a *government* to influence *population‖trend*.

policy, populationist *population policy* designed to encourage *population‖growth* or to check actual or incipient population decline.

policy, pro-natalist *population policy* designed to increase the *birth rate*.

policy, restrictionist *population policy* designed to check *population‖growth*.

policy-making determining *policy*, whether this involves *decision-making* or *problem-solving*.

politicization 1. the acquisition of political character by a *group, institution* or *activity*. 2. the acquisition by an individual of political interests and activities. 3. characteristic of behaviour of being aimed at acquisition or preservation of *power*. (Lasswell). **politicise** *vt*.

politics 1. the struggle for *power*. 2. the authoritative allocation of *values*. (Easton, D.). 3. see *activity, political*. 4. see *science, political*. 5. action in the name of the *state* or *government*. 6. the scientific study of governmental behaviour.

politics, comparative the comparative study of political phenomena.

politics, competitive the presence in a *political system* of *parties* in competition for *power*. (Dahl, R.A.).

politics, incremental *politics* in which political differences are only quantitative.

politics, machine *politics* involving *political machines*.

politics, manipulative *politics* involving not *coercion* or *terror*, but *manipulation* and *influence*.

politics, power international behaviour which is primarily power-orientated.

politics, pressure application of organized pressure on holders of political *office* to use their *power* to further *group goals*.

politization see *politicization¹*.

polity see *system, political*.

poll 1. the casting of votes in an *election*. 2. a *survey* of *public opinion* on a particular issue.

poll, straw a *survey* of electoral opinion prior to an *election*.

pollee a *respondent¹* in a *poll²*.

pollution a situation which is symbolic of disorder, confusion, or anomaly.

pollution, external 1. *pollution* caught from a polluted person or thing. (Orenstein, H.). 2. relatively mild pollution. (Stevenson, H.N.).

pollution, internal 1. *pollution* which is not caught from a polluted person or thing, but is the result of an act of *ego* towards a person or thing. (Orenstein, H.). 2. relatively severe pollution. (Stevenson, H.N.).

pollution, menstrual *pollution* resulting from menstruation.

pollution, relational *pollution* resulting not from an act or contact but from *consanguineal relationships* with others. (Orenstein. H.). see also *act-pollution*.

polyad a *group* of three or more persons.

polyandry 1. *marriage* of one woman to two or more men. *(usu.)*. 2. marriage of two or more men to one or more women. (rare).

polyandry, adelphic see *polyandry, fraternal*.

polyandry, attenuated see *levirate, anticipatory*.

polyandry, disparate *polyandry* involving *co-husbands* of unequal *status*.

polyandry, fraternal *polyandry* in which the husbands are brothers.

polyandry, nonfraternal *polyandry* in which the husbands are not brothers.

polyandry, serial having a succession of husbands on the part of one woman, but only one at a time.

polyarchy high degree of *liberalization* combined with high degree of *political participation²*. (Dahl, R.A.).

polychotomy a division into many parts.

polyethnic pertaining to more than two *ethnic groups*.

polygamy *marriage* involving plural wives, plural husbands, or both. **polygamous** *a*. see also *polygyny*; *polyandry*; *marriage, group*; *monandry*.

polygamy, double see *marriage, group*.

polygamy, tandem see *monogamy, serial*.

polygon, frequency graph formed by connecting the plotted points when the class frequencies are plotted at the midpoint of each respective class.

polygon, percentage a *frequency polygon* representing a *percentage distribution*.

polygyny *marriage* of one man to two or more women.

polygyny, disparate *polygyny* involving *co-wives* of unequal *status*.

polygyny, general see *polygyny, nonsororal*.

polygyny, nonsororal *polygyny* in which the wives are not sisters.

polygyny, serial having a succession of wives on the part of one man, but only one at a time.

polygyny, sororal *polygyny* in which the wives are sisters.

polykoity plural mating. (Fischer).

polysegmentary consisting of similar, mutually exclusive *groups* each of which is subdivided into similar, mutually exclusive groups, and so on.

polytomy see *variable, polytomous*.

pool, gene all the genes of a *breeding isolate*.

pool, kindred those members of an *ego-centric kindred* for whom active membership is optional. (Hudson, A.B.).

pool, spouse those persons eligible for *marriage* to ego.

pool, spouse, actual *ego's* potential *spouse pool* minus those members marrying before ego's *marriage*.

pool, spouse, potential *ego's* original *spouse pool*.

pooling 1. concentration of *wealth* of *group* members for subsequent redistribution. 2. amalgamating class frequencies to form one frequency.

pooling, chiefly concentration of *society*'s *wealth* in hands of *chief* for subsequent redistribution.

population 1. collection of distinct elements. 2. entire *group* from which *sample* is drawn. 3. the *aggregate* of persons or objects under investigation. 4. all the inhabitants of an area. 5. a *category* of the inhabitants of an area. 6. the number of persons who are in an area.

population, active sector of *population* active in economic or noneconomic *roles*.

population, actual see *population, de facto*.

population, agricultural *population* consisting of those engaged in *agriculture* plus their dependants.

population, agricultural, active *population* consisting of those engaged in *agriculture*.

population, binomial *population* the elements of which are classified according to possession or lack of a certain *attribute*.

population, bivariate *population* each element of which is measured on two characteristics.

population, breeding a *population* which differs markedly from other populations in *gene frequency*.

population, captive *population* whose members are unable to avoid being the objects of study.

population, civil the *de jure population* minus all members of the armed forces (of whatever country) that may actually be in the area at the time. see also *population, total*.

population, closed *population* without *migration* inwards or outwards.

population, daytime the *population* of an *urban area* at a particular time during the day. see also *population, nighttime*.

population, de facto those persons in a specified area on *census* day.

population, de jure those persons who are normally resident in a specified area.

population, enumerated see *population, de facto*.

population, home see *population, de jure*.

population, institutional 1. *population* in quasi-households. 2. population in penal, psychiatric and geriatric institutions. (US).

population, intrabreeding see *population, breeding*.

population, marriageable those persons legally free to contract *marriage*.

population, maximum 1. largest *population* supportable under specified conditions. 2. largest population supportable at a specified standard of living.

population, minimum smallest *population* consistent with *group* survival.

population, model see *population, simulated*.

population, multivariate *population* each element of which is measured on more than· two characteristics.

population, nighttime the *population* of an *urban area* at night. see also *population, daytime*.

population, non-marriageable those persons not legally free to contract *marriage*.

population, open *population* with *migration* inwards or outwards.

population, optimum the condition in which neither a decrease nor an increase in inhabitants will yield advantages to the remainder. see also *overpopulation*; *underpopulation*.

population, planned *population* the *growth* and composition of which is planned.

population, present-in-area see *population, de facto*.

population, psychiatric those persons suffering from mental disorders in a particular *population*.

population, research a *population* which is the object of reasearch.
population, resident see *population, de jure.*
population, rural 1. *population* not in cities and *urban fringes.* (USBC). 2. population of those *agglomerations[1]* which are under a specified size. see also *population, urban.*
population, rural, adventitious *population* living in *rural areas* by choice.
population, rural, primary that part of the *rural population* consisting of *farmers* and farm workers.
population, rural, secondary *rural population* the function of which is to service the *primary rural population.*
population, rural-farm all rural ·residents living on farms.
population, rural-nonfarm all rural residents not living on farms.
population, sampled the *population* of which a *sample* is representative. see also *population, target.*
population, saturated *population* which absorbs all resources in subsistence.
population, sedentary a *population* not *nomadic* or *transhumant.*
population, settled see *population, sedentary.*
population, simulated a hypothetical *population* employed in a *computer simulation.*
population, stable *population* with stable *age distribution.*
population, stationary *stable population* with zero growth rate.
population, stimulus the *population* exposed to a certain *stimulus.*
population, survey *population* represented by *sample* as distinct from the *target population.*
population, target 1. the *population* to which an investigator wants to generalize. see also *population, sampled.* 2. population which is the object of *social action[3].*
population, total the *civil population* plus members of the national armed forces (but not members of the forces of other countries) wherever they may actually be (at home or abroad) who belong to the area when on leave.
population, univariate *population* each element of which is measured on a single characteristic.
population, urban 1. *population* of cities and *urban fringes.* (USBC). 2. population of those *agglomerations[1]* which are over a specified size. see also *population, rural.*
population, working 1. the economically *active population.* 2. those persons working for pay. 3. those persons working for pay or seeking paid work during a specified period.
position 1. location within a *set[1]* of interconnected *roles.* (Lundberg). 2. totality of *ego's* relations with *groups* and individuals of *population.* (Sorokin). 3. see *category, social.* 4. a phase in an *encounter.* 5. locus of *set[1]* of forces in a *life space.*
position, achieved voluntary, open *position* open to *competition.*
position, ascribed involuntary, closed *position* not open to *competition.*
position, ecological position of an ecological unit in a *hierarchy* of *ecological dominance.*
position, formal *position* which is explicitly-formulated. (Galtung).
position, genealogical any one of the possible ways in which one person may be related by *kinship* to another.
Position, Index of Class (I.C.P.) *index* of individual's *social class,* based on *class identification* and *occupation.* (Ellis, R.).
Position, Index of Social (I.S.P.) *index* of individual's *social class,* based on *education, occupation,* and area of residence. (Hollingshead, A.).
position, informal *position* which is not explicitly-formulated. (Galtung).
position, marginal see *situation, marginal.*

position, power a *position* conferring *power* on incumbent.

position, social a person's *position* in *society*.

positivism the doctrine that tested and systematized experience should be substituted for undisciplined speculation. **positivist** *a.* & *pers n.*

positivism, logical see *empiricism, logical.*

possession, spirit the temporary possession and control by a spirit of a human body. see also *mediumship, spirit.*

possibilism the doctrine that man has freedom to choose, within the limits set by the *environment*. **possibilist** *a.* & *pers n.*

postcategorization 1. categorizing behaviour not at time of observation but from records. 2. progressive refinement of *system* of behaviour *categories* as a result of observational experience.

postdiction determining past data in terms of given observations. (Reichenbach, H.).

postmarriage *marriage* which follows cohabitation.

postremogeniture see *ultimogeniture.*

post-test test determining 'after' condition given to *subjects[1]* after application of *experimental stimulus.*

postulate 1. an assertion without proof in an *axiomatic theory.* 2. a basic *proposition* of a particular discipline. see also *axiom; theorem; corollary.*

postulate, cultural a broadly generalized *proposition* held by members of a *society.*

posture position of the body in relation to gravity. **postural** *a.*

potential, revolutionary the overall gap between the demands made on a *government* and its performance. (McAlister, J.T.). see also *space, revolutionary.*

poverty 1. individual or *family* insufficiency of assets, income and public services. 2. condition of having an income in the lowest one-fifth of the income distribution. (Miller, H.). 3. condition of having an income incompatible with a *society*'s national *objectives.* (Mencher, S.).

poverty, absolute *poverty* not defined in terms of a *partile* of an income distribution. see also *poverty, relative.*

poverty, case *poverty* which is the result of individual characteristics or some characteristics of the individual *family* afflicted. (Galbraith, J.K.).

poverty, crisis *poverty* resulting from a crisis such as injury, illness, or unemployment.

poverty, culture of the complex of *culture traits* common to the poor, transcending national, regional, and rural-urban differences. (Lewis, O.).

poverty, disreputable *poverty* which results in those suffering from it to live in disrepute. (Marza, D.).

poverty, insular an enclave in which everyone or nearly everyone is poor. (Galbraith, J.K.).

poverty, life-cycle *poverty* afflicting certain persons in characteristic stages of the *life cycle.* see also *cycle, poverty.*

poverty, primary *poverty* which is not the result of extravagance.

poverty, relative *poverty* conceived as possession of an income falling below a certain *partile.* see also *poverty, absolute.*

poverty, secondary *poverty* which is the result of extravagance.

poverty, tertiary *poverty* resulting from goods and services being unobtainable although requisite income and careful expenditure are present. (Marshall, T.H.). see also *poverty, primary; poverty, secondary.*

power 1. the ability to control the *actions* of others. 2. unauthorized ability to control the actions of others. (Nadel). 3. illegitimate *influence.* 4. the production of intended effects. (Russell, B.). 5. the ability to produce effects. 6. an *authority* of specified ʂcope attached to an *office.*

power, coercive *power* exercised through physical constraint.

power, delegated an *authority* of specified scope conferred on a subordinate.

power, discretionary *authority* to make *decisions* within prescribed limits.

power, dispensing *authority* to exempt individuals from a rule of law.

power, expert *power* based on *alter*'s belief in *ego*'s expert knowledge.

power, formal see *power, institutional.*

power, identitive see *power, referent.*

power, informal see *power, spontaneous.*

power, institutional *power* derived from *norms.*

power, normative *power* based on allocation and manipulation of *symbolic* rewards.

power, referent *power* based on *alter*'s *identification* with *ego.*

power, remunerative *power* exercised through actual or threatened deprivation of money or possessions, or deprivation of anticipated material rewards or privileges. (Etzioni, A.).

power, spiritual political *power* possessed by a *religious‖leader.*

power, spontaneous *power* not derived from *norms.*

power, sub-delegated an *authority* of specified scope conferred on a subordinate which is the result of further *delegation* of a *delegated power.*

power, utilitarian see *power, remunerative.*

power-subject a person under the *power* of another.

powers, delegation of downward transfer of *decision-making‖authority.*

practice 1. personal variant of *normative behaviour.* 2. performing an *act* one or more times for its fixation or improvement. 3. a single performance of an act for its fixation or improvement. 4. see *usage.*

practice, socialization any *activity* aimed at *socialization.* (Mayer, P.). see also *process, socialization[1].*

praetorianism 1. the intervention of the military in *politics.* 2. the intervention of the military of other *group* in politics in the absence of effective *political institutions.* **praetorian** *a.*

pragmatics study of the relations between *signs* and their users.

pragmatism doctrine that the meaning of a *proposition* depends on its practical consequences.

praxis 1. a *system* of *procedures* for the achievement of a practical *objective.* 2. an *action* in its totality which involves acquired co-ordination. (Piaget, J.).

prayer use of words to secure *spirit* aid.

prayer, petitionary *prayer* consisting of a petition addressed to a *spirit.*

prayer, supplicatory *petitionary prayer* characterized by humility. see also *obsecration.*

prayer, votive a *prayer* expressing a *vow.*

preanimism universal stage of *animatism* preceding *animism.*

precinct 1. minor division for casting and counting votes. (US). 2. minor division for police *administration* in city or ward. (US). 3. specialized *urban area* reserved for pedestrians. 4. the ground immediately surrounding a *religious* structure.

precision the closeness to true *value[6]* claimed of a measurement. see also *accuracy.*

precoding the advance assignement of *code‖symbols* to the various response or *observational categories.*

predelinquent individual with a high probability of becoming a *delinquent.*

predicament a situation characterized by the presence of a perplexing problem. (Farber).

prediction foretelling on the basis of a full knowledge of the *values[6]* of the *variables* involved. see also *forecast; projection[4].*

predictor a *variable, measure, measurement[2]* or *model* used to predict.

prefecture 1. the *office* of *prefect.* 2. a prefect's *administrative area.* see also *system, prefectoral.*

pre-government *political system* lacking *coercion.* see also *government.*

prehistory the study of past *preliterate‖cultures.* **prehistoric** *a.*

prehistory, primary the study of past *preliterate‖cultures* which is not through the written records of literate cultures.

prehistory, secondary the study of past *preliterate‖cultures* through the written records of literate cultures.

prejudice a *negative attitude* towards a *group.* see also *discrimination.*

prejudice, generalized *prejudice* which is not towards a particular *group.*

prejudice, primary *prejudice* with first-hand contact with the persons who constitute its object. (McKellar, P.).

prejudice, secondary *prejudice* without first-hand contact with the persons who constitute its object. (McKellar, P.).

prelinguistics the study of the physical and biological aspects of language. **prelinguistic** *a.*

preliterate (of a *society* of *culture*) before the appearance of writing. see also *nonliterate.*

prerequisites, functional conditions for a *social system* to come into existence. see also *requisites, functional*; *imperatives, functional*; *requirements, functional.*

prescriptions, role the formal expectations attached to a *position.* (Lundberg). see also *expectations, role*; *requirements, role.*

present, ethnographic using the present tense in *ethnographic* statements, irrespective of when the ethnographic observations were made.

present, ethnological see *present, ethnographic.*

press *set¹* of *stimuli* reacted to as a unit. (Murray, H.A.).

pressure, conformity see *pressure, social.*

pressure, group *social pressure* applied by the *group.*

pressure, population pressure of *population* on the means of subsistence.

pressure, role a *role expectation* sent to role-player.

pressure, social pressure applied informally to individuals to secure their *conformity.*

pressure, socializing force applied to an individual tending to induce *socialization.*

pressure, uniformity force applied informally to individuals tending to produce uniformity.

prestation a gift which creates social obligations.

prestige 1. *rank²* in *esteem.* 2. esteem not acquired automatically from holding of *office,* but from personal qualities. 3. social approval attached to a *position.* 4. group-approval power of a *status.* (Mandelbaum, D.G.). see also *esteem*; *status.*

prestige, halo the *prestige* accorded to an individual in one sphere of activity as a result of the prestige accorded to him for his known performance in another sphere of activity.

prestige, occupational social approval attached to an *occupation.*

pretest 1. test determining 'before' condition given to *subjects¹* before application of *experimental stimulus.* 2. a practice test. 3. see *survey, pilot.*

pretribal characterized by a cultural level below that of the *tribal.* see also *tribe.*

prevalence see *ratio, prevalence.*

primigravida woman having her first pregnancy. **primigravidous** *a.*

primipara woman having her first confinement. **primiparous** *a.* **primiparity** *n.*

primitive 1. see *nonliterate.* 2. see *preliterate.* 3. (White) see *tribal.* 4. stateless. (Sahlins). 5. societally simple. 6. societally homogeneous. (Redfield.). 7. not possessing a monetary *economy.* (Firth). 8. tradition-bound. (Boas). 9.

prescientific. (Bidney).

primitivism doctrine of superiority of that which is *primitive*. **primitivist** *a* & *pers n.*

primogeniture exclusive or preferential right in *inheritance* of eldest son. see also *ultimogeniture; unigeniture.*

principle any broad scientific or methodological generalization.

principle, exception referring only nonroutine cases to a superior for *decisions.*

principle, market the determination of prices by the forces of supply and demand.

principle, scalar the *principle* that *authority* and corresponding *responsibility* should flow in a clear unbroken line from the highest to the lowest official in an *organization.*

principle, triple-appeal *propaganda∥technique* of appealing simultaneously to the subject's self-interest, feelings, and morals. (Lasswell).

prisonization *socialization* into the *deviant* prison *culture.*

privatization 1. withdrawal of individual from political interests and activities. 2. characteristic of behaviour of not being in response to or directed towards other persons. (Lasswell). see also *socialization³.*

proaction *action* resulting from internal state. (Murray, H.A.).

probands persons with the clinical trait which is being investigated.

probation method for dealing with offenders, applied on selective basis; involving conditional suspension of *punishment,* and involving supervision and *treatment².*

probationer a person on *probation.*

problem, behaviour disapproved-of behaviour in a child, presenting a problem to be solved.

problem, personality a *behaviour problem* concerned with *personality* maladjustment.

problem, social a social state of affairs disapproved of by the dominant *social stratum* and presenting a problem demanding solution.

problem-solving choosing an alternative when the problem is given and the alternatives are given. see also *decision-making; policy-making.*

procedure prescribed sequence of steps for achieving *objective.*

procedure, discovery see *strategy, research.*

process, administrative a standardized series of administrative operations designed to achieve an *objective.*

process, adoption characteristic series of stages from initial information to final adoption of a practice.

process, art an artistic *concept* plus resulting behaviour, product, and *feedback* upon the concept. (Merriam, A.P.).

process, behaviour a standardized series of behaviours.

process, centralization a series of events resulting in political *centralization.*

process, communication see *system, communication¹.*

process, control the *administrative process* of defining *standards,* comparing results with the standards and taking corrective action.

process, cultural, directional long-run process involving a cumulative shift in the *culture.*

process, deterministic process the entire future of which is predictable.

process, intergroup a *social process* occurring between *groups.*

process, intragroup a *social process* occurring in a *group.*

process, irreversible a process the direction of which cannot be reversed unless *parameters²* are changed.

process, judicial a process of dispute settlement in which there is a judge, *norms* are important, and the social strength of the parties is of no importance. (Gulliver, P.H.). see also *process, political.*

process, learning a series of events resulting in *learning*.

process, legislative the process by which *legislation* is created.

process, measurement sequence of operations involved in *measurement*.

process, morphogenic a process tending to change or elaborate a *system's* form, *structure,* or state.

process, morphostatic a process tending to maintain a *system's* form, *structure,* or state.

process, policy process by which a *policy* is established.

process, political a process of dispute settlement in which there is no judge, *norms* are of little or no importance, and the social strength of the parties is the main determinant of the outcome. (Gulliver, P.H.). see also *process, judicial.*

process, revitalization characteristic series of stages by which *revitalization* is achieved. see also *movement, revitalization.*

process, scalar relationships amongst levels in an *organization.*

process, settlement any one of a standardized series of events resulting in permanent residence by a plurality of *migrants.*

process, single a concrete *social process.* (von Wiese).

process, social 1. characteristic series of social changes occurring to a person or *group.* 2. series of steps leading from one social state to another. 3. *chain* or *network of interaction.* 4. type of *interaction*, e.g., *co-operation, competition, conflict.*

process, socialization 1. a standardized series of events resulting in *socialization.* 2. a *mechanism* or type of social experience actually resulting in the inculcation of *role-playing[2]‖skills* and *attitudes.* (Mayer, P.). see also *practice, socialization.*

process, societal, directional long-run process involving a cumulative shift in the *social structure* or *culture.*

process, societal, recurrent short-run process recurring diurnally, seasonally or yearly in a *society.*

process, stochastic a process containing an element of *randomness.*

process, symbolic the utilization by an individual of *symbols.*

process, terror see *terror, process of.*

processing, content *techniques* for the *objective* and systematic comparison of the content of *communication.* (Levy, F.).

processing, data 1. changing the form, meaning, appearance, location, or other characteristics of data. 2. steps from *data collection* to the production of distributions. (Galtung, J.). see also *acquisition, data*; *reduction, data*; *handling, data*; *transcription, data*; *collection, data.*

processing, data, electronic (EDP) *data processing* performed by electronic equipment.

processing, data, mechanized (MDP) *data processing* performed by machines.

procession a movement of persons along a predetermined route. (Goffman, E.).

procreation, family of *nuclear family* which person establishes by his or her *marriage.*

productivity 1. *efficiency* in utilization of resources. 2. output per man-hour. 3. output per unit of *capital.* 4. ratio of output to input.

profane 1. technically functional. (Leach). (opposite of *sacred[1]*). 2. the ordinary and the *unholy.* (Davis, K.). 3. pertaining to things of ordinary concern. (Spiro, M.E.).

profession *occupation* characterized by skilled intellectual technique, *voluntary association,* code of conduct.

professionalization 1. increase in percentage of professionals in the *labour force.* 2. acquisition of professional characteristics by an *occupation,* without an increase in *skill.*

profile graphical representation of levels with respect to a *set[1]* of characteristics.

profile, community *profile* of the properties of a *community.*

profile, group *profile* of the properties of a *group.*

profile, job a list of the psychological and physical requirements for a particular *job.*

profile, occupational *profile* showing *percentage distribution* of workers by *occupational category.*

profile, personality graphical representation of individual's level with respect to a group of *personality traits.*

profile, psychic see *profile, personality.*

profile, semantic the *profile* resulting from the application of the *semantic differential* to a particular word or *concept.*

profile, test a *profile* representing the *values[6]* of the *variables* measured by a test.

profile, trait see *profile, personality.*

progeny-price *bride-price* through which rights over the offspring of the *marriage* are acquired by husband's *kin.* (Hoebel).

programme 1. plan involving quantification. 2. subplan or minor plan.

progress 1. change from the worse to the better. (Russell, B.). 2. increasing *adaptation.* (Boas). 3. movement in a desired direction.

pro-husband the *cicisbeo* in a *ghost marriage.*

projection 1. ascribing one's own traits, which are not disowned, to others. 2. ascribing one's own disowned traits to others. 3. reflection of one's *personality* in the interpretation of ambiguous *stimuli.* 4. a derivation concerning a future state from a given *set[1]* of assumptions. see also *forecast.*

projection, assimilative see *projection[1].*

projection, direct ascribing one's own disowned traits to others, who do not possess them. (Allport, G.W.).

projection, disowning see projection[2].

projection, harmonizing an overall *projection[4]* the constituent partial *projections[4]* of which are adjusted for consistency.

projection, overall a combination of partial *projections[4].*

projection, play reflection of *testee's personality* in *play‖activity.*

projection, population a derivation concerning a future state of a *population* from a given *set[1]* of assumptions. see also *forecast, population.*

prolicide killing one's child or children.

promotion attempting to secure the adoption of an *innovation.*

pro-natalist pertaining to *population policy* designed to increase the *birth rate.*

propaganda the technique of changing *attitudes* in a desired direction.

propaganda, black *propaganda* the source of which is concealed.

propaganda, covert see *propaganda, black.*

propaganda, mass *propaganda* involving *source-personal diffusion.*

propaganda, monopoly *propaganda* which does not have to compete with *counterpropaganda.*

propaganda, overt see *propaganda, white.*

propaganda, preparatory *propaganda* designed to control the effects of important events which are anticipated.

propaganda, white *propaganda* the source of which is not concealed.

prophecy 1. *prophetic‖activity.* 2. prophetic *utterance.*

prophet an individual who brings news of a personal god who reveals himself to man, the prophet's voice being the voice of this god. (Weber, M.). **prophesy** *vi.* & *vt.* **prophetic** *a.*

proportion, masculinity proportion of males in total *population.*

proposition 1. meaning of a declarative sentence. 2. a confirmed *hypothesis.* see also *axiom; postulate; theorem; corollary.*

propriety the conventional standards of proper behaviour.

proprioceptor *receptor* which is aroused by *stimuli* from muscles or joints. see also *interoceptor*; *exteroceptor*.

protest, status the rejection of a *status system* by a *group* having a low *status* within it.

proto-caste a rudimentary *caste*. (Balandier, G.).

proto-class a rudimentary *social class*. (Balandier, G.).

protocol 1. original record of investigation. 2. etiquette of *diplomacy* and state‖*ceremonies*. 3. international agreement less formal than a treaty or *convention*⁵. 4. the original which is being simulated or compared with a *model*.

protocol, observation original record of observations.

protoculture socially-learned, trans-generational behaviour without language, energy control or *technology*, found amongst pre-hominids and proto-hominids.

protohistory see *prehistory, secondary*. **protohistoric** *a.*

protolanguage an inferred language without records thought to be the ancestor of two or more languages of which texts are available.

proto-tool a slightly modified natural object, the modification involving little difficulty or sophistication, used as a tool by pre-hominids or nonhuman primates. (Gruber, A.).

proto-totemism ancient tales, customs and ideas which have relationships between man and animal as their subject. (Baumann).

province, culture see *area, culture*.

proxemics the study of how people handle space. (Hall, E.T.). **proxemic** *a.* **proxemicist** *pers n.* see also *sociofugality*; *sociopetality*; *space, personal*; *space, sociofugal*; *space, sociopetal*; *space, use*.

psephology the science of voting behaviour. **psephological** *a.* **psephologist** *pers n.*

pseudo-communication an unsuccessful attempt to communicate, with neither person aware of the failure. see also *communication*.

pseudo-kinship fictitious kinship ties maintained between *groups* for political purposes. see also *quasi-kinship*.

pseudo-moiety one of two divisions of a *community*, whether or not they are *descent groups*.

pseudo-mores *norms* generally believed to be generally accepted as *mores*, but in fact only so accepted by a minority.

pseudo-shaman individual unsuccessfully claiming *shamanistic* powers. (Boyer, L.B.). see also *shaman, real*.

psychegroup a *group* organized for social intercourse. see also *sociogroup*.

psychiatry branch of medicine concerned with the diagnosis, prevention, and treatment ⸜ ˙ mental disorders. **psychiatric** *a.*

psychiatry, community that branch of *psychiatry* concerned with the mental health care of a specified *population*.

psychiatry, comparative see *anthropopsychiatry*.

psychiatry, folk *psychiatric* beliefs and treatment found in *primitive* and *folk societies*. (Kiev, A.).

psychiatry, industrial that branch of *psychiatry* concerned with mental disorders in their industrial context.

psychiatry, political the application of *psychiatry* to *politics*.

psychiatry, preventive branch of *psychiatry* concerned with the prevention of mental disorders.

psychiatry, social the study of mental disorders in their social context.

psychoanalysis Sigmund Freud's psychological theory and *psychotherapy*. **psychoanalytic** *a.*

psychocultural involving both psychological and cultural *factors.*

psychodrama *psychotherapy* in which patient with the help of director and assistants or other patients acts out his private problems on stage. (Moreno).

psycho-ethnography the *psychology* of *culture.* (Herskovits).

psychogenic of psychological origin.

psychogeriatrics treatment of *psychiatric* problems of the aged. **psychogeriatric** *a.*

psychogram see *profile, personality.*

psychograph see *profile, personality.*

psychograph, job see *profile, job.*

psycholinguistics the science of the interrelations of language on the one hand and human behaviour and experience on the other. **psycholinguistic** *a.*

psychologism attributing to *psychology* supreme importance for the *explanation* of human behaviour. **psychologistic** *a.*

psychology the science of behaviour and experience.

psychology, applied the psychological *principles, methods* and *techniques* used in controlling human behaviour.

psychology, cognitive that branch of *psychology* concerned with the *cognitive.*

psychology, collective the *psychology* of *collective behaviour.*

psychology, correctional that branch of *applied psychology* concerned with criminal rehabilitation.

psychology, criminal that branch of *psychology* concerned with criminal behaviour.

psychology, differential the study of psychological individual and *group* differences.

psychology, educational that branch of *applied psychology* concerned with *education.*

psychology, engineering the study of human behaviour in relation to machines and tools.

psychology, general the study of what is common to human beings psychologically.

psychology, genetic the study of the development of individual *personality* and of changes occurring to human personality in the course of history.

psychology, industrial that branch of *applied psychology* concerned with *industry.*

psychology, mass the study of *mass behaviour.*

psychology, military the study of the psychological aspects of *military organization.* see also *sociology, military.*

psychology, organizational the *social psychology* of *organizations* and *general psychology* in so far as it is relevant to *organizational behaviour.*

psychology, perceptual that branch of *psychology* concerned with *perception.*

psychology, positional study of effect of *birth order* on *personality.*

psychology, social the science of the *responses* of individuals to their *interpersonal* and more extended *social environment.*

psychology, variational see *psychology, differential.*

psychopathology the pathology of mental disorders.

psychopathy see *personality, psychopathic.*

psychosocial involving both psychological and social *factors.*

psychosis, climacteric a psychosis associated with the climacteric.

psychosis, ethnic a psychosis or psychotic *syndrome* peculiar to a particular *ethnic group.*

psychosis, functional a psychosis not associated with organic disease.

psychosis, gestational a psychosis associated with pregnancy.

psychosis, manic-depressive psychosis characterized by cyclical movement from elation to depression.

psychosis, organic a psychosis associated with organic disease.

psychosis, prison a psychosis, irrespective of type, precipitated by anticipated or actual incarceration.

psychotechnics psychological *techniques* used in controlling human behaviour.

psycho-terror *terrorization* of individuals aimed at their *demoralization* in order to undermine the *authority structure*. see also *terror*; *terrorism*.

psychotherapy treatment of mental disorders through *verbal* or *nonverbal communication* with the patient. **psychotherapeutic** *a*. **psychotherapist** *pers n*.

psychotherapy, group *psychotherapy* given to *group* of patients, utilizing *interaction* of patients.

public 1. a *mass* with a common interest. 2. large *collectivity* with inter-member *communication*, each member influencing resultant *opinion*.

puerperium period following labour to involution of uterus. **puerperal** *a*.

punishment an unpleasantness imposed for an offence on an offender by a personal agency having *authority* to impose it. see also *penalty*.

punshment, collective *punishment* of a *collectivity* based on *collective responsibility*.

punishment, deterrent *punishment* intended to act as a deterrent.

punishment, exemplary a *punishment* of unusual severity for a given offence, which is thought to be necessary for a supposed need for increased *general deterrence*.

punishment, infamous *punishment* conferring on offender the legal status of infamy.

punishment, reformative *punishment* intended to reform or rehabilitate an offender.

punishment, superordinate *punishment* inflicted on an offender not by the *group* wronged but by a superordinate *chief* or *court*.

putsch 1. sudden attempt to overthrow a *government* based on a plot. 2. forcible overthrow of the government by a *faction* within the army. see also *revolution*; *rebellion*; *revolt*; *insurrection*; *uprising*; *insurgency*; *coup*.

pyramid, age-sex see *pyramid, population*.

pyramid, occupational an *occupational hierarchy* represented by *bar charts* placed one above the other.

pyramid, population two adjoining *bar charts*, each chart representing one of the sexes and each bar representing an *age-grouping*.

pyramid, power a *power hierarchy* represented by *bar charts* placed one above the other.

pyromancy *divination* from the behaviour of fire. **pyromantic** *a*.

Q-data data on *personality* from self-evaluative reports.

quadruple *group* of four persons.

quality—performance see *ascription—achievement*.

quantiles *values*[6] having below them a certain proportion of the observations arrayed in ascending order.

quantitativism the doctrine that phenomena should be quantified, if possible. **quantitativist** *a*. & *pers n*.

quartet see *tetrad*.

quartiles *quantiles* dividing *array* into four equal parts.

quasi-cession granting independence to a colony.

quasi-feudal characterized by extra-legal relationships involving adherence for protection between individuals and governmental *organizations*.

quasi-folk *groups* isolated from civilized *communities*. (Redfield, R.).

quasi-group unorganized *collectivity,* possessing common interests or behaviour, which may give rise to a *group.*

quasi-kinship extension of *kinship terms* and behaviour to non-*kin.* see also *pseudo-kinship.*

quasi-lineage a *group* of *cognates* approximating the structure of a *lineage* but based on *filiation* instead of *unilineal descent* or *non-unilineal descent.*

quasi-migrant an international migrant who does not intend to settle permanently in the receiving country. (Richmond, A.H.).

quasi-money special purpose medium of exchange.

quasi-totemism the first stage of *clan totemism.*

quasi-urban having an *urban* character but *nonliterate.* (Sjoberg).

quasi-variable *polytomy* having an intrinsic order.

quest, ceremonial an attempt by an individual, through dancing or other *ceremonial,* to encounter a particular *spirit.*

quest, vision a travel undertaken by an individual in order to visually encounter a particular *spirit.*

question, cafeteria see *question, multiple-choice.*

question, closed question with fixed-alternative answers.

question, closed-alternative see *question, closed.*

question, dichotomous question with two fixed-alternative answers.

question, direct question asking for information sought by investigation.

question, explanatory opinion question preceded by a statement giving *respondent[1]* information on the topic.

question, fixed-alternative see *question, closed.*

question, forced-choice see *question, fixed-alternative.*

question, free-answer see *question, open-ended.*

question, indirect question probing *personality* of *respondent[1]* whilst appearing to seek *survey data.*

question, information question asking for information or for separating informed from uninformed *respondents[1]* in an *opinion survey.*

question, multiple-choice see *question, closed.*

question, multiple-response question requiring more than one selection from the response-alternatives.

question, open see *question, open-ended.*

question, open-ended question to which any answer may be given.

question, precoded question having *code||symbols* printed against the response alternatives.

question, restricted see *question, closed.*

question, selective-answer see *question, closed.*

question, semi-structured question involving a free stimulus and a structured response, or a structured stimulus and a free response.

question, structured question which must follow the exact wording and order of the *schedule[1].*

question, unrestricted see *question, open-ended.*

question, unstructured question which need not follow the wording and order of the *schedule[1].*

questionnaire form filled in without assistance of interviewer. see also *schedule[1].*

questionnaire, precoded *questionnaire* on which *code||symbols* are printed against the response alternatives.

questionnaire, sociometric *questionnaire* requiring *subject[1]* to make sociometric choices. *(sociom.).*

questionnaire, structured *questionnaire* in which the form and order of all the questions are predetermined.

quintiles *quantiles* dividing *array* into five equal parts.

quintuple *group* of five persons.

race 1. class of *populations* based on *genetic[1]* criteria. 2. any population which differs genetically from others. 3. class of *genotypes*. 4. the individuals, irrespective of location, whose genotypes are of a certain class. **racial** *a.*

raciation the differentiation of humans into classes of *populations* based on *genetic[1]* criteria.

raciology the scientific study of *race*.

radix 1. original size of *birth cohort*. 2. standard number of births of a *life table*.

ramage ancestor-orientated *ambilineal kin group*.

random each item has equal probability of appearing. **randomness** *n.*

randomization *random* selection determines whether individual is in *experimental group* or *control group*.

range 1. difference between largest and smallest *value[6]*. 2. area over which a *nomadic* or *transhumant‖group* moves. 3. that part of *habitat* which is occupied by a *group*. 4. area within which a species is confined.

range, effective *range[1]* from which extreme, isolated *values[6]* have been eliminated.

range, interquartile difference between first and third *quartiles*.

rangers *nomads* or *transhumants*.

rank 1. a highly formalized *status*. (Nadel). 2. the precedence of an object in an ordinal series.

rank, birth precedence of birth amongst *siblings*.

rank, caste the *prestige* possessed by a *caste*.

rank, formal a *rank[1]* which is explicitly-formulated.

rank, informal a *rank[1]* which is not explicitly-formulated.

rank, percentile percentage of observations falling below a given *value[6]*.

rank, sociometric a *group* member's *rank[2]* on the number of choices received. (*sociom.*).

ranking 1. the order of objects in an ordinal series. 2. putting a *set[1]* of objects in an ordinal series.

ranking, complete a *ranking[1]* with no tied ranks.

rapport being able to have uninhibited *communication* with another.

rate, adjusted see *rate, standardized*.

rate, case-fatality the number of deaths from a certain cause per specified number of new cases of illness or injury from this cause over a specific period.

rate, cohort rate referring to lifetime of *cohort*.

rate, corrected 1. rate correcting published rate found to be based on defective data or inappropriate methods. 2. see *rate, standardized*.

rate, crime *incidence* of crime in a *population*.

rate, crude rate which is not related to certain *variables*.

rate, delinquency *incidence* of delinquent acts in a *population*.

rate, disability average number of days of *disability[3]* per person per specified period.

rate, final rate based on complete data.

rate, general rate calculated for *population* as a whole.

rate, incidence number of events in *population* at *risk[2]* during specified time, compared to mean population at *risk[2]* during that time.

rate, migration ratio of *migrants* to *population* at *risk[2]* during specified *migration interval*.

rate, morbidity measure of frequency, duration or severity of *morbidity*.

rate, occupancy number of persons per habitable room.

rate, pregnancy number of conceptions amongst women per unit of time during periods at *risk²*.

rate, prevalence see *ratio, prevalence*.

rate, provisional rate based on data known to be incomplete.

rate, revised rate correcting published rate found to be based on incomplete data.

rate, specific rate calculated for a homogeneous *sub-population*.

rate, standardized rate permitting comparability of *populations* with respect to a *variable*.

rate, stillbirth ratio of stillbirths registered in a given year to all births registered in the same year.

ratee person rated. see also *rater*; *rating*.

rater person who estimates on a *scale²* the degree of a specified characteristic.

rating 1. estimating on a *scale²* the degree of a specified characteristic. 2. such an estimate on a *scale²*.

rating, man-to-man see *rating, peer*.

rating, peer *rating* of individual by his peers.

rating, qualitative *rating* asserting presence or absence of characteristic.

ratio, basic-nonbasic the ratio of the production of the *basic industries¹* to the *nonbasic industries* of a particular *community*.

ratio, basic-service see *ratio, basic-nonbasic*.

ratio, behaviour ratio of strengths of opposed response tendencies at a choice-point.

ratio, child-woman number of children under 5 per 1,000 women of childbearing age.

ratio, choice-rejection ratio of number of choices received to number of rejections received by an individual. *(sociom.)*.

ratio, crop/rest see *ratio, cultivation/rest*.

ratio, cultivation/rest the ratio of the time that land is under cultivation to the time that it is at rest.

ratio, death see *mortality, proportionate*.

ratio, dependency ratio of number of persons in the dependent age groups to number of persons in the active age group.

ratio, divorce percentage of the *marriages* in a *sample* ended by divorce.

ratio, foetal death ratio of foetal deaths to *live births*.

ratio, illegitimacy number of illegitimate births per 1,000 total births.

ratio, man-land 1. number of inhabitants per unit area. 2. ratio of *population* to arable land.

ratio, masculinity ratio of males to females in a *population*.

ratio, military participation (M.P.R.) ratio of militarily utilized persons to total adult male *population*. (Andreski, S.).

ratio, morbidity see *rate, morbidity*.

ratio, noise-signal the ratio of *noise* to *signal* in a *message*.

ratio, parity-progression ratio of women of *parity* n + 1 to women of *completed fertility* of *parity* n.

ratio, prevalence proportion of *population* that exhibits phenomenon at particular time.

ratio, selection ratio of number chosen on a certain *criterion* to number available for choice.

ratio, sex 1. ratio of one sex to the other in a *population*. 2. number of males per specified number of females (100 or 1,000). 3. number of females per specified number of males (100 or 1,000).

ratio, sex, primary *sex ratio* at conception.

ratio, sex, secondary *sex ratio* at birth.

ratio, sex, sibling the average ratio of the sexes in the *sibling groups* in a *pop-*

169

ulation.

ratio, stillbirth ratio of stillbirths to *live births*.

rational 1. pertaining to beliefs determined by evidence instead of need-satisfaction. 2. having insight into one's motives. 3. (economics) acting according to one's economic interests. 4. (political) pertaining to *planning* instead of growth. 5. co-ordinating means to ends. 6. pertaining to purposeful behaviour. 7. selecting course of action leading to 'best' or 'most preferred' situation. (Simon, H.A.).

rationality, functional the functional *organization*[10] of *actions* directed to a *goal.* (Mannheim, K.).

rationality, substantial perceiving logical or empirical relationships. (Mannheim, K.).

rationalization 1. giving justifications for unconsciously motivated behaviour or beliefs which would otherwise be unacceptable to oneself or others. 2. co-ordinating and integrating an *industry.* 3. conferring a *rational* character on anything.

rationalization, cultural 1. a *rationalization*[1] which an individual adopts which is provided by his *culture.* 2. a *rationalization*[1] provided by a culture or *subculture* to explain away inconsistencies in its *norms* or deviation in the behaviour of the *group* from its *values.*

reaction 1. *act* elicited by *stimulus.* 2. *action* resulting from an external *stimulus.* (Murray, H.A.). 3. act which is not an object of expectation in a particular *culture.* (Lasswell). see also *response*[2]. 4. see *feedback, positive.*

reaction, circular 1. *behaviour cycle* which is *stimulus* for its own repetition. 2. *interaction* involving *schismogenesis.*

reaction, signal automatic *reaction* to a *signal.*

reactor an individual who reacts to a *stimulus* or *set*[1] of stimuli.

realism, cultural the doctrine that *culture* is ontologically distinct from the behaviour of individuals. see also *nominalism, cultural.*

realm, institutional *set*[1] of *positions* that produce, transmit, and receive a single *institutional value.* (Zetterberg).

rebellion 1. forcible overthrow of the *government.* 2. a *revolt* intended to overthrow the existing rulers without intending to change the form of government. 3. large-scale *insurrection.* 4. deliberate violation of *norms.* 5. rejection and replacement by an individual of the *cultural goals* and the institutionalized means of a *society.* (Merton, R.K.).

recall removal from *office* of elected official by popular vote.

receptor a sensory nerve terminal which is aroused by *stimuli.*

receptor, contact *receptor* which is aroused by *stimuli* from objects in contact with the body.

receptor, distance see *distoceptor.*

recidivism 1. committing another *crime* after completion of sentence. 2. habit of committing another crime after completion of sentence. **recidivate** *vi.*

recidivist repeater in *crime,* i.e., a person who commits another crime after completion of sentence.

recidivist, multiple *recidivist* with many reconvictions.

recidivist, primary *recidivist* with only one reconviction.

recipathy reciprocal *sympathy* between two persons.

reciprocation repayment by recipient to donor.

reciprocity 1. the use of *reciprocal terms.* 2. the reciprocity of obligations in a *community.* 3. the possession by both parties to a relationship of both duties towards and rights against the other. see also *complementarity.*

reciprocity, balanced *exchange* involving an equivalent return within a short period.

reciprocity, generalized *exchange* in which the *counter-obligation* is not stipulated by time, quantity or quality.

reciprocity, heteromorphic *reciprocity* in which exchangeables must be equal in *value* as defined by the *actors*, but need not be the same in form or in circumstances of *exchange*.

reciprocity, homeomorphic *reciprocity* in which exchangeables must be the same in form or in circumstances of *exchange*, but need not be equal in *value* as defined by the *actors*.

reciprocity, moiety *reciprocity* of obligations between *moieties*.

reciprocity, negative an *exchange* involving an acquisition by one party without the consent of the other followed by a counter-acquisition without consent when this becomes possible.

record an account of events written at the time of the events. (Madge, J.). see also *report*.

record, behaviour *record* of an individual's total behaviour over a given period of time.

record, vital a document attesting to a *vital event*.

recreation 1. *activity* or inactivity which is recuperative. 2. self-rewarding activity. 3. *leisure* activities. 4. active *play*. 5. socially-approved play.

recreation, community *recreation* provided for itself by *community*. (Bogardus).

recreation, escapist *recreation* which permits an individual to identify with a state of affairs which is not his own. (Levy, M.J.).

recreation, social *recreation* involving social contacts.

recruitment obtaining membership on the part of a *group*.

recruitment, bisexual *recruitment* from both sexes.

recruitment, closed *recruitment* involving conditions of entry. (Nadel, S.F.).

recruitment, contractual *recruitment* involving voluntary membership with entry into a *contract* to behave in a specified way for a specified period of time. (Udy, S.H.).

recruitment, custodial *recruitment* involving compulsory membership enforced by *penal sanctions*. (Udy, S.H.).

recruitment, familial *recruitment* involving compulsory membership based on ascribed *genealogical position*. (Udy, S.H.).

recruitment, open *recruitment* not involving conditions of entry. (Nadel, S.F.).

recruitment, role *recruitment* to a *role*.

recruitment, unisexual *recruitment* which is restricted to one sex.

recruitment, voluntary *recruitment* involving voluntary membership without entry into a *contract*. (Udy, S.H.).

redistribution sending of goods to an administrative centre and their reallotment by the authorities at the centre.

reduction the denial of *explanatory emergence*, which denial is, however, compatible with the affirmation of *descriptive emergence*.

reduction, data converting recorded data into desired useful forms. see also *acquisition, data*; *transcription, data*.

reductionism see *reduction*.

reductionism, biological treating phenomena belonging to a higher level of analysis as biological phenomena.

reductionism, ontogenetic regarding adult behaviour as being derived from early acquired *reactions*.

reductionism, phylogenetic regarding complex human behaviour as being only quantitatively different from the behaviour of lower animals.

reductionism, psychological treating phenomena belonging to a higher level of analysis as psychological phenomena.

redundancy, social multiplication of channels in *communication networks* to ensure *message* reception.

reference, frame of a *set[1]* of basic assumptions directing research.

reference, term of term used to name a relative when speaking about him to a third person.

referendum a direct *decision* by the people on a legislative or administrative matter. see also *plebiscite*.

referendum, compulsory a *referendum* involving the compulsory referral by the legislature of a measure to the voters.

referendum, initiative a *referendum* held on measures proposed by a *group* of citizens.

referendum, optional a *referendum* involving the legislature's option to refer the measure to the voters.

referendum, statutory submission of ordinary *laws* to the electorate after they have been approved by the legislature.

reflex 1. *response* plus its *eliciting stimulus*. (Skinner, B.F.). 2. see *response*. 3. simple automatic response.

reflex, chain an *innate* sequence of *acts*, each act being the *response* to the preceding act and the *stimulus* for the succeeding act.

reflex, circular *act* which is *stimulus* for its own repetition.

reflex, conditioned *reflex* resulting from stimulus-response connection formed by pairing original *stimulus* (*unconditioned stimulus*) with a new stimulus (*conditioned stimulus*).

reflex, postural *reflex* contributing to maintenance of a *posture*.

reflex, unconditioned *innate* or original *reflex*.

reflexology the study of *reflexes*. **reflexological** *a*.

reform limited social change involving piecemeal improvements.

reform, agrarian improvements in the *agrarian structure*. see also *reform, land*.

reform, land 1. a basic change in *land tenure* arrangements. 2. see *reform, agrarian*.

reformism the doctrine of social change by gradual, piecemeal improvements.

reformulation adaptation of borrowed cultural elements.

refugee 1. person who has left his native country through fear. (MDD). 2. person who has left his country through fear and intends to settle permanently in his new country. (Petersen). 3. person who is uprooted and lacking national protection and status. see also *exile*; *expatriate*; *emigré*; *person, displaced*; *expellee*.

refugee, internal see *refugee, national*.

refugee, international a *refugee* in a *state* other than his own.

refugee, national a *refugee[3]* in his own *state*.

region 1. area possessing common characteristics differentiating it from other areas or possessing characteristics giving it a unity. 2. a major subdivision of a *state territory* officially delimited for a specified function. 3. a *territory* consisting of two or more *states* delimited for a specified purpose.

region, administrative 1. see *area, administrative*. 2. see *region[2]*.

region, agricultural large, sub-continental area which is agriculturally homogeneous.

region, culture see *area, culture*.

region, depressed a sub-national area of declining or stagnant *economy*.

region, economic a technologically homogeneous area requiring its own development *policy*.

region, international see *region[3]*.

region, metropolitan see *area, metropolitan*.

region, nodal those areal units dominated by the same central place.

region, synthetic a *region* of contrasting but interrelated parts.

region, urbanized a *region* possessing an *urban* character.

regionalism 1. using the *region* as a basis for *planning* and development. 2.

social movement to revive regional identities and feeling. 3. the possession by regions of *group consciousness.*

regionalism, city the presence of *dominant cities* having dependent integrated *communities.* (McKenzie, R.D.).

regionalization the division of a *state territory* into *regions².* **regionalize** *v.*

register variety of a language defined with reference to the circumstances in which it is used. see also *dialect.*

register, population an official register of the *vital statistics* of the *population* which is kept continuously up to date.

registration, civil registration of *vital statistics* with the civil (i.e. non-religious) authorities.

registration, continuous *civil registration* involving the registration of *vital events* on their occurrence.

regression 1. predicting the *value⁶* of one of a pair of intercorrelated *variables* corresponding to a given *value⁶* of the other variable. 2. tendency for average measure of offspring on some characteristic to be closer to *population* average than is the parental average. 3. tendency for extreme *scores* on tests and *scales²* to be less extreme on retesting. 4. a return to less mature behaviour.

regression, filial see *regression².*

regression, cultural a similarity occurring cross-culturally in historically separate areas or *area co-traditions.*

reification attributing the reality of being 'things' to abstractions. **reify** *v.*

reinforcement 1. change in a *response* probability. 2. see *reinforcement, positive.* 3. the use of *authority* to prevent deviations from culturally-prescribed behaviour.

reinforcement, autogenic strengthening of a *response* tendency by *factors* within the organism.

reinforcement, negative decrease in a *response* probability.

reinforcement, positive increase in *response* probability.

reinforcement, social strengthening a *response* tendency by means of a social reward.

reinforcer event changing a *response* probability.

reinforcer, negative event decreasing a *response* probability.

reinforcer, positive event increasing a *response* probability.

rejectee 1. individual who receives many sociometric rejections and few sociometric choices. *(sociom.).* 2. an individual who is rejected. see also *rejection.*

rejection depriving an individual of appropriate and normal *interaction.*

relation, primary see *relationship, primary.*

relation, secondary see *relationship, secondary.*

relations, ethnic relations between *ethnic groups.*

relations, sustenance those social relations directly related to survival in a particular *habitat.*

relationship, associational a *social relationship* entered into by individuals as a means to an end. (MacIver).

relationship, avoidance extreme type of *respect relationship* involving mutual avoidance.

relationship, communal a *social relationship* entered into by individuals as an end in itself. (MacIver).

relationship, diagonal relationship which is neither between organizational peers nor is superior-subordinate.

relationship, dominance a *social relationship* involving the dominance of one individual over the other.

relationship, face-to-face a *social relationship* involving *face-to-face contacts.*

relationship, formal a *social relationship* which is explicitly-formulated.

relationship, functional a *social relationship* involving *segmental contacts*.

relationship, horizontal peer-to-peer relationship in *organization*.

relationship, individual see *relationship, social¹*.

relationship, informal a *social relationship* which is not explicitly-formulated.

relationship, joking relationship between relatives which involves *joking behaviour*. see also *partners, joking*.

relationship, joking, asymmetrical a *joking relationship* in which only one *joking partner* has the right to practise *joking behaviour* towards the other. (Radcliffe-Brown).

relationship, joking, symmetrical a *joking relationship* in which both *joking partners* have the right to practise *joking behaviour* towards the other. (Radcliffe-Brown).

relationship, line a relationship in an *organization* permitting the exercise of *line functions*. see also *relationship, staff*.

relationship, multiplex a *social relationship* involving several types of interest. (Gluckman).

relationship, personal an *individual relationship* which is not between mutually substitutable persons. (Paine, R.).

relationship, power a *social relationship* in which one or both parties can exercise *power* over the other.

relationship, power, bilateral a *social relationship* in which both parties can exercise *power* over the other.

relationship, power, unilateral a *social relationship* in which only one of the parties can exercise *power* over the other.

relationship, primary a *social relationship* which is intimate, personal, diffuse.

relationship, privileged a kinship relationship in which pre-marital and/or extra-marital intercourse is permitted.

relationship, respect prescribed relationship between relatives which involves maintaining respectful distance.

relationship, secondary a *social relationship* which is non-intimate, impersonal, specific.

relationship, segmental a *social relationship* involving only a segment of the other person's *activities*.

relationship, simplex see *relationship, single-interest*.

relationship, single-interest a *social relationship* involving only one type of interest. (Gluckman).

relationship, social 1. a series of modes of behaviour of A towards B and of B towards A. 2. that which a *set¹* of *individual relationships* have in common.

relationship, sociometric a relationship between two *group* members of interpersonal choice, rejection, or indifference.

relationship, staff a relationship in an *organization* permitting the exercise of *staff functions*. see also *relationship, line*.

relationship, totemic the relationship between *totemite* and *totem*.

relationship, vertical superior-subordinate relationship in *organization*.

relative, ablineal see *ablineal*.

relative, affinal a relative by *marriage*.

relative, bilateral a relative who is both a *patrilateral* and a *matrilateral relative* to *ego*.

relative, colineal see *colineal*.

relative, collateral a relative not related to *ego* as *ascendant³* or descendant.

relative, consanguineal a person socially-defined as genetically connected to a given person.

relative, distant relative more distant than a *tertiary relative*.

relative, effective see *relative, intimate*.

relative, genetic a relative by *genetic[1]* connection.

relative, intimate relative with whom *ego* is in intimate contact.

relative, jural a person socially-defined as a relative.

relative, lateral see *relative, collateral*.

relative, lineal a relative related to *ego* as *ascendant[3]* or descendant.

relative, maternal see *relative, matrilineal*.

relative, matrilateral a relative related to *ego* on the mother's side.

relative, matrilineal a relative related to *ego* through females.

relative, paternal see *relative, patrilineal*.

relative, patrilateral a relative related to *ego* on the father's side.

relative, patrilineal a relative related to *ego* through males.

relative, primary member of a person's *nuclear family*.

relative, secondary *primary relative* of a primary relative.

relative, tertiary *primary relative* of a *secondary relative*.

relative, uterine see *relative, matrilineal*.

relatives, avoidance relatives in an *avoidance relationship*.

relatives, cross-sex relatives of opposite sex.

relatives, joking relatives in a *joking relationship*.

relatives, parallel relatives or offspring of *siblings* of the same sex.

relatives, respect relatives in a *respect relationship*.

relativism, cultural 1. the doctrine that cultural phenomena should be evaluated in terms of their *function*. 2. the denial of the possibility of *cross-cultural‖value* judgments.

relativism, ethical 1. the doctrine that moral rules must be justified by their cultural context. 2. the diversity of *moral systems*.

releaser structural characteristic or behaviour of organism releasing a species-specific *response* in another organism.

reliability extent to which test reproduces measurements of what in fact it measures; consistency of repeated measurements. see also *validity*.

reliability, chance-half see *reliability, split-half*.

reliability, inter-coder degree to which coders agree on their *coding* of the same responses or observations.

reliability, inter-scorer degree to which scorers agree on their scoring of the same responses or observations.

reliability, parallel-form see *reliability, split-half*.

reliability, repeat see *reliability, test-retest*.

reliability, split-ballot see *reliability, split-half*.

reliability, split-half results compared of applications of two halves of test, the *items* of each half randomly selected.

reliability, test-retest results compared of two applications of test to the same *population*.

religion 1. belief in spiritual beings. 2. seeking aid of *spirits* through appeal of *prayer*. (Frazer). 3. *set[1]* of supernatural beliefs and practices conceived as an end in itself.(Malinowski). 4. *ideology* of the supernatural. (Piddington). **religious** *a.* see also *magic*; *sorcery*; *witchcraft*.

religion, comparative the comparative study of *religion*.

religion, redemptive a *religion* centred on salvation.

religion, sociology of the study of *religion* in its social context.

religion, state the official *religion* of a *state*.

religiosity an individual's degree of participation in religious *rituals* or the sum of those behaviours and *attitudes* of an individual which are judged to be *religious* within a *group* or *society*.

re-migration *migration* to area of departure of persons who have already migrated. **re-migrate** *v.* **re-migrant** *pers n.*

remission 1. reduction in a prison sentence made while it is being served. 2.

removal of part or whole of sentence, leaving conviction standing. **remit** *vt.* see also *pardon*; *amnesty*; *commutation*; *reprieve*; *respite*.

renegade ex-member who not only repudiates the *norms* of the *group* and membership in it, but joins the opposition. (Merton, R.K.).

repatriate a person who has been sent back or who has been assisted in returning to his own country. **repatriate** *vt.*

repatriation 1. sending back a person or assisting the return of a person to his own country. 2. resumption by an individual of a lost nationality.

replicate that which receives all the *treatments³* in a single *replication*.

replication 1. repeating *treatments³* on different *experimental units*. 2. any one of these repetitions.

replication, external *replication* using a larger *sample* or more samples to see whether the finding still holds. see also *replication, internal*.

replication, fractional a *replication* involving only a part of the total number of *treatment³* combinations.

replication, horizontal *replication* on further units or *variables* on the same level. (Galtung).

replication, intergroup *replication* using a new *group* of *subjects¹*.

replication, internal *replication* using independent *subsamples* to see whether the finding still holds. see also *replication, external*.

replication, intersubject *replication* using a new individual *subject¹*.

replication, intragroup *replication* using the same *group* of *subjects¹*.

replication, intrasubject *replication* using the same individual *subject¹*.

replication, item the use of several *questionnaire‖items* eliciting basically the same information as a means of testing *reliability* or studying the various dimensions of an *attitude*.

replication, vertical *replication* on subunits or superunits or on *subvariables* or *supervariables*. (Galtung).

report an account of events written after the events have occurred. (Madge, J.). see also *record*.

reportability probability of offence being reported to the police.

reprieve postponement of the execution of a sentence.

reproduction rate extent to which a hypothetical male of female *birth cohort* is replaced in the next *generation²*.

reproduction rate, effective average number of live daughters born to a hypothetical female *birth cohort* on assumption of current *age-specific fertility rates* and estimated future *age-specific death rates*.

reproduction rate, female average number of female births to a hypothetical female *birth cohort*.

reproduction rate, gross *reproduction rate* which assumes zero *mortality¹* until the end of the reproductive period.

reproduction rate, male average number of male births to a hypothetical male *birth cohort*.

reproduction rate, maternal see *reproduction rate, female*.

reproduction rate, net *reproduction rate* which assumes that *birth cohort* is subjected to current *age-specific fertility* and *mortality rates*.

reproduction rate, paternal see *reproduction rate, male*.

requirements, role *role prescriptions* or *role expectations*.(Lundberg).

requisites, functional conditions necessary for the survival of a *social system*. see also *prerequisites, functional*; *imperatives, functional*; *requirements, functional*.

research, field see *work, field*.

research, group see *research, organized*.

research, individual independent research by an individual.

research, nonreactive research employing *unobtrusive measures*.

research, observational nonexperimental research based on observation.

research, operations (OP) the application of *scientific method* to administrative problems.

research, organized co-ordinated research by a *group*.

research, survey see *research, observational*.

resegregation the re-establishment of *segregation* following *desegregation*.

reserve, labour those persons outside the *labour force* available for work in a national emergency.

residence place of residence of couple after *marriage*.

residence, ambilocal see *residence, bilocal*.

residence, amitalocal residence of couple with or near husband's father's sister.

residence, avunculocal residence of couple with or near husband's mother's brother.

residence, avunculouxorilocal residence of couple with or near wife's mother's brother.

residence, avunculovirilocal residence of couple with or near husband's mother's brother.

residence, bilocal residence of couple permitted with or near parents of either husband or wife.

residence, duolocal spouses apart in their *natal units,* husband visiting wife.

residence, duo-patrilocal *duolocal residence* for initial period followed by permanent *patrilocal residence*.

residence, fililocal residence of a parent with one of his married children.

residence, matricipient residence of couple in which mother of either husband or wife is a co-resident.

residence, matrilocal residence of couple with or near wife's parents.

residence, matri-patrilocal *matrilocal residence* for initial period followed by permanent *patrilocal residence*.

residence, matriuxorilocal residence of couple with or near wife's mother.

residence, matrivirilocal residence of couple with or near husband's mother.

residence, natolocal see *residence, duolocal*.

residence, neolocal residence of couple away from relatives.

residence, parenticipient residence of couple in which either parent of either partner is a co-resident.

residence, patricipient residence of couple in which father of either husband or wife is a co-resident.

residence, patrilocal residence of couple with or near husband's parents.

residence, patriuxorilocal residence of couple with or near wife's father.

residence, patrivirilocal residence of couple with or near husband's father.

residence, unilocal 1. residence which is not bilocal or neolocal. (Murdock). 2. residence of couple in the already existing *household* of husband or wife. (Titiev, M.).

residence, unilocal-matrilocal residence of couple in the already existing *household* of wife.

residence, unilocal-patrilocal residence of couple in the already existing *household* of husband.

residence, utrolocal *residence rule* under which couple must choose one of two places of residence.

residence, uxorilocal residence of couple with or near wife's relatives.

residence, virilocal residence of couple with or near husband's relatives.

residues *sentiments* motivating *nonlogical actions*. (Pareto, V.).see also *derivations*.

resocialization *socialization* of an individual following *desocialization*.

respite see *reprieve*.

respondent 1. person questioned by a *schedule, questionnaire, scale²*, in a *sur-*

vey or in an interview. 2. organism reacting to a *stimulus*. 3. a *response* to an *eliciting stimulus*.

response behavioural event consequent to behavioural or extraorganismal antecedent event.

response, abient *response* tending to remove organism from exposure to a given *stimulus*.

response, adient *response* tending to expose organism to more of a given *stimulus*.

response, bicultural *response* to *culture contact* in the form of *biculturism*.

response, circular see *reaction. circular[1]*.

response, conditioned *response* elicited by a *conditioned stimulus*.

response, dichotomous a *response* which can only take two *values[6]*.

response, differential one person turns to *crime*, whilst others in the same *environment* do not.

response, mimetic *response* copying behaviour of another.

response, motor *response* defined with the organism as the frame of reference. see also *response, orienting*.

response, orienting *response* defined in terms of *environment*. see also *response, motor*.

response, protective automatic protective movement.

response, statokinetic *postural reflex* serving to maintain stability and orientation while the body is in motion.

response, terminal *response* of *subject[1]* on the final *trial* to which he is exposed.

response, transactional an *action* in response to a *transactional stimulus*. (Berne, E.).

response, unconditioned *response* elicited by an *unconditioned stimulus*.

response, vacuum a *response* without any preceding external stimulation.

responsibility 1. imputation of an *action* to a person. 2. accountability.

responsibility, collective the accountability of a *group* for the actions of any its members. see also *responsibility, vicarious*.

responsibility, general accountability for a wide range of activities.

responsibility, legal accountability at *law* for an *action*.

responsibility, moral imputation of an *action* to a person.

responsibility, specific accountability for a narrow range of activities.

responsibility, vicarious the accountability of persons, *groups* or *states* for actions other than their own.

restratification the emergence of a new *stratification*.

retaliation socially-approved, controlled, limited acts of revenge. (Radcliffe-Brown).

retention (Herskovits) see *survival*.

retreatism rejection by an individual of both the *cultural goals* and the institutionalized means of a *society*. (Merton, R.K.).

retreatism, economic *retreatism* in which the individual is content to live at *subsistence level*. (Glaser, D.).

retreatism, juvenile *retreatism* in which the individual adopts a juvenile life style. (Glaser, D.).

retrocession ceding back of ceded *territory*. see also *cession*.

retrodiction (Rhyle, G.) see *postdiction*.

returnee see *re-migrant*.

revitalization the acquisition through a movement, of a more satisfying *culture* by rapid acceptance of a pattern of multiple *innovations*. (Wallace, A.F.C.). see also *movement, revitalization; process, revitalization*.

revolt a renunciation of subjection to those in *authority*. see also *uprising; insurrection; putsch; rebellion; revolution; coup*.

revolution 1. a radical change in the form of *society*. 2. a critical breakthrough in *cultural evolution.* 3. forcible overthrow of the *government.* 4. forcible change of the form of government. 5. a radical change in the form of government. 6. a radical change affecting a considerable portion of a *culture.* 7. any radical change. 8. a radical and rapid change in the form of society or a considerable portion of a culture. 9. a permanent change in a *polity* resulting in new ways of mobilizing and sharing *power.* see also *rebellion*; *revolt*; *putsch*; *insurrection*; *uprising*; *coup.*

revolution, agricultural see *revolution, food-producing.*

revolution, demographic fall from high to relatively low *fertility* and *mortality[1].*

revolution, economic a radical change in the *economic system.*

revolution, food-producing substitution of *husbandry* for *food-gathering.*

revolution, palace a *revolution* carried out by persons close to the rulers.

revolution, political a radical change in the *political system.*

revolution, rural the elimination of rural-urban differences.

revolution, scientific a shift in science to a new *paradigm[2].*

revolution, social a radical change in the *social structure.*

revolution, total the total transformation of *society.*

revolution, urban the first appearance of towns in the world.

revolution, vital see *revolution, demographic.*

rhabdomancy *divination* by means of the divining-rod. **rhabdomantic**[c] *a.* **rhabdomancer** *pers n.*

rhochrematics flow process from raw-material sources to final consumer.

right, junior see *ultimogeniture.*

rights, domestic rights in a married woman to her domestic services.

rights, genetricial rights in a married woman as a mother, i.e., rights to her children.

rights, kinship *genetricial rights* and *uxorial rights* in a married woman.

rights, uxorial rights in a married woman as a wife, i.e., rights to her domestic and sexual services.

rigidity, group unadaptability of *group* to changed conditions.

ring, market a *set[1]* of market places with meetings held in rotation.

ring, metropolitan that part of a *metropolitan area* lying outside the *metropolis.*

risk 1. a known probability. 2. probability of event occurring to element of a *population.* 3. probability of loss. see also *uncertainty.*

risk, categoric the *risk[2]* of an offender being convicted resulting from his *social category.*

risk, morbidity *risk[2]* of individual having illness during lifetime, if he lives long enough to pass period of *risk[2].*

rite element in a *ritual.*

rite, calendrical *rite* which is on the *ceremonial calendar.*

rite, critical *rite* intended to help an individual or *society* only in time of crisis.

rite, prescribing *rite* consisting of a prescribed *action.*

rite, proscribing *rite* consisting of an avoidance.

rite, scheduled see *rite, calendrical.*

rite, territorial *rite* marking the passage of a person or persons over a territorial boundary.

rite, unscheduled *rite* the performance of which cannot be anticipated and is thus not on the *ceremonial calendar.*

rites, puberty *ceremonies* marking transition to adult *status.*

ritual 1. *ceremonial* which symbolizes the *status structure.* (Leach). 2. *holy‖ceremonial.* 3. expressive, symbolic behaviour. (Beattie). 4. sanctioned, symbolic behaviour having a non-empirical referent and aimed at controlling human affairs. (Firth, R.). 5. behaviour which is more rigid than is technically justified. (Nadel).

ritual, avoidance a prescribed form of *deference behaviour* for maintaining *social distance.* (Goffman, E.).

ritual, constitutive *ritual* which expresses or alters *social relationships.* (Gluckman, M.).

ritual, ego-centred *ritual* for the benefit of an individual.

ritual, factitive *ritual* for increasing the material well-being of a *group.* (Gluckman, M.).

ritual, group-centred *ritual* for the benefit of the *group.*

ritual, presentational a prescribed form of *deference behaviour* which promotes *interaction[1].* (Goffman, E.).

ritualism 1. emphasis on the importance of *ritual.* 2. rejection by an individual of the *cultural goals* and acceptance of the institutionalized means of a *society.* (Merton, R.K.).

ritualization the making ritual of an *activity.* **ritualize** *v.*

rivalry personalized *competition.* see also *emulation.*

role 1. part meant to be played by a person. 2. the dynamic aspect of *status.* (Linton). 3. the processual aspect of status. (Parsons, T.). 4. *set[1]* of rights and duties with further characteristics which go beyond occupational requirements. (Nadel). 5. the prescribed ways of behaving attached to a *position.* (Newcomb). 6. the obligations attached to a position.7. *attitudes, values* and behaviour prescribed for and rights attached to a status. 8. *set[1]* of *norms* and expectations attached to a position. (Banton). 9. actual behaviour of status occupant. 10. individual's organized *system* of participation. (Parsons, T.). 11. enactment of rights and duties attached to a status. (Goffman, E.). 12. personal variant in carrying out the requirements of a particular status. (Mandelbaum, D.G.). 13. any position whether or not institutionalized. (Levy, M.J.). 14. part played by a player in a *heuristic game.*

role, age *set[1]* of *roles* peculiar to those persons lying within specified age limits. see also *age-group[1].*

role, age-sex *set[1]* of *roles* peculiar to the members of one sex lying within specified age limits.

role, basic 1. an important *role.* 2. a role which is always salient. 3. a role relevant to every social or physical situation.

role, counterfeit a *role* which an individual pretends is his own, but iş used as cover for his actual role. (Lemert, E.M.).

role, diffuse see *role, generalized.*

role, expressive a *role* contributing to an expressive *function.* see also *role, instrumental*; *role, maintenance.*

role, generalized a *role* governing a wide range of situations. see also *role, specific.*

role, group-building (Benne, K.) see *role, maintenance.*

role, index *rôle* determining a person's *status.* (Slotkin, J.S.).

role, instrumental a *role* contributing to an instrumental *function.* see also *role, expressive*; *role, maintenance.*

role, internalized a *role* played by an individual which has become part of his *self-concept.*

role, maintenance a *role* contributing to a maintenance *function.* see also *role, expressive*; *role, instrumental.*

role, neighbour the prescribed part of *neighbouring‖activities.* see also *neighbours*; *neighbouring*; *neighbourhood.*

role, non-relational a *role* capable of independent definition. (Nadel).

role, predicted a predicted *role performance[1].*

role, received a *focal person's* perception of a *sent role.* (Rommenveit).

role, relational 1. a *role* incapable of independent definition. (Nadel). 2. a role requiring two or more persons for performance. (Foddy, W.H.).

role, representative the *role* of representing a *group* to persons outside the group by behaving in a way which conforms to the group's *norms*.

role, sent the *role expectations* sent by the members of a *role-set* to the *focal person*. (Rommenveit).

role, sex the expected behaviour of members of the same sex.

role, sex, social the expected non-erotic behaviour of members of the same sex.

role, specific a *role* governing a narrow range of situations. see also *role, generalized*.

role, status the *role* attached to a *status*. (LaPiere).

role-playing 1. enacting a *role* which is not one's own role. 2. see *enactment, role*.

role-relationship a person may play the same *role* towards several persons, with each of whom he has a role-relationship.

role-sequence standardized sequence of *role performances* of an individual with a specified *status*.

role-set *set[1]* of *roles* associated with a *status*.

role-set, diversified *role-set* involving more than one class of *role senders*. (Snoek, J.D.).

role-taking 1. see *role-playing[1]*. 2. *role-playing* by children in anticipation of an adult *role*.

role-taking reflexive taking the *role* of another in order to perceive others' *perception* of oneself.

roles, multiple the complex of *roles* associated with the totality of *statuses* occupied by an individual.

rope *descent group* resulting from *alternating descent*.

rotation, crop growing different crops in a recurring succession on same piece of land.

rotation, field-forest see *cultivation, shifting*.

rotation, job rotating the operations to be performed amongst a *group* of workers.

rotation, land regular *shifting cultivation*.

round, holy see *circumambulation*.

routine 1. recurrent series of *acts*. 2. a pre-established action pattern unfolded during performances. (Goffman, E.).

routine, habit a *routine* maintained by a *habit* sequence.

routinization, ecological routinized movement of *population* and goods within a *metropolitan area*.

rule 1. regularity in behaviour recognized by members of a *society*. 2. regularity in behaviour discovered by observer. 3. prescribed regularity in behaviour. 4. statement that certain behaviour is preferential.

rule, merging *practice[4]* of applying same *kinship term* to offspring of same-sex siblings.

rule, rank-size the doctrine that the nth largest town will have a *population* one-nth that of the largest town.

rule, residence *norm* governing *residence*.

rule, skewing *practice[4]* of applying same *kinship term* to man's sister's relatives and daughter's relatives.

rumour talk concerning events or the *conduct* of persons, the sender rejecting *moral responsibility*, which does not follow specific channels. (Bailey, F.G.). see also *gossip*; *scandal*.

run 1. a *trial* of a *simulation model*. 2. one or a series of the same *attribute* or a series of increasing or decreasing *values[6]* in a series of observations.

rural 1. pertaining to a small *agglomeration, dispersed settlement*, or uninhabited *territory*. 2. not characterized by *urbanism*.

ruralism *rural* way of life.

ruralization 1. increase in proportion of *rural population*. 2. the process of becoming *rural*.

rurban having both *rural* and *urban* characteristics.

rurbanization the acquisition of *rurban* character by an area.

sacerdotalism the doctrine of the necessity for the *authority* of a priesthood.

sacred 1. technically non-functional. (Leach).(opposite of *profane¹*). 2. *social action* manifesting emotionalized reluctance to change. 3. segregated and forbidden. (Durkheim). 4. (Davis, K.). see *holy*. 5. pertaining to things of ultimate concern. (Spiro, M.E.).

sacrifice religious act which, through *consecration* of *victim¹* modifies condition of the moral person who accomplishes it or that of certain objects with which he is concerned. (Mauss, M.) **sacrificial** *a*.

sacrifice, building human *sacrifice* in which body is buried in a wall of or in or under the foundations of a building.

sacrifice, foundation human *sacrifice* in which body is buried in or under the foundations of a building.

sacrifice, objective *sacrifice* in which an object directly receives the *sacrificial* action. (Mauss, M.).

sacrifice, personal *sacrifice* in which *personality* of *sacrifier* is directly affected. (Mauss, M.).

sacrifice, vicarious the *sacrifice* of a proxy.

sacrifice, votive a *sacrifice* to fulfill a *vow*.

sacrificer person performing a *sacrifice*.

sacrifier the subject benefiting from the *sacrifice*. (Mauss, M.).

salience individual's awareness of his *group* membership.

salon, social non-institutionalized, informal *interest group* having highest degree of directness of member *interaction*. (Simmel, G.). see also *circle, social*; *set, social*.

sample representative part of group of units.

sample, adequate *sample* large enough to have a *sampling error* within the desired limits.

sample, master large *sample* drawn for future investigations from which samples are drawn when required.

sample, stratified *sample* consisting of *sub-samples* drawn from classes into which the *population* has been divided.

sample, stratified, disproportional *stratified sample* in which equal number of cases is drawn from each *stratum*.

sample, stratified, proportional *stratified sample* in which the same percentage of cases is drawn from each *stratum*.

sample, truncated *sample* omitting cases having *values⁶* outside certain limits.

sampling drawing *samples* from *populations*.

sampling, accidental nonprobability *sampling* involving nonsystematic selection of cases which happen to be available. see also *sampling, probability*.

sampling, area *sampling* involving the selection of sub-areas of a larger area, the *population* of sub-areas being stratified or unstratified.

sampling, areola see *sampling, area*.

sampling, behaviour *time sampling* of behaviour.

sampling, block see *sampling, area*.

sampling, cluster *sampling* in which each *sampling unit* consists of more than one element.

sampling, configurational see *sampling, grid*.

sampling, convenience see *sampling, accidental*.

sampling, domal a type of *area sampling* involving a systematic selection of houses in an area with a specification as to which persons in each selected house are to be included in the *sample*.

sampling, element *sampling* in which each *sampling unit* consists of only one element.

sampling, epsem *sampling* in which the *population elements* have equal probability of selection.

sampling, extensive 1. *sampling* involving a low density of sampling points, i.e. space-extensive. 2. sampling involving a superficial study of a large number of topics, i.e. item-extensive. 3. sampling covering a long period, i.e. time-extensive.

sampling, grid a type of *cluster sampling* in which a grid is placed on a map and grid areas are selected as clusters.

sampling, intensive 1. *sampling* involving a high degree of sampling points, i.e. space-intensive. 2. sampling involving a deep study of a small number of topics, i.e. item-intensive. 3. sampling covering a short period, i.e. time-intensive.

sampling, line *sampling* by taking cases of *sampling frame* falling on specified lines of lined paper.

sampling, list see *sampling, systematic*.

sampling, multi-phase *sampling* in which some data is obtained from the full *sample* and additional data is obtained, either at the same time or later, from *sub-samples*, the same type of *sampling unit* being used at each phase.

sampling, multi-stage *sampling* in which different types of *sampling unit* are sampled at different sampling stages.

sampling, ordinal see *sampling, systematic*.

sampling, population *sampling* in which the *population elements* are persons.

sampling, probability *sampling* in which every *population element* has a known nonzero probability of selection.

sampling, probability, area see *sampling, area*.

sampling, sequential see *analysis, sequential*.

sampling, situation *sampling* in which the *population elements* are types of situation.

sampling, space *sampling* over space as a protection against unknown sources of variation.

sampling, structural *sampling* in which the *sampling units* are connected by specified relations. (*sociometric*, dominance, *communication, interaction*).

sampling, systematic drawing *sample* by selecting from a file or list after random start from I to k of every kth *sampling unit*.

sampling, time *sampling* of periods for observation.

sampling, unitary *sampling* in which the ultimate units are selected directly from the *population*.

sanction 1. reward or *punishment*. 2. a promise of reward or threat of punishment. (Epstein, A.L.). 3. any measure taken in support of a social order. (Kelsen).

sanction, coercive *sanction* based on threat of or use of *force*.

sanction, diffuse *sanction* not involving a recognized *procedure* but consisting of spontaneous behaviour of members of the *community* acting as individuals. (Radcliffe-Brown).

sanction, ethical see *sanction, moral*.

sanction, external *sanction* applied to the individual by others.

sanction, formal see *sanction, organized*.

sanction, immediate *religious sanction* operating automatically without *spirit* intervention.

sanction, informal see *sanction, diffuse*.

sanction, internal *sanction* self-applied in the form of a psychic state.

sanction, jural a *sanction* imposed by a legitimate authority in a *society* lacking developed forensic *institutions*. (Radcliffe-Brown).

sanction, legal 1. a *sanction* imposed by *law*. 2. a sanction imposed by means of forensic *institutions*. see also *sanction, jural*.

sanction, moral a *sanction* consisting of *shame²* or guilt.

sanction, mystic see *sanction, religious*.

sanction, negative *sanction* in the form of a *punishment*.

sanction, normative *sanction* based on persuasion or suggestion.

sanction, organized *sanction* imposed by a recognized *procedure*. (Radcliffe-Brown).

sanction, penal an *organized, negative sanction*.

sanction, physical a *sanction* involving *violence* or physical restraint.

sanction, positive *sanction* in the form of a reward.

sanction, premial an *organized, positive sanction*. (Radcliffe-Brown).

sanction, public a *sanction* imposed by the *community*.

sanction, religious a *sanction* consisting of the modification of the individual's *religious* condition.

sanction, ritual see *sanction, religious*.

sanction, satirical a *negative sanction* consisting of ridicule.

sanction, supernatural see *sanction, religious*.

sanction, transcendental see *sanction, religious*.

satiation satisfaction of *drive*.

satiation, semantic a *symbol*'s loss of meaning for an individual resulting from prolonged repetition.

satisficing choosing the course of action having an acceptable instead of an optimum outcome.

saturation, channel the number of channels with which a given position must deal in a *communication network*. (Gilchrist, J.C.).

saturation, input the number of *messages* coming in to a given position in a *communication network*.

saturation, ouput the number of *messages* going out from a given position in a *communication network*.

scalar pertaining to the gradation of *authority* and corresponding *responsibility²* in an *organization*.

scale 1. a level of *measurement¹*. 2. any group of *items¹* employed to rank any group of individuals along any dimension.

scale, absolute see *scale, ratio*.

scale, acculturation a *scale²* for measuring degree of *acculturation*.

scale, a priori *scale²* the *items¹* of which are judgmentally ordered.

scale, Bogardus-type a *cumulative scale* measuring *attitude* towards *groups* by the closeness of relationship to which *subject¹* is willing to admit members of group.

scale, cardinal see *scale, interval*.

scale, category see *scale, nominal*.

scale, classificatory see *scale, nominal*.

scale, composite level of *measurement¹* at which there are both relations between the objects and relations between the distances between objects.

scale, continuous *scale²* with infinite number of possible *values⁶* between highest and lowest value.

scale, cumulative a *scale²* in which an affirmative *response* to a given *item¹* implies affirmative responses to all items scoring less.

scale, designatory see *scale, nominal*.

scale, differential a *scale²* consisting of *items¹* ordered on judges' *ratings²*.

scale, discontinuous see *scale, discrete*.

scale, discrete *scale²* with finite number of possible *values⁶* between highest and lowest value.

scale, genotypic a *scale²* measuring data on the *genotypic level*.

scale, graphic see *scale, rating, graphic*.

scale, Guttman a series of *items¹* in which *responses* to individual items are predictable from the *respondent's* total *score²*.

scale, intensity see *scale, rating*.

scale, interval level of *measurement¹* at which there are equal units but no true zero; thus we cannot say that one *measurement²* is twice as great as another.

scale, latent see *scale, genotypic*.

scale, manifest see *scale, phenotypic*.

scale, measurement level of *measurement¹*.

scale, metric, ordered level of *measurement¹* at which the relation of 'greater than' holds for some or all pairs of distances between adjacent objects on an *ordinal scale*.

scale, nominal level of *measurement¹* which consists of giving *symbols* to equivalence classes.

scale, numerical see *scale, rating, numerical*.

scale, ordered-ordered level of *measurement¹* at which the relation of 'greater than' holds for all pairs of distances between adjacent objects on an *ordinal scale*.

scale, ordered-partially ordered level of *measurement¹* at which the relation of 'greater than' holds for some but not all pairs of distances between adjacent objects on an *ordinal scale*.

scale, ordinal level of *measurement¹* which consists of ordering things according to size.

scale, partially ordered level of *measurement¹* at which the relation of 'greater than' holds between some but not all pairs of equivalence classes.

scale, phenotypic a *scale²* measuring data on the *phenotypic level*.

scale, rank see *scale, ordinal*.

scale, rating *scale²* on which is given an estimate of the degree of a specified characteristic.

scale, rating, compound a *rating scale* consisting of two or more individual rating scales, the *scores* on which are combined to form a total score on the total *variable* for each *subject¹*.

scale, rating, descriptive a *rating scale*, continuous or discontinuous, having descriptions of various intensities.

scale, rating, graphic a *rating scale* which is continuous and which consists of a line any position on which can be marked, the significance of the two ends and the middle being shown by words or *scale numbers* or both.

scale, rating, itemized a *rating scale* which is discontinuous and which consists of descriptions of intensities with or without *scale numbers*.

scale, rating, numerical a *rating scale* which is discontinuous and which consists of *scale numbers* with or without descriptions of intensities.

scale, ratio highest level of *measurement¹* at which there are equal units taken from a true zero; thus we can say that one *measurement²* is twice as great as another.

scale, stimulus *continuum* of *stimulus‖values⁶*.

scandal 1. defamatory talk, without an overt moral evaluation, not following specific channels. (Bailey, F.G.). 2. talk intended to discredit other persons. (Paine, R.). see also *gossip; rumour*.

scapulimancy *divination* by means of scapulae. **scapulimantic** *a*.

scarification producing scars for non-medical purposes. **scarify** *v*.

scarifier a person who scarifies.

scarnimento cutting the flesh from a corpse before burial.

scatophagy the eating of excrement, whether or not culturally regulated.

scatophagous *a.*

scatoscopy *divination* by means of excrement.

scatter see *dispersion.*

scattergram see *diagram, scatter.*

scatterplot see *diagram, scatter.*

scedasticity in the relationship between two *quantitative variables,* the *dispersion* of the *values[6]* of one *variable* for each of the *values[6]* of the other variable. **scedastic** *a.*

scenario a description or representation of a hypothetical sequence of events showing the alternative *decisions* at *decision points* and the possible consequences of each decision with their estimated probabilities.

schedule 1. form, filled in by interviewer or with assistance of interviewer. see also *questionnaire.* 2. a table showing how one *variable* responds to changes in another variable. 3. plan specifying when each operation is to be carried out.

schedule, census *schedule[1]* employed in a *census.*

schedule, collective *census schedule* on which *enumerator* enters successively data for all persons enumerated by him.

schedule, household *census schedule* concerning each and every member of a *household.*

schedule, individual *census schedule* concerning single individual.

schedule, institutional *census schedule* concerning each and every member of a quasi-household.

schedule, observation *schedule[1]* consisting of *observational categories.*

schedule, precoded *schedule[1]* on which *code‖symbols* are printed against the response alternatives.

schedule, reconstructed *schedule[1]* filled up by interviewer after interview.

schedule, structured *schedule[1]* in which the form and order of all the questions are predetermined.

schema, analytical a *system* of definitions plus a *set[1]* of analytical statements derived from it.

schema, definitional a *system* of definitions.

schema, paradigmatic see *paradigm[2].*

scheme, conceptual *system* of *concepts* employed in research.

scheme, sampling see *plan, sampling.*

schismogenesis cumulative interaction in a *society.* **schismogenetic** *a.*

schismogenesis, complementary cumulative interaction in a *society,* involving a cleavage between dissimilar types of behaviour.

schismogenesis, symmetrical cumulative interaction in a *society,* involving a cleavage between similar types of behaviour.

schizophrenia a psychosis the symptoms of which are delusions, hallucinations, thought disorder, emotional blunting, volitional disorders and disorders of locomotor function. **schizophrenic** *a.* & *pers n.*

science, administrative the scientific study of *administration.*

science, normal the activities of developing in full the strengths and weaknesses of *theories* within a *paradigm[2]* tradition. (Kuhn, T.H.).

science, philosophy of the philosophical aspects of science, such as *determinism,* causation, types of *theories, models, paradigms[2], epistemology.*

science, policy 1. any science contributing to the study of the *policy process.* 2. any science contributing to the information needs of *policy.*

science, political the scientific study of political *norms,* political *groups* and *quasi-groups,* political activity, political action and political behaviour.

science, revolutionary the activities involved in the overthrow of a *paradigm[2]* tradition and its replacement by a new *paradigm[2].* (Kuhn, T.H.).

scientism the misapplication to other disciplines of the *methods* of the natural sciences. **scientistic** *a*. see also *physicalism*.

sciomancy 1. *divination* by consulting the shades of the dead. 2. divination from shadows. **sciomantic** *a*.

sciosophy supposed knowledge based on *tradition*.

scopelism 1. throwing enchanted stones on to a neighbour's ground. 2. casting stones on a grave.

score 1. *value*[6] assigned to a test *response*. 2. sum of individual scores by an individual.

score, sociometric an individual's *score* on number of choices received from the other *group* members. *(sociom.).*

scrying *divination* by inspecting colourless quartz or water. **scry** *v*. **scryer** *pers n*.

secession 1. formal withdrawal of an area from a *state*. 2. withdrawal of organized subset from *group*. **secede** *v*.

seclusion, menstrual the institutionalized seclusion of menstruating women.

sect 1. non-accomodated religious *group*. 2. minority religious group formed in protest against another religious group. 3. small, doctrinal group of a *religion*. 4. a group, religious or non-religious, formed in protest against a societally adapted group.

section 1. see *section, marriage*. 2. a *marriage class* in a *four-class system*. 3. an *ethnic group* in a *plural society*.

section, marriage any one of the *sections*[1] from which women can be taken in accordance with the *rules* of a *section system*.

section, sedentary part of a *nomadic society* which is *sedentary*.

sector, role that part of a *role* having to do with a particular type of *role other*. (Goffman, E.).

secular 1. non-religious or civil. 2. pertaining to acceptance on rational grounds as opposed to acceptance on the grounds of veneration and inviolability. 3. very long-term.

secularization transfer of non-religious *functions* from religious to secular *organizations*.

sedentarism the state of being *sedentary*.

sedentarization the acquisition by or the imposition of *sedentarism* on a *group*.

sedentarization, definitive permanent *sedentarization*.

sedentarization, temporary *sedentarization* which is not permanent.

sedentarization, total see *sedentarization, definitive*.

sedentary non-*nomadic* and non-*transhumant*.

segment, horizontal a *sub-society* crosscutting the *vertical segments* of a complex *society*. (Steward, J.).

segment, vertical a local unit of any sort. (Steward, J.).

segmentary consisting of similar, mutually exclusive *groups*.

segmentation 1. division into social structural units performing the same *function*. 2. a state of internal subdivision of a *group*. (Fortes). 3. the process by which a group becomes subdivided internally while retaining its unity. (Barnes). 4. a state of internal subdivision of a group involving a merging series of segments.(Goody, J.). see also *juxtaposition*. 5. the contraposition of *political units*. (Smith, M.G.). 6. the division of a *message* into units at various levels.

segregate a terminologically-distinguished *set*[1] of objects. (Conklin, H.C.).

segregation 1. voluntary or involuntary concentration of particular *population* types or *organizations* in particular areas. 2. separation of persons of different *ethnic groups* in the course of their use of public facilities or the exclusion by the dominant *ethnic group* of persons of other ethnic groups from certain *associations*.

segregation, class *segregation* of *social classes*.

segregation, cultural *segregation* based on cultural differences.

segregation, de facto *segregation* which is not enforced by *law*.

segregation, de jure *segregation* which is enforced by *law*.

segregation, ecological see *segregation, residential*.

segregation, ethnic *segregation* of *ethnic groups*.

segregation, involuntary *residential segregation* not resulting from the preferences of the individuals segregated.

segregation, racial *segregation* based on racial differences.

segregation, residential *segregation* of persons from the point of view of residence.

segregation, rite of a preparation of the individual for his new *status* and *role*. (Van Gennep).

segregation, spatial see *segregation, residential*.

segregation, voluntary *residential segregation* resulting from the preferences of the individuals segregated.

seigniory a piece of land giving the holder *seignorial jurisdiction*. see *fief*; *benefice*; *appanage*.

seignorialism the predominance of *seignorial jurisdiction*.

selection, migratory nonrandom selection of *migrants*, resulting in distributions of migrants according to various characteristics differing from distributions of nonmigrants.

selection, social 1. sorting of individuals into *social positions*. 2. elimination of individuals for various social positions. 3. preferential survival of individuals resulting from social *factors*.

self, looking-glass *self-concept* resulting from *ego*'s perception of others' perception of ego.

self, reflected see *self, looking-glass*.

self, social 1. that aspect of the individual which is perceived by others in social intercourse. 2. those characteristics of the individual which are most important in determining *social interaction*. 3. the socially-determined part of the *personality*. 4. see *self, looking-glass*.

self-actualization developing one's capacities, accepting oneself, and integrating one's motives. (Maslow, A.).

self-appraisal an explicit evaluation of one's own *personality traits*.

self-assessment evaluation of one's own *personality traits*.

self-attitude an *attitude* directed towards the self.

self-check see *self-rating¹*.

self-concept that organization of qualities that an individual attributes to himself.

self-consciousness over-involvement with himself as an *interactant* on the part of a participant in a conversation. (Goffman, E.). see also *interaction-consciousness*; *other-consciousness*.

self-correlation *correlation* between two administrations of test or between comparable forms or random halves of test.

self-enumeration completion of *census schedules* by *respondents¹*.

self-evaluation 1. an evaluative *self-attitude*. 2. the process by which an individual arrives at a decision as to his own worth.

self-hate hate of an individual towards his own *group*.

self-help 1. carrying out of part or whole of right-enforcement process by individual concerned. 2. enforcement of both appearance and judicial decision by individual concerned. 3. community improvement carried out by the *community* itself.

self-ideal a personal condition towards which one strives.

self-image see *self-concept*.

self-insight the recognition, emotionally repugnant or threatening to self-esteem, of one's *personality* characteristics.

self-inventory a self-rated inventory of traits.

self-orientation—collectivity-orientation the incompatible alternatives facing an *actor* of pursuing private interests or *group* interests. (Parsons, T.).

self-perception see *self-concept.*

self-perception, sociometric a *group* member's *perception* of his own *sociometric status.*

self-ranking the action of *ranking* oneself on one or more *variables.*

self-rating 1. estimate of own *personality trait* or performance. 2. the action of estimating own personality trait or performance.

self-rating, sociometric estimate of own *sociometric score.*

self-realization the realization of one's potentialities.

self-recruitment *self-selection* of members for a *group.*

self-report a report made by an individual on himself.

self-segregation see *segregation, voluntary.*

self-selection selection for a *sample* or *social selection* in which the individuals select themselves.

self-sentiment *sentiment* towards the self.

self-survey a *community survey* carried out by the *community* itself.

semantics the science of meaning. **semantic** *a.* **semanticist** *pers n.*

semantics, anthropological branch of *semantics* consisting of *ethnographic semantics* and *ethnologic semantics.*

semantics, descriptive the study of natural languages. (Carnap, R.).

semantics, ethnographic 1. the *semantic* description of particular *cultures.* 2. the description of culturally revealing semantic characteristics.

semantics, ethnologic *semantics* of the terminology of *comparative ethnology.*

semantics, ontogenetic *semantics* of the learning and development of the meaning of words in the individual's *life cycle.*

semantics, pure the study of *formal languages.* (Carnap, R.).

semantics, structural the study of meaning interrelations based on assumption of discrete *semantic* differences and contrastive semantic relations.

semantogenic pertaining to maladjustment resulting from failure to understand the *denotation* of an emotive word or from the *connotation[2]* a word possesses for the individual.

semasiography the study of ideographic, pictographic, and logographic writing systems. (Gelb).

semasiology see *semantics.*

sematology see *semantics.*

semiology the science of *signs* in general. (de Saussure).

semiosis the process in which something functions as a *sign.*

semiotics the study of *sign* phenomena. (Weinreich, U.).

semi-autobiography life-history produced by direct questioning of *subject[1].* (Kluckhohn). see also *autobiography, focused.*

semi-pastoralism the *herding* and *husbandry* of domesticated animals combined with cultivation or some other form of livelihood. **semi-pastoral** *a.* **semi-pastoralist** *pers n.*

semisquatter one who first squats and then rents or buys the land. see also *squatter.*

sending 1. a *familiar* or a *sorcerer,* transformed, on an errand of injury or death. 2. an evil *spell* directed at a *victim[2].*

senicide see *senilicide.*

senilicide the killing of the senile.

senders, role individual's *role* partners in a *role-set.* (Rommetveit).

sensation uninterpreted awareness resulting from stimulation of *receptors.* see also *perception.*

189

sentence, definite a prison sentence with the period fixed by the *court*.

sentence, extended sentence for the protection of the public which is greater than the maximum sentence for the offence.

sentence, fixed see *sentence, definite*.

sentence, indefinite see *sentence, indeterminate*.

sentence, indeterminate a prison sentence with the minimum and maximum periods or only the maximum period fixed by the *court*.

sentence, suspended sentence which does not take effect unless the person convicted commits a further offence within a specified period or breaks a specified *court* order.

sentiment 1. idea plus affect. 2. feeling (Homans). 3. culturally-conditioned affective disposition. (Parsons, T.).

sentiment, collective a *sentiment* shared by a *collectivity*.

sentiment, mass a *sentiment* shared by a *mass*.

sentiment, moral a *sentiment* directed towards a moral idea.

sentiment, national *sentiment* of supreme loyalty to the *nation*.

separation, rite of a symbolic announcement of an imminent change of *status*. (Van Gennep).

separation, structural absence of *primary contacts* between the members of different *ethnic groups* within a society.

separatism the belief that a particular area should be separated from the *state* of which it forms a part. **separatist** *a.* & *pers n.*

sept see *group, descent, ambilineal*.

serendipity *discovery* resulting from chance events. **serendipitous** *a.*

serf an agricultural labourer bound to the soil. **serfdom** *n.* see also *servitude*; *slavery*.

seriation 1. arrangement of data into a series. 2. determining the series of changes undergone by an *artifact*.

series, control see *group, control*.

series, experimental see *group, experimental*.

series, role a complete *set¹* of *role* attributes. (Nadel, S.F.).

service the duty owed by a tenant to his lord.

service, community any service to *groups* in the community or to the community as a whole.

service, military military duties owed by a tenant to his lord.

service, social an *activity* designed to promote *social welfare*.

servitude lack of personal *freedom*. see also *serf*; *slavery*.

set 1. collection of objects satisfying a given property. 2. disposition for selective behaviour resulting from expectations. 3. part of *network²* classified by *ego* according to a certain *criterion*. (Barnes, J.A.). 4. the persons with whom *ego* interacts.

set, classificatory see *set³*.

set, interactive see *set⁴*.

set, kinship *category* of relatives bound together by one or more kinship ties.

set, lexical a *set¹* of *lexemes*.

set, mental readiness for a certain *activity*.

set, perceptual readiness to perceive in a certain way.

set, research *set¹* of cases studied in an investigation.

set, social non-institutionalized, informal *interest group* having lowest degree of directness of member *interaction*. (Simmel, G.). see also *circle, social*; *salon, social*.

setting, behaviour the *behaviour patterns*, independent of particular individuals, attached to a particular place, behaviour objects and time.

settled see *sedentary*.

settlement 1. *group* of *sedentary* persons. 2. the act of peopling a new country.

3. the establishment of permanent residence by *migrants*. 4. see *settlement, social*.

settlement, chain a *migration settlement* resulting from *chain migration*.

settlement, concentrated a *settlement¹* of concentrated dwellings.

settlement, dispersed a *settlement¹* of dispersed dwellings.

settlement, dry-point a *settlement¹* on higher dry land amidst wet land.

settlement, migration a *settlement¹* resulting from *migration*.

settlement, nucleated a *settlement¹* the dwellings of which are concentrated round a central point.

settlement, residential a *social settlement* having resident staff.

settlement, scattered see *settlement, dispersed*.

settlement, social a social agency for the overall development of a *neighbourhood* or cluster of neighbourhoods.

sextiles *quantiles* dividing *array* into six equal parts.

shaman 1. a religious practitioner who acts as a vehicle for *spirits* and is able to control them. 2. person who communicates with spirits. (Lowie, R.H.). 3. person who offers magical services. (Piddington, R.). 4. magical healer. (Bouteiller). 5. *magico-religious* practitioner manifesting trance behaviour.

shaman, real individual successfully claiming *shamanistic* powers. (Boyer, L.B.). see also *pseudo-shaman*.

shamanism the practice of the *shaman*. **shamanistic** *a*.

shamanism, inspirational *shamanism* in which *spirit* is believed to speak through *shaman*.

shamanism, possessive *shamanism* in which the *shaman* is believed to be possessed by a *spirit*.

shamanship the *office* of *shaman*.

shame 1. lack of *honour*. 2. embarrassment over being different from others.

shame, conventionalized *shame²* which is culturally-determined.

shame, spontaneous *shame²* which is not culturally-determined.

shock, culture *psychic strain* resulting from shifting to another *culture*. see also *shock, transitional*.

shock, transitional personal *stress* resulting from shifting from one *group*, *social class* or *culture area* to another. see also *shock, culture*.

sib (US) see *clan¹*.

sib, maternal see *matrisib*.

sib, paternal see *patrisib*.

sib, totemic a *sib* constituting a *totem group*. see also *totemism*.

sib-mates fellow-members of a *sib*.

sibling, residual the *sibling* in a *patrilineal system* or a *matrilineal system* through whom rights are not transmitted.

siblings brothers or sisters.

siblings, cross-sex *siblings* of opposite sex.

siblingship the state of being a *sibling*.

sibship see *group, sibling*.

sign 1. external *stimulus* triggering off *response*. 2. a thing that stands for something else. 3. an abbreviated expression of a known thing. (Jung). see also *symbol*; *signal*.

sign, conventional a thing that stands by intention and convention for something else.

sign, door object placed on or above a door to avert evil.

sign, iconic a *sign* involving a geometric similarity between the *sign-vehicle* and its denotata.

sign-vehicle anything carrying a meaning.

signal 1. *sign* indicating *action* to be performed. 2. medium carrying encoded *message*. 3. pattern of *stimuli* eliciting *response*. see also *sign*; *symbol*.

signs, diacritical see *characteristics, diacritical.*

signs, syncretic see *characteristics, syncretic.*

significance, level of shows the probability that the *association*[4,5] is not due to chance, i.e. sampling variability; usually .95 or .99.

significs see *semantics.*

simplification, job removing some of the more difficult elements in a *job.* see also *enlargement, job*; *extension, job.*

simulation construction and manipulation of an *operating model.*

simulation, all-man *simulation* involving a purely human *operating model.*

simulation, analogue *simulation* involving the manipulation of an *analogue*[2].

simulation, computer *simulation* performed by a computer.

simulation, iconic *simulation* involving the manipulation of an *iconic model.*

simulation, man-machine *simulation* involving an *operating model* partly mechanical and partly human.

simulation, pure-machine *simulation* involving a purely mechanical *operating model.*

simulation, real-time *simulation* in which operations of *operating system* have same duration as those of *real system.*

simulation, symbolic *simulation* involving the manipulation of a *symbolic model.*

simulator training situation or device employing equipment and conditions imitating those in which learner will later perform.

sister-exchange exchange of sisters by two men to obtain wives.

site 1. place where *artifacts* of a former *culture* are located. 2. place where a *settlement*[1] is located.

site, crop *site*[1] revealed by differential crop growth.

site, habitation a place where a *group* of people centred their daily activities. *(archaeol.).*

site, occupation see *site, habitation.*

site, soil *site*[1] revealed by the discolouration or disturbance of the soil.

situation a complex of things and events temporarily affecting an organism. see also *surround.*

situation, incompatibility the existence of a plurality of persons whose *goals* are incompatible.

situation, marginal non-membership or incomplete membership of a co-existing privileged *group* into which entry is barred. (Mann, J.W.).

situation, observational properties of observer, individual or *group* under observation, *environment,* and *procedures* employed.

situation, social relation of *goals* to persons, giving rise to a *social process.*

situationalism stressing the *situation* as a determinant of behaviour.

situses equally-valued vertical divisions of the *social structure.*

situses, occupational equally-valued vertical divisions of the *occupational structure.*

skewness (of a *frequency distribution*) lack of symmetry.

skewness, negative *skewness* with longer tail to the left.

skewness, positive *skewness* with longer tail to the right.

skill 1. anything that an individual has learned to do with ease and precision. 2. the degree of learnt ease and precision.

slash the cut undergrowth prior to burning in *shifting cultivation.*

slash-and-burn see *cultivation, shifting.*

slavery 1. condition of a person over whom any or all of the rights of ownership are exercised. (L of N, 1926).2. condition of unfree *status.* (Leach, E.R.). 3. any extreme form of *servitude.* 4. condition of a person over whom all the rights of ownership are exercised. see also *serf*; *servitude.*

slavery, chattel see *slavery*[4].

slavery, penal *slavery* imposed as a *punishment*.

slavocracy rule by slave-owners. **slavocratic** *a.*

slogan a summarizing assertion which is systematically ambiguous and which is capable of interpretation to any level of specificity desired.

sloganizer an individual who creates *slogans*.

slum an area of unsanitary, highly deteriorated buildings.

slum, company a *slum* owned by a company for the housing of its employees.

slum, disorganized a *slum* characterized by *social disorganization*.

slum, ethnic a *slum* in which members of a particular *ethnic group* are segregated.

slum, stable a *slum* without *social disorganization*.

smallholding small unit of agricultural land farmed by a single *family* without paid labour.

snap-reading using *sample* of momentary observations made at random intervals. see also *time-intercept*.

social 1. see *societal*. 2. pertaining to interpersonal behaviour. 3. pertaining to *social processes*[3,4].

socialization 1. process of communicating the *culture* to a child. 2. process of communicating a culture or *subculture* to an individual. 3. characteristic of behaviour of being in response to or directed towards other persons. (Lasswell). see also *privatization*; *acculturation*; *enculturation*.

socialization, adult process of communicating a *culture* or *subculture* to an adult.

socialization, anticipatory adoption by individual of the *values* of a *group* to which he aspires but does not belong. (Merton, R.K.).

socialization, child process of communicating the *culture* to a child.

socialization, cognitive process of communicating to a child the *cognitive* aspects of its *culture* or *subculture*.

socialization, deviant process of communicating *deviant norms* to an individual.

socialization, diffuse *socialization* by informal means. see also *socialization, systematic*.

socialization, heterogeneous *socialization*[1] occurring in a *group* in which members are socialized differentially according to their *category*.

socialization, initial see *socialization, primary*.

socialization, linguistic process of communicating to a child its first language.

socialization, occupational process of communicating an *occupational culture* to an individual.

socialization, post *socialization* of new *group* member where affiliation precedes *identification*. see also *socialization, situational*.

socialization, primary *child socialization* in the *primary group*.

socialization, professional process of communicating a *professional culture* to an individual.

socialization, situational *socialization* of new *group* member where affiliation follows *identification*. see also *socialization, post*.

socialization, systematic *socialization* by formal means. see also *socialization, diffuse*.

sociation form and content of psychological *interaction*. (Simmel).

sociempathy see *socioempathy*.

societal 1. pertaining to *society*. 2. pertaining to society-wide phenomena.

societary see *societal*.

society 1. (broad sense) a *group* with a *culture* organized for the satisfaction of all human *needs* and interests. 2. (narrow sense) a *social structure* (excludes culture) . 3. see *unit, political*. 4. the widest *population* most effectively held together in a group. (Nadel). 5. a *social system* which includes all the *actions* necessary for its existence. (Parsons, T.).

society, abstract a *society* which operates on the basis of *role* or *status* and not on the personal characteristics of its personnel. see also *society, concrete; society, face-to-face.*

society, atomistic a *society* possessing only individual allegiances and ties. (Benedict, R.).

society, caste a *society* possessing a *caste system.*

society, collecting a *society* based on *collecting.*

society, concrete a *society* which operates on the basis of the personal characteristics of its personnel. see also *society, abstract.*

society, core see *subsociety, core.*

society, corporate a *society* which is itself a *corporate group* or consists of corporate groups. (Benedict, R.).

society, estate a *society* possessing an *estate system.*

society, extractive a *society* based on hunting, fishing, *food-gathering* or *collecting.*

society, face-to-face see *society, concrete.*

society, feudal a *society* characterized by *feudalism.*

society, folk (ideal type) *society* small, isolated, *nonliterate,* homogeneous, high solidarity; in which behaviour traditional, spontaneous, uncritical, personal; no *legislation* or experiment or intellectualizing; *family* is unit of *action; sacred* prevails over *secular; economy* one of *status* rather than market. (Redfield). see also *society, urban.*

society, foraging a *society* based on *foraging.*

society, graded *association* having a series of grades through which the members pass.

society, guilt a *society* having a *guilt culture.*

society, host the dominant *subsociety* of a *society* receiving *immigrants.*

society, hydraulic a *society* based on large-scale *irrigation.*

society, industrial *society* characterized by *industrialization.*

society, manorial a *society* based on *manorialism.*

society, mass a *society* characterized by *mass behaviour* and *mass culture.*

society, nomadic a *society* based on *nomadism.*

society, organic a *society* based on *organic solidarity.* (Durkheim, E.).

society, peasant a *society* based on a *peasant economy.*

society, planned a *society* under *state planning.*

society, plural a *political unit* in which there are separate *cultures* and no common culture, order resting on political *force* and economic expediency. (Furnivall).

society, praetorian a *society* characterized by *praetorianism.*

society, secret a *voluntary association* with an element of secrecy, entrance and promotion purchaseable.

society, seignorial a *society* characterized by *seignorial jurisdiction.*

society, shame a *society* having a *shame culture.*

society, small-scale a *society* whose *population* is small or which consists of small segments.

society, stateless *society* lacking a *state¹*.

society, subsistence *society,* all the production of which is internally consumed.

society, traditional !. an illiterate *peasant society.* 2. a *society* based on *traditional action.* (Rostow).

society, transitional a *society* which is changing from a *traditional society* to an *industrial society.*

society, urban (ideal type) *society* with characteristics the opposite of those of the *folk society.* see also *society, folk*

socifact any element of *social organization.* (Bidney, D.). see also *artifact; agrofact; mentifact.*

sociocentre recipient of the largest number of sociometric choices. (*sociom.*).

sociocracy *government* in which the social sciences are systematically utilized. **sociocratic** *a.*

sociocultural possessing a social or cultural character or both.

socio-demography see *demography, social.*

sociodrama method of exploring and treating a *group* problem by individuals representative of the *culture* acting out problem on stage. (Moreno, J.L.). see also *psychodrama.*

sociodynamics the study of the structure of *social aggregates*, single *groups*, and group clusters. (Moreno, J.L.). **sociodynamic** *a.*

socioeconomic 1. possessing a social or economic character or both. 2. involving both social and economic *factors.*

socioempathy awareness of another's *status.*

sociofugality the property possessed by an area or spatial orientation of decreasing *social interaction*. **sociofugal** *a.* see also *sociopetality.*

sociogenic of social origin.

sociogram diagram showing pattern of attractions, repulsions and indifferences among members of a *group*. (*sociom.*).

sociogram, developmental a *sociogram* showing a sequence of changes in a *sociometric structure.*

sociogram, target *sociogram* consisting of a network superimposed on concentric circles, the nearer a node to the centre of the concentric circles, the higher the *choice status* represented.

sociogrammetry the quantitative study of settlement and agricultural patterns and growth by means of aerial photography.

sociography descriptive *sociology.* **sociographic** *a.*

sociography, regional the descriptive *sociology* of *regions.*

sociogroup a *group* organized for a *task.* see also *psychegroup.*

sociolegal involving both social and legal *factors.*

sociolinguistics the study of language in its social context. **sociolinguistic** *a.*

sociologism attributing to *sociology* supreme importance for the *explanation* of human behaviour. **sociologistic** *a.*

sociology 1. the encyclopaedic science of *society*, absorbing the other social sciences. (Comte). 2. a superscience unifying the generalizations of the other social sciences. (Spencer, H.). 3. the scientific study of *social structure*. 4. the science concerned with the form of human *actions* in society. (Simmel). 5. the science concerned with the common characteristics and interrelations of the other social sciences. (Sorokin). 6. the *methodology* of the social sciences. (Lazarsfeld).

sociology, applied the application of *sociological theory* to the solution of concrete problems.

sociology, biological see *biosociology.*

sociology, clinical see *sociology, concrete.*

sociology, comparative the systematic and explicit comparison of data from two or more *societies*. (Marsh, R.M.).

sociology, concrete that branch of *sociology* concerned with intensive, small-scale investigations of *groups* and *organizations.*

sociology, cultural the scientific study of *society* at the *cultural* level.

sociology, economic the study of *economic systems* in their social context.

sociology, educational the study of *education* in its social context.

sociology, electoral the study of *elections* in their social context. see also *psephology.*

sociology, evolutionary body of *theory* in *sociology* based on social evolutionism.

sociology, folk the *sociology* of *folk societies.*

sociology, formal the study of the form of human *actions* in *society*. (Simmel).

sociology, general the study of the relations between the most general aspects of *social life*.

sociology, genetic *sociology* involving *diachronic analysis*.

sociology, historical that branch of *sociology* concerned with the *synchronic analysis* and *diachronic analysis* of historical data to obtain generalizations.

sociology, industrial that branch of *organizational sociology* which is concerned with *economic organizations²*.

sociology, legal see *law, sociology of*.

sociology, managerial branch of *sociology* concerned with *management*.

sociology, medical that branch of *sociology* concerned with medicine in its social context.

sociology, military the study of *military organization* in its social context. see also *psychology, military*.

sociology, occupational analysis of the *professions* and *occupations* and their interdependence with the *social structure*.

sociology, organizational the sociological approach to the study of *organizations*.

sociology, philosophical see *metasociology*.

sociology, political the study of the *political system* in its relationship to the rest of *society*. see also *science, political*.

sociology, psychiatric that branch of *sociology* concerned with mental disorder and its *treatment²* in its social context.

sociology, regional the scientific study of *regions* as *social systems*.

sociology, rural that branch of *sociology* concerned with social phenomena peculiar to *rural areas* and to problems in which their *rural* context is relevant. see also *sociology, urban*.

sociology, synthetic (Aron, R.) see *sociology, general*.

sociology, systematic total body of interrelated sociological generalizations.

sociology, systems the application of *systems theory* to *sociology*.

sociology, urban that branch of *sociology* concerned with social phenomena peculiar to *urbanized areas* and to problems in which their *urban* context is relevant. see also *sociology, rural*.

sociomatrix a *matrix* showing the choices and rejections made and received by the members of a *group* arranged to reveal the *subgroups*. (*sociom.*).

sociometrics see *sociometry²*.

sociometry 1. quantitative study of interpersonal preferences. 2. quantitative study of interpersonal relations. 3. quantitative study of social and interpersonal phenomena. 4. (Chapin, F.S.). see *measurement, social*. **sociometric** *a.* **sociometrist** *pers n.*

sociometry, preferential quantitative study of interpersonal preferences.

sociomorphism attributing social characteristics to cosmic processes. **sociomorphic** *a.*

socionomics the study of the place of nonsocial *factors* in social phenomena.

socionomy generalizations concerning social phenomena. (Moreno, J.L.).

sociopathy disposition towards antisocial behaviour. **sociopathic** *a.* **sociopath** *pers n.*

sociopetality the property possessed by an area or spatial orientation of increasing *social interaction*. **sociopetal** *a.* see also *sociofugality*.

sociopharmacology the study of drug-usage in its social context.

sociotechnical pertaining to both the social and technological aspects of the work situation.

sociotype 1. *stereotype* widely held by a *group*. 2. an objectively derived summary description of the characteristics of a *category* of persons.

sodality 1. *group* which is not a *kinship group*. (Lowie). 2. *religious* brotherhood.

solidarity, family solidarity possessed by a *family*.

solidarity, functional *social integration* based on occupational interdependence. (Durkheim, E.).

solidarity, mechanical *social integration* based on similarities. (Durkheim, E.).

solidarity, organic *social integration* based on complementary differences. (Durkheim, E.).

solidarity, sibling solidarity possessed by a *sibling group*.

somatogenic of somatic origin.

somatomancy *divination* from examination of the human body. **somatomantic** *a*. **somatomancer** *pers n*.

somatotype a series of three numerals, each expressing the approximate strength of one of the primary components in a physique, i.e., *endomorphy, mesomorphy, ectomorphy*. (Sheldon, W.H.).

somatotyping the determination of type of body build.

somatotypology a *classification* of persons according to body build.

somatotypy see *somatotyping*.

sorcery 1. see *magic, protective*. 2. see *magic, positive*. 3. *magic* which is attempted by a person. see also *witchcraft*. **sorcerer** *pers n*.

sororate custom whereby a man must marry his dead wife's sister.

sororate, junior custom whereby a man must marry his dead wife's younger sister.

sororilateral pertaining to a relationship traced through a sister. (Goody, J.).

sortilege *divination* by lot.

sortition selection by lot.

soul immaterial aspect of *personality*. (NQ). see also *spirit; ghost; supernaturals*.

soul, animal a *soul* of the dead, reincarnated in an animal.

soul, bird 1. a *soul* in the form of a bird. 2. a soul of the dead reincarnated in a bird.

soul, bush a *soul* of a human being dwelling in a wild animal in the bush.

soul, dream a *soul* which leaves the body during sleep.

soul, external see *soul, separable*.

soul, separable a *soul* that can reside away from the body.

soul-animal 1. an animal which is an individual's co-existent double. 2. an animal in which a *soul* of the dead is reincarnate.

sources, contemporary *sets[1]* of data compiled at the time of the event.

sources, primary original *sets[1]* of data produced by the persons who collected them.

sources, retrospective *sets[1]* of data compiled after the event.

sources, secondary *sets[1]* of data not collected at first-hand but drawn from other persons' original data.

sovereignty, coercive supreme *coercive power*.

sovereignty, influential the strongest political *influence*.

sovereignty, legal the supremacy of a *norm* in a legal *hierarchy*.

sovereignty, legislative the omnicompetence, or supreme competence within its field, of a legislative organ.

sovereignty, political supreme *power* in a *political unit*.

sovereignty, popular *political sovereignty* vested in the people.

space, action *set[1]* of all possible *actions*.

space, attribute *set[1]* of all possible *attributes*.

space, behaviour *set[1]* of all possible behaviours.

space, decision *set[1]* of all possible *decisions*.

space, genealogical *set[1]* of all possible *genealogical positions*.

space, household 'the quarters occupied or normally occupied by a private household' (Registrar-General).

space, life all the *factors* in person and *environment* determining individual's behaviour at given moment. (Lewin, K.).

space, outcome *set¹* of all possible outcomes of an *experiment* or *decision*.

space, personal the space carried around by a person entry into which by another individual is felt to be an intrusion.

space, preference *set¹* of all possible preferences.

space, property *set¹* of all possible properties.

space, psychological see *space, life*.

space, revolutionary any one of the gaps existing in a *society* between the demands made on the *government* and its performance. (McAlister, J.T.). see also *potential, revolutionary*.

space, sample the *set¹* of *sample points* corresponding to all possible *samples* which may be drawn from a given *population*.

space, semantic a space in which meanings can be located.

space, social *set¹* of all possible social phenomena.

space, sociofugal area which decreases *social interaction*.

space, sociopetal area which increases *social interaction*.

space, use space immediately around or in front of person, his claim to which is respected because of apparent instrumental *needs*. (Goffman, E.).

span, life the maximum possible length of human life. (MDD).

specialization making *activity* or the *function* of something specific.

specialization, economic *specialization* concerning economic activity.

specialization, functional *specialization* by *function*.

specialization, geographical see *specialization, territorial*.

specialization, individual *specialization* by person.

specialization, institutional *functional specialization* of *institutions*.

specialization, intercommunal *specialization* between *communities*.

specialization, international *specialization* by *nation*.

specialization, intracommunal *specialization* within a *community*.

specialization, labour the *specialization* of a person in his economic activity.

specialization, local see *specialization, territorial*.

specialization, organizational *specialization* by *organization*.

specialization, regional *specialization* by *region*.

specialization, territorial *specialization* by area.

specialization, tribal *economic specialization* by *tribe*.

specialization, job *job description* combined with *job grading*.

spell the words spoken in a performance of *magic*.

spiralism combination of *upward mobility* and *areal mobility* through a number of *communities*.

spiralists individuals characterized by *upward mobility* and simultaneous *areal mobility* through a number of *communities*. (Watson).

spiralists, blocked *spiralists* stopped from further *upward mobility*.

spirit a supernatural believed to be imperceivable by human beings. see also *ghost*; *soul*; *supernaturals*.

spirit, astral *spirit* located in a star.

spirit, directional *spirit* associated with a particular direction.

spirit, familiar *spirit* which is the servant of *witch* or *wizard*.

spirit, guardian see *spirit, tutelary*.

spirit, nature *spirit* controlling a particular category of natural phenomena.

spirit, neutral a *spirit* which does not have any active influence on the affairs of the living. (Tatje, T.A.).

spirit, protective see *spirit, tutelary*.

spirit, tutelary a *spirit* protecting a particular person, place or thing.

spiritism 1. belief in freely moving *spirits*. see also *animism*. 2. belief in discarnate spirits. 3. belief in the possibility of communication with discarnate spirits. 4. attempting communication with discarnate spirits.

spodomancy *divination* by means of ashes. **spodomantic** *a.* **spodomancer** *pers n.*

spread see *dispersion.*

squatter one who settles on land without being legally entitled to do so.

squatter, owner a *squatter* who owns his dwelling.

squatter, speculator one whose aim in squatting is to receive a reward for leaving.

squatterism the practice of settling on land without being legally entitled to do so.

stability, marital absence of divorce or separation of married couple.

staff 1. the personnel of an *organization.* 2. the personnel of the *staff organization.* 3. see *organization, staff.*

staff, personal *staff¹* which only advises a particular line official.

staff, specialized *staff¹* which gives specialist advice to all parts of the *organization,* both *line* and *staff.*

standard something against which comparisons can be made. see also *criterion; baseline.*

standard, group 1. a *standard* of performance of a *group.* 2. a *value* adopted by a group.

standardization 1. establishing fixed *procedures* for administering and scoring a test. 2. establishing *norms³* for tests. 3. establishing fixed procedures in an *organization.*

star 1. recipient of large number of sociometric choices. (*sociom.*). 2. *communication network* in which no person, except the *central person²* who is in direct communication with all the others, can communicate with any other person except indirectly through the central person.

star, isolated *group* member receiving many sociometric choices but making no choices. (*sociom.*).

star, sociometric see *star¹.*

state 1. *organization* which exercises *coercive authority* over all the inhabitants of a *territory.* 2. a *society* possessing such an organization. 3. *population* having a territory and under its own sovereign *government.* 4. one specific *set¹* of *values⁶* of the *variables* of a *system.*

state, buffer a weak *state* between two or more powerful states which reduces the probability of *conflict* between them.

state, conquest *state* resulting from *conquest¹,* the conquerors constituting the *ruling class.*

state, consanguineal *state* in which the *subjects³* are *consanguineal relatives.*

state, dependent a *state* under the control of another state.

state, federal *state* characterized by *federalism.*

state, garrison a *state* characterized by *militarization.*

state, irrigation a *state* based on large-scale *irrigation.*

state, steady a relationship which is invariant with respect to time between the *variables* of a *system.*

state, unitary *state* not characterized by *federalism.*

state-description description of a particular state of the whole *system* in terms of specified *variables.* see also *state-variables.*

state-variables *variables* employed in a *state-description.*

state-ways rules of law created by legislatures. (Sumner). see also *law-ways.*

statics, administrative analysis of the *administration* of an *organization* at a fixed point of time. (Caiden, G.E.).

statics, cultural *functional analysis* of coexisting cultural elements.

statics, organizational analysis of an *organization* at a fixed point of time.

statics, social *functional analysis* of coexisting social facts. (Comte).

station 1. *set[1]* of *statuses* which tend to be combined in one person. 2. an early *site[1]* with *artifacts* that typify a *culture. (archaeol.).*

statism state intervention in the *economy.*

statist 1. pertaining to *statism.* 2. advocate of statism.

statistics 1. the collection, reliability, organization, representation, analysis and interpretation of numerical data. 2. numerical data. 3. *sample||values[6].*

statistics, demographic see *statistics, population.*

statistics, descriptive methods for describing the distributions of the characteristics of a *set[1]* of units.

statistics, generalizing see *statistics, inductive.*

statistics, health *statistics[2]* concerning *morbidity, cause mortality,* or any other aspect of the health of a *population.*

statistics, inductive methods for estimating the distributions of characteristics in the *population* from which a *sample* has been drawn.

statistics, inferential see *statistics, inductive.*

statistics, judicial *statistics[2]* concerning trials and their results.

statistics, literacy *statistics[2]* dealing with literates, illiterates and semi-literates. (MDD).

statistics, morbidity *statistics[2]* of disease.

statistics, order see *quantiles.*

statistics, police *statistics[2]* concerning *crimes* known to the police, arrests, and the age, *race* and sex of arrested persons.

statistics, population 1. that branch of *statistics[1]* concerned with population data. 2. numerical data concerning *populations.*

statistics, psychiatric *statistics[2]* concerning the *incidence* or *prevalence* of psychiatric disorders in a *population.*

statistics, tract official *statistics[2]* concerning *census tracts.*

statistics, vital numerical data, basic or derived, concerning *vital events.*

statocentrism evaluating in terms of the *values* of one's own *status* level. **statocentric** *a.*

status 1. a *position* in *society.* 2. the static aspect of *role.* (Linton). 3. the positional aspect of role. (Parsons, T.). 4. a more institutionalized role. 5. *set[1]* of rights and duties without further characteristics which go beyond occupational requirements. (Nadel, S.F.). 6. position of an individual relative to other individuals. (Hyman, H.H.). 7. *prestige* attached to position. 8. position in a *hierarchy.* (Benoit-Smullyan). 9. see *status, general.* 10. see *status, societal[1].* 11. the rights attached to position. 12. position which is not an *office.* (Davis, K.). 13. sum total of an individual's ideal roles. (Levy, M.J.). 14. a person's legal position, i.e., his *set[1]* of legal rights and duties, capacities and incapacities. see also *prestige*; *esteem*; *station*; *position*; *office*; *role.*

status, accorded the *status* given to an individual by others.

status, achieved voluntary, open *status* open to *competition.* (Linton, R.).

status, acquired *status* which a person is not born into.

status, age an individual's *status* resulting from his age.

status, ascribed involuntary, closed *status* not open to *competition.* (Linton, R.).

status, associational *status* in an *association.* (Weber, M.).

status, assumed voluntary, open *status* not requiring *competition.*

status, choice see *rank, sociometric.*

status, ephemeral an individual's temporary *status* while in a transitional state.

status, familial *status* of *family.*

status, fringe membership of *small group* involving exclusion from *primary group* but not involving *out status.*

status, functional *prestige* in *organization* deriving from type of *work* performed.

status, general a person's general *prestige* in *society*.

status, generic a *status* granted by all or most of the persons of a *society*. (LaPiere).

status, legal a person's legal position, i.e., his *set[1]* of legal rights and duties, capacities and incapacities.

status, marginal see *situation, marginal*.

status, mobility *status* of person with regard to spatial movement or nonmovement or type of spatial movement during a specified period.

status, object the *status* of an *alter*. see also *status, subject*.

status, out membership of *small group* or the larger *organization* involving rejection by all members of the *primary group*.

status, private individual's *status* not held in the *community*.

status, public individual's *status* held in the *community*.

status, scalar *prestige* deriving from *formal rank* in *organization*.

status, self-assigned see *status, self-rated*.

status, self-rated the *status* which an individual believes himself to possess.

status, social see *status, general*.

status, societal 1. the *status* of an individual in his *society*. 2. the status of a society in the *international system*.

status, sociometric see *rank, sociometric*.

status, specific a *status* granted by a small number of persons. (LaPiere).

status, subject the status of *ego*. see also *status, object*.

status, subjective individual's assessment of his own *status*.

status, transitional *status* attached to an individual's transitional state.

status-assent the acceptance by an individual of his *status*. (Mogey).

status-dissent the rejection by an individual of his *status*. (Mogey).

status-sequence standardized sequence of *statuses* of an individual.

status-set the complex of *statuses* occupied by an individual.

stereogram any diagram showing a three-dimensional figure on a plane surface.

stereotype the most frequent combination of traits assigned by one *group* to another.

stereotype, ethnic *stereotype* held concerning an *ethnic group*.

stereotype, national *stereotype* held concerning a *nation*.

stereotype, occupational *stereotype* held concerning the members of a particular *occupation*.

stereotypy degree of repetition of any sequence of *responses* in a given behaviour *sample*.

sterility 1. see *infecundity*. 2. childlessness. **sterile** *a*.

sterility, primary absence of reproductive capacity in a woman who has never had children.

sterility, secondary absence of reproductive capacity in a woman who has had children.

stigma blemish, defect, or sign of such, which has a serious negative effect on the afflicted individual's social acceptance. (Goffman, E.). **stigmatize** *v*.

stimulus antecedent of a *response*.

stimulus, aversive anything which by combination with a *response* reduces the response tendency.

stimulus, conditioned *stimulus* eliciting a particular *response* only after conditioning.

stimulus, distal event in *environment* which is part of process leading to the *proximal stimulus*. see also *stimulus, proximal*.

stimulus, eliciting a *stimulus* which elicits a *response*.

stimulus, environmental *stimulus* which is not intraorganismic.

stimulus, mass *stimulus* intended to influence a large number of persons who are treated for the purpose as similar.

stimulus, neutral *stimulus* unable to elicit a particular *response.*

stimulus, proximal *stimulus* applied to *exteroceptor.* see also *stimulus, distal.*

stimulus, social 1. a social phenomenon which acts as a *stimulus.* 2. a stimulus which produces a social *response.*

stimulus, transactional an *action* of an individual which initiates a *transaction².* (Berne, E.). see also *response, transactional.*

stimulus, unconditioned *stimulus* eliciting a particular *response* without prior conditioning.

stirpiculture the deliberate breeding of humans for *eugenic* purposes.

stock an ad hoc, *ego*-focused grouping consisting of all the descendants of a married couple.

strain 1. *reaction* of individual to *stress.* 2. impairment of interrelations of systemic elements and resultant malfunctioning of *system.* 3. disruptive pressure in system. see also *stress; stressor; tension.*

strain, cumulative *strain* resulting from successive life *stresses.*

strain, organizational *strain* existing within an *organization.*

strain, psychic intrapsychic pressure producing psychic malfunctioning.

strain, role the felt difficulty in fulfilling *role* obligations.

strata (stratum *sing.***)** 1. successive levels of a *society.* 2. *sub-populations* of a *population.* 3. see *sub-universe.*

strata, occupational 1. differentially-valued horizontal divisions of the *occupational structure.* 2. *aggregates* of persons in *occupational categories,* each occupational category demanding approximately the same degree of *skill.*

strata, population *sub-populations* each of which is homogeneous with respect to a specified *variable.*

strata, social *aggregates* in a *society,* each aggregate consisting of persons of approximately equal *status.*

strategy 1. a *procedure* having alternatives at various steps. 2. bargaining manoeuvre aimed at altering power limits. 3. that body of *theory* and *techniques* with which science attacks its problems. (Washburn, S.L.).

strategy, compromise a *decision-making‖strategy* in an *organization* involving disagreement as to the order of priority amongst the *objectives,* the means to which are fully known. (Blau).

strategy, computational a *decision-making‖strategy* in an *organization* involving agreement on *objectives,* the means to which are fully known. (Blau).

strategy, inspirational a *decision-making‖strategy* in an *organization* involving disagreement on *objectives,* the means to which are not fully known. (Blau).

strategy, judgmental a *decision-making‖strategy* in an *organization* involving agreement on *objectives,* the means to which are not fully known. (Blau).

strategy, research 1. a *procedure* having alternatives at various steps, used in research. 2. see *strategy².*

stratification 1. a grading into successive levels. 2. see *stratification, social.* 3. division of *population* into *sub-populations.*

stratification, class the grading of a *population* into *social classes.*

stratification, economic the grading of a *population* into income groups.

stratification, ethnic the grading of a *population* into *ethnic groups.*

stratification, multidimensional coexistence of two or more *stratification systems* based on different principles. see also *stratification, plural.*

stratification, occupational the grading of a *population* into *occupational groupings.*

stratification, plural *social stratification* consisting of overlapping *stratification systems* in a particular *society.* see also *stratification, multidimensional.*

stratification, social 1. the existence of a *hierarchy* of *groups* in a *society*. 2. differential *status* existing in society. 3. process by which status is differentiated in society.

stratification, unidimensional the existence in a *society* of a single *stratification system*.

stratocracy rule by the military. **stratocratic** *a*.

stream, migration body of *migrants* with a common area of origin and a common area of destination over a specified period.

stress 1. environmental pressure on individual. 2. environmental or intraorganismic pressure on individual. 3. environmental pressure on individual and the resulting internal state. see also *stressor*; *strain*; *tension*.

stress, biological pressure on individual which is intraorganismic.

stress, cognitive *stress* resulting from *cognitive dissonance*.

stress, environmental pressure on individual which is not intraorganismic.

stress, frustrating *stress* resulting in *frustration*.

stress, organizational *stress* to which an *organization* is exposed.

stress, physical *stress* not involving mediation of noxious *stimulus* by c.n.s.

stress, psychic environmental or intraorganismic pressure on individual resulting in *psychic strain*.

stress, psychological *stress* involving mediation of noxious *stimulus* by c.n.s.

stressor anything producing *stress*.

strip, conurbated built-up strip connecting two *settlements* of a *conurbation*.

structuralism the attempt to explain *sociocultural* phenomena by the determination of *structures* consisting of *sets[1]* of *rules*. **structuralist** *a*. & *pers n*.

structure 1. *set[1]* of interrelated elements. 2. *set[1]* of interdependent *variables*. 3. *set[1]* of relations between elements of a *system*. 4. *set[1]* of *rules* generating phenomena.

structure, age see *distribution, age*.

structure, agrarian all the social and economic *institutions* surrounding farm life.

structure, analytic a *structure* the elements of which are abstractions from concrete *actions*.

structure, authority the *structure* of *authority* in a group.

structure, character 1. *organization[10]* of an individual's *character traits*. 2. see *personality, nuclear*.

structure, communication see *network, communication*.

structure, concrete a *structure* the elements of which are concrete *actions*.

structure, dominance the network of *dominance relationships* amongst a *set[1]* of *statuses*. (Bartos, O.J.). see also *pattern, dominance*.

structure, ecological 1. spatial pattern resulting from *ecological distributions*. 2. physical features affecting ecological processes.

structure, farm 1. the areal distribution of farms and the plots within farms. (OECD). 2. the *structure* of the comparatively permanent *factors* involved in the *set[1]* of farms found in a specified area. (OECD).

structure, formal 1. see *structure[3]*. 2. see *organization, formal*.

structure, group the interrelated *group* elements at a given time.

structure, informal see *organization, informal*.

structure, kinship a *structure* consisting of a *set[1]* of *kinship‖rules[3,4]*.

structure, normative a *structure* the elements of which are *norms*.

structure, occupational the *structure* of *occupations* in a particular *society*.

structure, opportunity the means to the achievement of a *success-goal*.

structure, personality the *personality* treated as a *structure*.

structure, personality, basic the socially-required *personality*.

structure, political a *society*'s *structure* of political elements.

structure, population 1. distribution of the *population* by sex and age. 2. unalterable characteristics of population.

structure, power the *set[1]* of *power relationships* in a community.

structure, revolutionary an opposition *political structure* aiming at *revolution.* (McAlister, J.T.).

structure, risk-reward the degree and probabilities of *risk[3]* and reward for the *actor* attaching to an *action.*

structure, rural a delimited, structured, *rural agglomeration.*

structure, social 1. *structure* of *statuses.* 2. *network* of statuses and associated behaviour. (Gibbs, J.L.). 3. *set[1]* of *social processes* at a particular point of time. (Vogt). 4. the relatively permanent features of a *society.* (Evans-Pritchard). 5. formal pattern of a society. 6. ideal pattern of a society. 7. *set[1]* of *individual relationships.* (Radcliffe-Brown). 8. pattern and network of *social relationships.* (Nadel). 9. 'set[1] of ideas about the distribution of *power* between persons or *groups* of persons'. (Leach).

structure, sociometric the *structure* of *sociometric relationships* in a group. (sociom.).

structure, urban a delimited, structured, *urban agglomeration[2].*

structure, wage the *set[1]* of interrelationships amongst a *set[1]* of wages.

stub first column of *statistical table* containing the *row captions.*

study, area the study of a particular geographical area as distinguished from research in a particular discipline.

study, community analysis of a *community* undertaken to understand a *nation* or *region.*

study, exploratory see *survey, exploratory.*

study, field social investigation less representative, deeper, involving observation of *social interaction,* and more theoretical than *survey.*

study, formulative see *survey, exploratory.*

study, pilot final testing of *schedule* before *survey* undertaken.

sub-aggregate *aggregate* which is part of another aggregate.

subception see *perception, subliminal.*

sub-clan a *clan* which is part of a larger clan.

subcollectivity a *collectivity* which is part of a larger collectivity.

subcommunity 1. members of a particular *ethnic group* within a *community.* 2. unit of a *subsociety* found within a community based on ethnic group and class membership.

subcultural 1. pertaining to *subculture.* 2. pertaining to human social phenomena resulting from primate *drives.*

subculture 1. the *culture* of a *group* or *social class* which is at variance with the dominant culture. 2. the culture of a group hostile to the dominant culture. 3. cultural or behavioural features common to all *societies.* 4. culture of a *subsociety.* 5. those *culture traits* peculiar to a particular *collectivity* within a *cultural group.*

subculture, community those *culture traits* peculiar to a particular *community* within a *society.*

subculture, conflict see *contraculture.*

subculture, core see *culture, core.*

subculture, delinquent a *subculture* in which certain forms of *delinquent‖activity* are a necessary condition for the performance of the dominant *roles* of the subculture.

subculture, occupational the *subculture* of a particular *occupation.*

subculture, regional those *culture traits* peculiar to a particular *region* within a *political unit.*

subculture, retreatist a *subculture* implying *retreatism* on the part of those sharing it.

subculture, territorial those *culture traits* peculiar to a particular *territory.*

sub-delegation further *delegation* of *delegated authority*.

sub-ethos the *ethos* of a *subculture*.

sub-fecundity subnormal reproductive capacity of individual, couple, or *group*.

sub-fertility subnormal reproductive performance of individual or *group*.

sub-goal *goal* which is a means to another goal.

subgroup *set[1]* of *group* members who interact more with one another than with other members of the group.

subgrouping process by which *subgroups* are formed.

subincision partial or total slitting of penile urethra.

subinfeudation grant of whole or part of land held by a tenant in *feudal tenure* to a sub-tenant to hold of him in feudal tenure.

subirrigation *irrigation* by subterranean conduits.

subjects 1. persons who are the subject of an *experiment* or investigation. 2. things, whether persons, *groups* or characteristics, categorized by *items* of *scale[2]* or *questionnaire*. 3. persons fully subject to the *power* of a *state*.

sub-lineage a *lineage* which is part of a larger lineage.

sub-model *model* the *output[2]* of which is one of the *inputs[2]* of a superordinate model.

submoiety subdivision of *moiety*. (Murdock, G.P.).

sub-network a *network* which is part of another network.

sub-objective *objective* which is a means to another objective.

subplan plan which is part of a larger plan.

sub-population a *population* which is part of a larger population.

sub-process the most specific class of *social process*. (von Wiese).

subsection a *marriage class* in an *eight-class system*.

subsib subdivision of *sib*. (Murdock, G.P.).

subsistence, mixed see *farming, mixed*.

subsocial pertaining to phenomena below the social level of analysis or to *genetic[1]* ||*factors* in the behaviour of individuals and *populations*.

subsociety social unit within a *society* possessing *groups* and *institutions* serving entire *life cycle*.

subsociety, core the dominant *subsociety*.

substruction the reformulation of a *set[1]* of *concepts* through the analysis of an *attribute space* based on them.

substructure a *society*'s techno-economic base. see also *superstructure*.

subsystem a *system* which is part of a larger system.

subsystem, adaptive a *subsystem* of a *social system* having the *function* of *adaptation[7]*. (Parsons, T.).

subsystem, functional any one of the four *subsystems* of a *social system* which perform the functions of *adaptation, goal-attainment, integration[6]*, and *pattern-maintenance*. (Parsons, T.). see also *subsystem, adaptive*; *subsystem, goal-attainment*; *subsystem, integrative*; *subsystem, pattern-maintenance*.

subsystem, goal-attainment a *subsystem* of a *social system* having the *function* of *goal-attainment*. (Parsons, T.).

subsystem, integrative a *subsystem* of a *social system* having the *function* of *integration[6]*.

subsystem, leading *subsystem* having most influence on the activities of the *organization*.

subsystem, pattern-maintenance a *subsystem* of a *social system* having the *function* of *pattern-maintenance*. (Parsons, T.).

subsystem, societal any one of the *functional subsystems* of a *society*. (Parsons, T.).

sub-universe a *universe* which is part of a larger universe.

suburbanization the acquisition by an area of suburban characteristics.

subvaluent, social see *decrement, social*.

subvariable a *variable* which is a component of another variable.

success-goal an individual's *goal* of success, as defined by the individual or culturally-defined.

succession 1. following another natural or juristic person in possession of *authority, rank, office,* rulership, *function,* sovereignty, or *territory.* 2. see *succession, ecological.*

succession, adelphic see *succession, fraternal.*

succession, bureaucratic transmission of *bureaucratic office.*

succession, cultural complete displacement, in an area, of one *culture* or *subculture* by another.

succession, demographic complete displacement, in an area, of one *population* type by another.

succession, ecological complete displacement, in an area, of one *population* type or land-use type by another.

succession, filial inheritance of *authority* by a son.

succession, fraternal inheritance of *authority* by a brother.

succession, goal the replacement of one *goal* by another.

succession, household *succession* to the headship of a *household.*

succession, institutional complete displacement, in an area, of another land-use type by commercial or industrial *organizations.*

succession, land-use complete displacement, in an area, of one land-use type by another.

succession, lateral inheritance of *authority* by a *lateral relative.*

succession, lineal inheritance of *authority* by a *lineal relative.*

succession, matrilineal inheritance of *office* in the mother's line.

succession, occupational inheritance of an *occupation.*

succession, patrilineal inheritance of *office* in the father's line.

succession, political acquisition of *power* by a new *government* or transmission of rulership.

succession, racial complete displacement, in an area, of one *race* by another.

succession, residential complete displacement, in an area, of one *population* type by another.

succession, state *set[1]* of rights and duties attached to acquisition of *territory* by a *state.*

succession, territorial following another *state* in possession of a certain *territory.*

succession, universal *inheritance* of entire estate, with assets and liabilities.

suggestibility susceptibility to *suggestion.*

suggestibility, mass susceptibility to *suggestions* on the part of a *mass.*

suggestibility, primary susceptibility to bodily *suggestions,* e.g. subject will sway.

suggestibility, secondary susceptibility to *cognitive||suggestions,* e.g. as to smell, weight.

suggestibility, tertiary susceptibility to *prestige suggestion.*

suggestion 1. unreasoned acceptance. 2. object of unreasoned acceptance. 3. intended object of unreasoned acceptance.

suggestion, crowd unreasoned acceptance resulting from membership of a *crowd.*

suggestion, negative *suggestion* intended to produce a particular *inhibition.*

suggestion, prestige unreasoned acceptance resulting from another person's *prestige.*

suggestion, therapeutic *suggestion* with therapeutic aim.

suicide, altruistic suicide for the good of the *group.* (Durkheim, E.).

suicide, anomic suicide resulting from *anomie.* (Durkheim, E.).

suicide, egoistic suicide due to strong value system, low group integration, and an overpowering sense of personal responsibility. (Durkheim, E.).

suicide, fatalistic suicide resulting from a sense of helplessness in the face of environmental constraints.

suicide, individualistic socially-proscribed suicide. (Davis, K.).

suicide, institutionalized socially-prescribed suicide. (Davis, K.).

suitor-service see *bride-service*.

supercision see *superincision*.

superincision longitudinal slitting of prepuce.

supernaturals supernatural beings. see also *spirit*; *ghost*; *soul*.

superstructure that part of a *society* determined by its *substructure*.

supersystem see *suprasystem*.

supervariable a *variable* composed of *subvariables*.

supervision, span of see *control, span of*.

supplantment, military *military intervention* taking the form of the replacement of the civilian *government* by a military *junta*.

supply, labour the amount of *labour* offered at a given wage.

suprasocietal pertaining to *organizations* superordinate to *societies*.

suprasystem the *system* of which a given system is a part.

surrogate, parent an individual acting as a substitute for a parent.

surround things and events temporarily affecting an organism, less inclusive than *situation*. see also *environment*.

surplus, agricultural excess of agricultural production over that necessary for the subsistence of a particular agricultural-producing *group*.

surplus, economic a *society*'s excess of production over that necessary for subsistence.

surplus, rural surplus *rural population*.

surplus, social 1. see *surplus, economic*. 2. a *society*'s excess of social energy over that necessary for subsistence.

survey 1. direct, systematic collection of representative data from a *population* or *sample* of a population. 2. inquiry involving more than a statistical count.

survey, administrative a *survey* whose aim is not scientific but administrative.

survey, analytic *survey* involving more than statistical counts.

survey, cadastral a *survey* concerning land ownership.

survey, community a *survey* of a *community* whether or not carried out by the community itself.

survey, complete a *social survey* covering the entire *research population*.

survey, descriptive *survey* not investigating interrelationships of *variables*.

survey, diagnostic *survey* of *population* employing diagnostic tests to detect one or more morbid conditions unknown to the persons affected.

survey, enumerative *survey* involving no more than statistical counts.

survey, explanatory *survey* investigating relationship between one or more *dependent variables* and one or more *independent variables*.

survey, exploratory *survey* prior to formulation of *hypothesis*.

survey, field *survey* using *personal interview* for data collection.

survey, household *survey* of the distribution of *households* of various types in a specified area.

survey, incomplete a *social survey* not covering the entire *research population*.

survey, industrial *survey* of the distribution of the *industries* of a specified area.

survey, local a *survey* of a particular locality.

survey, opinion see *poll²*.

survey, pilot see *study, pilot*.

survey, poverty a *survey* of the different types of *poverty* and their distribution in a *population*.

survey, pre-pilot an *exploratory survey* preceding a *pilot study*.

survey, psychiatric *survey* of the *prevalence* and *incidence* of various mental disorders in a *population*.

survey, regional a *social survey* of a *region*.

survey, research a *survey* of the research which has been done in a specified field.

survey, sample *survey* based on the study of a *sample*.

survey, test-tube see *study, pilot*.

survey, theoretical *survey* aimed at contributing to *theory*.

survey, trial see *study, pilot*.

survival a nonfunctional social or cultural element which formerly had a *function*.

survivors persons studied who are available for later tests or *surveys*.

swidden 1. see *cultivation, shifting*. 2. a field under shifting cultivation. (Hudson, A.B.).

symbiont see *symbiote*.

symbiosis 1. co-existence and interdependence of unlike *groups* or persons. 2. co-existence of unlike groups or persons, involving interdependence, in which both partners are benefited. **symbiotic** *a*. see also *mutualism*; *parasitism*; *helotism*; *commensalism*.

symbiosis, civil-military joint rule by civilian officials and the military.

symbiosis, industrial the clustering of interdependent *productive units*.

symbiote *symbiotic* partner.

symbol 1. a thing that stands for something else. 2. a thing that stands by intention and convention for something else. 3. vehicle of meaning plus meaning. 4. best possible expression of a relatively unknown fact. (Jung). see also *sign*; *signal*.

symbolate a product of symboling. (White, L.A.).

symbolatry the *worship* of symbols. **symbolatric** *a*.

symbolism 1. the use of *symbols*. 2. see *system, symbol*.

symbolization 1. attaching *symbols* to references. 2. process of symbol emergence. 3. re-interpretation of *myth*, by persons accepting it, as symbolic of certain *values* or truths.

symbology the science of *symbols*. see also *semiology*; *semiotics*.

sympathy reproduction in onself of the suffering of another person plus the appropriate affect aroused by this. see also *empathy*; *identification*.

sympatric (of a *group*) not possessing a totally exclusive *territory*. see also *allopatric*.

syndrome 1. *set[1]* of associated symptoms. 2. *set[1]* of associated characteristics.

synectics the study of the creative solution of problems by *groups* of diverse individuals.

synergism tendency to form *groups* for the attainment of ends.

synergy goal-seeking energy of *group*.

synergy, maintenance energy expended to maintain *group*.

synergy, task energy expended to execute *group task*.

syngenism natural solidarity manifested in spontaneous association of individuals into *groups*. (Glumplowitz, L.).

synoecism the coalescence of neighbouring *villages* into a town. **synoecize** *v*.

syntactics study of the relation between *signs* without reference to their meaning.

syntality *effectiveness* of *group* in carrying out external *task*.

system 1. *set[1]* of interrelated elements. 2. *set[1]* of interdependent *variables*.

system, abstract a *system* the elements of which are abstractions.

system, action 1. a *set[1]* of causally related *actions*. (Parsons, T.).2. pattern of *activities* integrating members of organized *group*. (Lundberg).

system, activity *set[1]* of different behaviours which can be substituted for each other as a means to attainment of a specified *goal*.

system, adaptive *system* which continuously moves towards *stable equilibrium*.

system, administrative a type of *administration*.

system, administrative, integrated *administrative system* in which central government agencies directly administer all technical services, with central government area co-ordinators responsible for field co-ordination.

system, agrarian *system* of *rural\||land tenure*.

system, allodial see *allodialism*.

system, Auburn see *system, silent*.

system, authority a *set[1]* of interrelated *authority* centres.

system, axiomatic (Galtung) see *theory, axiomatic*.

system, behaviour stable sequence or *organization[10]* of *actions*.

system, belief a *set[1]* of beliefs constituting a *system*.

system, binary a *system* with two possible states.

system, bipolar an *international system* having two main *blocs[1]*.

system, bipolar, loose a *bipolar system* possessing different kinds of *actors* such as *states, blocs[1]*, bloc leaders, bloc members, nonbloc members.

system, bipolar, tight a *bipolar system* of very high tension in which nonbloc members have no *role*.

system, career the *set[1]* of interrelated graded *careers* in an *organization*.

system, caste 1. *system* of *social stratification* with the lowest degree of *social mobility* and in which the differences between the *social strata (castes)* are maintained and expressed ritually. 2. system of social stratification in which *upward mobility* is only possible through *passing*. (Myrdal). 3. system of social stratification with the lowest degree of social mobility. (Berreman).

system, category any ordering of *categories*.

system, category, continuous *category system* the *categories* of which are located along a *continuum*.

system, category, discrete *category system* the *categories* of which are not located along a *continuum*.

system, class *system* of *social stratification* in which the *social strata* are *social classes*. see also *system, estate*; *system, caste*.

system, closed *system* unaffected by changes in its *environment*.

system, closed-class *class system* with low *social mobility*.

system, communication 1. a *system* consisting of an information source, transmitter, *communication channel*, receiver, and destination. 2. see *network, communication*.

system, complex 1. a *system* with many elements and interrelations. 2. a system possessing *subsystems*.

system, component see *subsystem*.

system, conceptual a *set[1]* of *concepts* constituting a *system*.

system, concrete a *system* the elements of which are concrete and not abstract.

system, conflict a *system* of individuals or *groups* in *conflict*.

system, conserving *system* which does not lose elements.

system, contract system of *prison labour* involving letting-out the *labour* of prisoners to a contractor, the contractor supplying the raw materials and undertaking supervision.

system, control the components of a *social system* which produce *social control*. (Price, J.L.).

system, controlled *system* which is maintained in *equilibrium*.

system, correctional the *set[1]* of *norms, sanctions*, and *groups* in a particular *society* intended for the rehabilitation of offenders and *general deterrence*.

system, cultural 1. the *system* of cultural features constituting a *whole culture*. 2. any one of the several systems of cultural features, each system consisting of cultural features of a particular type, which constitute a culture.

system, cybernetic see *system, controlled.*

system, data-handling see *system, data-reduction.*

system, data-reduction automatically operated equipment used to interpret data gathered by instrument installations.

system, deductive 1. an interpreted *axiomatic system.* 2. a *system* of *valid hypotheses.* (Galtung).

system, descent a *society's set[1]* of *descent‖principles.*

system, descriptive *set[1]* of qualitative *categories* or types.

system, deterministic a *system* successive states of which are perfectly predictable.

system, deterministic, complex a *system* with many elements and interrelations and whose successive states are perfectly predictable.

system, deterministic, simple a *system* with few elements and interrelations and whose successive states are perfectly predictable.

system, domestic see *system, putting-out.*

system, dynamic a *system* which passes through a succession of states.

system, dysfunctional a *system* which frustrates the attainment of the *objectives* for which it is intended.

system, ecological a *system* of ecological *variables.*

system, economic 1. see *economy.* 2. type of economy.

system, eight-class a *section system* possessing eight *marriage classes.*

system, electoral the *norms* governing a particular type of *election.*

system, empirical (Parsons, T.) see *system, concrete.*

system, energy-tight see *system, closed.*

system, engineering complete instrumentality for performing a specified task.

system, equilibrium a *system* characterized by *stable equilibrium.*

system, estate *system* of *social stratification* in which the *functions* of the *strata* are legally determined and the distinctions between them predominantly enforced by *legal sanctions.*

system, ethnic a *set[1]* of interrelated *ethnic groups.* (Cox, O.C.).

system, external *system* of *sentiments, activities* and *interactions* required by external problem of *group.* see also *system, internal.*

system, formal 1. see *organization, formal.* 2. see *theory, formal.*

system, four-class a *section system* possessing four *marriage classes.*

system, homeorhetic a developing *system* characterized by *homeorhesis.* see also *chreod.*

system, homeostatic *cybernetic system* maintaining one particular state.

system, inductive a *system* of *tenable hypotheses.* (Galtung).

system, inductive-deductive a *system* of *valid hypotheses* most of which are *tenable hypotheses.* (Galtung).

system, informal see *organization, informal.*

system, information 1. a *system* involving the integration of user, information and retrieval system. 2. *engineering system* designed to perceive, transmit, store, compute, interpret, or reproduce information.

system, information, urban an *information system* serving the *government* of an *urban agglomeration.*

system, institutional *set[1]* of *institutions* whose main *functions* are of the same type.

system, internal *system* of *sentiments, activities* and *interactions* over and above those required by external problem of *group.* see also *system, external.*

system, international the system of relationships between the total *set[1]* of *states.*

system, interpreted an interpreted *axiomatic system.*

system, isolated see *system, closed.*

system, kinesic the *set[1]* of *kinemes* employed by the members of a particular *group.*

system, kinship the *system,* of *kinship norms, kinship behaviour,* and *kinship terminology* of a *society.*

system, language a language viewed as a *system.*

system, leading the *subsystem* having the greatest influence on the *suprasystem.*

system, lease system of *prison labour* under which a contractor assumes entire control of the prisoners.

system, legal 1. a *society's system* of *legal norms.* 2. a society's *set¹* of *norms, roles, behaviour patterns* and personnel pertaining to judicial, legislative, executive, and administrative processes. (Evan, W.M.). 3. see *family, legal.*

system, list *electoral system* based on PR of *parties* each of which presents a list of candidates, the voter being directed to cast his vote for one of the lists as a whole or permitted to alter the content, order, or both, of the list itself.

system, manorial the *system* of *land tenure* and *economy* in a *society* resulting from the prevalence of *manors.*

system, market the interdependent formation of market prices.

system, marks a remission method based on awarding marks to a prisoner or subtracting from a total of marks debited against him.

system, matrilineal a *kinship system* characterized by *matrilineal descent.*

system, mechanical *set¹* of relations between positions of mass at various points of time.

system, medical a patterned *set¹* of ideas and *practices⁴* concerning illness. (Glick, L.B.).

system, miniature see *theory, miniature.*

system, moral a *system* of moral *rules* and *principles.*

system, naming the *set¹* of *norms* regulating the giving of personal names.

system, normative *set¹* of *norms* constituting a *system.*

system, nutritional *system* of knowledge, *technology, sentiment,* and social and *magico-religious* practices by which the *need* for food is satisfied and regulated in a particular *culture.*

system, observer *system* of *observational categories* used by observer.

system, one-ballot *electoral system* lacking the *second ballot.*

system, open *system* affected by changes in its *environment.*

system, open-class *class system* with high *social mobility.*

system, oscillating *system* continually losing and regaining *stable equilibrium.*

system, parliamentary see *government, parliamentary.*

system, party the *set¹* of *parties* which constitute a *system* in a given *polity.*

system, patrilineal a *kinship system* characterized by *patrilineal descent.*

system, Pennsylvania see *system, separate.*

system, persisting *system* having structural continuity.

system, personality the *personality* treated as a *system.*

system, piece-price system of *prison labour* under which a contractor, who does not undertake supervision, supplies the raw materials and pays the prison for each unit accepted by him.

system, political 1. the *system* formed by a *political structure* and its *environment.* (Bailey, F.G.). 2. the *goal-attainment subsystem* of a *society.* (Parsons, T.). 3. the legitimate, order-maintaining or transforming system of a society. (Almond, G.).

system, postulate see *theory, axiomatic.*

system, prefectoral type of *field administration* in which there is a generalist representative of the central government exercising *delegated authority* in each *administrative area.* **prefect** *pers n.*

system, prefectoral, integrated *prefectoral system* in which local government officials and field officials of the central government are subordinated to the *prefect.*

system, prefectoral, unintegrated *prefectoral system* in which local government officials and field officials of the central goverment are not subordinated to the *prefect.*

system, presidential see *government, presidential.*

system, probabilistic a *system* successive states of which are a matter of probability.

system, probabilistic, complex a *system* with many elements and interrelations and whose successive states are a matter of probability.

system, probabilistic, simple a *system* with few elements and interrelations and whose successive states are a matter of probability.

system, proxemic a *system* of standardized *proxemic behaviours.*

system, public account system of *prison labour* involving complete direction of employment by the authorities, the production being sold for mutual benefit of public and prisoners.

system, putting-out productive system involving domestic production by individual or *family,* raw materials being supplied by entrepreneur to whom finished product is sold.

system, real that *system* represented by a given *model* or *operating model.*

system, real-time EDP system permitting processing fast enough to keep up with events in the real world.

system, relationship see *system, kinship.*

system, ritual *set[1]* of interrelated *rituals.*

system, role a *set[1]* of *roles* constituting a *system.*

system, second-ballot *electoral system* employing the *second ballot.*

system, section *marriage‖rule* according to which a man can only marry women from a certain *section[1]* of the opposite *moiety.*

system, self-other the perceived relationship of self to others.

system, semiotic *set[1]* of interrelated *signs.*

system, sentient *social system* which demands and receives loyalty from its members. (Miller, E.J.). see also *group, sentient.*

system, separate form of imprisonment in which all prisoners serve their whole sentences in solitary confinement.

system, silent form of imprisonment characterized by congregate labour and a rule of silence.

system, simple 1. a *system* with few elements and interrelations. 2. a system lacking *subsystems.*

system, slogan a *set[1]* of interrelated *slogans.*

system, social 1. a *system* of social elements. 2. an *action system* in which the interdependent *actions* are performed by interacting individuals. (Parsons, T.).

system, sociocultural a *system* of *sociocultural* elements.

system, sociotechnical a *system* consisting of the *social relationships* and the man-machine relationships of a *work* situation.

system, status the *system* of *statuses* within an *organization, community,* or *society.*

system, steady-state *system* the relationship between the *variables* of which remains invariant with respect to time.

system, stratification *set[1]* of *social strata* constituting a *system.*

system, symbol *set[1]* of interrelated *symbols.*

system, task *set[1]* of interrelated *tasks.*

system, technological *set[1]* of interrelated technological devices.

system, terror see *terror, system of.*

system, theoretical *set[1]* of interconnected *propositions[2].* (Parsons, T.).

system, two-ballot see *system, second-ballot.*

system, uncontrolled *system* which is not maintained in *equilibrium.*

system, uninterpreted see *system, axiomatic, uninterpreted*.

system, universal an *international system* in which supreme *power* resides in a universal *organization*.

system, urban urban nucleus plus dependent *settlements*.

system, value a *system* of *terminal values* and *instrumental values*.

system-problems the *functional prerequisites* of any *social system*. (Parsons, T.).

systematics science of *classification*.

systematist one who attributes supreme importance to *systems theory* for the study of social phenomena. (Thompson, L.).

table, actuarial see *table, life*.

table, derived a *summary table* derived from a *general table*.

table, general *statistical table*, relatively large, presenting original, varied numerical data for reference purposes.

table, general-purpose see *table, general*.

table, life a *statistical table* showing *mortality*, survivorship, and *life expectancy* in a *cohort* over time.

table, life, cohort see *table, life, generation*.

table, life, current a *life table* derived from *mortality rates* for one or a few years.

table, life, generation a *life table* showing, through observations in successive years, the actual *mortality* and survivorship in a *cohort*.

table, manning table giving the personnel requirements of a particular *organization*.

table, mortality see *table, life*.

table, prediction table of social-background or *personality‖factors* for predicting probability of *recidivism* or commission of *crime* or *delinquency*.

table, primary see *table, general*.

table, reference see *table, general*.

table, special-purpose see *table, summary*.

table, statistical a systematic arrangement of numerical data in columns and rows.

table, summary *statistical table*, relatively small, presenting selected, summary numerical data in order to show certain relationships.

table, text see *table, summary*.

taboo prohibition involving automatic *penalty[1]* of supernatural origin.

taboo, incest the prohibition of *incest*.

taboo, menstrual the prohibition on sexual intercourse with a menstruating woman.

taboo, name a *taboo* on speaking or writing the name of a person or a *supernatural*.

taboo, postpartum the prohibition on intercourse with a woman for a certain period following childbirth.

taboo, pregnancy a *taboo* in operation during pregnancy.

taboo, twin-birth a *taboo* on the birth of twins, resulting in the killing of one or both twins.

tabulation sorting completed *schedules* or punched cards into classes according to various characteristics, counting them, and preparing *statistical tables*.

tabulation, hand *tabulation* carried out by hand.

tabulation, machine *tabulation* by mechanical means.

tactics bargaining manoeuvres within the power limits. see also *strategy[2]*.

tale, catch story intended to trick listener into making remark which will make him the butt of the joke.

tale, chain *folktale* based on a series of things.

tale, cumulative *folktale* which is cumulative in some element, e.g., characters, names.

tale, endless *formula tale* having endless repetition of a certain incident or *set[1]* of words.

tale, formula *folktale* following a pattern to which the plot is secondary.

tallying the process of recording *raw data* on a tally sheet.

target 1. quantitatively specified short-term aim. 2. area or *population* which is the object of *social action[3]*.

task *subsystem* of a *role* defined by a *set[1]* of physical operations. (Parsons, T.).

task, coactive *group task* involving *coaction*.

task, group a *task* undertaken by each of the *group* members independently or a task undertaken by a group and involving the *interaction* of the members.

task, interactive *group task* involving *interaction*.

tattooing decorating the skin with dyestuff inserted in pricks, scratches or under the skin. see also *kakina*.

tattooing, prick decorating the skin with dyestuff inserted in pricks.

tattooing, thread decorating the skin by pulling a sooty thread under the skin.

taxis reflexive orienting *response*.

taxon a *taxonomic‖category*. see also *taxonomy*.

taxon, terminal a *taxon* which includes no other taxon.

taxonomy *category system* in which *categories* are ordered by relations of contrast and inclusion. **taxonomic** *a*.

taxonomy, deep a *taxonomy* possessing many levels of inclusion.

taxonomy, numerical the numerical evaluation of the affinity or similarity between taxonomic units and the ordering of these units into *taxa* on the basis of their affinities. (Sokal, R.R. and Sneath, P.H.A.).

taxonomy, perfect a *taxonomy* which is represented by a *branch diagram* in which each node corresponds to a *lexeme*.

T-data data on *personality* from *objective tests*.

team a plurality of persons organized for a specific project.

teasing persistent irritation of another person by *actions* intended to produce distress, discomfort, or ridicule. (Loudon, J.B.).

teasing, competitive *teasing* which is an expression of *rivalry* between the participants. (Loudon, J.B.).

teasing, domestic *teasing* in a domestic context. (Loudon, J.B.).

teasing, public *teasing* in a public context, in which members of the *audience* do not participate. (Loudon, J.B.).

technique 1. manufacturing process. 2. *set[1]* of operations used in *measurement* or *experimental manipulation*. 3. *set[1]* of operations for achieving a *goal*. 4. a process derived from *theory* used in *planning*.

technique, mid-range a *technique* sufficiently general to be common to all or a significant part of the sciences. (Kaplan, A.).

technique, social any method of moulding behaviour to fit into the prevailing patterns of *interaction* and *organization*. (Mannheim, K.).

technocracy 1. *government* using science and engineering for the solution of problems. 2. government by technical experts. **technocratic** *a*. **technocrat** *pers n*.

technology 1. the body of knowledge concerning manufacturing and extractive processes. 2. the whole or an organized sector of the industrial application of science. 3. a *society*'s *set[1]* of *techniques* for obtaining sustenance. 4. pattern of all the practices for utilizing resources in pursuit of *values*. (Lasswell). 5. all existing means for achieving *organizational goals*.

technology, information the *technology* utilized in the collection, storage, retrieval, and processing of information.

technology, material *techniques* employed in the production of material things. (Radcliffe-Brown).

technology, nonmaterial *techniques* which are not employed in the production of material things. (Radcliffe-Brown).

technology, social 1. see *technology, nonmaterial*. 2. the applied social sciences underlying *social planning*.

technostructure *set¹* of members of an *organization* who contribute to its *group decisions*. (Galbraith, J.K.).

teknonym a name applied to a person by virtue of his relation to his child.

teknonymy custom of naming parent from his or her child, e.g. 'Father of so-and-so'.

teknophagy the eating of children. **teknophagous** *a*.

teleceptor see *distoceptor*.

telexis mate selection according to social standards of desirability.

telic having a *goal*.

telotaxis a goal-oriented *taxis*.

tenants, cash agricultural tenants who pay a fixed cash rent for use and occupancy of land.

tenants, crop-share agricultural tenants who pay a share of the crops only.

tenants, full agricultural tenants who rent all the land they operate.

tenants, livestock-share agricultural tenants who pay a share of the livestock and/or livestock products, and who may or may not pay a share of the crops.

tenants, share agricultural tenants who are either *crop-share tenants* or *livestock-share tenants*.

tenants, share-cash agricultural tenants who pay part of their rent in cash and part in a share of the crops and/or livestock and livestock products.

tenants, squatter *squatters* who rent huts from other squatters. see also *landlord, squatter*.

tenants, statutory tenants whose tenancies have contractually expired, but who have rights by statute to pay rent and continue in occupation.

tension 1. physiological or psychological pressure in individual. 2. state existing in individual who has *need* or intention. (Lewin). 3. physiological or psychological state in individual resulting from *stressors*. 4. unpleasant internal psychological pressure. 5. disequilibrium or imbalance in *system*. see also *stress*; *stressor*; *strain*.

tension, intergroup *tension* existing between *groups*.

tension, intragroup *tension* existing within a *group*.

tension, need *tension* resulting from presence of *need*.

tension, organizational disequilibrium or imbalance in an *organization*.

tension, revolutionary any disequilibrium or imbalance in a *society* conducive to a *revolution*.

tension, role *tension* resulting from *role conflict*.

tension, social 1. state existing in individuals resulting from friction or *opposition* in *group*. 2. disequilibrium or imbalance in a *social system*.

tension-binding ability to inhibit an *act* on perception of *stimulus* to the act.

tentation *innovation* which is not synthesis or application to new situation but is the result of trial-and-error learning.

tenure 1. see *tenure, land*. 2. continuance of an individual in *office*. **tenurial** *a*.

tenure, allodial *tenure¹* under which land is held in absolute ownership.

tenure, collective *tenure¹* under which land is held collectively.

tenure, communal *tenure¹* under which the land belongs to the *community*, each member having a right to individual occupation of a portion of the land

215

when available according to his requirements.

tenure, feudal 1. *tenure[1]* under which land is held on condition of rendering *military service*. 2. *tenure[1]* under which land is held on condition of rendering military service and entailing *seignorial jurisdiction*.

tenure, hereditary *tenure[1]* under which land is inherited by an individual or *group*.

tenure, individual *tenure[1]* under which land is held by an individual.

tenure, land the rights of individuals and *groups* over land.

tenure, military *tenure[1]* under which land is held on condition of rendering *military service*. see also *tenure, service*.

tenure, semi-feudal *tenure[1]* under which land is held on condition of rendering *military service* but without *seignorial jurisdiction*.

tenure, service *tenure[1]* under which land is held on condition of rendering a service.

terciles see *tertiles*.

term, classificatory term covering *kinship categories* delineated by sex, *generation[2]* and specific genealogical connection, e.g. 'uncle'.

term, denotative term used for only one *kinship category*, e.g. 'mother'.

term, derivative term consisting of *kinship term* and another lexical component, e.g. 'stepson'.

term, descriptive term consisting of two or more basic terms which describe the relative.

term, egocentric a *kinship term* the application of which is relative to *ego*. see also *term, sociocentric*.

term, elementary term not having lexical components with kinship meaning, e.g. 'father'.

term, particularizing see *term, denotative*.

term, sociocentric term referring to a position in a *kinship group*, application being irrespective of *ego's* position. see also *term, egocentric*.

terminology, classificatory *kinship terminology* in which *lineals* are not distinguished from *collaterals*.

terminology, descriptive *kinship terminology* in which *lineals* are distinguished from *collaterals*.

terminology, kinship a *system* of *kinship terms*.

terminology, mixed *kinship terminology* employing both *classificatory terms* and *denotative terms*.

terminology, particularizing *kinship terminology* employing only *particularizing terms*.

terms, kin see *terms, kinship*.

terms, kinship terms used in a *society* for different classes of relatives.

terms, observational scientific terms whose applicability to particular situations is determined by direct observation. (Hempel, C.G.).

terms, reciprocal two terms for a kin relationship, each term being used by a participant to denote the other participant.

terms, theoretical scientific terms which do not refer to directly observable entities. (Hempel, C.G.).

terrace a constructed horizontal step on a hill-slope with the soil retained by earth banks or stone walls.

territorialism 1. concentration of political *power* in large land-owners. 2. see *territoriality*.

territoriality the behaviour of an animal in defending its *territory[3]*.

territory 1. the land and waters, or any given portion of it, under the jurisdiction of a *government[1]*. 2. see *dependency[1]*. 3. area maintained, marked, and defended against intrusion.

territory, dependent see *dependency[1]*.

216

territory, neutral *territory* set aside as neutral by mutual agreement of two or more *tribes*.

territory, state the *territory[1]* of a *state*.

terror 1. *tyranny* characterized by failure of obedience to guarantee safety and the infliction of arbitrary *punishment* to create fear and paralyze resistance. 2. see *terrorism[2]*.

terror, agitational see *terrorism[1]*.

terror, defensive systematic use of *terrorization* by *groups* in a *population* to defend the status quo or traditional rights.

terror, enforcement see *terror[1]*.

terror, offensive see *terrorism[2]*.

terror, process of the act or threat of *violence* aimed at defending the *authority structure* or undermining the authority structure, the extreme fear created, and the social effects. (Walter, E.V.).

terror, regime of (Walter, E.V.) see *terror[1]*.

terror, repressive systematic use of *terrorization* by a *government* or by rebels to eliminate rivals, coerce popular support, or maintain *conformity* within the rebel *organization*.

terror, seige of (Walter, E.V.) see *terrorism[1]*.

terror, system of a sphere of *social relationships* controlled by a *terror process*. (Walter, E.V.).

terror, zone of a *system of terror* which is part of a larger *society* which does not itself constitute a *system of terror*. (Walter, E.V.).

terrorism 1. systematic *violence* aimed at undermining the *authority structure* through creating fear. 2. violence taking the form of a *regime of terror* or a *seige of terror*.

terrorism, external intimidation and surveillance of non-members by a *party*. (Duverger, M.).

terrorism, internal intimidation and surveillance by a *party* of its own members. (Duverger, M.).

terrorization the act of terrorizing. see also **terrorize** *v.*

terrorize to dominate or coerce by fear.

tertiles *quantiles* dividing *array* into three equal parts.

test, chastity *ordeal* given to a woman to discover whether or not she has been faithful.

test, culture-free test independent of *testee's culture*.

test, cycle see *test, omnibus, cycle*.

test, group test for administration to more than one person at a time.

test, individual test for administration to one person at a time.

test, multiple-choice test involving *multiple-choice questions*.

test, multiple-response test requiring more than one selection from each *set[1]* of response-alternatives.

test, objective test the scoring of which is *objective[5]*. see also *test, subjective*.

test, omnibus test in which *items[1]* are not grouped according to type.

test, omnibus, cycle *omnibus test* in which *items[1]* of different type are arranged in a recurrent pattern.

test, omnibus, spiral *omnibus test* in which *items[1]* of different type are arranged in a pattern recurring with increasing difficulty.

test, performance test scored on nonverbal *responses*.

test, selective-answer see *test, multiple-choice*.

test, self-marking a test the *responses* to which are automatically recorded as right of wrong.

test, sociometric a test used to reveal a *sociometric structure*. (*sociom.*).

test, son-in-law a test given to a man by his prospective parents-in-law to determine his suitability as the husband of their daughter.

test, spiral see *test, omnibus, spiral.*

test, subjective test lacking *objective*[5] scoring. see also *test, objective.*

testee person tested.

tetrad *group* of four persons.

thanatomania the *psychosomatic* production of death by a *magical* action or death curse accepted as fatal by the *victim*[2].

thaumaturgy the working of miracles. **thaumaturge** *pers n.*

theme 1. see *theme, cultural.* 2. meaning-unit in *communication* content.

theme, cultural 1. the explicit or implicit affirmations giving character, *structure,* and direction to a *culture.* (Opler). 2. a deep structure which is implicit in a culture.

theocracy *government* involving the application to the minutiae of *social life* of what the rulers believe to be divine law. **theocratic** *a.*

theogony beliefs concerning the origin of gods. **theogonic** *a.*

theolepsy possession by a deity.

theoleptic a person possessed by a deity.

theomancy *divination* through *oracles* believed to be divinely inspired. **theomantic** *a.* **theomancer** *pers n.*

theophagy the sacramental eating of a god. **theophagous** *a.*

theophany a personal manifestation of a deity to an individual.

theorem 1. a *proposition* derived from a *postulate*[1] or *set*[1] of postulates. 2. a *hypothesis* or part of a hypothesis expressed in a testable form. 3. see *hypothesis, valid.*

theorem, sociologistic *principle* that individual *motivation* tends to be congruent with the *value system* of the *society.* (Parsons, T.).

theorem, Thomas the *proposition*[2] that situations defined as real are real in their consequences.

theory 1. *set*[1] of interconnected *propositions*[2]. 2. (Galtung). see *system, inductive-deductive.* 3. see *scheme, conceptual.*

theory, action *theory* which seeks to understand *society* through the analysis of *social action.*

theory, alliance *theory* which explains *kinship* phenomena predominantly in terms of *marital alliances.*

theory, analogical *theory* expressed in a physical *model.*

theory, anthropological see *anthropology, theoretical.*

theory, axiomatic *set*[1] of *postulates* with entailed *propositions,* the terms clearly defined.

theory, broad see *theory, wide-range.*

theory, cognitive a theoretical approach in *psychology* which emphasizes the *cognitive.*

theory, communication the technology that deals with *communication* in all its aspects.

theory, concentric zone Burgess's *hypothesis* that typical urban *growth* involves five concentric land-use zones.

theory, cumulative *theory* built on the successive revision of preceding theories.

theory, decision the mathematical *theory* of *decision-making.*

theory, descent *theory* which explains *kinship* phenomena predominantly in terms of *descent.*

theory, dissonance *theory* concerning *cognitive dissonance.*

theory, eclectic a *theory* employing two or more *models.*

theory, ethnographic *theory* concerning *criteria* for the evaluation of alternative *ethnographic* descriptions, the ethnographic methods most effective for deriving generalizations, and criteria such as completeness, conciseness, and accuracy, for evaluating ethnographies.

theory, explicit a *theory* which is explicitly-formulated.

theory, field 1. the study of behaviour as the function of the entire, immediate situation. (Lewin, K.). 2. the study of psychophysiological energy patterns. (Köhler, W.).

theory, formal see *theory, axiomatic.*

theory, formalized see *theory, axiomatic.*

theory, game the mathematical *theory* of *interaction* seen as the *strategy* of people engaged in contests.

theory, general a *theory* embracing the whole of a particular field.

theory, grand see *theory, wide-range.*

theory, implicit a *theory* which is not explicitly-formulated.

theory, information the study of the transmission of *messages* and the *communication* of information, i.e., that which reduces the uncertainty or ambiguity of a message.

theory, kinship *theory* explaining *kinship* phenomena. see also *theory, alliance*; *theory, descent.*

theory, location *theory* of locational choice for economic units.

theory, measurement 1. *theory* of *measurement,* whether qualitative or quantitative. 2. theory of *quantitative measurement.*

theory, methodological *theory* concerning *methodology* per se.

theory, middle-range a *theory* explaining a medium number of empirical generalizations. (Merton, R.K.).

theory, miniature a *theory* explaining a very small field of phenomena.

theory, multi-nuclear *hypothesis* that urban land-use zones develop from several nuclei, either simultaneously or in succession.

theory, narrow-range a *theory* explaining a small number of empirical generalizations.

theory, normative 1. *set[1]* of interconnected *propositions* stating the means to specified ends. 2. *theory* concerning *norms.*

theory, organization *theory* concerning *organizations* in general.

theory, over-arching see *theory, wide-range.*

theory, partial a *theory* embracing part of a particular field.

theory, political 1. the moral theory of *politics.* 2. the history of political ideas in their social context. 3. the analysis of the language of politics. 4. *substantive theory* concerning political phenomena.

theory, role a scheme of *role concepts* or a *set[1]* of interconnected *propositions* employing role concepts.

theory, scaling *theory* of *qualitative measurement,* i.e. of the *ordered metric scale* and *scales[1]* of lesser power.

theory, sector *hypothesis* that urban land-use zones grow radially from city centre. (Hoyt).

theory, sociological the body of *theory* and *meta-theory* concerning social phenomena.

theory, special see *theory, partial.*

theory, stage any *theory* that *societies* or economic or other *systems* pass through common stages.

theory, substantive *set[1]* of interconnected *propositions* making assertions about reality.

theory, systematic see *theory, axiomatic.*

theory, systems a body of *theory* concerning *systems* as such.

theory, verbal *theory* expressed in words.

theory, wide-range a *theory* explaining a large number of empirical generalizations.

therapy *treatment[1]* seeking to ameliorate or cure a disorder suffered by an individual.

therapy, drama see *psychodrama.*

therapy, semantic the process of correcting *semantogenic* disorders.

they-group see *out-group*.

through-put the processing within a *system* of the *input* to it.

thrust, culture the thrust of *material culture* ahead of *nonmaterial culture*. (Quinn, J.A.). see also *lag, cultural*; *lag, cultural, inverse*.

threshold point on *stimulus scale* below which *perception* or *response* does not occur.

tillage, brand see *cultivation, shifting*.

tillage, hand see *horticulture*.

time, discretionary time when individual is free from *activity* that it is necessary to perform.

time, free time that is neither *work* time nor work-related time (time spent to appear at work) nor subsistence time (time spent maintaining healthy state of organism).

time, reaction see *latency, response*.

time, residual nonwork time.

time-binding transmitting *culture* from *generation²* to generation.

time-intercept using *sample* of momentary observations. see also *snap-reading*.

tinsit tendency-in-situation, i.e., frequency of *type-response* in a *type-situation*. (Coutu, W.).

tinsit, personal *tinsit* involving acquired *responses*. (Coutu, W.).

tinsit, somatic *tinsit* involving *innate‖responses*. (Coutu, W.).

title 1. an appellation or address of dignity. 2. the right to ownership of property. 3. a complex of rights, privileges, or powers with respect to some subject matter. (Murdock).

token, chastity personal object given by spouse or lover believed to expose unfaithfulness of recipient.

token, life object chosen by or born with a person which is believed to reveal when he is in danger, may die, or is dead.

to-name a person's additional name, bestowed or derived from a description.

toponomasiology study of the place names of a given language or area.

toponomastics see *toponomasiology*.

toponomatology see *toponomasiology*.

toponymic 1. place name. 2. term for a geographical feature.

toponymy study of the derivation of place names.

totalitarianism permanent governmental control over totality of *social life*. **totalitarian** *a.* see also *autocracy*; *dictatorship*; *despotism*; *absolutism*; *tyranny*.

totem a class of animate or inanimate things with which a *totem group* is associated.

totemism the association of different *groups* (*totem groups*) with different classes of animate or inanimate things (*totems*). **totemic** *a.*

totemism, clan association of a *clan* with a *totem* or totems.

totemism, conceptional *totemism* in which a child belongs to the totemic centre nearest the spot where its mother first became aware of her pregnancy.

totemism, group association of a *group* with a *totem* or totems.

totemism, individual association of an individual with a *totem*.

totemism, linked *group totemism* involving several *totems* with an underlying order.

totemism, multiplex *group totemism* involving several *totems* without an underlying order.

totemism, personal see *totemism, individual*.

totemism, sex *totemism* in which each sex has a different *totem*.

totemism, twin *group totemism* in which the human *group* and the animal species have common *ancestors*.

220

totemites people who practise *totemism.*

tract, census a small, permanent, relatively homogeneous area of a city delimited for the collection of *census* data. (USBC).

tract, urban a continuous urban built-up area. (Dickinson, R.E.).

trade, administered trade in which the traders are political representatives of their *communities.*

trade, depot see *trade, silent.*

trade, silent exchange of goods without direct social interaction.

trade, symbiotic 1. see *barter, silent.* 2. trade between *societies* in which the less advanced society develops a trading surplus only in response to the trade need.

trade, transit trade in which traders transport goods from one people to another, non-contiguous people.

tradition 1. socially-inherited belief or beliefs accepted uncritically. 2. socially-inherited belief or beliefs involving piety for what is thought to have always existed. 3. an *institution* whose perpetuation is institutionalized. (Levy, M.J.).

tradition, great the reflected-upon, systematized *culture* of a *society.* (Redfield, R.).

tradition, little the unreflected-upon, unsystematized *culture* of the *peasant* ‖ *communities* within a particular *society.* (Redfield, R.).

tradition, oral belief or beliefs or a cultural feature transmitted from one *generation*[2] to the next by word of mouth.

tradition-directed characterized by a *behavioural conformity* to *tradition.* (Riesman, D.). see also *inner-directed; other-directed.*

traditionalism 1. the uncritical acceptance of socially-inherited beliefs. 2. the acceptance of socially-inherited beliefs, based on piety for what is thought to have always existed. **traditionalist** *a.* & *pers n.*

training teaching *skills* and giving instruction.

training, entrance see *training, orientation.*

training, external *training* for the public service provided by an *organization* which is not part of the public service of the country whose officials are being trained. (UN).

training, induction *in-service training* which goes beyond *orientation training* and is concerned with the *tasks* connected with a particular *position.* (UN).

training, in-service *training* given to an employee after beginning *job.*

training, observer *training* gained by observing trained workers.

training, off-the-job *training* which is not given in a work situation.

training, on-the-job (OJT) *training* given in a work situation.

training, orientation *in-service training* designed to adjust a new employee to the procédures and personnel of the *organization.* (UN).

training, out-service see *training, external.*

training, portal see *training, induction.*

training, post-entry see *training, in-service.*

training, pre-entry *training* given to an employee before beginning *job.*

training, simulated *training* on equipment withdrawn from the work situation or on *simulators.*

training, vestibule see *training, induction.*

trait, character a relatively consistent and enduring aspect of an individual's *character,* which is manifested in many situations.

trait, complex a *culture trait* which is divisible into other culture traits.

trait, culture 1. minimum transmissible unit of *culture.* 2. smallest identifiable unit of culture. (Herskovits). 3. minimal definable element of culture. (Kroeber).

trait, negative absence of a particular *culture trait.* (Wissler).

trait, personality a relatively consistent and enduring aspect of an individual's *personality*, which is manifested in many situations.

trait, positive a *culture trait* present in a *culture*. (Wissler).

trait, secondary any part of a complex *culture trait* which is unnecessary for its use.

trait-list inventory of the *culture traits* found in a *culture* or *culture complex*.

transaction 1. *exchange* with accompanying *negotiations*. 2. unit of social intercourse. (Berne, E.).

transaction, primitive a *transaction*[1] occurring on a non-price level. (Firth, R.).

transactor an individual involved in a *transaction*.

transcription, data conversion of data from one recorded form to another. see also *acquisition, data*; *reduction, data*.

transculturation reciprocal *acculturation*. (Ortiz, F.).

transhumance regular seasonal movements on the part of a whole people. **transhumant** *a.* **transhumants** *pers n.*

transhumance, local *transhumance* involving a relatively short distance. (Arbos, P.).

transhumance, pastoral *transhumance* practised by *pastoralists*.

transhumance, regional *transhumance* involving a relatively long distance. (Arbos, P.).

transition, demographic period between fall in *mortality* and fall in *fertility*.

transvection the flying of a *sorcerer* to attack a *victim*[2].

transvestism see *transvestitism*.

transvestitism 1. the psychopathological desire to dress in the clothing of members of the opposite sex. 2. any culturally-prescribed dressing in the clothing of the opposite sex.

treatment 1. subjecting something or someone to an action or influence. 2. any measure to ameliorate an undesirable condition. 3. any one variation in the *experimental stimuli*.

treatment, custodial *treatment*[1] restricted to custody applied to a psychiatric or criminal case.

treatment, dummy a *treatment*[3] which is not in fact applied, included in an *experimental design* to preserve its symmetry.

treatment, experimental any one variation in the *experimental stimuli*.

tree see *diagram, branch*.

tree, decision a *tree* representing a *decision‖structure*.

tree, game a *tree* representing the *moves* of a player. see also *theory, game*.

trend a smooth growth or decline in a quantity, that is, smooth over periods that are long in relation to the unit of time.

trend, curvilinear see *trend, nonlinear*.

trend, empirical a *trend* found in a *set*[1] of data for which the investigator has no *explanation*.

trend, linear a *trend* in which rate of change is constant.

trend, nonlinear a *trend* in which rate of change is not constant.

trend, rational a *trend* found in a *set*[1] of data for which the investigator has an *explanation*.

trend, rectilinear see *trend, linear*.

trend, secular a very long-term *trend*.

trend, social a *trend* displayed by a social phenomenon.

triad *group* of three persons. **triadic** *a.*

triadism the structural or territorial division of a *community* into three parts. (Lévi-Strauss). see also *dualism*.

trial one series of *experimental manipulations*.

tribalism the existence of total tribal *cultures* or *tribal* ties and loyalties.

tribalism, rural total participation in the *tribal‖culture* of a *rural‖community*.

tribalism, urban *tribal* ties and loyalties, *supertribalism,* and inter-tribal relations existing in towns.

tribe 1. a *group* with conscious cultural uniformity. (Nadel). 2. a group which is the object of *ethnographic* analysis. 3. a *society* basing its membership on *kinship.* 4. a society more complex than a *band* but less complex than a *chiefdom.* 5. one of the *political units* of a *cultural group.* (Mair, L.). **tribal** *a.*

tribe, centralized a *tribe* which is not *acephalous* and *segmentary.*

triple *group* of three persons.

truce type of *accommodation* in which individuals or *groups* in active *conflict* temporarily or permanently suspend hostile actions without the conflict being resolved or the issues settled.

turnover, labour replacement rate of employees.

turnover, residential replacement rate of residents in an area.

tutelary see *spirit, tutelary.*

type, classificatory a type which is construed as a class in a *typology²* possessing the logic of *classification.*

type, constructed a *construct* which is a *model* resulting from research. (Becker, H.).

type, cross-cultural a complex of *cultural cores* of *culture area types* occurring two or more times in historical independence of one another.

type, culture 1. a class of *cultures.* 2. an ideal-typical culture. 3. the culture in a *culture area* where the complex of *culture traits* peculiar to the area is found in its most extreme form.

type, culture area a locally distinctive *sociocultural system.*

type, extreme a type constituting a conceptual point of reference under which individual cases cannot be subsumed but can only be characterized as to the extent to which they approximate it. (Hempel, C.G.).

type, ideal a *concept* in which one or more characteristics are exaggerated and the concept purified of elements not required. (Weber, M.).

type, personality any one of the types belonging to a *classificatory typology* of *personality.*

type, pure see *type, extreme.*

type, social see *sociotype¹.*

type-response type of *response.* (Coutu, W.). see also *tinsit.*

type-situation type of *situation.* (Coutu, W.). see also *tinsit.*

typology 1. the study of types. 2. any ordering of types.

typology, classificatory a *typology²* possessing the logic of *classification.*

tyranny 1. a *government* felt by a substantial part of its *subjects³* to be cruel and oppressive. 2. the type of government which secures obedience mainly or entirely through the fear of *punishment.* 3. the manner of exercising *authority* which involves very frequent recourse to punishments of utmost severity. 4. the exercise of *power* beyond the scope permitted by existing *norms.*

tyranny, erratic *tyranny* under which *punishments* are not *norm*-controlled. (Andreski, S.).

tyranny, regular *tyranny* under which *punishments* are *norm*-controlled. (Andreski, S.).

ultimogeniture exclusive or preferential right in *inheritance* of youngest son. see also *primogeniture; unigeniture.*

umland see *hinterland, urban.*

umpire person who supersedes arbitrators if they cannot agree. see also *arbitration.*

uncertainty 1. an unknown probability. 2. incomplete predictability of alternative outcomes. 3. state of doubt or indecisiveness. see also *risk*.

uncertainty, affective indecisiveness resulting from *subjective uncertainty*.

uncertainty, objective incomplete predictability of alternative outcomes with all available information.

uncertainty, subjective belief in the incomplete predictability of alternative outcomes.

underdevelopment 1. condition of a low level of *economic development*. 2. suboptimum utilization of natural and human resources.

under-enumeration incomplete coverage of *enumeration*.

undernutrition hypocaloric state. see also *malnutrition*.

underpopulation the condition in which an increase in inhabitants will yield advantages to the remainder. see also *overpopulation*; *population, optimum*.

under-registration incomplete coverage in registration of *vital statistics*.

under-represented less frequent in a *sample* than in the *population*. see also *over-represented*.

understanding, empathetic process and *technique* whereby *psychotherapist* empathizes with patient. see also *empathy*.

understanding, sympathetic see *Verstehen*.

unholy whatever is thought to contaminate the *holy*. (Davis, K.).

unicultural 1. in which one *culture* is represented.2. pertaining to one culture.

uniformity, cultural a similarity in the form or content of *culture* characterizing a single area or *area co-tradition*.

unigeniture exclusive or preferential right in *inheritance* by one son as opposed to equal inheritance by sons. **unigenitary** *a.* see also *primogeniture*; *ultimogeniture*.

unilineality see *descent, unilineal*.

unilocality see *residence, unilocal*.

unimodal (of a *frequency distribution*) having one *mode*.

union, cohabiting a stable sexual union involving cohabitation see also *union, visiting*.

union, conjugal a stable sexual union whether or not constituting a *marriage*.

union, consensual a stable union not constituting a *marriage*.

union, free see *union, consensual*.

union, ritual copulation performed as part of a *ritual*.

union, visiting a stable sexual union not involving cohabitation. see also *union, cohabiting*.

unit, accomodation unit of housing occupied by one *household*.

unit, commensal *set[1]* of persons who regularly eat together.

unit, consumption *set[1]* of persons who pool resources for consumption.

unit, decision-making individual or *group* having a *decision-making||function*.

unit, descent corporate or non-corporate *descent group[1]*. (Schneider, D.M.).

unit, dwelling see *dwelling*.

unit, ethnographic a *group* which is the object of *ethnographic* analysis.

unit, experimental that which receives a *treatment[3]* in a single *replication*.

unit, geosocial *territorial group* plus *habitat*.

unit, housing room or group of rooms occupied or intended for occupancy as separate living quarters. (USBC).

unit, housing, improvised an independent makeshift shelter constructed of waste materials intended for habitation by one *household*. (SOUN).

unit, housing, mobile *housing unit* constructed to be transported or which is a moving unit. (SOUN).

unit, listing see *listing*.

unit, migratory a *migratory group* or individual *migrant*. (Hägerstrand, T.).

unit, natal the *kinship group* in which an individual was born.

unit, neighbourhood a planned residential area having a physical unity which is designed to become a *neighbourhood*. see also *neighbours*; *neighbouring*; *role, neighbour*.

unit, observational unit from which observations are obtained as distinct from *population element, sampling unit* or *listing*.

unit, political a *population* characterized by *law* within and *war* without.

unit, productive *group* organized temporarily or permanently for production.

unit, residential *set[1]* of co-resident persons treated as a unit for purposes of analysis.

unit, sampling one of the elements or groups of elements of a *population* included in a *sample*.

unit, social 1. smallest unit possessing a *social* character. 2. unit employed in social analysis. 3. *observational unit* employed in the compilation of social statistics.

unit, spending *set[1]* of persons who pool resources for spending.

unit, utterance stretch of speech bounded by a change of speaker. (Fries, C.C.).

universalism—particularism the incompatible alternatives facing an *actor* of treating a social object as a member of a class or in terms of some particular relationship it has to him. (Parsons, T.).

universals, cultural features common to all *cultures*.

universals, linguistic properties common to natural languages.

universe see *population[1,2]*.

uprising a localized *revolt*. see also *revolution*; *rebellion*; *putsch*; *insurrection*; *coup*.

urban 1. characterized by *urbanism*. 2. pertaining to a large *agglomeration*. see also *rural*.

urbanism city way of life.

urbanization 1. the extension of urban patterns to new areas and *populations*. 2. increase in proportion of *urban population*. 3. the process of becoming *urban*. 4. urban population divided by total population. 5. the process of population concentration. (Eldridge).

urbanization, arterial *urbanization* along the transportation routes joining urban nodes.

urbanization, subsistence *urbanization* in which the majority of urbanites live at *subsistence level*. (Bresse, G.).

usage 1. probability of uniformity of *social action*. (Weber, M.). 2. *action* learnt from other members of *group*. (Slotkin). 3. a mode of behaviour which is usual in a particular *community*. (Radcliffe-Brown). see also *custom*; *convention*; *mores*; *folkways*.

usufruct right to the use and produce of something belonging to another. *(jurid.)*.

usufructuary person possessing a *usufruct*. *(jurid.)*.

utterance 1. an act of speech. 2. any self-sufficient unit of speech.

utterance, free *utterance* that can stand alone.

uxorilateral on the wife's side.

uxorilocality see *residence, uxorilocal*.

valence attracting or repelling quality of object.

valence, negative repelling quality of object.

valence, positive attracting quality of object.

validity extent to which test measures what it is intended to measure.

validity, a priori see *validity, logical*.

validity, assumption see *validity, face*.

validity, concept see *validity, construct*.

validity, concurrent *correlation* between test results and concurrent performance of *testees*.

validity, congruent see *validity, construct*.

validity, construct *validity* involving a *criterion* which is a *construct*.

validity, content the degree to which the test *items[1]* are representative of the *variable* to be measured.

validity, convergent *validity* established by the agreement of a *measure* with a measure whose validity has already been established.

validity, criterion-orientated see *validity, empirical*.

validity, definitional the *variable* to be measured is defined in terms of the test *items[1]*.

validity, empirical *correlation* between test results and an external *criterion*.

validity, face the test *items[1]* superficially appear to be representative of the *variable* to be measured.

validity, factorial *correlation* between test and a *factor* found by *factor analysis*.

validity, intrinsic the test *items[1]* necessarily elicit the type of behaviour to be measured.

validity, item 1. degree to which a test *item[1]* measures what it is intended to measure. 2. degree to which a test *item[1]* discriminates between persons.

validity, logical the test *items[1]* superficially appear to elicit the behaviours assumed to belong to the *variable* to be measured.

validity, predictive *correlation* between test results and future performance.

validity, rational see *validity, logical*.

validity, status *correlation* between test results and *testees'* concurrent status which is believed to require the *variable* the test is intended to measure.

value 1. the object of an interest, terminal or instrumental. 2. object possessing a *valence*. 3. a character trait culturally-defined as desirable. 4. anything culturally-defined as desirable. 5. the rate of exchange between commodity A and commodity B. 6. any one of the possible magnitudes of a *variable*.

value, cultural a *value* embraced by a *culture* or culturally-prescribed for an individual.

value, explicit a *value* which is explicitly-formulated.

value, focal any one of the *terminal values* of a *society* which is inferable from a *set[1]* of other *values*.

value, implicit a *value* which is not explicitly-formulated.

value, institutional a *value* served by an *institution*.

value, instrumental a *value* which is a means to another value.

value, normative (Barton, A.) see *value[4]*.

value, occupational any *value* pursued by people in their *occupation*.

value, preference (Barton, A.) see *value[1]*.

value, scale 1. number assigned to an object in accordance with a *scale[2]*. 2. number assigned to one of the divisions or reference points of a *scale[2]*.

value, social 1. a *value* pursued by a *group* or *society*. 2. the way in which a thing affects or is capable of affecting *social life*. (Radcliffe-Brown).

value, societal a *value* pursued by a *society*.

value, stranger the advantages to social investigation accruing from fact that investigator is a stranger. (Piddington, R.).

value, terminal a *value* which is not a means to another value.

value, ultimate see *value, terminal*.

value-freedom the doctrine that science excludes the making of value judgments.

variable quantity which varies.

variable, all-or-none see *variable, dichotomous*.

variable, autonomous see *variable, exogenous*.

226

variable, background a *variable* which is public and permanent within a given *system* of interaction. (Galtung).

variable, binary see *variable, dichotomous.*

variable, binomial see *variable, dichotomous.*

variable, composite a *variable* composed of *subvariables.*

variable, confounding *variable* producing a *correlation* between two other variables by its correlation with each of the variables.

variable, contaminating see *variable, confounding.*

variable, continuous *variable* with infinite number of possible *values*[6] between highest and lowest value, e.g. height, weight.

variable, decision a manipulation *variable* in a *decision model.*

variable, dependent 1. *variable* observed by experimenter to discover whether it changes in response to change in *independent variable.* 2. variable completely determined by one or a combination of other variables in the *system.*

variable, determining *variable* which by itself or in combination with others determines another variable.

variable, dichotomous a *qualitative variable* which can only take two *values*[6].

variable, discontinuous see *variable, discrete.*

variable, discrete *variable* with finite number of possible *values*[6] between hignest and lowest value, e.g. number of persons in household.

variable, distal *variable* concerning part of a psychological process which had its location in the *environment* beyond the boundary of an organism.

variable, effect see *variable, dependent.*

variable, endogenous a *variable* within the *system.*

variable, exogenous a *variable* outside the *system.*

variable, experimental see *variable, independent.*

variable, extraneous a *variable* affecting the *dependent variable* but not recognized by the *research design.*

variable, independent *variable* manipulated by experimenter.

variable, instrument a *variable* influenced by planners in order to give a certain *value*[6] to the *target variable.*

variable, intervening a *mediating construct* to which reality is not attributed.

variable, multinomial see *variable, polytomous.*

variable, nonnumerical see *variable, qualitative.*

variable, numerical see *variable, quantitative.*

variable, polylog see *variable, polytomous.*

variable, polytomous a *qualitative variable* with many *categories.*

variable, private a *variable* the *values*[6] of which are not necessarily public knowledge, although an individual may choose to make a *value*[6] known. (Galtung). see also *variable, public.*

variable, proximal *variable* concerning that part of a psychological process which has its location at the boundary of an organism and its *environment.*

variable, public a *variable* the *values*[6] of which are necessarily public knowledge, e.g. age, sex, race. (Galtung). see also *variable, private.*

variable, qualitative *variable* consisting of named *categories.*

variable, quantitative *variable* that is measured.

variable, random see *variate.*

variable, resultant see *variable, dependent.*

variable, target the *variable* of which it is the object of *planning* to give a certain *value*[6].

variable, treatment see *variable, independent.*

variable, two-point see *variable, dichotomous.*

variance square of the *standard deviation.*

variance, analysis of the analysis into components, associated with defined sources of variation, of the total variation, as measured by the *variance,* displayed by a *set¹* of observations.

variate a quantity which may take any of the *values⁶* of a specified *set¹* with a specified relative frequency or probability.

variation, mean see *deviation, mean.*

vassal holder of land by *feudal tenure.* **vassalic** *a.*

vassalage 1. the state of being a *vassal.* 2. the services due from vassal to lord. 3. the whole body of vassals or the vassals of a particular lord. **vassalize** *vt.*

vassalry the whole body of *vassals.*

vector force with both direction and magnitude.

vendetta lasting mutual homicidal relationship between two *groups* in a *society* which is not ,socially regulated. see also *feud.*

verifier, code a person who codes a *sample* of *schedules* or *questionnaires* already coded to check coder's work.

Verstehen discovering the *explanation* for the behaviour of another through *empathy* followed by introspection.

veto 1. rejection of *legislation* by a *collectivity* or individual. 2. *authority* or *power* to reject legislation.

veto, absolute *veto¹* incapable of being overruled.

veto, permanent *veto¹* operable for an unlimited period.

veto, qualified *veto¹* capable of being overruled.

veto, suspensive *veto¹* operable for a limited period.

victim 1. object destroyed in an *oblation.* 2. person harmed for the benefit of another.

victimization creating a *victim².* **victimize** *vt.*

victimology the study of the *victim²*'s behaviour as one of the determinants of the *crime.* **victimological** *a.* **victimologist** *pers n.*

village 1. permanent, small *settlement¹*, irrespective of settlement pattern. 2. small, consolidated agricultural *community.*

village, centrifugal a *village* possessing *norms* which tend to drive out its members.

village, centripetal a *village* possessing *norms* which tend to hold or draw back its members.

village, compact see *village, nucleated.*

village, company a *village* owned by a company and inhabited by its employees.

village, kinship *village* most of the inhabitants of which are *consanguineal relatives.*

village, line a *village* the dwellings of which stretch along one or both sides of a single road or along the bank of a river.

village, nucleated a *village* the dwellings of which are concentrated round a central point.

village, semi-nucleated see *village, line.*

village, subsistence *village* all the production of which is internally consumed.

violence the application of injurious physical force to persons or property. see also *force; coercion; manipulation; domination; influence; power; authority.*

violence, legitimized *violence* which is accorded *legitimacy* by a given *society* or *group.* (Wolfgang, M.E.).

violence, social *violence* to persons or their property because of the *social category* into which they fall.

virifocal male-centred.

virilateral on the husband's side.

virilocality see *residence, virilocal.*

viripotestal with *domestic authority* concentrated in the men.

viscidity *group* solidarity.

visibility the degree to which members of an *ethnic group* are identifiable through physical appearance, *posture, gestures* and other perceptual characteristics. see also *pandiacritic*; *macrodiacritic*; *mesodiacritic*; *microdiacritic.*

volume, acquaintance number of persons *ego* has communicated with over a given period.

volume, role proportion of *group* members who are active *role players.*

vote, floating the overall change in *party* support.

voting, colonized voting by persons resident in a constituency in order to support a particular *party.*

voting, preferential voting in which voter indicates his order of preferences.

voting, split voting for candidates of different *parties* at the same or different electoral levels.

votive 1. offered or erected in fulfilment of a *vow.* 2. consisting of or expressing a vow.

vow a solemn promise to a *supernatural.*

war 1. organized fighting between *communities.* 2. a *conflict* between *political units* carried on by armed forces relatively large for the political units concerned. 3. a legal condition which equally permits two or more hostile *groups* to carry on a conflict by armed force. (Wright, Q.).

war, absolute a *war* the aim of which is the extermination or unconditional surrender of the enemy. see also *war, limited[1].*

war, catalytic a *war* precipitated between two or more powers by an outside power.

war, conventional 1. a *war* limited by conventions.(Andreski, S.). see also *war, unlimited.* 2. a war in which only conventional, i.e. nonnuclear weapons are used.

war, imperial a *war* between *states* belonging to different communities of nations.

war, international a *war* between *states* in the same community of nations.

war, interregional a *war* between *states* belonging to different *international regions.*

war, intraregional a *war* between *states* belonging to the same *international region.*

war, limited 1. a *war* having limited aims. see also *war, absolute.* 2. a local, nonnuclear war.

war, local a *war* which remains confined to the original pair of belligerent *states.*

war, total a *war* involving the mobilization of the entire *population.*

war, unlimited a *war* not limited by conventions.(Andreski). see also *war, conventional[1].*

ward subdivision of a *local group.* (NQ).

waste, conspicuous waste which ipso facto confers *prestige.* (Veblen, T.). see also *consumption, conspicuous.*

wealth that which possesses utility and has a price.

we-feeling feeling of solidarity amongst the *group* members and feeling of group distinctiveness.

we-group (Sumner) see *in-group.*

welfare, economic welfare concerned with subsistence, goods, and recreational services.

welfare, occupational welfare activities which are incident to employment. (Titmuss, R.M.).

welfare, social 1. the welfare of the *community* as a whole. 2. welfare involving health, *education* and other concerns excluding subsistence, goods, and recreational services. 3. activities that directly advance the economic and social well-being of individuals and *families*.

witchcraft 1. see *magic, destructive.* 2. *black magic* which is thought to be involuntary. **witch** *pers n.* see also *sorcery.*

withdrawal rejection by an individual of both the *cultural goals* and the institutionalized means of a *society.* (Merton, R.K.).

wizardry *witchcraft* or *sorcery.*

women, exchange of obtaining wives by exchanging sisters or other female relatives.

work 1. any overt motor performance. 2. expenditure of energy in performance of task. 3. instrumental activity. 4. productive activity. 5. gainful productive activity. 6. instrumental activity involving direct or indirect economic obligation.

work, case application of the *case method[2].*

work, centre highly specialized distributive and control activities in the *economy.* (McKenzie, R.D.).

work, direct *work* that can be conveniently, economically, and accurately attributed directly to specific units of product. see also *job, direct.*

work, extension *work* in the field of *extension education.*

work, field studying actual phenomena under natural conditions, as distinct from laboratory or library methods.

work, group social work with *groups.*

work, indirect *work* that cannot be conveniently, economically, or accurately attributed directly to specific units of product. see also *job, indirect.*

worship reverance, honour or service given to *supernaturals.* see also *prayer*; *sacrifice.*

worship, ancestor veneration or *worship* of ancestral *spirits.*

xenocentrism positive orientation to *nonmembership reference groups.* **xenocentric** *a.*

xenoglossia purported use in a trance of a language unknown to the individual. see also *glossolalia.*

zoanthropy a condition in which a person believes himself changed into an animal and acts like one. **zoanthropic** *a.*

zonation possession by city or *community* of areas having distinctive land-use.

zone 1. an area distinguished on some characteristic from surrounding or adjoining areas. 2. subdivision of an area, delimited for a specific purpose.

zone, census an area of variable size assigned to an *enumerator.*

zone, central the innermost of the concentric land-use zones of a city.

zone, conversion see *zone, transition.*

zone, criminogenic a crime-producing zone.

zone, ecological an area having a distinctive land-use.

zone, transition area of mixed land-use, adjacent to commercial or industrial district of city.

zoning dividing area into zones in which land-use and character of the buildings is legally prescribed.

zoning, ethnic dividing city into zones for involuntary *ethnic segregation.*

zoning, regional any prescribed *specialization* by *regions[2].*

zoning, rural *zoning* applied to *rural areas*.
zoning, urban *zoning* applied to *urban areas*.
zoolatry the *worship* of animals. **zoolatric** *a*.